# GOLD DUST WOMAN

ALSO BY STEPHEN DAVIS

Reggae Bloodlines

Reggae International

Bob Marley

Hammer of the Gods

Say Kids! What Time Is It?

Moonwalk

Fleetwood

Jajouka Rolling Stone

This Wheel's on Fire

Walk This Way

Old Gods Almost Dead

Jim Morrison

Watch You Bleed

To Marrakech by Aeroplane

LZ-'75

More Room in a Broken Heart

William Burroughs / Local Stop on the Nova Express

Miles Davis / 1973

# GOLD DUST WOMAN

## WOMAN

THE BIOGRAPHY OF

# STEVIE
# NICKS

## STEPHEN DAVIS

St. Martin's Press ⚏ New York

www.stmartins.com

Designed by Donna Sinisgalli Noetzel

The images in this book are used with the permission of © Getty Images.

The Library of Congress Cataloging-in-Publication Data

Names: Davis, Stephen, 1947- author.
Title: Gold dust woman : a biography of Stevie Nicks / Stephen Davis.
Description: First edition. | New York : St. Martin's Press, 2017.
Identifiers: LCCN 2017023621| ISBN 9781250032898 (hardcover) | ISBN 9781250032904 (ebook)
Subjects: LCSH: Nicks, Stevie. | Singers—United States—Biography. | Fleetwood Mac (Musical group) | Rock musicians—United States—Biography.
Classification: LCC ML420.N6 D38 2017 | DDC 782.42166092 [B] —dc23
LC record available at https://lccn.loc.gov/2017023621

Our books may be purchased in bulk for promotional, educational, or business use. Please contact your local bookseller or the Macmillan Corporate and Premium Sales Department at 1-800-221-7945, extension 5442, or by email at MacmillanSpecialMarkets@macmillan.com.

First Edition: November 2017

10  9  8  7  6  5  4  3  2  1

Fan is short for fanatic.

This biography is dedicated to all the fans of Stevie Nicks

(and Fleetwood Mac) past and present,

*memor et fidelis. Non nobis solum nati sumus.*

Blessed Cecilia, appear in visions

To all musicians, appear and inspire:

Translated Daughter, come down and startle

Composing mortals with immortal fire.

— W.H. AUDEN


Chiffon lasts forever if you take good care of it.

— STEVIE NICKS

Back then . . . she's a complete unknown, the new girl in an old band.

She's standing on a soundstage in Los Angeles, about to make her national television debut. She's trembling slightly as she waits on her taped mark while the director explains that if she steps away from the microphone, she'll be off camera.

If she's scared, she's determined, she said later, not to let it show. While she waits, she holds the microphone stand with both hands to keep steady. She tells herself to clear her mind.

It's June 11, 1975, and semi-washed-up English blues band Fleetwood Mac is making its first video with its new-look Anglo-American lineup. The song they're about to play is "Rhiannon," written by the new girl in the band, Stevie Nicks. She's about to sing her most important song to America for the first time.

She should tremble, other than from the excitement of the video shoot in front of a small studio audience. This "Rhiannon" performance is Make or Break for the not-young singer-songwriter. An elderly ingénue at the age of twenty-eight, she's been kicking around California's booming music business for seven years already, with little to show for it other than a bulging songbook and an interesting boyfriend, who's standing next to her on the stage with his guitar, getting ready to inject a dose of "Rhiannon" into the American consciousness, like an enchantment from the misty mountains of farthest Wales.

Do or die—because if this new iteration of Fleetwood Mac fails to catch on, for Stevie Nicks it's back to waiting tables wearing a corny period uniform in West Hollywood. And the auguries aren't great at this point. Her singing had been panned—put down—by *Rolling Stone* magazine in its review of Fleetwood Mac's new album. She also knew that she was only in Fleetwood Mac because her boyfriend told the band that if they wanted him as their new guitar player, they had to take her as well.

As the stage manager counts down the time, Stevie Nicks looks over at the boyfriend—Lindsey Buckingham. "Linds." He's a year younger than she is. He's in his stage outfit, a floppy silk kimono top, very Robert Plant, with lots of visible chest hair and an ample 'fro of dark curly locks. He smiles at her and winks—he's nervous, too. But *this is their moment*—what they've been after, for years. She's all in black, her blond hair layered in a feathered shag perm with platinum highlights. She's a breath over five feet, a tiny girl really, but the fashionably stacked heels of her black boots add an extra four inches. A lacy black cape made of light chiffon completes the ensemble. She's wearing a lot of eye shadow. She looks amazing, made for television like all the rock stars. (The formal, witchy top hat will come later. This is pre-*Rumours*. One day in the next century there will be websites devoted to her collection of shawls.)

But now the red studio light flashes on, Stevie takes a half step back, and Lindsey starts the song, cuffing his electric guitar. Drummer Mick Fleetwood pulses the rhythm forward with bassist John McVie, whose wife Christine sits at her electric keyboards, stage left, playing bluesy chords. Now Stevie steps forward and speaks into the microphone her first-ever words to her future rabid fans:

"This is a *song*," she intones in a western drawl, "about an old Welsh witch." And then she lets Rhiannon cast her magic cathode-ray spell. The song lasts almost seven minutes. Stevie pushes the beat with an arm gesture, and Fleetwood kicks it. "Rhiannon rings like a bell through the night and wouldn't you love to love her? She rules her life like a bird in flight, and who will be her lover?" Stevie sways with the beat, in close eye contact with Lindsey by her side. She wails "taken by the sky, taken by the wind," a powerful female spirit vanishing in the ether, leaving no trace except the pretty guitar licks, and this young woman dancing power twirls on her mark between the second and third verses. She sings lyrics slightly different from those on the records: "Once in a million years / A lady like her . . . rises." She and Lindsey and Christine all sing together the keening, breathy chorus— "Rhiaaaaa-nnon. Rhiaaaaaaaaaa-nnon."

Lindsey is rocking out and smiling. It's totally happening now. Fleetwood Mac is nailing this. "She is like a cat in the dark, and then she is the darkness . . . Would you stay if she promised you heaven? Will you ever win?"

Then the music softens as Christine plays a bluesy keyboard solo that sets up the sonic whirlwind to come. Stevie stretches her gauzy black cape out like a pair of wings, fluid stagecraft before the song's next movement. ("Rhiannon" in performance can be seen as a five-scene playlet.) At just after four minutes the beat recedes, and Stevie sings the midsection: "Dreams unwind / Love's a state of mind." And then, with two minutes to go, the band launches into a militant 4/4 march with Stevie in a hieratic trance—shouting, yelling, *wailing* lyrics, waving arms, strutting and stomping, acting out, wild-eyed. She's shaking and vibrating, screaming like a bloody Bacchant, ready to tear the soul out of your body, her gesturing fingers making portents and prophesies in the smoky air.

The song crashes finally to a halt—"You cry / But she's gone"—as she lets out a final howl that lasts ten seconds, descending by octaves. Then Stevie bends way down into a deep floor bow, grasping the microphone stand with both hands to prevent an exhausted collapse. The performance is complete; the studio audience applauds, and the image fades from the screen.

When the "Rhiannon" video was broadcast months later on *The Midnight Special,* the syndicated (nonnetwork) rock concert program shown late on Friday nights in the seventies, it changed everything for Fleetwood Mac. The band's eponymous new album, released the previous summer, had been chugging along, selling the usual mid-chart numbers to the band's loyal audience, although the first single, Christine's "Over My Head," had gotten airplay on FM radio's soft rock/adult contemporary format and had jumped to *Billboard* magazine's #20 chart position.

Then the "Rhiannon" 45-rpm single was released in February 1976 and exploded like a radio grenade after the enormous rock audience saw Stevie Nicks celebrate the rite of the old Welsh witch on national television. Suddenly a million American girls went out and bought the new Fleetwood Mac album. Then a million more. The "Rhiannon" album track immediately jumped on every American FM rock station's playlist, while the remixed single—which sounded hotter on a tinny car radio—crossed from FM onto AM radio and into the A&W Root Beer drive-ins of middle America. The White Goddess's momentum turned into massive album sales, and to the shock of everyone (but the band), the *Fleetwood Mac* album hit #1 on the *Billboard* Hot Hundred, and stayed there for weeks.

When Fleetwood Mac found out about their number-one album, they were already making their next album—*Rumours*. But whenever they turned on their car radios, now "Rhiannon" was riding the airwaves with them. The old Welsh witch had done her job.

Who is Rhiannon?

The song doesn't give away any information on her, but it offers a transcendent signal—the sky, the wind, flying—that was picked up by the daughters of the enormous Welsh-descended population of North America, like an occluded racial memory from olden days, before the time of memory. Even Stevie Nicks, who had so ardently conjured Rhiannon, admitted that she hardly knew what she was writing about. ("I read this novel, I loved the name. We felt she was a queen, and her memory became a myth.") Later, Stevie learned much more. Rhiannon was an ancient Welsh goddess, and this affected the spiritually minded singer, because Stevie was of almost pure Welsh extraction herself.

Wales and its legends are important to this story—how a beautiful Welsh-descended daughter of the American Southwest became a rock goddess herself and then sustained a decades-long international career, at the very top of her profession.

Wales occupies the westernmost territory of Great Britain, a land of misty mountains, drowned cities, and legendary giants. The Celtic tribes of the British Isles regarded Wales as a holy and haunted place since time immemorial, a sere landscape imbued with tremendous spiritual power. When the priestly Druids built Stonehenge, their prehistoric solar observatory on Salisbury Plain, they obtained the enormous bluestone monoliths from the Preseli Mountains in Wales, a hundred miles away. Even today nobody knows how the Druids rolled their stones down to Wiltshire.

Julius Caesar invaded Britannia, and the Romans ruled for centuries. After they left, Britain was occupied by migrating German nations. The native Celtic tribes were pushed west to Wales, a less fertile and hospitable landscape. Over the next thousand years, the Welsh people assumed the traits that still describe their intense nationality and a love of poetry and singing, especially choral music. The Welsh also came to be associated with otherworldliness and magic. Merlin, the magician of the Arthurian legends, was born in Wales. So was Morgan le Fay, King Arthur's sister, another old Welsh witch. The "blessed island" of Avalon is just offshore. This national propensity for magic and spells cannot be discounted when thinking about Stevie Nicks.

Life in Wales was hard for its people, who farmed the stony fields, raised sheep and cattle, and fished in the violent swells of the craggy Welsh coastline. The other occupation was mining, first for tin and copper, later for iron and coal. The women worked as hard as the men. They found relief at the famous Welsh festivals that featured choral competitions and riotous, mead-fueled word games where poetic champions composed spontaneous verse to determine the national poets laureate. The Welsh bards and minstrels sang of Dylan, "the son of the wave," a child-god in the shape of a fish; of the sisters of the holy wells; of sacred twins; and of the Three Birds of Rhiannon, the goddess who seems to change from a little moon to a mare goddess, or to a nightmare, according to the old stories in the *Welsh Triads* and *The Mabinogion*.

William Shakespeare had a Welsh grandmother, Alys Griffin. The heir to the English throne is the Prince of Wales. The wild

Welsh spirit inhabits the cultures of England, the United States, Canada, Australia, and New Zealand. It preserves something of the essence of the older Celtic-romantic traditions of the west—Western civilization.

Beginning in the 1600s, Welsh people joined the migrations to North America for opportunity and a better life by the tens of thousands, later swelling to millions. Many fleeing poverty arrived in bonded or indentured servitude. In return for passage from Cardiff to ports in Maryland, Virginia, and the Carolinas, the bonded servant owed his or her master seven years of service. Then they were free to go their own way. So was the American South and Mid-South populated in the seventeenth and eighteenth centuries. By 1900 more than half the names in American telephone directories—Jones, Lewis, Evans, Wilson, Williams, Thomas, Hopkins, Jenkins, Perkins, Davis—were descended from the epochal Welsh migrations to North America.

Some researchers think Stevie Nicks's ancestors arrived sometime in the mid-1700s, when the surname Nicks appeared in ship manifests in the Baltimore area. (In northern Celtic folklore, a "nixie" is a female sea sprite, a water-wraith related to the kelpie, the mythic sea spirit of the Scottish Isles. "There are nicks in sea, lake, river, and waterfall," according to the old books of fairy lore.) The migrants from Wales were mostly Protestant, often Methodist, and the choral culture of their churches is thought to have been absorbed by slave religion in the South; some musicologists link the Welsh harmonic influence to the development of African-American gospel choirs.

By 1950, a crucial Welsh influence had appeared in America in the form of the roaring young poet Dylan Thomas, from Swansea, south Wales; his stirring, bardic cadences, delivered in a mellifluous Welsh baritone, spread from coast to coast through recordings and readings during the 1950s, a major inspiration for the Beat Generation writers and other modernist poets.

In the mid-fifties, Welsh-descended musicians invented rock & roll music in America's Mid-South. The Welsh name Elvis means what it sounds like—elfin, impish, otherworldly. And Presley is another way to spell Preseli, the Welsh mountains that provided the Druidical "sarsen stones" of Stonehenge. Just the name "Elvis Presley" must have conjured an atavistic signal. Welsh mountain spirit! Could this help to explain the hysterical reactions of white Southern girls to Elvis the Pelvis's uninhibited gyrations in Tennessee and Arkansas, Alabama and Louisiana, in 1954? Was an ancient and forgotten Welsh god reborn as a young one in Tupelo, Mississippi, in 1935? Most of the other early rockers were Welsh, too: Jerry Lee Lewis from Ferriday, Louisiana; Carl Perkins and the Everly Brothers from Tennessee; Conway Twitty (born Harold Jenkins) from Arkansas. Same with Ronnie Hawkins and Levon Helm. Even Johnny Cash and a lot of the country and western stars: Loretta Lynn. Buck Owens. Kitty Wells. Hank Williams.

A few years later, in 1960, when a young folk singer from Minnesota named Robert Zimmerman moved to New York City to try his luck, and he needed a new identity for credibility in the commercial folk revival, he changed his name to Bob Dylan.

The founder of the Rolling Stones, Brian Jones (born Lewis Brian Hopkin-Jones), had Welsh blood. David Bowie's real name was David Jones. Ray Davies. Robert Plant and Jimmy Page both had Welsh ancestors, and even retreated to Wales to write music for Led Zeppelin. "Bron-Yr-Aur." Misty Mountain Hop, indeed. Stevie Nicks, herself a poet of sometimes exquisite technical skill in terms of cadence and scansion, is firmly in this tradition, the venerable Welsh legacy of professional bardic championship.

Now, more than forty years after the mid-seventies' success of "Rhiannon," Stevie Nicks herself is an old Welsh witch. She's the acknowledged Fairy Godmother of Rock. Fleetwood Mac went on to make *Rumours,* one of the bestselling recordings in history, then on to worlds beyond, and the Rock & Roll Hall of Fame. It's the same with Stevie Nicks, whose wildly successful solo career continues into the time of this writing. In fact, she's bigger than ever, with legions of loyal fans thronging her concerts, dressing like her, identifying with her—*beyond the music itself.* (Other than Stevie, only Led Zeppelin enjoys this sort of mystical bond with its multigenerational audience.) Since 1981, Stevie's fans have immersed themselves in the dark velvet rooms she creates in her songs, from the epic to the heartbroken, through loss and failure, from addiction to recovery. For her fans, Stevie Nicks fills many different roles. She's an elegist and an analyst of romantic longings. She's a chronicler of remorse and regret. Her work has an organic core of a woman artist according a tragic dignity to a failed marriage between two ambitious people, as well as to the oblique charms of a broken life. Always in her songs there are notes of tailored elegance amid the agonies of her disasters. Through the music, she's able to override her own troubles and move on. Stevie Nicks is too busy working on the next project to worry about redemption. She seems to tell us that we're all worth more than what "happens" to us. She's a mood of her own, "a will to wistfulness," a candle of hope, or maybe just a wish. Through the songs comes self-realization and emotional commitment. They are cathartic for her and her audience. Memories, dreams, and the passing of time are her special subjects. Stevie's fans owe her greatest songs to her compulsion to externalize her experiences, to let them all hang out, to use them to express her feelings: first in poems and drawings, then in songs, recordings, costume, and performance, with the ultimate goal of ensuring that her life, and her life's work, can never fade beyond memory. The appropriate response of her fans to this golden presence, which seems to embody the idea that we all have sacred powers within us, is worship and love.

In 1979, "Gold Dust Woman" was a chilling prophesy of excess and failure that came true. This biography is an attempt to describe its subject as a fully externalized public woman with an ongoing career, in and out of Fleetwood Mac. Anyone who writes about Stevie Nicks soon learns that there are things she doesn't want anyone to know and which no one will ever know. Any biographer should think this challenging, seductive, admirable. "I'm stranger than most people," Stevie said awhile ago. In the end, her songs and music tell most of her story, certainly the important parts of it. To current interviewers, Stevie insists she has more work to do. Her fans know that her art will last as long as it remains in the keeping of those who understand its emotional value, its deepest meanings, and the transcendental distinction of her music and her life.

—S.D. 2017

# GOLD DUST WOMAN

CHAPTER 1

## 1.1  Teedie

The frontier state of Arizona is the keystone of the American Southwest, wedged between California and New Mexico. The climate is arid and dry, the landscape monumental and gigantic. In the years after the Second World War when she was born, Arizona still had a Western frontier look. The people were the grandchildren of frontier families, solid and outgoing. The cactus was the state emblem. Native American tribes lived on their reservations, a world apart from "Anglo" society, as it was called. The bigger cities—Phoenix and Tucson—were expanding out into the desert, fueled by postwar migration to a promised land of opportunity and bright sunshine in the winter.

Into this western land was born Stephanie Lynn Nicks on May 28, 1948, at Good Samaritan Hospital in Phoenix. Her mother, the former Barbara Alice Meeks, was just twenty, having married the previous year when she was nineteen. Her father, Aaron Jess Seth Nicks, Jr., was twenty-three. They met when both were working at *The Arizona Republic* newspaper. Barbara wrote in her diary that it was love at first sight, and they were married a month after they met. Jess Nicks was a confident, ambitious young man, beginning to pursue what would become a successful, if itinerant, career in business in the booming Southwestern corporate economy.

Barbara Nicks's pregnancy had been difficult. She was quite small, only just over five feet tall, and the child was very active in utero, a real dancer, the young parents joked. She was nauseous much of the time and existed mostly on Mexican food, enchiladas, and refried beans. But the birth went well, and the couple was delighted with their tiny, dark-eyed daughter.

Stephanie was the couple's first child, and as an especially pretty little girl she was doted on by her parents' families. Jess had two younger brothers, Bill and Gene, who married two sisters, Carmel and Mary Lou Ruffin. Jess and Barbara were closest to Bill and Carmel, whose son Johnathan was the cousin Stevie was closest to. They mostly lived near each other in Paradise Valley, near Phoenix.

Jess and Barbara started calling their daughter Stevie right away, but she couldn't say this until her teeth came in, so she called herself Teedie (which Barbara called her for the rest of her life). Barbara was a devout Catholic, always wearing a silver or gold cross on a chain, and a practical, frugal homemaker who kept her little girl very close, making most of her clothes from pattern books ordered by mail. Stevie was soon put on a pony like all the little Arizona cowgirls, and she learned to ride not long after she learned to walk.

Almost every summer the family would go to visit Barbara's mother, Alice, who lived in the town of Ajo, a long and dusty drive into Pima County, near the Mexican border. Alice Harwood was from an old copper mining family. She had been a good singer as a young woman and had two children while living in Bisbee, Arizona, with a man nobody would ever talk about. After she divorced him, Stevie's mother and her uncle Edward were adopted by Alice's second husband, a Mr. Meeks, who worked in the rich Bisbee copper mines; he was said to have been abusive, and later died of tuberculosis. "My mother had a hard life," Stevie would recall. "She was very poor, she was only nineteen when she married, and she had me at twenty."

Grandma Alice—"Crazy Alice" to the family—lived alone near Ajo (which means garlic in Spanish). Beginning when Stevie was about four, she spent part of every summer in Ajo with her grandmother—and loved it. Alice liked to sing old lullabies to little Stevie. Alice read books to her and told her the first fairy tales Stevie ever heard.

When Stevie was five, her grandfather started her singing career. This was her father's father, Aaron Jess Nicks, a local country singer (born, like Stevie, on May 28, in 1892 in Phoenix) known as "A.J." He and his wife, Effie, had split up—she'd gone to California—and by then he was living in a collection of shacks and trailers up in the hills above Phoenix. A.J. made something of a living playing billiards and singing in taverns and saloons, doing songs by Jimmy Rogers, Hank Williams, and Red Sovine; playing guitar, fiddle, and harmonica, sometimes alone, sometimes with a little band—whatever he could scrabble together. He was sometimes heard on local radio, singing jingles for commercials. A smart, sharp, and wiry man, he frequented poolrooms and had spent time during the Great Depression hopping freight trains, riding the rods, living that life. He may have met Woody Guthrie in the hobo camps and rail yards of the sprawling Southwest. He drank.

Starting in 1952, when Teedie was four, A.J. started coming by the house and singing with her. He taught her harmony by having her sing "Darling Clementine" while he took the higher harmony. Then he reversed it, and she picked up the harmonic immediately, by ear. It was complicated for a child, but she could do it. He could tell Stevie was a gifted harmony singer. They sang "Are You Mine" by Red Sovine and other songs. Stevie couldn't even read yet, but she had the natural singer's innate ability to repeat the words of a song after hearing them only a few times.

A.J. Nicks started taking his tiny granddaughter along to parties (with her parents), where they sang for friends. The reaction was always sheer delight, and Stevie seemed to love the attention. When she was five, she started singing in local saloons with her grandfather. They had a little act. A.J. would sing a few songs, and then Jess would lift Stevie onto the bar in her cute cowgirl outfit her mother had made. The drinkers loved the harmony singing, and the raucous applause at the end of their act was the best response A.J. had ever gotten in his mostly futile career. For a brief while, A.J., who had been trying his entire life to make it in the country music business, got the idea that little Stevie could be the real deal. Maybe their singing act— an old coot and his granddaughter—could be A.J.'s winning ticket to the Grand Ole Opry. He started paying her fifty cents a week to sing with him.

Her parents stopped it. No, they told him when he asked to take Stevie along to bookings outside the Phoenix Valley. Out of state? Out of the question. A.J. pleaded with them, but Barbara Nicks was adamant. She told A.J. that her five-year-old daughter, who hadn't even started school yet, was not going on the road with a sixty-year-old man, and that was the end of it. A.J. left the house, angry. He retreated to his lair in the hills, and the family didn't see him for more than two years. Stevie always had a great fondness for her grandfather, and she would dedicate her first recording to him. But she was also firm in her feeling that "he was a real good singer, but he wasn't a great musician."

Right around then, the Nicks family moved to Albuquerque, New Mexico.

Barbara Nicks kept Stevie close to home once she began school. She didn't exactly discourage friendships for Stevie, but she didn't seek them out, either, because she knew the family would be moving all over the Southwest over the next fifteen years as her husband moved from post to post, almost like a military family, as he climbed the corporate ladders of big companies: Armour & Company meat packers, the Greyhound Bus Company, and Lucky Lager Brewing. She knew her children would be changing schools a lot, and that some of these lost friendships could be sad. Instead, she signed Stevie up for various lessons: piano, drawing, ballet, and tap. Barbara had an inkling that adorable Stevie could be an actress or even a movie star and kept pushing acting lessons, although Stevie, who was naturally shy, told her mother not to. It was Barbara, an expert, who taught Stevie how to twirl a baton. Barbara also realized that Stevie was nearsighted, and she got her first pair of glasses in the first grade.

In late 1954 the Nicks family moved to El Paso, the bustling Texas border city. A year later Barbara had her second and last child, Christopher Aaron Nicks, born December 18, 1955. Now seven-year-old Teedie had a brother. She hated him, she later said. She'd been the focus of the family's attention, and now this. She says she's still telling Chris how sorry she is for being such a bad sister when they were kids. She's frank about it. "I hated Chris," she told an interviewer.

Stevie started the third grade at a Catholic girls' school called Loretto, but she didn't like it: it was too hard for her, she said later, and she didn't do well. Also, Stevie proved to be left-handed, and the nuns tried to get her to write with her right hand, which was like being tortured. So she started fourth grade in 1957 at nearby Crockett public school and fit in better. This was really where she learned to sing with other kids. She was a star singer in the school chorus, and even allowed her mother to talk her into being in the class play. "It was called *The Alamo,* Stevie remembered later, "or something like that. There were only two girls in the play and I was one of them because I could sing. When it was time to say my lines I totally froze. I couldn't remember. It was the worst moment of my life. When I got home I told my mother, 'I am *not* an actress. Don't *ever* sign me up for any more plays ever again.'"

Stevie may not have been an actress, but she was a performer. Primal rocker Buddy Holly was from nearby Lubbock, and in the fourth grade Stevie and her best friend, Colleen, brought the house down when they did a tap dance to a record of Holly's "Everyday." "I wore a black top hat," Stevie recalled, "and a black vest, a black skirt, a white blouse, black tights, and black tap shoes with little heels. I had a definite knowledge of how I should look—even then."

Holidays were a big deal in the Nicks household, and Stevie's mother particularly liked Halloween. But Barbara could never understand why Stevie always wanted to go out trick-or-treating as a witch. "I always had a great love for Halloween," she recalled, "and for being a witchy character from when I was six years old. My mom and I argued about it every single year, and she was very tired of making witch costumes." When Stevie was in fourth grade Barbara made a yellow Martha Washington costume and then finally gave up when Stevie dyed it black.

In 1958, Pappy A.J. showed up in El Paso. Barbara told close friends that Stevie had been kept away from him, but now there was a reconciliation, and once again the family was singing together around the table. A.J. brought Stevie a lot of records, 45-rpm singles, songs that he thought she might want to learn. There were a lot of Everly Brothers and other country-influenced rock & rollers. Come along and be my party doll. A.J. taught Stevie to duet with him on "It's Late" by Dorsey Burnette. "Once again A.J. picked up that I could do this. He'd say to me, 'You're a *harmony singer,* honey.'" But Stevie's grandfather wasn't doing well. He may have borrowed some money from Jess. Stevie later remembered her father's upset with A.J., his anguish as he "watched A.J. going down the tubes, trying to make it" in the music world.

In 1959, Jess Nicks was transferred to Salt Lake City, Utah, where Stevie would start the sixth grade. Stevie had made some good friends in El Paso and she was very upset at having to start all over again. Barbara sat her down and told her that all she has to do is to open herself up and make some new friends. Her mother told her, "You will go to school, and you will be independent, and you will *never* be dependent upon a man. And you'll have a really good education, and you'll be able to stand in a room with a bunch of very smart men and keep up with them, and never feel like a second-class citizen."

## 1.2   The New Girl in School

Stevie's family spent the next three years—the late 1950s—in Salt Lake City, one of the most conservative in the United States. But her two years there—eighth and ninth grade at Wasatch Junior High—were spent immersed in the music that was changing America. The Nicks family loved music, especially country and western, as country music was then known. Jess had a good hi-fi record changer in the living room, and Barbara had the radio on for most of the day. (Stevie's mother liked working and had enjoyed many part-time jobs, but her husband's business success in old-fashioned Salt Lake City now put social pressure on her to stay home with the children, like all the other wives of Jess's colleagues.) So Stephanie Lynn spent these crucial years between twelve and fourteen glued to the radio. She had spent her childhood listening to the early fifties hit parade: the doggy in the window, "The Tennessee Waltz," "Sixteen Tons." Of the early rockers, she liked Buddy Holly and the Everly Brothers the best, especially their heavenly harmonies on "All I Have to Do Is Dream" and "Wake Up Little Susie." She learned to dance the Lindy, down and up, the prevailing dance of the day. Chubby Checker's "The Twist" came late to Utah and when it did arrive, it was banned at school dances and country club socials as immoral. The Mormons who dominated the town didn't think white teenagers should be gyrating like savages. They wouldn't even let them play the record at the hops. Salt Lake fans could only see the twist on Dick Clark's *American Bandstand* TV program, broadcast Monday through Friday from far-away Philadelphia.

Stevie was a baton twirler at school events. Her mother signed her up for dancing classes and guitar lessons. She started writing song lyrics in a little notebook in her looping, left-handed script. She was the most popular girl in the school.

In 1960 the family was enthralled by the presidential election. At the end of the fifties, America was up for grabs between the Republican vice president Richard Nixon and the charismatic young Democratic senator from Massachusetts, Jack Kennedy. Kennedy was a handsome war hero with a stunning wife, some new ideas, a charming Boston accent, and a plea for renewed American vigor (pronounced "vigah"). Stevie's father, an Arizona frontier Republican, supported Nixon. But Stevie's Catholic mother adored Kennedy and his beautiful young wife, Jacqueline, and so did Stevie. When Kennedy was elected in November 1960, Stevie at age twelve could identify with the newly branded national notion of the Kennedy family's ascendancy as a rebirth of Camelot, evoking the legendary Knights of the Round Table, a lost world of romantic legend and myth.

Stevie failed math in the ninth grade, so her parents enrolled her at Judge Memorial Catholic High School for tenth grade. She hated being away from her junior high friends, but this only lasted about a month as Jess Nicks accepted another job. So in 1962 the family relocated again, this time to Arcadia, California. Stevie remembers crying over this news with her best Salt Lake friend, Karen Thornhill, on her front steps: "Well, we moved—a lot. So I was always the new girl. I knew I wasn't going to have much time to make friends, so I made friends quickly and I adjusted really well, and when I'd say, 'I'm gonna miss my room,' my mom would always say, 'There's always a better house.'"

Arcadia is one of the wealthier towns in Los Angeles County, at the foot of the majestic San Gabriel Mountains, where Stevie was enrolled in tenth grade at Arcadia High School. The AHS football team was the Apaches, but it doesn't seem that Stephanie Nicks (as she now called herself) joined the Apache Princesses, the baton-twirling marching team. "[It] was a very hoity-toity school," she remembered, "very cliquey, and a lot of rich people went there." But she did join the school's elite A Capella Choir, where she met a beautiful classmate named Robin Snyder. A great singer, graceful dancer, and one of the most popular girls in the school, she would become much more than a best friend; gorgeous Robin Snyder was more like the twin sister that Stevie never had.

At home Stephanie spent a lot of time in her new bedroom with the door closed, listening to KHJ on the radio, especially loving the girl groups that ruled early sixties airwaves: the Chiffons, the Shi-relles, the Supremes, Martha and the Vandellas. She liked the sound of the Shangri-Las singing "Remember (Walking in the Sand)." She was starting to notice how songs were put together, with verses and choruses and instrumental hooks. She remembered, "Moving from Utah made me take all the guitar lessons and stuff I'd written on the side and get serious about my music. I was depressed and hurting, and that's usually the best time for a writer."

One time Stephanie was in the backseat of the family car when a song came on the radio and her mother began to speak to her. "Hush!" Stevie shouted. "I'm *concentrating* on this." This was when her some-what bewildered parents began to realize that music might mean more to their daughter than just a hobby.

Stephanie wore her hair short in 1962–63. Her natural color was now a light brown, sometimes called dirty blond. She'd begun to have her period back in Salt Lake. She had almost reached her full height, just over five feet, just like her mother. Her myopia had worsened and she needed stronger glasses to read. Coming from Utah, she dressed modestly compared with the California girls, who tended to show a lot of skin. Instead, Stevie dressed conservatively, sometimes in volu-minous dresses and skirts, some of which her mother still made. Later her classmates would remember her as a bohemian or "beatnik" pres-ence among the big school's athletes, cheerleaders, hot-rodders, and surfers—a tiny girl wearing thick glasses and carrying her books in a Mexican straw basket. Stevie said later that she *was* kind of odd, and that her classmates probably thought she was crazy.

The year 1963 was when surf music took over California popular culture, with local bands the Beach Boys and Jan & Dean riding the wave of striped shirts, churning bass lines, and throbbing pipeline guitars. (Surf music guitar god Dick Dale was of Lebanese extraction, and later said that the style he pioneered was an ancient Middle Eastern way of playing the oud.) At the end of the year, President Kennedy was murdered in a bloody public assassination in Dallas, Texas, dashing the high hopes of a nation. Years later Stevie would talk about what a loss of innocence this felt like to her generation. And then, only a few months later, as if obeying an occult summons to cheer up America, the Beatles arrived from England and charmed America with new songs and insouciance on Ed Sullivan's Sunday night variety show, the same way Elvis Aaron Presley had in 1956. The Beatles rode a wave of their own in 1964 with "She Loves You" and "I Want to Hold Your Hand," and became the vanguard of the cultural shockwave known as the British Invasion. Along with a host of new bands from England came new styles, new accents, new clothes, new hair (long for boys, long and ironed for girls), new movies, and, of course, James Bond. (At the tail end of this invasion a few years later, Fleetwood Mac would make its American debut as a virtuosic English blues band.)

For her fifteenth birthday, her parents gave Stevie six weeks of guitar lessons with a young man who played in the classical Spanish style. He loaned Stevie a small Goya parlor guitar, and she took to it immediately. After the six weeks he announced that he was leaving for Seville, and Stevie begged her parents to buy the guitar for her. She'd spent so much time practicing in her room that they knew this wasn't another fad, and so Stevie got her first guitar in 1963.

Around this time Stevie's father bought a bar nearby in the San Gabriel Valley, with the idea of turning it into a music venue where A.J. could come and play. Stevie's mother cooked some of the bar food, and she and Stevie would often bring the catering to the bar. On weekends they'd sometimes find Jess and his brothers singing with A.J. and some of the players and pickers from the local country music scene. A.J. wanted Stevie to sing with them, but her mother always demurred and said she had homework to do.

Arcadia High had an annual father-daughter dinner, and in tenth grade Stevie invited Jess to come and sing with her. Jess was a good singer, and he suggested country music star Roger Miller's current hit song "King of the Road." They practiced a few times, but when they got up in front of the audience Stevie was so embarrassed that she lost it. She began laughing, couldn't stop, then Jess started up, and it was a fiasco. Her father later told a magazine interviewer that Stevie wet her pants while on the stage with him.

Stevie kept up her guitar practice and soon was singing with a school group, the Changin' Times, inspired by Bob Dylan's stirring protest song "The Times They Are A-Changin'." This quartet harmonized on Dylan's "Blowin' in the Wind" and "Puff, the Magic Dragon" as sung by Dylan's folk revival colleagues Peter, Paul & Mary. "The Times They Are A-Changin'" is a rather dark song that speaks to the political and cultural convulsions of the era. The Cold War was raging, the Bomb hung over everything, Martin Luther King was agitating for civil rights, Kennedy was dead, and the Beatles were here. The song was confrontational. "Your old road is rapidly agin' / Please get out of the new one if you can't lend a hand." Stevie would later remember how much Dylan's song meant to her, and she resolved to somehow be part of the big changes to come, and especially to somehow do work that she, too, would be remembered for.

## 1.3   California Dreamin'

At the end of 1963, Stevie Nicks fell in love. He was a little older, a "really handsome boy," she said later. He broke up with the girl he'd been going steady with, a girl who was a good friend of Stevie's, and he and Stevie went out for about six months. But then—on May 28, 1964, Stevie's sixteenth birthday—he went back to his previous girlfriend. When she found out about this, that she'd been dumped for her friend, Stevie went home, shut herself in her room, and began to cry. "I had fallen for this incredible guy, and he ended up going out with my best friend. And they both knew that I was going to be crushed."

A ballad is a simple narrative poem composed in short stanzas, often with a romantic theme, often set to music. It's one of the oldest forms of musical communication still extant. Stevie Nicks wrote her first ballad—called "I've Loved and I've Lost"—on this unhappy occasion, which also happened to be her birthday, which made it even worse.

"I was totally in tears, sitting on my bed with lots of paper, my guitar, and a pen, and I wrote this song about your basic sixteen-year-old love affair thing that I was now going through." It was a country-style song that went, "I've loved and I've lost, and I'm sad but not blue / I once loved a boy who was wonderful and true / But he loved another before he loved me / I knew he still wanted her—'twas easy to see." (Stevie clearly had an ear for verse; like Bob Dylan, she wrote in "common measure," the simple meter of many ballads and hymns, as well as most of Emily Dickinson's poems.)

Stevie: "When I said, 'I'm sad but not blue,' I was accepting the fact that they were going to be together. I was horrified but I really loved both of them, and I knew they didn't do it purposefully to hurt me.

"I finished that song, hysterically crying. And I was hooked. When I played my own song later that night, I *knew*—from that second on—that I was not going to sing a lot of other people's songs. I was going to write my own. From that day forward, when I was in my room playing my guitar, nobody would come in without knocking, nobody disturbed me. They even let me miss dinner if necessary, it was that important to me. They could hear that I was working, at sixteen years old, and they would leave me alone. I started singing a lot more at school, and I sang whenever I could, for whatever I could possibly find to do. If it had anything to do with music or singing, I did it."

At the same time that she knew she could sing a love song, and really put it over, Stevie also knew that she could use some romantic experience. "At sixteen I could sing a love song pretty well," she said later. "My dad would go, 'That's a good song, honey.' And my mom would go, 'That's just beautiful, Stevie.' And they would be thinking, 'We know for a fact that she's only been on one date, and she was back in two hours.' "

In June, Stevie and Robin Snyder got their hair streaked by a friend who was going to a beauty school. "I had my hair streaked at the end of my tenth-grade year and got in a lot of trouble for it," Stevie recalled thirty years later, laughing. "They didn't just streak it blond, they streaked it silver. My hair was totally ivory. I was grounded for six weeks. But when my hair changed, everything changed. I got to wear grayish plum eye shadow. There was no way I was going back."

In the summer of 1964 Stevie bid a sad farewell to Arcadia High and her friend Robin Snyder—they vowed eternal friendship—because the Nicks family was on the move again. This time they were headed north, to the wealthy suburban towns halfway up the great peninsula between San Francisco and San Jose. They fetched up in San Mateo, and Stevie began her junior year at Menlo-Atherton High School in nearby Atherton.

M-A, as the school is known, was and is one of the great American public high schools, and it has a reputation for academic rigor. Many graduates went on to prestigious Stanford University in nearby Palo Alto. Today these towns are better know as Silicon Valley, legendary birthplace of personal computing, but in 1964 the San Francisco peninsula was mostly still farmland, with vast strawberry fields stretching along California Highway 101, backing up to the San Francisco Bay.

Stevie Nicks was at first intimidated by M-A, a wealthy, politically conservative school whose parking lot was full of Detroit's finest: Corvettes, Sting Rays, GTOs, the early Ford Mustangs. The car-crazy greasers drove '57 Chevies, and there were even a few '32 Ford coupes, the little deuce coupe of Beach Boys fame. But her mother gave her the pep talk about opening herself up and making new friends, and as always Stevie was encouraged. She was also the living embodiment of "The New Girl in School," Jan & Dean's hit single from that summer— a beautiful California girl that the guys wanted to date and the girls wanted to be like (or hate). Stevie's classmates took to this guitar-toting new girl immediately—these kids knew star quality when they saw it—and soon Stevie found herself a close runner-up for 1964 homecoming queen and then was nominated for vice president of M-A's Class of 1966. She established her musical aptitude quickly and soon was a regular at school assemblies and talent shows, appearing at M-A's Sports Night Dinner in a demure skirt, low heels, and a low-key beehive hairstyle, de rigueur for girls in those days. She did well in class and began keeping journals, expressing herself in private jottings, poetry, and drawings. She dressed herself in the preppy "Ivy League" style common to all the kids from well-to-do homes. She was a "good girl," a self-described "prude," unlike some of the faster girls in class with serious reputations for backseat love during *The Carpetbaggers* at the drive-in.

"If you were going out with somebody," she remembered later, "you went to a movie, and then you came home and parked in your driveway, and you made out—in a not-a-big-deal way—and then you came in the house."

Stevie's senior year at M-A began in September 1965, the pivotal year of the American sixties. The civil rights movement and the Vietnam War were the big issues of the day, with student protests at the University of California in nearby Berkeley gaining national attention. California bands like the Byrds were adapting Bob Dylan songs and inventing a new style, folk rock. And the local music scene was in full boil as well. Two garage bands from nearby San Jose, the Count Five and the Syndicate of Sound, would have coast-to-coast hit singles ("Psychotic Reaction" and "Little Girl") in 1966. Up in San Francisco new bands were forming; within a year the Grateful Dead, Jefferson Airplane, and Big Brother and the Holding Company would coalesce with a dozen other groups into an organic movement that would spread the so-called San Francisco Sound around the planet.

Locally, Stevie bought her guitar strings at Dana Morgan's Music Store in Palo Alto, where all the aspiring young players hung out. She acquired an "official" boyfriend, Charlie Young, a handsome star of the M-A Bears football team. She scored an ace in English class when she set Edgar Allan Poe's morbid poem "Annabel Lee" to music in order to make it easier to memorize as a song, and then sang it in class. (Poe has long appealed to teen readers who instantly recognize a fellow sufferer.) She would record her version of "Annabel Lee" forty-five years in the future. (Another original ballad Stevie sketched in 1965, "Rose Garden," would appear on her album *Street Angel* thirty years later.)

Late in 1965 a new folk rock group from Los Angeles calling themselves the Mamas and the Papas (Hells Angels slang for gang members and their girlfriends) released a new song, "California Dreamin'," written by the group's leader, John Phillips. The celestial four-part harmonies the quartet specialized in appealed to singers like Stevie, and the song became a national hit record. When the group's album came out a few months later, it introduced passionate, brokenhearted classics like "Monday Monday," "Got a Feelin'," and "Go Where You Wanna Go," and Stevie was hooked on this harmonically sophisticated new way of getting folk rock songs across.

Around the end of the year, Stevie took her guitar over to a local church that offered Wednesday evening sessions for young musicians. "It was called Young Life," she said. "Everybody went just to get out of the house on a school night. It was fun. Even I went, and I didn't go anywhere."

She was talking with some kids from school when a tall boy with longish dark hair walked in. She recognized him from M-A; he was a junior, a year younger than she. After a bit, Lindsey Buckingham, age sixteen, sat down at the piano and began playing the opening chords of "California Dreamin'."

"Well, I just happened to know every word and could sing the harmony, and I thought he was absolutely stunning. So I kind of casually maneuvered my way over to the piano." Stevie chimed in, singing Michelle Phillips's high harmony part while Lindsey sang the melody. They glanced at each other; she noticed his eyes, cold blue like lake ice. They sang the whole song while the room went quiet, everyone mesmerized. Then it was over. People clapped a bit. Lindsey was, she guessed, "ever-so-slightly impressed. Not to let me know it, but he did sing another song with me, which let me know he did like it a little." Nothing more was sung that evening. "It wasn't any kind of big deal," Stevie remembered. "He was singing 'California Dreamin',' and I joined in. It was just a one-off, three-minute moment."

Stevie Nicks wouldn't see Lindsey Buckingham again for three years. But she later said that she never stopped thinking about him from time to time.

Then, in the middle of her senior year, Stevie Nicks got herself a recording contract. She described this to England's *Guardian* newspaper much later. "I had a record deal early on. When I was a senior in high school, a friend of a friend of my dad was a big deal at 20th Century Fox [the movie studio, with its own record label]. So I flew to LA with my guitar, sang for them, and signed a contract with a producer called

Jackie Mills. But he quit soon after, and luckily there was a 'main man' clause in my contract that meant that now I was released from it. I wasn't upset. Even at that age I was smart enough to realize that I didn't want to be stuck on a label with people that I didn't know."

After the 1966 new year, Stevie's senior year flashed by. She needed stronger glasses. She applied to colleges at her parents' insistence. "I wanted to go to hairdressing school," she later maintained, "but they didn't go for that idea at all." She kept up her music; her favorite song was Bob Dylan's "Just Like a Woman" from *Blonde on Blonde,* especially the line "But she breaks just like a little girl." ("Just Like a Woman" would appear much later on *Street Angel* as well.) She was photographed in a modest off-shoulder sack dress at the M-A senior prom in June, and shimmied and shook while doing the frug, the most popular high school dance of the day.

In September 1966 she began classes at La Canada Junior College. Stevie continued to live with her family, close to her loving mother, Barbara, commuting to school in a little car that she could hardly drive because she was so nearsighted. The following year she transferred to San Jose State College, where she was often seen on campus carrying her guitar. "I should have gone to hairdressing school," she insists, "because that would have really benefited me more." Soon, "I was singing with Lindsey the whole time, and found it real difficult to study."

## 1.4   Fritz

Lindsey Adams Buckingham was born on October 3, 1949, in Palo Alto, and grew up in Atherton. His father, Morris "Buck" Buckingham, owned a coffee importing company, Alta Coffee, in Daly City, which had been founded by his own father in the 1920s. Lindsey was the youngest of his mother Rutheda's three sons, the older brothers being Greg and Jeff. Lindsey has described his childhood being like *Ozzie and Harriet,* a popular fifties TV comedy about a "normal," typically contemporary suburban family in California. (The program launched the successful music career of the couple's youngest son, Ricky Nelson, who often performed at the end of the show.) A big part of the Buckingham family's life centered on the swimming pools of the Menlo Country Club and the famous Santa Clara Swim Club, where all three boys swam competitively. (Lindsey's older brother Greg, who swam for Stanford University's world-class program, would win a silver medal at the 1968 Olympics in Mexico City.)

When Lindsey was about six years old, he saw cowboy star Gene Autry strumming a guitar on television and asked his parents to buy one for him. So from the Atherton five-and-dime store came a little plastic Mickey Mouse guitar. To Buck and Rutheda's surprise, Lindsey showed some rhythmic aptitude, strumming along to his brother Jeff's collection of 45s. A bit later he appeared at a grade school assembly in black slacks and a starched white shirt, playing a thirty-five-dollar Harmony guitar, singing (or miming) Elvis Presley's "Heartbreak Hotel."

Lindsey was deeply influenced at an early age by local heroes the Kingston Trio, calypso collegians who emerged from Palo Alto with the hit single "Tom Dooley" in 1958 and went on to a successful and enormously influential career playing college concerts around the country. The Trio was really the vanguard of the folk revival to come a few years later, and young Lindsey was captivated by the series of Trio albums his brothers brought home: *The Kingston Trio; . . . From the "Hungry i"; At Large*. He was especially enthralled by the banjo playing of Trio founder Dave Guard, whose fluid style would affect Lindsey's own unusual finger-picking way of playing guitar. By the age of thirteen, even though he never took lessons and couldn't read musical notation, Lindsey was developing into a good guitarist himself through constant, obsessive practice.

Another major influence came in 1963, when the Beach Boys' records started getting airplay in California. Brian Wilson's dreamy reveries about surfing, girls, and cars were delivered with moody blue chord changes and soaring vocals unlike anything heard in rock & roll and pop music. Their 1966 album *Pet Sounds* made an indelible impression on Lindsey, to the point where Brian Wilson's melodic sensibility would have a major impact on Lindsey's musical direction. These two archetypal California groups—the Beach Boys and the Kingston Trio—were the two foundations on which Lindsey's career as a musician, songwriter, and arranger were based.

Lindsey played guitar and banjo while in high school, copying records by the Beatles, Elvis, the Everly Brothers, and country music stars Hank Williams and Marty Robbins. He was much more interested in music than swimming, and when he finally quit the M-A swim team, the coach told him he was a loser. But by then he didn't care, because Lindsey had joined his first real band, Fritz, composed of friends from high school.

Fritz was formed in the fall of 1966 by Lindsey (on guitar and bass) and classmates Bob Aguirre on drums and Javier Pacheco on keyboards. Jody Moreing was the singer and her cousin Cal Roper played bass. The original name of the band was the Fritz Rabyne Memorial Band, named for a rather awkward German exchange student at M-A who reportedly didn't appreciate this honor, so they shortened it to just Fritz. They started playing Top 40 songs like "So You Want to Be a Rock 'n' Roll Star," the Byrds' great satire on the Monkees, the artificial band cynically created in Los Angeles for a TV show. Satire or not, the song's ending—"Don't forget who you are / You're a rock 'n' roll star"—made a deep impression on a lot of aspiring young musicians.

At the time he joined Fritz, Lindsey didn't own an electric guitar, so Bob Aguirre borrowed a Rickenbacker twelve-string from a friend he was playing with in another band. Javier Pacheco was an aspiring songwriter, and they began working on his songs in the garage of the big Buckingham ranch house in Atherton. They gradually worked out band arrangements for a set list that included numbers called "Dream Away," "Lordy," "Sad Times," and "John the Barber" (Pacheco's father was the Buckingham family's longtime barber). Fritz's first real gig was at a senior class assembly at M-A in the spring of 1967. Lindsey's brother Greg came by with some of his Stanford buddies, one of whom, David Forest, liked the band and said he could maybe book them into fraternity house parties for decent money.

Now the young musicians began having delusions of grandeur. Maybe, after a lot of hard work and gigging, Fritz could join the growing roster of the San Francisco bands, playing original songs in front of psychedelic light shows in the city's repurposed old ballrooms and auditoriums: the Grateful Dead, Jefferson Airplane, Country Joe & the Fish, Quicksilver Messenger Service, the Charlatans, Moby Grape, the Sons of Champlin, Ace of Cups, Spirit, and Big Brother and the Holding Company. In Oakland across the bay, Sly & the Family Stone were fomenting a revolution in dance music, combining the funk of soul music with the hard rock of the other Bay Area bands. These groups played almost every weekend, often on bills with top English bands—Cream, the Who, John Mayall's Bluesbreakers—at a handful of venues around San Francisco. Top rock promoter Bill Graham had been putting on rock concerts at the Fillmore Auditorium at the corner of Fillmore and Geary since 1966. The Family Dog hippie commune staged shows at the Avalon Ballroom at 1268 Sutter Street, a favorite venue of the communitarian Grateful Dead. In 1968 Bill Graham would lease the Carousel Ballroom at Market and South Van Ness Avenue and rename it the Fillmore West. These shows were promoted with avant-garde psychedelic posters and on the new FM rock stations pioneered by San Francisco's KSAN. They inspired a new kind of audience, "girls dancing like they were catching butterflies on acid," according to guitarist Carlos Santana, a Bill Graham protégée.

Graham also showcased San Francisco bands in San Jose, and these sometimes wild shows in 1967 were the first time Stevie Nicks saw the two women who would become her role models: Grace Slick, the elegant lead singer of Jefferson Airplane; and Janis Joplin, whose raw, bluesy vocals powered Big Brother and the Holding Company. Little did Fritz know it then, but a year later they would be opening for a lot of these legendary bands.

Lindsey graduated from M-A in June 1967 and would start at San Jose State in September. He wanted to keep Fritz going, because the more they rehearsed, the better they sounded. But then Jody Moreing left to join the New Invaders, a bigger band working out of San Jose. Cal Roper left for college, and Lindsey moved over to play bass. Javier hired Brian Kane to play lead guitar. Fritz auditioned two girl singers, but neither had the onstage presence that Jody had. Finally, at a band meeting at Lindsey's house, he mentioned that there'd been a girl a year ahead of him at M-A who was kind of cute and could really sing. He'd seen her at college toting a guitar case. Maybe she would do. Her name, he said, was Stevie Nicks. Javier said he knew her from M-A. Lindsey said, yeah, give her a call.

Stevie was in her first year at San Jose State (where she had decided to study speech therapy, since it was the major closest to her aspiring singing career). A few months earlier, in the fall of 1967, she'd had an epiphany when she first heard Linda Ronstadt (from Tucson, Arizona) of the Stone Poneys sing "Different Drum" on Top 40 radio in a powerful voice that delivered a passionate message about a young woman wanting her independence from a man who just wants to settle down. Much later, looking back, Stevie remembered, "I heard Linda Ronstadt, and I just said, 'That's *it!* *That's* what I want to do' . . . although I didn't look as good as her in cut-offs."

More than ever, an ambitious Stevie now knew what she needed to do: write songs and sing them with a band behind her, like Linda, Grace, and Janis. She wrote in her journal that nothing was going to get in her way. But where could she find a band? It was at this fortuitous moment that the phone rang, and on the other end of the line was Bob Aguirre from high school, saying that "Linds," the bass player in his band, recommended her as a good singer, and would she be interested in coming by his house for an audition?

And so Stevie Nicks, in her twentieth year, packed up her guitar, and a friend drove Stevie, in her own car, over to Lindsey Buckingham's house in Atherton, and into a future that she might have faintly foreseen at that moment in her life, a glimmer of what was to come.

## 1.5   Hands Off Stevie Nicks

They hired her. Sometime in the summer of 1968 Stevie Nicks joined Lindsey Buckingham and friends in Fritz. And this was only one of many big changes to come that year. Her father was reassigned to Chicago, so the family home was sold and Stevie moved into a little apartment with friends so she could continue at San Jose State. (The college made headlines that summer when two of its star sprinters won Olympic medals in Mexico City and raised black-gloved fists at the awards podium to protest against racism in America.)

Joining Fritz was a big deal for her. Bob was a good drummer and Lindsey was versatile, could play almost anything. "They were good," she recalled. "They were really playing, so it was almost as bad as join-ing a big rock-and-roll band, because they were serious. I was the only girl and I was always late for everything, but now it was 'You be there!' But I was one on-time person, mostly. I had no social life at all, but I would get paid, at least."

Stevie learned Javier's songs, and he thought she did them as well as or better than Jody. She brought along two songs of her own, "Funny Kind of Love" and "Where Was I?" and played them on her guitar. She seemed to fit right in as a band singer, working with the micro-phone and moving to the rhythms in an attractive way, kind of slinky like Grace Slick. The band's first paying gig with Stevie Nicks onstage was arranged by Greg Buckingham in the fall of 1968, playing to a huge crowd in the main quad at Stanford.

Bob Aguirre: "I knew right away what she would bring to the party, and it worked! I remember that her first gig with us was at the Quad at Stanford—a big deal with lots of people there—and Stevie did a ver-sion of Linda Ronstadt's "Different Drum" that brought the house down, that *we had to do again,* by popular demand. The writing was on the wall."

After the concert the band was approached by a Stanford freshman who was so impressed by Fritz's performance that he wanted to be their booking agent. His name was David Forest and he was the so-cial chairman of his Stanford dormitory. He realized that he could make money by booking the top local bands he was hiring for other gigs at high schools and college fraternities. Forest asked if they wanted to work more, and explained that he could get Fritz regular gigs at $125 for four 45-minute sets per night. He took a $25 fee on top of that. Fritz came back and said they'd do three sets for $150, take it or leave it. Forest took the deal, even though Fritz absolutely refused to play the most requested songs by the frat boys: "Gloria," "Louie Louie," and "Satisfaction."

And so Fritz started playing around Santa Clara County, up and down the peninsula, hairy young Bob Aguirre driving the decrepit Ford equipment van, working the Stanford frat parties and local high school dances, plus the Bay Area community colleges like La Canada

Junior College in Redwood City and De Anza in Cupertino, performing mostly Javier's songs but also quirky numbers like "Bonnie and Clyde," which was actually Lindsey playing "Foggy Mountain Breakdown" (from the 1967 hit movie about the bank-robbing lovers) on the banjo. They worked up a version of "Codine," folk singer Buffy Sainte-Marie's song about codeine addiction, with Stevie dramatically acting out the ravages of addiction withdrawal that often got the most applause of the evening. (The band would be eye-rollingly annoyed every time Stevie stole the show this way.)

Gradually, the guys in the band began to get frustrated that Stevie Nicks seemed to be getting all the attention. People clapped politely when the band members were introduced at the end of their sets, but Stevie usually provoked a roar and general cheering. David Forest reported that when clients—especially the fraternities—called to book a band, they first asked for the group that had the cute little chick singer with the dirty blond hair.

Things were looking good for the former high school band. They even got a permanent place to rehearse, in the unused banquet room of the Italian Gardens restaurant in San Jose. At Fritz's peak they rehearsed there four days a week and did shows on Friday and Saturday nights.

Meanwhile, Fritz had a policy: Hands off Stevie Nicks. This was from day one. It was barely discussed, but there wasn't going to be any intraband dating going on with Fritz. And this was fine with her. The guys all had girlfriends, anyway. (Lindsey was going with a girl called Sally.)

Recalling her days on the road with Fritz, Stevie said, "Nobody in that band wanted me as their girlfriend because I was too ambitious for them. But they didn't want anyone else to have me either. If anyone else in the band started spending any time with me, the other three would literally pick that person apart—to the death. They all thought I was in it for the attention. These guys didn't take me seriously at all. I was just a girl singer, and they hated the fact that I got a lot of the credit."

Years later, an interviewer asked Stevie when was the first time she ever felt like a rock star. She replied that shortly after joining Fritz, she was walking across her college campus in 1968, carrying her guitar, and that's when she knew in her bones that she was going to be a rock star someday.

All this time, she kept writing poems and lyrics in the journals she always carried. In early 1969, thinking about the boy who broke up with her in high school, she wrote a sexy lyric called "Cathouse Blues."

By late 1969, Fritz had graduated to San Francisco's legendary electric ballrooms. It was a thrill to open for Moby Grape at the Fillmore West or for Creedence Clearwater Revival at Bill Graham's Winterland, an old skating rink at the corner of Post and Steiner that the impresario had opened as a rock venue in 1968. For the next eighteen months Fritz opened shows for Leon Russell, Chicago, and the Santana Blues Band. They appeared twice on Ross McGowan's local TV dance show. They opened a huge concert called Earth Day Jubilee at Cal Expo, the big state fair in Sacramento, the other acts being B.B. King and the Guess Who. They supported Santana again at the Monterey/Carmel Pop Festival, right before Woodstock in the summer of 1969. They tried and failed to get a gig opening for Led Zeppelin in San Francisco, but Bill Graham wanted a bigger act for Jimmy Page's new English band—which was the hugest thing at San Jose State that year. "Their music was everywhere," Stevie remembered. (Somewhat oddly, Fritz never opened shows for Fleetwood Mac, the surging British blues band starring London guitar god Peter Green. Fleetwood Mac—reliable, crowd-pleasing, virtuosic—was a favorite of Bill Graham's, who actively promoted them and gave the band all the work they wanted in the San Francisco area.)

Janis Joplin had left Big Brother to go solo, an industry trend as talent managers separated the biggest rock stars from their original bands and started over with hired musicians. Fritz opened for Janis's new Kozmic Blues Band at the Fillmore West in early 1970. Stevie: "When I first saw Janis she was very angry. The first band had run overtime and she came on the stage screaming, scared me to death. I was hiding behind the amps. She told them to get the fuck off her fucking stage—and they wrapped it up! Twenty minutes later, on walks this girl in silky bell bottoms, a beautiful top, lots of gorgeous jewelry, wearing sling-back low heels, feathers in her crazy big natural hair. Lots of attitude, arrogance, sang like a bird, the crowd in the palm of her hand. . . . She was not a beautiful woman, but very attractive. I was very taken with her."

Less taken with the hard-living singer were the guys in Fritz, who hung out with her and her band in the dressing room. Janis was swigging from a bottle of Southern Comfort, chain-smoking and cussing out everyone in her Texas drawl. They thought she was coarse, vulgar, and not someone you'd want to be in a band with.

In the spring of 1970 there was a student strike at San Jose State to protest the American invasion of Cambodia. Strike organizers put together a concert with Fritz as the main act, and they played for hours, and in the end Stevie lost her voice for the first time.

That summer Fritz opened some of Bill Graham's rock concerts at the Santa Clara County Fairgrounds. These drew big crowds, and big acts. They opened for Janis Joplin's new Full Tilt Boogie Band at the Fairgrounds on July 12, 1970, and also for Jimi Hendrix's Band of Gypsies that summer in front of a reported 75,000 fans. Jimi noticed Stevie backstage, and he seemed to her to be a very humble, sweet, unpretentious person. During his act, as he was tuning his guitar, Hendrix looked over and saw Stevie watching him from behind the amplifiers. He stepped up to the microphone, pointed at Stevie, and told the crowd, "I want to dedicate a song to that girl over there." Legend has it that the song he played for her was "Angel."

"I saw him play once," she later said of Hendrix, "and I remember thinking, *I want to wear white fringe. I want to tie a beautiful scarf in my hair.*"

Through all this Stevie Nicks watched and learned, taking her lessons as she found them. "So from Janis I learned that to make it as a female musician in a man's world is going to be tough, and you need to keep your head held high. From Jimi, I learned flamboyance, grace, and humility."

But neither star would see the end of 1970. A few months later, both Janis Joplin and Jimi Hendrix died of drug overdoses, a national tragedy, both at the age of twenty-seven.

## 1.6   The Music Machine

Much later, Stevie recalled this period with her first band as one of the happier times in her life, "when I first lived on my own, with my friend Robin." Certainly the sense of style, costume, and fashion that would underpin her future career were formed in the intense cultural matrix of the San Francisco Sound. Stevie moved in both music circles and student circles. She was impressed by the early groupies' original style that scrambled genres and broke fashion rules in the same way these girls also aggressively broke sexual norms. The groupies mixed contemporary styles (which they often sewed or knocked off themselves) with vintage clothes and outdated mod stuff from thrift stores. They used feathers, boas, and fishnet to attract attention. Heavy on the makeup, lots of flashy dyed hair. They liked costumes—flapper dresses, bordello-chic lingerie, Barbarella sci-fi outfits, velour suits with kinky masculine brogues, Native American buckskins—all topped with floppy broad-brimmed hats or classic veils.

(But Stevie also was well aware that the real lives of the so-called groupies weren't all dressed-up glamour. Their world was competitive and often tawdry, even dangerous because of the drugs, and many a dirty-look dagger did Stevie receive backstage from these feral girls hunting rock stars. Some of this sordid atmosphere would surface ten years later in the song "Gold Dust Woman.")

Then there was the prevailing style of the college coeds, and the hippie girls milking goats in the new farm communes sprouting north of San Francisco, listening intently to Joni Mitchell's confessional albums and reading Sulamith Wulfing, the visionary German artist who painted vivid depictions of angels and fairies (and a major inspiration for Stevie Nicks): these were young women in shawls, woolens and long tweed skirts, hair long and straight, wearing sturdy boots, peasant blouses, tie-dyed dresses, turquoise, jet, and silver, with the occasional brocaded sheepskin vest that someone had brought back from Afghanistan.

Stevie liked to shop at an ultrahip San Francisco boutique called Velvet Underground, where Janis Joplin and Grace Slick bought much of what they wore onstage. If anyone, it was Grace Slick—electrifying siren of acid rock—whom she most admired as the archetypal female

rock star. Grace was tall and aristocratic, a former debutante from suburban Chicago. She was older than most, born in 1939, and performed
the Airplane's anthemic, hard-rocking songs with the élan of someone who'd had sophisticated dance training, moving across a stage
with slinky feline assurance. Stevie liked that it wasn't "Grace Slick
and the Jefferson Airplane," that Grace was part of a band and not on
a solo trip like Janis had been in the end. Grace looked great in silk
bell-bottoms and stiletto-heeled boots. She wore Victorian blouses and
antique clothing to photo shoots. Her soaring vocal bravado on the
band's 1967 Top 10 singles "Somebody To Love" and "White Rabbit"
had turned the Airplane into a national brand, a group of hippie artists with commercial clout. Some of Grace's distinctive style definitely
rubbed off on Stevie, in those years when Fritz was one of the better
local bands in the Bay Area.

In fact, people remember Fritz as an exciting psychedelic rock band.
Back in the early days of the group, Fritz had competed in a battle of
the bands in San Jose with the Count Five and the Syndicate of Sound,
both groups with national hit singles behind them. Count Five won
the battle, but afterward Stevie got in their faces. "You're good," she
told the astonished Counts, *but you're not as good as me.*

But then, in 1971, it all fell apart. Fritz would disband that year. It
would be a months-long process, and it ended in a lot of recrimina-
tion and remorse for everyone involved. When it was over, Stevie and
Lindsey Buckingham would embark on the most important relationship of their lives.

It started to change when David Forest, the band's de facto manager, decided to move to Los Angeles, and he wanted Fritz to go with
him. He would get them studio time, they'd demo their songs, he'd
get them a record deal. LA was where it was happening in the music
business. San Francisco was so 1967. What Forest didn't tell Fritz was
that Bill Graham had taken an interest in the band, and thought he
might be able to do something with the group. But Forest had a point.
The big LA bands—the Doors, Buffalo Springfield, Love, the Flying
Burrito Brothers—sold more records nationally than the Bay Area
bands. They had much more exposure to the media. And he may have

noticed that when Stevie and Lindsey sang together, it sounded a lot more like Southern California country rock than anything else.

This LA move was controversial, and the band meetings were heated. Stevie didn't much want to go to LA, which was generally thought of as plastic, crass, and uncool by the hippie musicians in San Francisco. Javier Pacheco, who wrote the songs and ran Fritz (according to Stevie) "with an iron hand," was against the idea as well. He protested that there were sharply different regional values at work here. Did Fritz want to be overproduced, like Crosby, Stills & Nash? He said that Fritz was already beyond the commercial limitations of the polished Tinseltown record business. Later he wrote, "How do you [re]fashion a group whose music is inspired by the Dead and the Airplane to suddenly turn into the Monkees?" But in the end, Javier would be outvoted by his band mates. Fritz would try to head south. The next step was to find a producer interested in recording the band in Los Angeles.

In 1971 Keith Olsen was the chief engineer at a grungy, second-rate recording studio in Los Angeles called Sound City. Olsen was a little older and had played bass guitar with the Music Machine, an ahead-of-its-time Los Angeles garage band that dressed in all black and played with black leather gloves. They had a national hit single with "Talk Talk" in 1966. Like many ambitious recording engineers, he aspired to the greater satisfaction and rewards of producing records, taking a band's songs and reshaping them into a commercial format that would sell to the huge postwar baby boom, an audience that bought so many millions of records that by the mid-1970s the music industry was the most lucrative entertainment component of the American economy, even bigger than Hollywood.

Olsen was at the end of a long list of producers that another agent named Todd Shipman was trying to persuade to go to San Francisco and see Fritz. Every LA studio pro with any record company connections said no—except Olsen, who was always up for a free trip north to hear a promising new band. At the least he could record demos of some of their songs if they were any good. He flew in and was met at the airport by Bob Aguirre driving the seatless Fritz van; Olsen sat on the drum cases on the way to the band's gig, a Friday night dance at a Catholic high school.

"They were OK," he recalled, "but not the super band of the future." But Keith Olsen was struck by the harmony singing and the sexy rapport between Stevie and Lindsey. There was definitely energy there. He allowed that he could get Fritz some free studio time, on a Sunday, if they came down to make some song demos with him in LA.

Stevie didn't much want to do this, and neither did Javier, but soon the band piled in the van and made the long drive to Los Angeles on a Saturday. They checked into the famously band-friendly Tropicana Motel on Sunset Boulevard. When they got to Sound City Studio in industrial Van Nuys on Sunday morning, they found the door locked. They had to take it off its hinges to get inside. The studio was a dump, with rotting Chinese take-out food containers and overflowing ashtrays from the previous night's sessions. Soon Javier noticed that Lindsey's demeanor was changing as he watched Keith Olsen, a seasoned studio engineer, manipulate the knobs and faders of the sixteen-track recording console for the first time. Lindsey was fascinated, entranced. Worse, he looked bored when the band listened to the tapes they'd made. The mostly hook-free tunes kind of sucked; they may have sounded OK at a beer-sodden fraternity party, but they just didn't have the dynamics of a great record. Javier could almost feel his band slipping from his iron fist while they were still in the studio.

They cut demo tapes with Keith Olsen of four of Javier's songs. "Something wasn't right," Olsen recalled. "There were too many weaknesses." Before Fritz went home, Olsen recalls, "I took Lindsey and Stevie aside and said to them, 'You two really have a unique sound together . . . but the rest of your band will hold you back. I'd like to continue to work with you, but I think you'd do *much* better as a duo.'"

They looked at each other, then told Olsen that they would talk it over and get back to him. The race was now on for real.


## 1.7  Trading Old Dreams for New

When Stevie Nicks and Lindsey Buckingham returned home, they took a few days to think about what Keith Olsen had offered. Stevie called her mother. Lindsey spoke with his father and brothers. At one point she asked Lindsey what would happen if she decided to stay, and he said he didn't know what he'd do in that case. Everyone felt bad for the other guys in Fritz, but that's show business. Unspoken were the social and racial implications of the two cuter and more talented Anglos leaving behind the two journeymen Hispanics, Pacheco and Aguirre. But that's California. Stevie saw it as a betrayal. Lindsey didn't think so. They had something major going between them, he told her, and they were just taking it to the next level. There was a lot of talk between them about races to be run and about winning as opposed to losing.

But she still wasn't sure she wanted to be in Los Angeles. The city had just had that big earthquake: bridges flattened, cracks in the earth, the sky turned yellow for days. "I didn't want to go that much," she said later. "I never thought that I'd make it in Hollywood. And I *never* thought that I'd want to stay."

But in those fraught days Stevie and Lindsey were growing closer. Sometimes she had stayed overnight in the Buckinghams' guest room when the band came home late. Now she started sleeping there more. Lindsey broke up with his girlfriend Sally. "We started spending a *lot* of time together," she recalls, "working out songs" with lots of shared intimacy and eye contact. When they finally made the decision to break up the band, they kept it to themselves for a few days, and it wasn't the only secret they shared.

There may have been an erotic aspect to killing this attachment of five years and taking off to greener pastures. Stevie later said that she never felt entirely comfortable with what happened. "All through Fritz Lindsey and I were dating other people. I'm not sure we would have even become a couple if it wasn't for us leaving that band. It kind of pushed us together."

Stevie and Lindsey dreaded the last band meeting. Later Stevie told *Behind the Music:* "We had to tell these other three guys—that we *loved*—that we were going to break up the band, and that Lindsey and I were going to Los Angeles. And it was very difficult." They said they couldn't resist Keith Olsen's offer to produce them, that it was a main chance for them. They held hands, the first time anyone had seen this. (Bob Aguirre: "They weren't real out in the open about it. All of a sudden they were together.") They said they were both dropping out of college—Stevie was only a few credits shy of graduation—and running for the rainbow in LA. And that was basically the end of Fritz. Bob Aguirre stayed friends with them, but Javier was bitter and later complained about the "lying and manipulative" way that David Forest had treated them, just as Bill Graham had (supposedly) taken an interest. Forest himself went on to a checkered career as an agent, a pimp, a gay-porn producer, and eventually went bankrupt.

But it was the beginning of the epic love of Stevie and Lindsey. She was twenty-three; he was a year younger. "I loved him before he was famous," she said on TV later. "I loved him before he was a millionaire. We were two kids out of Menlo-Atherton High School. I loved him for all the right reasons." And, to an interviewer: "We did have a great relationship at first. I loved taking care of him and the house. I washed his jeans and embroidered stupid moons and stars on the bottom of them, and made it so he was perfect."

This love would become greater with time. The Stevie & Lindsey Saga would inspire some of the greatest love songs of their generation, and indeed of the entire rock movement. The songs are in heavy rotation even now, decades on. This love would then suffer neglect and jealousy and finally would expire, but only on the surface. Their love would burrow underground, forgotten by everyone but the lovers, where it would smolder for decades like a dormant volcano, occasionally erupting into passionate explosions of romantic fire and magma. (Some say this love still exists.)

September 1971. The deed was done, and Stevie and Lindsey prepared to move south. Keith Olsen invited them to stay at his house in the Hollywood Hills until they could get on their feet. But then fate intervened and Lindsey got sick. The symptoms were low fever, lassitude, and weakness. The diagnosis was glandular fever or mononucleosis. The doctor told Lindsey to rest, nothing else until he started to feel better.

So while they waited (and waited, for seven months) for Lindsey to recover, and while Stevie looked after him, they started making songs. The Hand of Fate may have dealt Lindsey a bad card, but now Dame Fortune favored him with a timely family inheritance of $12,500, enough to live on for a year. He and Stevie went shopping and bought a used BMW, a pre-owned electric guitar, and an old Ampex half-inch, reel-to-reel tape recorder. The inheritance came at just the right time, Stevie remembered. "It was a goodly amount of money, especially then, and especially for two people who had no money. Lindsey bought an Ampex four-track—he's very brilliant and I can't even plug in the stereo—and his dad let us have this tiny little room in his coffee plant. All the workers would leave around seven [P.M.] and we'd get there around seven-thirty and leave at six in the morning. It was this big, huge building; it was scary, and we'd lock ourselves in and work. It was just me, Lindsey, and the Ampex, everything we owned on the floor of this tiny room, and we'd just sing, and play, and record. We did seven songs and it took us a year. We thought they were really good."

As the months at the coffee plant in Daly City dragged on, Stevie's new song lyrics started to take on issues about their relationship. Lindsey was not an easy boyfriend to have. She found him to be bossy, hyperopinionated, and overcontrolling. He made her study records by the Beatles and the Kingston Trio so she could learn songwriting form—verses, chorus, a bridge. It was annoying. Forbidden to smoke marijuana by his doctor, major pothead Lindsey was often irritable and short with her. New songs like "Races to Run" and "Lady from the Mountains" explored relational issues like mastery and jealousy. "Without You" was about adjusting to a tense new relationship. "After the Glitter Fades" and "Nomad" mirrored her unease about moving to LA. This didn't seem to faze Lindsey, who was focusing more on turning her words into music than on what they actually might mean. "I loved her lyrics," he said later. "I loved providing the styles in which we would interpret these songs."

And Lindsey was writing, too, in an amazing burst of artistic creativity. He was, after all, a bass player who was also teaching himself how to play electric lead guitar. Early in his recovery he was too weak to sit up, so he taught himself to play while lying flat, using downward strokes. This developed into an almost unique personal style: playing a "bass" part on the lower strings with his thumb while using the first three fingers—and mostly his fingernails—for melody and rhythm. One of the first songs he completed this way was a lovely instrumental for his new girlfriend, called "Stephanie."

Lindsey was also teaching himself the craft of sound engineering with his four-track machine. Stevie would watch him intently, for hours, concentrating under his headphones, recording with one little microphone, obsessing over details, dubbing in her vocals over the lead and bass guitar parts, with Bob Aguirre's drums on the bottom of the rock songs. She noticed that he would vigorously rub his hands together in pleased enthusiasm when he achieved an effect he was seeking. This is where Lindsey's earliest songs—"So Afraid" and "Frozen Love"—came from.

In late 1972 they had seven songs they thought were good enough to bring to Keith Olsen. They packed their clothes, a few possessions, the tape recorder, and Lindsey's guitars, and made the six-hour drive to Los Angeles. They found Olsen at busy Sound City, supervising the electricians and crew that was installing the studio's brand-new recording console, and generally being elated at the prospect of making records at this gleaming desk. At the end of the day they followed Olsen home to his house off Coldwater Canyon Boulevard and moved into his back room until they could land a place of their own.

So Stevie Nicks was dragged reluctantly, if not kicking and screaming, to Los Angeles by her new boyfriend Lindsey Buckingham. He was so sure this was the right road to follow, and she was so devoted to him that she went along, and indeed, she never lived to regret it.


## 1.8   Sound City

Stevie Nicks remembered that she and Lindsey Buckingham were apprehensive the first night they were taken to Doug Weston's Troubadour nightclub on Santa Monica Boulevard in late 1972. The Troub, as it was known, had been the social clubhouse of the LA music scene for more than ten years. Everyone played there, and many went on to become legends. The bar scene was intimidating.

By then the previous generation of sixties California rock stars had moved on (or died). The Byrds, Buffalo Springfield, the Mamas and Papas, the Burrito Brothers, Joni Mitchell, and all the laid-back sixties musicians were now living up in Topanga Canyon and Malibu and couldn't be bothered to drive into West Hollywood and be seen in the Troub's noisy, smoky bar area, packed with musicians, dealers, and hustlers, all on the make.

Their places were taken by a glamorous and talented new breed, many of them singer-songwriters: Linda Ronstadt, the braless beauty from Tucson; handsome young Jackson Browne; lanky Texan John David Souther; Hollywood brat Randy Newman; nasty drunk Warren Zevon; and especially charismatic Don Henley and Glenn Frey, the two principals of "Eagles" (as they insisted on calling themselves), the hottest group in America right then. They were surfing the crest of a new wave of psychic energy as California recovered from the serial traumas of the American sixties, which in Los Angeles had ended with the gruesome multiple murders by the so-called Manson Family and the subsequent trials and recriminations about an era of revolt and license that had gone horribly wrong.

But now there was a change in the air. The American seventies had an air of promise. In Los Angeles the music scene was alive with possibility and confidence, typified by the amazing success of the ultracommercial Eagles. The band had actually come together at the Troubadour bar when Linda Ronstadt, the greatest voice of her generation, hired singer-guitarist Frey (from Michigan and in Longbranch Pennywhistle with John David Souther) and the band Shiloh's singing drummer Henley (from Cass County, Texas) to play in her band. This mutated into Eagles, and all year Stevie and Lindsey had been listening to their irresistible Top 10 smash hits on the car radio: "Take It Easy," "Witchy Woman," and "Peaceful Easy Feeling." The Eagles were hated by establishment rock critics for their glossy superficiality and slick production values, but their records sold in the millions (mostly to women) and the songs were everywhere. (Many fans didn't think the Eagles were even the best band in Los Angeles. That honor went by popular acclaim to guitarist Lowell George's jazzy rock band, Little Feat.)

"We were scared to death when we first moved to LA," Stevie later recalled, but they needn't have been. They were immediately perceived as a sexy, star-bound couple. People who encountered them recall an aura about them, a radiance. They were Mr. and Mrs. Intense, he in his curly locks and icy blue eyes and she in her long straight hair and her piercing gaze when you talked to her. (This was because she could barely see you without her reading glasses.) They seemed to share an internal strength as magnified individuals. When they walked into the room—whether at the Troubadour or the Ash Grove or the Palomino Club or McCabe's Guitar Shop in Santa Monica—heads turned to check out this power couple newly arrived in LA, trying to make it big. Few who met them doubted that they would. Even brilliant but crazy Warren Zevon was nice to them.

But their demo tape of seven songs couldn't get arrested.

Lindsey had brought the Ampex and the tapes, which Olsen plugged into Sound City's new recording desk, and made a bunch of copies, which he tried to pedal to recording executives eager, even desperate, to sign the next Eagles. In early 1973 their demos were rejected by all the big labels: Columbia, Warner Bros., Reprise, Elektra, Atlantic, RCA, Polygram, Mercury, ABC-Dunhill, and talent manager David Geffen's new Asylum Records. Nobody heard a hit record in "Rhiannon," "I Don't Want To Know," and "So Afraid."

"Every record company in the world passed on us," Stevie said later. "We were devastated, but we still knew we were good." And Keith Olsen still believed in them, knew they had something special together, and he encouraged them to keep going. Olsen worked it out with Sound City's owners so the duo could work on new song demos, for free, in unused studios and after hours. This was at least something for the disappointed pair. Stevie and Lindsey had no record deal, and no management; they were lonely in these early days, were running out of money, and they missed their families. But now at least they had the Sound City Studio family behind them, and it *was* something like a family, and that was a good reason for them to keep going. It was a help to know that people they liked had faith in them.

Sound City was a former warehouse behind the railroad tracks in Van Nuys, then the industrial heart of the San Fernando Valley, northwest of downtown Los Angeles. There was a Budweiser brewery nearby, so the neighborhood always smelled of burned hops and fumes from the diesel beer trucks that rumbled through the streets day and night. 1540 Cabrito Road had been the Vox guitar factory in the sixties. The Rolling Stones had famously visited during their first American tour in 1964; it's where Stones founder Brian Jones got his iconic white teardrop-shaped guitar that was frequently seen on TV from 1964 to 1967. The building itself was shabby and in ill repair. The parking lot flooded when it rained.

The recording studio was started by local businessman Joe Gottlieb a few years later to cash in on the record boom in the wake of the big LA bands. There were two studios, control rooms, and a reception and lounge area. The whole complex was carpeted in brown shag, even some of the walls, and it was widely regarded as unsanitary. There was no janitor. The girls at the front desk were supposed to help keep the place tidy, but sessions often ended long after the receptionist had left for the day, and the facility was awash with coffee cups, empty bottles, and full ashtrays. One of Sound City's claims to fame was that Neil Young had sung the wonderful vocals for his multiplatinum album *After the Goldrush* there in 1970. On the album sleeve Young is depicted lying amid the empty soda cups and grungy shag of the studio lounge.

That year Gottlieb sold an interest in Sound City to a West Virginia entrepreneur called Tom Skeeter, who was moving to California to get into show business. When Keith Olsen joined the company a year later, he persuaded Skeeter to order a new mixing console from British sound engineer Rupert Neve. Then Neve's company took more than a year to custom-build the console to Sound City's specifications. Neve boards were then (and still are) considered the holy grail of analog recording. They were extremely rare (especially in America), custom made, and highly coveted. Sound City's board, when it arrived in Van Nuys at about the same time as Stevie and Lindsey, was the only one of its kind in North America. Tom Skeeter paid a whopping $76,000 for the console; by contrast he also bought a three-bedroom house in Teluca Lake for $36,000, so this was a sizeable investment.

Stevie and Lindsey had a bunch of new ideas they wanted to try out, so as it happened the first song that Keith Olsen worked on with the brand-new Neve board was one of Stevie's new songs, "Crying in the Night." It was an auspicious beginning for the musicians, the producer, and Sound City, a studio taking a chance on two scared and lonely kids from out of town. For the next two and a half years, Stevie and Lindsey basically lived at Sound City. "It was like our home," she later agreed. "[Owners] Joe and Tom were like our parents."

## 1.9  "Not for Long"

Summer 1972. While Stevie and Lindsey were crashing in the back bedroom of Keith Olsen's house, he was called to New York to mix a James Gang show in Central Park. Their old car's transmission had died, so he loaned them his car—a new Corvette Sting Ray, gold colored, with 350 miles on it—on the condition that they drive him to the place where the limousine would be picking up the band—at five in the morning—and then pick him up three days later. At dawn on the appointed day, Stevie appeared in a nightdress, her hair in a towel, and blearily drove Keith down steep Coldwater Canyon Boulevard to the rendezvous in the Valley. Olsen: "Stevie in a long, heavy cotton robe, trying to drive a stick-shift car, which she'd never done before, where the end of the robe got caught up in the pedals. As she rode away after dropping me off, the lead singer of the James Gang said, 'Keith, you'll never see that car again.'"

When Olsen got to his hotel in New York, there was a message waiting for him to call home. "Lindsey got on the phone and told me everyone was OK but the car was in my neighbor's bedroom. Stevie had parked the car [on the steep hill], pulled on the brake—one click—and went back to bed. Forty minutes later, the car rolled down the hill, went over a cliff, was hurled into the air and into the bedroom of the house below me. (Come to think of it, I think Stevie still owes me for that car . . . )"

Stevie and Lindsey may have felt lonely when they first arrived in Los Angeles, but that wouldn't last long. One of the first friends they made was Richard Dashut, the twenty-two-year-old assistant engineer at Sound City. He was local, from West Hollywood, with dark long hair, friendly eyes, and a great laugh. He'd started out as the janitor at Crystal Sound in Hollywood, keeping an eye on the big stars of the day as they worked in the studio: James Taylor, Joni Mitchell, Jackson Browne, Crosby, Stills & Nash. He wasn't allowed to even touch the sixteen-track mixing board outfitted with the big Dolby units that every studio used to have. Richard met Keith Olsen and talked himself into a job doing maintenance at Sound City. But after a couple of weeks he was promoted to Olsen's number-two engineer, which is when he met Buckingham Nicks, as the duo was called in the production deal they had just signed with the studio.

Richard recalls: "They were staying at Keith's house and working with him on songs. Lindsey and I were friends five minutes after we met, smoking a joint in the parking lot. This was my first day in my new job. I met Stevie next, and twenty minutes later the three of us decided to get a place together, since I was looking around and they had to move out of Keith's. Eventually we rented an apartment in North Hollywood, near Universal Studios. It quickly became a madhouse. I'd come home after twenty hours working with Keith at the studio and literally trip over Lindsey's microphone cables because he'd be up late working with his Ampex four-track machine. Various other musicians would be passed out on the floor sleeping off the effects of all the pot and hash that we smoked, all the time. Sometimes I'd go into my room and find Stevie sleeping in my bed because she'd had another big argument with Lindsey, who liked to boss her around. It wasn't an easy life for us. You had to be resilient, but we were young."

One of those other musicians on the floor was Robert "Waddy" Wachtel, who had migrated to LA from Brooklyn. He was a spectral, gangly guitarist with long wild blond hair and wire spectacles perched on a big Brooklyn nose. He was a Stones-inspired hard rock musician who'd already been featured on Linda Ronstadt's albums, and like Buckingham Nicks he had a quasi-production deal going with Sound City. Wachtel recalls, "I was working at Sound City, doing my stuff, trying to get up the next rung on the ladder, and so were they. And we became very tight friends, you know? Stevie was still very innocent at that point. She was like this little folksinger girl. Lindsey and I were both totally addicted to the music. He had a four-track Ampex tape machine, and they were making these great demos of their songs. I started working on their album, and from then on the three of us were always together, basically. I was *always* at their house. We were just sitting around, on the floor, talking and playing our guitars and smoking lots of hash."

It was around this time that Stevie and Lindsey (pka—"professionally known as"—Buckingham Nicks) signed their deal with Pogologo Productions, a new company owned by Keith Olsen and Tom Skeeter, who recalled, "We signed them to a production deal. They wrote the songs. We provided the studio, the engineers, and the tape." There would be no retainer or salary for them until they got a recording contract with a major label, so they would have to get jobs. Also signing Pogologo contracts at this time were their pals Waddy Wachtel and the hot young percussionist Jorge Calderon.

There had been some contention about "Buckingham Nicks." Band names were important. Was it quite right? There were a lot of duos working in those days: Delaney & Bonny; Loggins & Messina; Brewer & Shipley; Seals & Crofts; Batdorf & Rodney. They all had the ampersand. Some thought the registered name should be "Nicks & Buckingham" since she was obviously going to be the draw, not him. Then someone said the name Buckingham Nicks might be *too* English. Like, Buckingham Palace. Like, Buckinghamshire. The Duke of Buckingham, et cetera. Then Warren Zevon came to—he was often out cold—and pointed out that Buckingham Nicks had four syllables but all the big English bands of the day had three: Led Zepp'lin, Jethro Tull, Judas Priest, Humble Pie, Spooky Tooth, Wishbone Ash, Blodwyn Pig, Steeleye Span, Savoy Brown, Fleetwood Mac. Even Rolling Stones. But they signed their deal, in the end, as Buckingham Nicks.

Keith Olsen now really put them to work. For this producer "preproduction" really meant rehearsal: shaping songs, working out arrangements, putting the ideas on paper because the reefer-addled musicians would forget what they'd done the day before. The next step after agreeing on an outline was to build the foundation of the song on cassette. The cassette tape was the template; the rest was built from there. It meant long and often tedious, detailed work in the studio as ideas and sounds were added and subtracted using the miraculous Neve board, which produced a hyperreal playback that everyone loved. While this was going on, when Stevie wasn't singing she curled up on the control room sofa, her legs tucked under her, watching everything, with her journals, tissues, and remedies because she was usually not feeling well.

When she wasn't needed in the studio, she went to work. They weren't making any money, and Lindsey's inheritance was spent. He and Richard Dashut would take turns bouncing checks at the International House of Pancakes and the Copper Penny, two chain restaurants where a lot of music-friendly people had jobs. Lindsey worked briefly at painting houses and telephone sales, but he gradually moved into Sound City to work on their songs full time. Someone had to make the rent.

Stevie started out cleaning Keith Olsen's house. She was the daily. She'd show up with her mops and brooms, a rag on her head. If no one was at home she'd play Spinners records on Olsen's massive home stereo rig. (She was really into "Mighty Love.") Once she padded through a meeting that Olsen was having at home. Someone said, "Who's that?" and Olsen said, "That's the maid." (*Not for long,* Stevie thought to herself.)

Stevie got a temp job as a dental assistant, but only lasted one day. She waited tables at the Copper Penny, did well in tips, always had a little silver in her pocket. She did hostess shifts at Bob's Big Boy, a burger chain. "I made the money that supported Lindsey and me," she remembered for the *London Telegraph* years later. "I paid for the apartment, for the car, for everything. And I loved that!"

But there was resentment as well. She gave *Rolling Stone* a different spin on that period: "We were broke and starving. I was cleaning the house of our producer for fifty dollars a week. I come home with my big Hoover vacuum cleaner, my Ajax, my toilet brush, my cleaning shoes on. And Lindsey has managed to have some idiot send him eleven ounces of opiated hash. He and all his friends are in a circle on the floor. They'd been smoking hash for a month, and I don't smoke because of my voice. I'd come home every day and have to step over these bodies. I'm tired, and I'm lifting their legs up so I can clean up and empty the ashtrays. And all these guys are going, 'I don't know why I don't feel very good.' I said, 'You want to know why you don't feel so good? I'll tell you why—because you've done nothing else for weeks but lie on my floor and smoke hash and take my money!' "

After recording a few demos, Stevie and Lindsey auditioned for the head of 20th Century Records, who said he liked them but couldn't sign them without proper management, which they didn't have. They went to see Lou Adler, a talent manager who owned Ode Records and who had signed the Mamas and the Papas. Adler listened to half of one song and told them thank you very much.

Through these difficult times Stevie kept writing lyrics in her omnipresent journal. "Without You" was from then; also "Planets of the Universe." (Both would show up on albums years—decades—later.) "Gold Dust Woman" in its earliest form was from then. "Designs of Love" became "That's Alright" on *Mirage,* ten years in the future. They got their first piano when Keith Olsen gave them an old carved upright, painted white. Learning to write on piano for the first time, Stevie came up with "Lady from the Mountains," which became "Sorcerer" later on. She was the lady from the mountains, Northern California. Lindsey was the sorcerer. "Who is the master?" the singer asks, in their continual struggle for control. " 'Lady' is me figuring the piano out," Stevie later averred.

Also around this time, Stevie read *Triad,* a romance novel by Mary Leader set in Wales, a tale of witchcraft and possession, sorcery and magical powers. She was also hearing Led Zeppelin's majestic "Stairway to Heaven" on the car radio every day as that epic anthem invaded the mass consciousness of her generation in those times. If Zeppelin could sing about mysterious ladies and bustles in hedgerows, she figured she could, too. All of these were part of the backstory of "Rhiannon," which was beginning to come together as Stevie sat, for hours, at her white piano, hunting for the music that would take her where she wanted to go.

## 1.10    Frozen Love

While Buckingham Nicks were pursuing a recording contract, other currents were swirling around in the musical torrents of Los Angeles.

They had been there for a year now, and people were starting to take notice. But when they tried to get paying gigs around town, promoters instead offered them deals to form a Top 40 cover band and play the steak-and-lobster circuit from San Diego to Santa Barbara, playing "Take It Easy," "Witchy Woman," and "Peaceful Easy Feeling" at Chuck's Steakhouse three nights a week for good money, five hundred dollars a week. The gigs were there for them, they were told, all the work they could handle, and they should take the offer because nobody was going to pay money to see Buckingham Nicks in the foreseeable future. They agreed that if they did this, it would be like prostituting themselves, and they would lose whatever they had going for them, even at that low point.

So no gigs, but Keith Olsen arranged a showcase for Buckingham Nicks at Art LaBoe's on the Sunset Strip so label executives could take a look at them, up close. They rehearsed for this together, and it wasn't sounding right. Stevie was nervous. Stage fright was rare for her. She told people that she was born to get up on a stage and sing, that she'd been *trained* to do this by her grandfather when she was five years old. That evening the only ones to show up were Waddy Wachtel and a friend of his.

Then Waddy had this notion that Stevie should sing country songs. "When I met Stevie and I heard her sing, I was very much into Dolly Parton at that point, which was wild because I never heard a note of country music when I lived in New York. And so I gave Stevie a Dolly Parton album and I said, 'You've got to learn this girl's work. You gotta get a load of this chick!' And she couldn't believe it. So we started to play around town, doing Dolly Parton tunes, some other country songs, a couple of [their] originals, and Lindsey and I would play guitar great together. We had another friend, Jorge Calderon, who played bass with us. It was the four of us, just knocking around town like that."

They were still working on their stuff at Sound City (for free, unheard of) with Richard Dashut, when Buckingham Nicks suddenly got a recording contract. Keith Olsen had played their tapes to a guy who was partners in an independent label, Anthem Records. He said he wanted to sign Buckingham Nicks and send them to London to record at Trident Studios, where the Rolling Stones often worked. But then the partnership broke up, and that deal fell through. But then the Anthem guy got a distribution arrangement with Polydor, a major label. For once, someone said yes to Buckingham Nicks. The Anthem/Pogologo deal was said to be worth about $400,000, huge money back then, but Pogologo recording artistes Buckingham Nicks were told only that their album had a green light with a most generous recording budget of $25,000.

They were ecstatic, so relieved. There'd be an album and a tour. Fame and riches were in the future. The album would be released late in 1973, and then another. What they had foreseen and what people had predicted for them would come true.

Stevie quit working at Bob's Big Boy.

For the next six months they cut ten new tracks under Keith Olsen's supervision. Waddy Wachtel and other friends played on the sessions, but now Olsen brought in some of the top studio musicians in Los Angeles. Drummer Jim Keltner (widely considered the best in town) played with Delaney & Bonnie and Eric Clapton. When Keltner wasn't available, Elvis Presley's drummer Ronnie Tutt was flown in from Las Vegas and paid double scale, $220 an hour. Bassist Jerry Scheff also played with Elvis and had worked with the Doors. Stevie attended all the sessions, often wearing long charcoal-colored skirts over her ballet leggings, watching everything from the control booth sofa. She wrote letters to her parents (now living in Phoenix again) on Sound City letterhead that famous people were playing on their record, and that Lindsey himself was going to be famous someday.

They finished sequencing the record in late spring, 1973. Stevie's "Crying in the Night" began the LP's first side and was an acoustic plea for a man to beware of a woman who was back in town, a dangerous woman. It had a sense of Joni Mitchell fronting the Eagles, and Stevie's rattling tambourine was way up in the mix. Lindsey's "Stephanie" was a guitar portrait of Stevie, touching and tinkling, also an homage to Brian Wilson's musical direction. Lindsey's "Without a Leg to Stand On" came next, sounding like a song by Cat Stevens, the very precious (and popular) English minstrel. Lindsey sang lead on Stevie's new ballad "Crystal," which described romantic love as a quest, a journey through mountains and fountains, sustained by a string section. ("Crystal" was New Look Fleetwood Mac *avant la lettre,* and would be reprised on that band's first album.) The album's first side ended with an actual anthem, Stevie's "Long Distance Winner," about a romance with a difficult, untamable man. "Winner" emerged as somewhat epic in scope, with a blowout jam at the end.

The album's flip side began with Lindsey's "Don't Let Me Down Again," a fast California rocker with the brilliant Jim Keltner driving the train. "Django" was Lindsey's tribute to gypsy guitar genius Django Reinhardt, and also to the song's composer, John Lewis of the Modern Jazz Quartet. Stevie's "Races Are Run" followed, an oddly modulated song about winning and losing at life's competitions, and about a relationship that had to end. (When Javier Pacheco heard "Races," he thought it was about them leaving Fritz in the lurch.) Two of Lindsey's songs wound up the sequence. "Lola (My Love)" sounded like another homage, this time to Ry Cooder. And "Frozen Love" (cowritten with Stevie) was astute, about a love that had gone stale, with layers of strings and synthesizers and a major Lindsey Buckingham rock guitar symphony with three separate movements, a Big Statement from a new guitarist. Close reading of Stevie's lyrics could suggest that, from her point of view at least, the Buckingham Nicks romance was nearly over.

With the recording completed, it was time to make the album jacket photographs. They wanted Waddy's brother Jimmy Wachtel to shoot them, but that was vetoed by Polydor's art director. Stevie and Lindsey duly reported to the Burbank studio of photographer Lorrie Sullivan, whose brief from the company was to make it sexy. This was an album from and about a hot couple; sex was what the label thought they were selling. So Stevie went shopping and with her last hundred dollars bought a loose, filmy white blouse that exposed a little skin, figuring that would do it. They went through hair and makeup while the set was lit for a close-up of the charismatic pair. Lindsey came out blow-dried and darkly handsome, with a carefully groomed moustache. Stevie was more brunette than blond, with long colored feathers dangling from her ears. The photographer snapped off a few rolls of film, and then she asked the couple to take off their shirts.

Stevie balked. She told Sullivan that she was a prude, and that her family would not approve of a bare breast on her first album, let alone a nipple. She was wearing a flesh-colored bra; maybe they could work with that instead. The photographer explained that it would be too hard to retouch the bra under the dangling feather; it would look fake. That's when already bare-chested Lindsey lost patience with her. "Don't be *paranoid*," he snapped at her. Then he lowered his voice and growled, "Don't be a fucking *child*. This is art!"

"This is not 'art,'" she hissed. "This is me taking a nude photograph with you, and I don't dig it."

Stevie was intimidated. She felt trapped by the people looking at her. Under pressure, she took off her blouse, then her bra, and was directed to pose behind Lindsey's right shoulder, exposing the side of her right breast. In the resulting picture she looked directly into the camera with her dark eyes. She looked like someone else. She also looked tense.

After this, Stevie went to her parents' home near Phoenix and had an ovarian cyst removed. She was in bed for five weeks after that. When the proofs of the album jacket were sent to her, Stevie showed them to her mother. Barbara Nicks told Stevie, "We're going to have to think about this before we show it to Dad." Stevie wanted it kept from her father, but this wasn't possible. When Jess Nicks saw his daughter's album jacket he was annoyed, and he let Stevie know it.

Around this time, Stevie wrote a song lyric titled "Garbo," after the film star Greta Garbo, who refused to wear revealing costumes on screen. The lyric was a tribute to all the Hollywood actresses who were forced into doing scenes they didn't really want to do.

This incident really bothered her. When the album came out later in 1973 she was mortified, even though it was quite chaste by contemporary standards. Her father was still not amused. Even A.J. complained. She tried to explain that she'd been bullied into taking off her shirt. "From the very beginning," she said later, "Lindsey was *very* controlling and very possessive. And after hearing all the stories from my mother and how independent she was and how independent she'd made me, I was never very good with controlling people and possessive people." She told herself that she would never let anything like this happen again.

## 1.11   Heartbreaker

Polydor Records released the *Buckingham Nicks* album in September 1973, when Stevie Nicks was twenty-five years old. The record promptly bombed.

The album jacket was dark gray and somber. The singers radiated an off-putting anxious glamour. (The same image, dyed in the solarization process, was on the jacket's reverse.) Stevie's name was misspelled "Stevi." There was no track listing, just lyrics. Jimmy Wachtel's insipid interior photo showed the pair smiling, dressed casually in bell-bottom jeans, with Lindsey's hand insinuatingly close to Stevie's crotch. The album bore a dedication to A.J. Nicks, identified as "the grandfather of country music." (In Nashville, they must have wondered about this.)

No one seemed to like the record. Polydor executives hadn't even wanted to release it. They said the songs lacked imagination and had no commercial potential, but their deal with Anthem meant that they were contractually obligated to put the album out. There was no radio promotion budget (i.e., bribes of cash and cocaine to program directors), and barely any publicity at all. Radio DJs told the Polydor promo guys that the songs weren't original enough, and that Stevie's voice was too "nasal" for the FM stations. Hard-rocking "Don't Let Me Down Again" was released as a single. (Polydor advertised it in the trade publication *Record World:* "A beautiful single by two beautiful people.") There was little airplay, except for in the college town of Madison, Wisconsin, and in Cleveland, where disk jockey Kid Leo played the single and album tracks on hard-rocking WMMS-FM.

The single didn't make the *Billboard* sales charts. Neither did the album. The press ignored *Buckingham Nicks,* which wasn't reviewed by *Rolling Stone, Creem,* or *Hit Parader,* the most important American music publications. In the only published interview Lindsey did, he was asked about the duo's inspirations. He answered that their songs were influenced by Cat Stevens, and his guitar playing owed something to Jimmy Page's acoustic work with Led Zeppelin.

Lindsey then put together a band so Buckingham Nicks could play out. Bob Aguirre came down to LA at Lindsey's request and played drums, and Tom Moncrieff, their old friend from Fritz days, played bass. Buckingham Nicks played another showcase at the Troubadour and only twenty people showed up. There were a couple of reviews in local papers, neither very supportive. *Billboard,* the weekly bible of the record business, dismissed them as "a lackluster male-female duo." Then Waddy Wachtel joined on second guitar, which took the Buckingham Nicks Band up a major notch. This is the band that played at the Starwood in West Hollywood (which usually featured glam bands) in late 1973. In November they opened for stellar songwriter John Prine at the Troubadour, and played other shows as well. Set lists (according to drummer Aguirre, who'd quit Dr. Hook's Medicine Show to make the gig) included "Lola," "I Don't Want To Know" (just written for the next BN album), "Monday Morning" (same), "Races Are Run," "Crystal," the guitar instrumental "Stephanie," "Lady from the Mountain," "You Won't Forget Me," and "Don't Let Me Down Again." A cover of Led Zeppelin's "Heartbreaker" was a star turn for Waddy. The encore was heavy-duty anthem "Frozen Love," Lindsey Buckingham's electric guitar showpiece.

Buckingham Nicks made their East Coast debut at a showcase for press and radio at Manhattan's Metro club. Stevie arrived in New York with a sore throat and a streaming cold. *Billboard* sent a writer, who thought Lindsey seemed overwhelmed by his duties as both lead singer and lead guitar. As for Stevie: "Ms. Nicks also encounters problems, chiefly in her solo style, which points up the occasional roughness of her voice and the strident quality to her top end that makes duets bracing, but proves less than fruitful when she takes the stage alone." Later the cold turned into the flu.

After that, Buckingham Nicks went south and opened some shows for headliner bands. They opened for LA country rock band Poco in Atlanta and for guitarist Leslie West's thunderous Mountain in Birmingham, Alabama. The local rock station had been playing cuts from *Buckingham Nicks,* and so they were pleasantly surprised when the fans seemed to know some of the songs, and they got an ovation and were called back for an encore.

Then, in the late winter of 1974, they were fired. Polydor dropped Buckingham Nicks. The label execs said that returns of *Buckingham*

*Nicks* were enormous (retailers could return unused product for credit), and that Polydor's sales staff now had to prepare for Eric Clapton's big comeback album after years of heroin addiction.

Stevie: "We were dropped by Polydor after about three months, and Lindsey and I were devastated, because we'd just had a taste of the finer things of life, and now we were back to square one.

"So Lindsey went back to writing his angst-laden songs [like "So Afraid"], and I went back to being a waitress: *'Can I get you anything? More coffee? Some cake?'* I was all right with that—I didn't mind being a waitress—but we couldn't believe it! We thought we had made it! Famous people played on our record! We were living the highlife! We were *stunned!*"

Discouraged, somewhat humiliated, Stevie told Lindsey she wanted to quit music, at least for a while. She thought seriously about going home, but during long soul-searching phone calls, Barbara Nicks advised her to try to keep going. "My mother would say, 'Stevie, don't forget—you're on a *mission.*'"

But somehow the contentious couple's luck managed to hold. Keith Olsen and Joe Gottlieb had put too much energy into them to stop now. They told Stevie and Lindsey that they could keep working at Sound City for free, same as before, until they had enough new songs to try to get a new deal with another label.

It was a hard time for them. There were bruising fights with harsh words about winners and losers that left Lindsey sleeping on the living room sofa with his guitar and Stevie in their bedroom with her toy poodle, Ginny. But later that spring, Lindsey and Richard Dashut got to work on their new songs while Stevie and her friend Robin Snyder (who'd relocated to LA) worked waitress shifts in corny flapper outfits at Clementine's, a Roaring Twenties theme restaurant in West Hollywood.

Stevie: "I'd get home at six [P.M.], fix dinner and straighten up, 'cos they'd been smoking dope and working on songs. Then from nine to three [A.M.] I'd join Lindsey on the music. Then I went to bed, got up, and went to my waitress job."

And so they pressed on, determined to make new music against hard odds.

The year 1974 would be an important year for Stevie and Lindsey. It was a time of political upheaval, with the agony of the Watergate scandal hearings and that summer's resignation of President Nixon, the first in American history. The Vietnam War was still in progress, with defeat looming over the horizon—another first for America. American cities were riddled with crime and prone to bankruptcy. It was the era of killer bees, Deep Throat, *The Exorcist,* and the kidnapping of the California publishing heiress Patricia Hearst by an armed radical faction that styled itself the Symbionese Liberation Army. (Most of them died in a fiery shootout in Los Angeles, shown live on TV.)

What impacted most Americans were the long lines at gas stations during the Arab oil embargo in the wake of the 1973 Middle East War. Not since the Second World War, when gasoline was rationed, did Americans have to line up for fuel. Sometimes the lines seemed endless, and frustrations could boil over into arguments and fights. It was in one of these gas lines that spring that Lindsey's father suffered a heart attack and died in his car while waiting his turn to fill his tank. He was only fifty-seven years old. Brother Greg Buckingham called to tell Lindsey the sad news.

Stevie: "I answered, and had to hand him the phone." She'd never seen Lindsey cry before. They went back to Atherton for the funeral, with Stevie doing her best to comfort Lindsey's distraught mother. Lindsey was subdued for a long time after that. "I don't think he ever got over his dad," Stevie said later.

Richard Dashut: "I had moved out to a one-bedroom apartment near Fairfax [Avenue, in West Hollywood]. After Buckingham Nicks bombed, Stevie and Lindsey ran out of money, so they moved in with me. Back went the four-track, the cables, the stoned musicians sprawled on the floor, and we worked on the demos for the next Buckingham Nicks album: 'So Afraid,' 'Monday Morning,' and 'Rhiannon.'"

———

Then opportunity knocked in the form of Don Everly, of the legendary Everly Brothers. Brother Phil had angrily thrown down his guitar and walked out of the long fraternal partnership during a show at Knott's Berry Farm in California, leaving Don to go it alone. He had recorded an album of new songs, and Warren Zevon put together a touring band with himself on keys and Waddy on guitar. When Waddy left to do session work he got Lindsey the job, with Lindsey also singing Phil's harmony parts with Don. The money was OK and much needed, and the tour would give Lindsey good experience and national exposure. He'd be away for about six weeks.

At least the place was clean while he was gone, and Stevie needed a break from her grueling routine of working all day and then singing on demo tapes until three in the morning. She could come home in her Clementine's outfit and collapse. "Stevie is so friendly, and such a good woman," Richard said later, "and we laughed all the time when we weren't out slaving."

While Lindsey was on tour, Stevie was invited to stay at a ski lodge owned by Warren Zevon's in-laws in Aspen, Colorado. Aspen then was still fairly rustic, with faint echoes of the old frontier mining town, and cool movie stars like Jack Nicholson gathering nightly for drinks in the funky saloon of the Jerome Hotel. Stevie thought she could use some time alone in Aspen to work on new songs. She packed herself, her guitar, and tiny dog Ginny into their old Toyota, and made the long drive to the Colorado mountains.

Stevie later wrote, "I was in somebody's living room, sitting cross-legged on the floor with my Goya guitar, . . . thinking about what to do with my life. Should I go back to school, or should I go on pursuing a music career with Lindsey?" She was thinking about the rejection they had suffered, how much it had shattered their pride and hurt them as a couple. "And we weren't getting along. I sat looking out at the Rocky Mountains, pondering the avalanche of everything that had started to come crashing down on us [and] at that moment, my life truly felt like a landslide in many ways."

She'd only been there for a few days when Lindsey showed up—in a rage. Don Everly had cut short his tour in frustration after disrespectful fans ignored his new songs and demanded to only hear the

hits, from "Bye Bye Love" to "Cathy's Clown." Stevie was having problems of her own—breathing in the rarefied alpine air was difficult for
her, leaving her with a a chronic sore throat—and she was, in Lindsey's opinion, less than comforting to him. This led to the inevitable
shouting match (and maybe worse) before Lindsey stormed out, abandoning his girlfriend—ill and alone—in the freezing Colorado ski
town.

Stevie later wistfully recalled this incident, which led to one of her
best, most popular, and enduring songs: " 'Landslide' I wrote in Aspen. That's where the snow-covered hills came from. And I was definitely doing a lot of reflecting when I was up there. Lindsey was on
the road with the Everly Brothers [sic], and I was very unhappy and
very lonely . . . and trying to figure out why he was out with the Everly
Brothers and I was in Aspen with forty dollars and my dog, and my
Toyota that went frozen the day we got there. And we thought he
would make like, lots of money. He didn't. He came back to Aspen
and he was very angry with me. And he left me. [He] took Ginny the
poodle and the car and left me in Aspen . . . [on] the day that the Greyhound buses went on strike. I had a bus pass because my dad was the
president of Greyhound. I had a bus pass; I could go anywhere. I said,
'Fine, take the car and the dog—I have a bus pass.' I also had a strep
throat. He drove away. I walked in and the radio is saying that Greyhound is on strike all over the United States. I'm going 'Oh no—I'm
stuck.' So I had to call my parents, and they—unwillingly—sent me a
plane ticket because they didn't understand what I was doing there in
the first place. So I followed him back to Los Angeles. That was like
October [1974]. It was all around Halloween."

## 1.12    Landslide

When Stevie returned to Los Angeles she couldn't bring herself to go
back to the apartment she shared with Lindsey and Richard. Instead,
she briefly camped out in Keith Olsen's back room in Coldwater
Canyon and wrote most of "Landslide." It was a song about romantic
disaster, the seismic upheaval of a woman of twenty-six years losing
her partner, the ground, sickeningly, giving way under her feet. The
"children" are getting older, and she's getting older, too, her biological

clock ticking, she could feel it. Would she ever even have children? She had hopes, but she also had her doubts. She'd been waiting tables and cleaning houses for three years. She was tired, emotional, exhausted. Keith Olsen could hear Stevie Nicks softly crying down the hall as she worked on her heartbroken new song.

Adding to her sadness was the death of her grandfather, A.J. Nicks. Her father told her she didn't have to go to his funeral in Phoenix, and she was relieved. She'd written a song for him while he was dying but never played it for him.

Barbara Nicks became alarmed at how Stevie sounded during their phone calls. It was like talking to a sickly old woman, not her little Teedie. She dispatched her husband to Los Angeles to see what was going on. Jess Nicks was shocked to see his daughter so thin and unhappy. Stevie: "There were times when my dad would say, 'How long are you going to do this? You have no money, you're not happy, you work constantly, you work at restaurants, you clean houses, you get sick very easily, you're living in Los Angeles, you don't have any friends—*why are you doing this?*' And I would just say, 'Because this is what I came here to do.'"

Jess Nicks then strongly suggested that Stevie put a time limit on her quest. Give it six more months, he advised, and if it doesn't happen, go back and finish college. The family was behind her, but there should be an end game. Her parents had been sending her a little money almost every month, but it couldn't go on forever. Reluctantly, Stevie agreed to some kind of vague timetable.

She recalled, "I think they saw in me shades of my grandfather A.J. He was a country-and-western singer who never made it and drank too much. He was so unhappy, trying to make it. He turned into a very embittered person and died that way." A few months later, Jess Nicks suffered a cardiac arrest, but Stevie couldn't get to Phoenix in time before her father underwent an open-heart operation. She was afraid he might die before she could make something of herself, which would make him so proud of her.

Now Stevie Nicks was even more determined to keep at it. When she eventually returned to their apartment she looked at Lindsey and read him the riot act. "I basically walked back into the house and said,

'Lindsey, let's go. *Let's do this.*' I wrote 'Landslide' about whether or not I was going to give it all one more chance. You know the rest of the story."

She played the first verse and chorus of "Landslide" for Keith Olsen, who agreed that the melancholy ballad had strong possibilities, but it needed more inspiration. Stevie: "I was over at Keith's house, and he had these great speakers that were as tall as me. And Joni [Mitchell]'s record [*Court and Spark*] had just come out, and I put it on. He went away; it was just me. I took some LSD—it felt like a safe place to do it and it was the only time I ever did it—and I listened to this record for three days. She was able to stuff so many words into one sentence and not have them sound crowded. She was talking about what it was to be very famous, and to be a woman living in a man's world. She had been in the world of fame much longer than me, and she had gone out with every famous rock star that there was. And she was such an amazing guitarist that they all respected her. That was unheard of. She was in the boys' club. She talked about what I saw coming. Even though Buckingham Nicks had tanked, I knew that we were going to be very famous, very rich, and that this fame thing was going to overwhelm us. So when I listened to this record, it was like a great old premonition just being laid out in front of me."

Stevie also noted that it sounded like most of Joni's new songs had obviously been written on the piano, not the guitar (or her mountain dulcimer).

So, on piano, Stevie began reworking the song she thought could make this prophesy come true. Her interest in the Rhiannon material had started with the sound of the name itself. It rang a bell for her. Stevie had bought a novel called *Triad: A Novel of the Supernatural,* by Mary Leader, at an airport bookstore the year before. (*Triad* was published in 1973.) "It was about a girl named Rhiannon and her sister and mother, or something like that. I just thought the name was so pretty that I wanted to write something about a girl named Rhiannon. It was only later I found out that Rhiannon was a real mythical character!"

The book was a story of sorcery and witchcraft inspired by the old

Welsh myths. The writing style was impossibly romantic; reading the novel, Stevie felt like she was watching scenes in a film:

> And down the glorious pathway flew three singing
> birds. One was white, and one was green, and one
> was gold as morning. Their singing was sweet, the
> thundering of hooves was loud. The sound flowed
> like water over his tired aching body. The words
> of his old nurse came back to him: the three birds
> of Rhiannon . . .

But Stevie's vision of Rhiannon was different than the book's narrative. "It was the *name* that interested me," she insisted. "It was a kind of superbeing that I made up. She was the only supernatural character that I've ever written a song about." Her vision of the Welsh goddess was numinous—something that could be felt and experienced but not actually seen. The various poems she wrote about Rhiannon were paired with an older melody in her head called "Will You Ever Win?"—a variation on the theme of winning and/or losing that had preoccupied her and Lindsey ever since they left home for LA.

When she moved back into their cramped apartment around Thanksgiving, she got up late one morning to go to work at her waitress job at Clementine's. She left a C-60 cassette containing a piano demo of "Rhiannon" propped against the coffeepot, with a note for Lindsey that read: HERE IS A NEW SONG. YOU CAN PRODUCE IT, BUT *DON'T* CHANGE IT.

November 1974. Stevie and Lindsey continued to work on the new songs at Sound City: "Monday Morning," "So Afraid," and "Rhiannon," also versions of "Nomad" (aka "Candlebright"), "Lady from the Mountain," "Castaway," "Mistaken Love," and the earliest attempts at "Gold Dust Woman." But they weren't really working together. Stevie complained that Lindsey was changing her songs too much from her original intentions, and that they didn't sound the way she wanted them to sound. This was a huge problem and an issue between the two of them. According to Keith Olsen, this simply couldn't be helped. He recalled, "Stevie writes these little repetitive loops that she crafts melodies around. This is one of the unique aspects of the way she writes, [but] sometimes this gets old—quickly. So a more commercial, chordal form needs to be implemented, and this is what she sometimes considers too much change from the original material."

Even Stevie had to admit that she was very dependent on Lindsey to remake her poems and melodic notions into actual songs. "He takes my little skeleton songs and turns them into finished pieces," she said later, but she was adamant that he took too many liberties with her music, and she told him so. This "hostile dependency" was tearing the couple apart. She needed Lindsey's creative mind, his fluid music, and resented this intrusion on the treasured independence her mother had instilled in her. Lindsey lately had been paranoid and cold to her; she told friends that Lindsey was more interested in his guitar than in her, and this left Stevie feeling drained by the conflicting emotions of their arrangement. They'd been through three hard years of stress together. Now the fights and harsh words grew worse. Sometimes Stevie was physically afraid during Lindsey's rages. Even their Toyota was broken, its reverse gear having given up the ghost.

Stevie couldn't take it anymore—being anxious all the time—and moved in with Robin Snyder. Stevie remembered, "Lindsey and I couldn't be together [as a couple] and try to work together. It wouldn't leave us anywhere to go at the end of the day." The once loving friendship between the two ambitious young musicians was beginning to fray and unravel.

And then something happened. Early in December, Stevie was working in Sound City's Studio B, at the rear of the building. Richard Dashut was at the controls, listening to her play a piano rendition of the entire "Rhiannon" cycle, including the much faster storm-dance segment toward the end. She wondered aloud into the microphone whether some "really important" bird sounds could be added to the track. She asked, "Don't you think Rhiannon is a beautiful name?" Just then, as if in answer to an occult summons, there was a commotion in another part of the building. Stevie walked into the hall and could hear the sound of Lindsey's guitar solo on "Frozen Love" blasting at top volume from Studio A.

Then she saw him. He was a giant, six-foot-six, with long straight hair under his weathered cowboy hat and a big, aquiline nose. He had on a flannel western shirt and sported a tweed vest with an old-fashioned pocket watch and chain across his skinny frame. With him were two little blond girls in frilly dresses and sandals, obviously his daughters. He was listening to the guitar solo with big ears, his head bobbing to the throbbing pulse of the hard rock guitar as he pounded the track's rhythm on his knee. She thought she recognized him. She'd seen him on TV, maybe. He was a rock star, an English rock star. She whispered to Richard, "Who is that?"

"That's Mick Fleetwood," he answered, "from Fleetwood Mac."

# CHAPTER 2

## 2.1 Heroes Are Hard to Find

In December 1974 Fleetwood Mac was a band on the run, a band in exile, a band in serious trouble.

The group had formed in London in 1967 when guitarist Peter Green, who had succeeded Eric Clapton in John Mayall's Bluesbreakers, decided to go out on his own. Green was a brilliant guitarist in the same league as the more famous London virtuosos Clapton, Jeff Beck, and Jimmy Page. (When the CLAPTON IS GOD graffiti began appearing in unfashionable Notting Hill in 1966, it was soon answered in ultrachic Chelsea by PETER GREEN IS BETTER THAN GOD.)

Peter Green also took his Bluesbreakers band mates, drummer Mick Fleetwood (whom Mayall had just fired for bad behavior) and bassist John McVie, and proceeded to name his new band after them—Peter Green's Fleetwood Mac. A comic second guitarist called Jeremy Spencer, who specialized in hellacious Elmore James blues playing, completed the first lineup, and Fleetwood Mac became a huge act in England on the strength of Peter Green's run of hit records: "Black Magic Woman," "Oh Well," and especially the moody, soulful guitar instrumental "Albatross."

Fleetwood Mac then took the electric ballrooms of late sixties America by storm. Promoters liked them because they were serious blues scholars and musicians who actually had an act. After the fiery guitar playing of Peter Green, the band would perform a hilarious rock & roll oldies set fronted by Jeremy Spencer in a gold lamé jacket. The fans loved this, and Fleetwood Mac became headliners at the Fillmore East in New York, Philadelphia's Electric Factory, and the Boston Tea

Party. In San Francisco they were taken up by Bill Graham and performed up and down the state.

But after a few years Peter Green left the band in bizarre circumstances (LSD), followed by Jeremy Spencer in even stranger ones (hippie religious cult). Between 1971 and 1974 musicians came and disappeared like gypsies. In a notorious incident in 1973, the band's management sent a fake version of Fleetwood Mac to play "Black Magic Woman" in America after the real musicians were too exhausted and freaked out by the latest defections to continue. But the band had regular fans who protested this outrage, and the promoters pulled the fake band off the road, leading to wearying litigation between Fleetwood Mac and its English manager that was still ongoing in December 1974.

By then the core lineup was at least stable. Mick Fleetwood, twenty-seven, was from a military family and considered Fleetwood Mac to be his life's mission. He had left school at sixteen, moved to London with his drum kit, and began a fast rise through the London beat scene in the sixties; his band the Cheynes had opened for the Rolling Stones early on, and then Mick married into Swinging London's aristocracy when he wed Jenny Boyd, sister of Patty Boyd, archetypal dolly-bird fashion model who was married to Beatle George Harrison. Mick had been with the Mac from the beginning and now found himself managing the band, since their old manager kept filing lawsuits against them.

John McVie, twenty-nine, was nominally the band's comanager. The affable bassist in the cloth cap with the humble stage presence was more of a perennially tipsy sidekick than a deal-maker. He was also a superb bass guitar player. He had to be, or perfectionist British blues purist John Mayall never would have hired him in 1963, when he was only seventeen. He was somewhat precariously married to Fleetwood Mac's lead singer and keyboard player, Christine McVie, thirty-one, originally Christine Perfect. She was a pretty blond former art student from the British Midlands, a great blues singer under her maiden name (and with the blues band Chicken Shack). Chris was Fleetwood Mac's spokeswoman onstage, greeting "the punters" (as they called their fans), announcing the numbers, and introducing the band.

Bob Welch completed the quartet lineup, a twenty-nine-year-old guitarist from California who joined Fleetwood Mac in England after working in a Paris-based band. He was the band's lead guitarist and wrote many of their later songs. An artist ahead of his time, Bob Welch (and there's the Wales thing again) was producing spacey, mystical, jazz-informed music for Fleetwood Mac, and songs like "Hypnotized" were chart hits in America and got played on progressive FM radio all the time.

It was Bob Welch who convinced Fleetwood Mac to move to California in April 1974. The band was finished in England for the time being, what with human resources problems and lawsuits. But Fleetwood Mac could work in America, could get on television when their albums came out, and Los Angeles was where their label, Reprise Records, was located. So, with some misgivings about leaving parents and families behind, the band migrated to Southern California. The band's financial assets were transferred to Bob Welch's American bank account, which gave him a whopping tax headache later on. No one thought about visas, immigration, working papers, or anything. Mick and Jenny Fleetwood, their two daughters Amy and Lucy, the McVies, Bob Welch, and veteran road manager John Courage (and a container of the band's road gear) landed at LAX in April 1974.

Before she left England, Christine McVie told her mother that Fleetwood Mac was in trouble, and that it was going to take a miracle to get the band going again in America. Her mother—who some thought had a gift for prophesy—told Chris not to worry, because they would find their miracle in a sunny California orange grove.

When Mick Fleetwood had settled his family in an old cabin in rural Topanga Canyon, he assumed his managerial duties and called Fleetwood Mac's longtime label, Reprise Records, to set up an appointment. He was put through to Mo Ostin, the president of parent company Warner Bros. Records. A few days later, at Warner headquarters in Burbank, somewhat to his surprise, Mick and the band's loyal American attorney, Mickey Shapiro, were warmly received by label executives. They told them that they *loved* Fleetwood Mac. The 1969 masterpiece album *Then Play On* was still outselling the Grateful Dead.

*Mystery to Me* was moving product, too. The band's master tapes were always delivered on time, they always had good songs, some of them radio hits, and you didn't have to put paper down for them when they came to the office. Their recent albums, Mick was told, sold a reliable 350,000 copies to the same 350,000 fans—every time. They joked that Fleetwood Mac took care of Warner Bros.' annual light bill in Burbank. Sure, they'd heard about the fake Mac disaster and were concerned about the resulting public relations nightmare, but they were in sympathy with the band over this painful issue. They even presented Mick with a framed gold record for the band's most recent album, *Heroes Are Hard to Find*, recorded in LA the previous summer, and which had reached #36 on *Billboard's* Hot Hundred chart. Best of all, despite the band's legal troubles in London, Warners would support Fleetwood Mac with a large advance on earnings and also support the group's new album—if they could get it out the following year. They shook hands on this, and Warners said the lawyers would start on the paperwork right away.

Much relieved, Mick Fleetwood left Burbank with the label's firm commitment to keep Fleetwood Mac going. As he drove up Highway 101, the Ventura Freeway, bisecting the San Fernando Valley on his way north, he set his mind to its next task—finding an affordable studio in which to make the veteran band's tenth album. Something told him that, way against all odds, this move to California might just work out for Fleetwood Mac.

## 2.2   Little Magic Star

One sunny day in late 1974, Mick Fleetwood loaded his daughters Amy and Lucy into the back of the old white Cadillac he was leasing from Rent-A-Wreck, which supplied vintage cars to people—mostly new arrivals to LA—who needed a little style at the right price. He drove up Topanga Canyon Boulevard until he reached the car turnout at the top of the mountain. He often stopped there to admire the cinematically stupendous view of the San Fernando Valley spread out for miles below, the very essence of Southern California in the seventies. Then they careened down the other side of the mountain, with its hard curves and switchbacks, until the boulevard emptied into Woodland Hills. Mick Fleetwoood was on a mission—for groceries.

But in the supermarket parking lot, Mick ran into an acquaintance, Thomas Christian. They had met when the Mac had recorded their last album in LA the previous summer. Mick mentioned that he was looking for production on the band's next album, and Thomas Christian said he was now associated with a studio in Van Nuys called Sound City.

Mick: "He told me I should check the place out, so I piled the groceries and the kids into the back of my seedy old Cadillac and followed this guy over to this studio. At Sound City I was introduced to Keith Olsen, the engineer. To demonstrate the sound of the studio, he played me a track called 'Frozen Love,' from an album he had recorded there."

Mick was impressed not only by the sound of the guitar but with the obvious talent of whoever was playing. This guy rocked out. He was fast, clever, arena-ready. But there was also something else, even more interesting. "My attention had been caught by what I saw through the thick glass that separated Sound City's two studios. It was a girl, and she was rehearsing a song in the next room. A piano track was playing, and I could hear her say something to the assistant engineer about wanting to have bird songs somewhere in the final mix of the song she was working on. I even remember what she was wearing: a long, sort of Indian-y cotton skirt and a little blouse—really pretty."

Mick Fleetwood was smitten. He wanted to meet the girl but managed to keep his very English reserve together as he airily inquired of Keith Olsen, "Who's that pretty girl in there?"

Her name, he said, is Stevie Nicks.

While Mick was digging "Frozen Love," Keith Olsen asked if he wanted to meet the guy who wrote the song. Mick said sure, and Lindsey Buckingham came in and was introduced. They shook hands and then Mick turned to Olsen, asking about the studio's availability and the hourly rates. Mick said he wanted to think it over and would be in touch. For the next ten days Fleetwood Mac would be on the back end of the *Heroes Are Hard to Find* tour, promoting their latest album. The band was playing in Las Vegas, just before Christmas, when Bob Welch told Mick he was leaving the band.

It wasn't exactly unexpected. Bob had long felt the band was floundering, repeating itself, and needed new blood to survive. He also wanted his own career and outlet for his style of music. If he didn't try this now, maybe he never would.

Mick pleaded with him to stay. Fleetwood Mac, he insisted, was like a marriage. You don't want to just walk away. But Bob and Chris had exchanged some harsh words after a rough gig in Vegas, and Welch was fed up.

This was a few days before the new year. Veteran Mac tour manager John Courage freaked out at this latest defection and threw Welch's guitar amp out the window. The band's road crew liked Welch, and there was talk of mutiny. Mick told them not to worry, that he had a plan, and things would work out, with a little patience.

Mick: "I rang up Keith Olsen over at Sound City and asked what was the name again of the chap whose music and guitar playing I had liked so much when I visited the studio.

"'Lindsey Buckingham,' he said.

"I told him that I wanted Lindsey Buckingham to be the new guitarist in Fleetwood Mac, and what did he think?"

Olsen explained that Lindsey was part of a duo, Buckingham Nicks, and the other half was also his girlfriend. They were a working couple, Olsen said. "If you want him, you'd probably have to take her, too." Olsen then gave Mick the outlines of their career so far: from his meeting them in Fritz and their coming to LA; working on their songs; Stevie cleaning his house and waiting tables all over town; making their record, a little touring; getting fired by Polydor but keeping at it; and working for free on their next album as Sound City's resident mascots when Mick Fleetwood just happened to stop in, looking for production.

Stalling for time while thinking this over, Mick explained that Fleetwood Mac always did everything on instinct. No one had ever auditioned to be in the band; musicians were hired on reputations, recommendations, plus smiles and vibes. Nothing ordinary, he explained, had ever happened to Fleetwood Mac precisely because of this. (And, by God, Mick could easily see himself in a band with that extremely hot little girl in the sexy blouse he had seen in the studio.)

"Without hesitating," as he later claimed, Mick told Olsen that he wanted them both. He'd take the whole package if they were agreeable. "I said, 'Those two kids—do you think they'd want to join my band?'" Olsen—totally surprised—replied that although it was New Year's Eve, he'd get in touch with Lindsey and Stevie, inform them of Mick's offer, and get back to him on the following day, January 1, 1975.

Mick hung up the phone and sat down in their rustic canyon kitchen with Jenny, who'd made him a cup of tea. The sun was down behind Saddle Peak, and holiday lights were twinkling on the other side of the creek. He told her about the phone call. "What about John and Chris? They don't know about this?" Mick told her not to worry. All would turn out well. "Somewhere up there," he told his beautiful young wife, "is a little magic star, looking out for us."

Later that night, Lindsey and Stevie had a few friends over for smoke and champagne, a quiet New Year's Eve gathering, and they were talking about whether 1975 was going to be a better year for them. That's when Keith Olsen walked in with a big grin on his face. "Hey, I've got some news . . . Fleetwood Mac want you to join them."

Stevie was shocked. Lindsey, Keith, and Richard Dashut just started to laugh; 1975 was looking better already! But Keith Olsen said he had to spend the rest of the night trying to convince Lindsey Buckingham to take the offer.

Keith had told Mick that he would get back to him about the Fleetwood Mac offer after the new year, so Stevie and Lindsey had a couple of days to think about it. At first Lindsey didn't think it was such a great idea. It meant the best songs they'd been working on all year would be presented to music fans as a Fleetwood Mac product. Buckingham Nicks would be over for good. Was this, he wondered, a total sellout of their hard work and integrity? Or were they so dead broke that they should just sign on the bottom line and just do it?

Stevie's outlook was quite different. She was tired of waiting tables. And joining Fleetwood Mac was a way of getting her boyfriend back. "We were breaking up when Fleetwood Mac asked us to join," she told

*Billboard* years later. "And I was working as a waitress to keep our little Toyota running. We weren't making five hundred dollars a week playing four sets a night at Chuck's Steakhouse because Lindsey wanted to play original music, so I went along with that."

When they got Mick Fleetwood's amazing offer, according to Stevie, "I said, OK, this is what we've been working for since 1968. And so, Lindsey, you and I have to sew this relationship back up. We have too much to lose here. We need to put our problems behind us. Maybe we're not going to have any more problems, because we're finally going to have some money. And I won't have to be a fucking waitress."

Lindsey wasn't totally convinced. As much as he liked Peter Green's playing, which he mentioned he would now have to replicate onstage every night if they joined Fleetwood Mac, he said he wasn't sure what this band was—now. They'd gone from one lineup to the next. Why had their guitar player quit? He told Stevie he felt ambivalent, not about getting back with her as a couple, but about casting their lot with this English blues band from the sixties.

The next day, Stevie "scraped together every dime I could find, went to Tower Records [on Sunset Boulevard in West Hollywood], and bought all the Fleetwood Mac records they had. And I listened to all of them. Lindsey only listened to the songs that had been hits in England. And I told Lindsey that I thought we could do a lot for this band. 'We'll do it for a year, save some money, and if we don't like it, we'll quit.'"

Lindsey argued, somewhat irrationally, that *Buckingham Nicks* in his opinion could still—somehow—break out and be a success. Stevie: "I said, '*You* wait around. I'm sick of being a waitress. *We are joining Fleetwood Mac, and we are going to be great!*'"

There was also another idea Stevie was working through here. After listening to the albums, looking for a thematic thread that ran through their songs, she came up with a word—"mystical." From "The Green Manalishi" of 1968 to "Hypnotized" in 1973, the songs had an inner core of wonder and the mystic that appealed to her. Later she recalled, "Since I have a deep love of the mystical, anyway, this really appealed to me. I thought, this might really be the band for me because they *are* mystical, they play wonderful rock and roll, and there's another lady, so I'll have a pal."

Nevertheless, she decided to keep her waitress job at Clementine's for another couple of weeks, just in case things didn't work out. With the benefit of hindsight, she later recalled that "Fleetwood Mac came along at the right time, because it was about to become not much fun anymore."

## 2.3    Tough Little Thing

Early January, 1975. Waddy Wachtel got a phone call at his place in North Hollywood. He was just back from playing guitar on a Linda Ronstadt tour. "The phone rings, and it's Lindsey. And he goes, 'Man, I gotta run something by you. I got a strange situation here.' And I go, 'What?' And he goes, 'Well, this guy named Mick Fleetwood came to Sound City looking for production with Keith Olsen. And Keith played him our stuff. And he wants us to join Fleetwood Mac.' And I went, 'Yeah? What the problem?' And he goes, 'I don't know if we want to do it, you know? We still got Buckingham Nicks.' And I said, 'Lindsey, the only mistake you're making right now is that you're on the wrong phone call. I want you to hang up, and call Mick Fleetwood, and tell him—Yes! Call him—now! Call him now—and say *yes!*' And I added that the only thing wrong with the equation was that they didn't want me also."

Still, Lindsey had deep reservations. "Listen to me, Stevie," he pleaded one night. "A hundred fucking people have been through Fleetwood Mac. It's like a meat grinder."

"You listen, Lindsey," she retorted. *"We're doing this.* I'm tired of being a waitress!"

So Lindsey did call Mick, who invited them to dinner at a Mexican restaurant so they could get together socially before any decisions were made. Lindsey accepted and later regretted it. Stevie: "I said, 'Lindsey, we're starving to death here. If we don't like them we can always leave.'"

The real purpose of the dinner was for Christine McVie to meet Stevie. Mick had played the *Buckingham Nicks* album for the McVies, and they both quite liked it, but, as Mick put it, "Christine had to meet Stevie first, because there would have been nothing worse than two women in a band who didn't like each other."

The dinner was set up by Judy Wong, an old friend of the band from both London and San Francisco. She was now part of Seedy Management, Mick and John's fledgling attempt to manage themselves. Fleetwood recalled, "Lindsey had come up to our house on Fernwood in Topanga Canyon. Judy Wong was there, and we soon adjourned to a Mexican restaurant in the Valley called El Carmen to meet John and Chris, who were driving in from their beach house in Malibu. Stevie Nicks was waiting for us, still dressed in her twenties flapper outfit from her waitress job."

Stevie: "I saw Fleetwood Mac drive up in these two old clunky white Cadillacs, with huge tail fins, and I was in *awe*." (She was in even greater awe a bit later when she found out that Jenny Fleetwood's sister Patti was married to George Harrison.)

Mick: "We settled in at our table, ordered drinks, and then just started smiling. We were checking each other out, and we all felt there was something magic in the air. We were also getting off on the margaritas. Lindsey offered to play an audition, and I explained that we didn't think it would be necessary. In fact, nobody had ever auditioned to be in the band."

Mick knew that Chris had some reservations about having another woman in the band. She'd told him earlier, "Do me a favor. As long as me and Stevie hit it off, everything will be fine. Otherwise . . ." But as the evening cruised on, Mick could see that Stevie was sympathetic to Chris's position, and that Chris got this, and the two girls were getting along very well. Christine asked Stevie where she lived and laughed when Stevie said she had an apartment on Orange Grove Avenue in West Hollywood. She told Stevie about her mother's words, finding their miracle in an orange grove. As Stevie chatted to Chris about the trials and tribulations of Buckingham Nicks, Chris regarded Stevie closely and thought to herself: *"Tough little thing."*

But the tough little thing was already smitten. "Mick was dressed beautifully in a velvet three-piece suit with a fob watch in his vest pocket. John was so handsome. We were just having the best time with them. And I kept thinking, *Oh my God, I can be in this band*." As for Christine McVie—blunt, tough-talking, hard-drinking, chain-smoking rock road queen—Stevie sensed that she had found an older sister, one who would be her friend and mentor in this possible new life.

Mick: "Before the dessert came, I leaned across the table and simply asked them: 'Do you want to join?' Stevie and Lindsey looked at each other, and Lindsey said yes. I said, 'We'd love to have you in the band.' And that was it."

Next, Mick explained Fleetwood Mac's situation, which was tenuous. Mick, John, and Chris were in California on tourist visas. They had no immigration papers or "green cards" that would allow them to work and earn money in America. The lawyers were working on this. The $200,000 advance from the record company (about a million dollars in current money) was still in Bob Welch's bank account. Keith Olsen had said Stevie and Lindsey were broke, so they were immediately put on a salary of $200 per week, each, as new members of the band. Some of their back rent was paid as well.

"We were breaking up, Lindsey and me, when Fleetwood Mac asked us to join," Stevie said later. "But then I got an apartment on Hollywood Boulevard and he moved back in with me, and we kind of put our relationship back together. Things were better between us. We weren't fighting about money, we had a really nice place, and we were going to work with these hysterically funny English people every day, making great music."

After this meeting, Christine returned to England to see her mother. The new Fleetwood Mac began when Lindsey found a garage on Pico Boulevard in Santa Monica and began rehearsing with Mick and John. He hadn't played with a veteran rhythm section of such high voltage, and this new energy took his own guitar work to a higher level. Stevie worked on songs at their apartment and was actually feeling happy for the first time since they'd moved to Los Angeles. She remembered, "We got paid in cash, two hundred dollars a week for each of us, so I had hundred-dollar bills everywhere. And since we hadn't spent any money in five years, we didn't even know *how* to spend money. I was putting hundred-dollar bills through the wash and then finding them all crumpled and bleached out, and then hanging them on the line with the rest of our stuff." Stevie had a premonition that they would soon be rich. "I said, 'That's it. I'm never looking at another price tag again.' And I meant it."

For almost the next two years Stevie and Lindsey would remain a couple, a relatively contented one. "How could you *not* be happy," she said later. "You were going with a drop-dead gorgeous man who sang like an angel, and the world was yours, and you were in a band that was already famous . . . I mean, things were looking up!"

## 2.4   Nothing Ordinary

Mick Fleetwood's idea was to rehearse the new band for a month and then take it directly into the recording studio in February 1975, even before they ever played in public. Stevie and Lindsey brought their demo tapes of new songs to the McVies' modest apartment on the beach in Malibu. They played in-progress versions of "So Afraid," "Monday Morning," "Landslide," and "Rhiannon." There was approval all around and smiling faces. Then Chris played them two of her new songs, which she'd written on a beat-up Hohner portable electric keyboard while gazing out at the roiling winter ocean: "Over My Head" and "Say That You Love Me." She also had a bluesy song called "Sugar Daddy" and a lulling tune, "Warm Ways." Lindsey suggested recording Stevie's "Crystal" from the *Buckingham Nicks* album, but in a different tempo and better production.

The first vocal rehearsal took place a few days later in the basement of the band's agency, International Creative Management on Beverly Boulevard. It was the first time that Christine, Stevie, and Lindsey heard how their voices sounded together, and it was immediate choral magic. Christine recalled, "This was my first rehearsal with them. They were in the band, but I'd never played with them before. I started playing "Say That You Love Me" and when I reached the chorus, they started singing with me. I heard this *incredible* sound—our three voices—and said to myself, 'Is this me singing?' I couldn't believe how great this three-voice harmony was. My skin turned to goose flesh, and I wondered how long this feeling was going to last."

Fleetwood Mac worked out their new music over the next few weeks. Mick was over the moon as he watched Stevie Nicks dance around the agency basement as he played changing rhythms for her. He knew there was nothing like this out there, and the punters were going to love her. And Lindsey was proving to be the most original guitar player the band had heard since the halcyon days of Peter Green's Fleetwood Mac.

One Sunday evening Mick invited Stevie and Lindsey to his house in Topanga for supper—shepherd's pie and salad and not a little red wine—and a history lesson. As Jenny got the meal together, and the little girls played with toy ponies, Mick told them he felt the urge to give them the full story of the band, to give them the sense, as he put it, that "nothing ordinary ever happened to Fleetwood Mac."

He began with Peter Green, who'd formed the band. Peter was Mick's idol—he only referred to him as the Green God—and would have been one of the major rock stars if he hadn't gotten bored with the band after four years. Peter was so self-effacing that he wanted two other guitarists—Jeremy Spencer and Danny Kirwan—in the band. But when Fleetwood Mac arrived in San Francisco for the first time in 1968, they were met at the airport by Judy Wong, Jerry Garcia, and Phil Lesh of the Grateful Dead, who wanted to meet the famous English guitar hero, Peter Green. Playing in San Francisco a lot, Fleetwood Mac's three-guitar attack developed a rambling, jamming style akin to the Dead's. But in 1970 the band was playing in Germany, and Peter Green had fallen in with a spiritualist LSD cult and taken way too much acid with them, after which he quit Fleetwood Mac, got rid of his material possessions, and became a recluse. He grew his fingernails so long that he couldn't play the guitar anymore. He asked the band's management to stop sending him royalty checks for hit records "Albatross" and "Black Magic Woman." When the checks kept coming in the post, he took an air rifle to the management office and threatened them, for which he was arrested and barely escaped prison. Mick often tried to contact him, but the Green God never returned his calls.

Fleetwood Mac pressed on without their leader, and British blues star Christine Perfect, now married to John McVie, was persuaded to join the band. In 1971 they were in California when a powerful earthquake hit Los Angeles and wrecked the city. Fleet-wood Mac was due to play the Whisky a Go Go on Sunset Strip, but the band's manic rock guitarist Jeremy Spencer didn't want to go after having awful premonitions of doom. When the band checked into the Hollywood Hawaiian Motel, Jeremy said he was going out for a walk and never returned. Four days later the roadies found him in a locked warehouse belonging to the Children of God, a notorious robe-wearing religious cult whose emissaries snatched runaways off the streets of Hollywood and brainwashed them into joining the sect. Jeremy now answered to the name Jonathan. He told them he was quitting the band and abandoning his young wife and child, who were back in England at Fleetwood Mac's communal country house. No one could believe this, but it happened. To save the tour, Peter Green agreed to sign on for a few concerts on the condition that they would be instrumental jams and little else.

Spellbound by this cinematic narrative (Mick punctuated the story with his emphatic body language and bug-eyed wonder), Stevie asked what happened to Jeremy. Mick said he was still with the Children of God (and indeed would remain so for decades to come).

Now the band slunk home to England and tried to figure it all out. This was when their friend Judy Wong recommended Bob Welch, who'd been playing in a band in Paris. Hired without an audition on the basis of good vibes when he visited the band's house in Surrey, Welch was credited by Mick for saving the band because he started writing good songs and generally was organized and friendly, and they loved having an American in the band. Back on the road in America in 1972, driving from show to show in a pair of rented station wagons, Fleetwood Mac carried on, but not without friction. John McVie was drinking and fighting with Christine. He'd thrown a wood-working awl at her in the Gorham Hotel on 55th Street in New York. She ducked just in time, and the tool stuck in the door where her head had been. Then Danny Kirwan had a mental breakdown on the back end of a long tour of American colleges. He'd been acting unprofes-sionally for weeks, getting the others upset. Mick described him as a walking time bomb. Just before one show he broke his guitar, and then smashed his head against a toilet wall. Danny's blood was spattered everywhere. The band went onstage without him, and that was Danny's last gig after four years. Mick had to tell him he was fired, the first musician ever let go from Fleetwood Mac.

Despite all the band's troubles, their albums continued to sell, and another round of American concerts was booked for 1973. Needing new people *tout de suite*, they hired guitarist Bob Weston away from Long John Baldry's band and blustery blues belter Dave Walker from Savoy Brown, another English blues band. Walker, Mick explained, was a little rough around the edges for the band, but he was great with crowds and was a master at *"Howyadoin, Cleveland!"* Back to the U.S.A. went Fleetwood Mac and things seemed to go well, with Mick's wife on the road with him for the first time. Halfway through, Mick was clued in that Jenny was having an affair with Bob Weston. There was a big row, and Mick admitted to Stevie and Lindsey that he wasn't a good husband, that he was more married to the band than to Jenny, whose birthday he could never seem to remember. Anyway, Jenny was sent home and Mick tried to carry on under emotionally fraught conditions, but finally couldn't take playing with Bob Weston, whom he had befriended and who had betrayed him. The tour was stopped in the Midwest. Mick called their manager, who exploded that he was sick of their antics. The band flew back to England, and the management sent out a substitute band to fulfill the remaining tour dates. (These new musicians were falsely told that Mick would be joining them for the rest of the tour, and were subsequently bottled off the stage when they tried to tell fans they were Fleetwood Mac, causing an industrywide scandal.)

All this, Mick went on, put Fleetwood Mac out of action for almost a year. Mick went to southern Africa to put himself back together, and eventually Jenny told him to come home to her. Bob Welch convinced them to move the band to California, and they basically knew the rest of the story.

Lindsey then asked Mick about how he thought the fans would react to having two couples in the band. Mick said he wasn't sure, and pointed out that John and Chris's marriage was strained after she'd tired of his heavy drinking and then had an affair with their English sound guy the previous year. Mick said that Keith Olsen had told him that Stevie and Lindsey weren't living together, either, and they replied that they were back together and in it for the long run. Relieved,

Mick said that he hoped this lineup could hold together and show the doubters—and there were not a few—that Fleetwood Mac could keep calm, carry on, and be a great band again.

Later, driving down the Pacific Coast Highway on their way home, Stevie and Lindsey talked things over. Neither of them had realized, they agreed, how much was at stake for Fleetwood Mac. These guys were trying to keep their band from failing, and now Mick, Chris, and John were depending on them to help make it happen.

## 2.5    Buckingham Nicks, Slight Return

And just then, late January 1975, came an urgent message from the South, asking Buckingham Nicks to headline some shows in Alabama.

Lindsey had been right, almost.

More than a year after the release of *Buckingham Nicks,* a rock station in Birmingham, Alabama, was playing tracks from the album alongside their usual Southern rock heroes: the Allman Brothers, Lynyrd Skynyrd, Black Oak Arkansas, Wet Willie. Fans were jamming the station's phones, asking for more. Viral radio miracles sometimes happened this way, with bigger stations adding the band to their playlists, going from Birmingham to Atlanta to St. Louis to Memphis to Chicago and then the coasts, until a band broke out nationally, dreams fulfilled.

Now a promoter was offering Buckingham Nicks headlining slots at the University of Alabama at Tuscaloosa, and then two shows in Birmingham. Lindsey decided to take the gig. Waddy Wachtel signed on first. Tom Moncrieff would handle the bass. Since the biggest Southern rock band—the Allmans—featured a two-drummer attack, Lindsey decided Buckingham Nicks needed a double battery as well. Hoppy Hodges had played on the album. He was joined, at Lindsey's urgent request, by Bob Aguirre, who'd been playing in Dr. Hook's Medicine Show in the Bay Area. They rehearsed the old Buckingham Nicks set, including album tracks and "Lady from the Mountains." Needing another fast number, they added "Rhiannon," which no one had ever heard yet.

They flew to Alabama and discovered they'd sold out a bunch of six-thousand-seat auditoriums. Unknown in LA, unable even to get a cheap gig, they were local heroes in Alabama. The fans went crazy when Stevie came onstage, and they went over great, with cheering and calls for more. This really shook Lindsey. He'd had a feeling this would happen, and it did.

At breakfast the next morning, along with the coffee, grits, and hotcakes, came multiple requests for autographs from fans who had tracked down the band at their motel.

At the sound check in Birmingham the next day, Stevie complained that they were taking "Rhiannon" too fast, that she couldn't keep up. That evening, at the second public performance of the piece, Stevie announced, "This is a song about an old Welsh witch." Then she turned to the band and admonished, "And remember: *not too fast.*"

At evening's end, Lindsey announced that this was the last show of Buckingham Nicks's Farewell Tour, because he and Stevie were joining Fleetwood Mac. This was met with almost dead silence; the English band hadn't ever made much impact in the deep South. Back at the motel, Lindsey wondered, *What have we gotten ourselves into?*

He and Stevie sat for an interview with a local paper before flying back to LA.

The major reason behind the breakup [of Buckingham Nicks] is the lack of recognition. Buckingham Nicks all feel that they have been overlooked by their recording label, Polydor. "Hopefully we can get our name known, instead of being buried within the name Fleetwood Mac. People will hear the difference in the music and take notice," hopes Lindsey. "It would take us years to build up the reputation they have. And Warner Brothers are really into Fleetwood Mac. They're not a monster or a giant act, but they consistently sell more albums than they did the last time."

"They're going to put us on a fine, major tour where we'll be playing to everyone," says Stevie. "And they are super nice people, so we figure it will be a tremendous learning experience. They

can help us, and we can help them, so it will be a
give-and-take thing."

The new Fleetwood Mac began to record at Sound City in February 1975, starting with work on Christine's new songs. Keith Olsen
saw "Say That You Love Me" as a potential single, and so they started
there. Stevie attended every session even when she wasn't needed to
sing. She curled up on the couch with her notebooks and sketchpads
to doodle or write snatches of verse. She'd chat with assistant engineer Richard Dashut. She was observing the new chemistry between
Lindsey and these veteran English pros. He was certain how he wanted
his new band to sound and not shy about giving direction. He'd sit
down at the drums and say, "Mick, why don't you try something like
this?" Mick didn't mind, but after a few days Lindsey's personality began to grate on John McVie. John was a drinker and Lindsey a stoner,
and sometimes this didn't work. "I'm not sitting here," John would
murmur, "being told what to do by someone who's just joined the
fucking band." John also seemed to be irritated by some of Lindsey's
nervous tics in the studio, like rubbing his hands together when he
was happy, or anxious, or both. Lindsey would suggest something to
John, who would just attack him. "Hang on, my son, hold on a sec—
*you're talkin' to McVie here.*"

Mick would take Lindsey aside and explain that, whereas Buckingham Nicks had been his exclusive thing, now he was in a band, and
that from day one Fleetwood Mac had always been a democracy.

Stevie also noticed that Lindsey behaved himself better around
Christine, who could kill you with a look. He was careful and polite
to her. "She was the only one who could buffer Lindsey," Stevie recalled. "She could totally soothe him and calm him down, and that
was great because I wasn't very good at that." In fact, it usually went
the other way, ending in hurt feelings and long silences.

Stevie was being watched, too, by Mick Fleetwood, and not just
because he found her attractive. Mick had staked the band's future
on  these two American kids, and while he displayed an air of semi-
befuddled detachment in most things, he was sharply observant of
the Sound City sessions. The most obvious thing he took notice of

was the control Lindsey maintained over Stevie. It wasn't a Svengali-like brainwash, but she deferred to him in all matters, and he would either ignore her rare suggestions or speak to her more sharply than one wanted to hear. He was also, in Mick's experience, unusually protective of her. If he saw someone trying to get her attention or get friendly with her, he would intervene and just vibe the person out. Stevie seemed oblivious to this and would keep on coloring in the drawings of angelic spirits she liked to work on in the studio (when she wasn't crocheting a blanket for someone's baby).

John McVie was observing her as well. One evening, John and Keith Olsen were watching Stevie twirl to a playback of "Rhiannon," leaping about the big, boxy studio wearing a gauzy dress and ballet slippers. McVie muttered to Olsen, "You know, mate, we're a fucking blues band." Olsen replied, "Yeah, man, but this is the shortest road to the bank."

After a few weeks the late California winter was turning into spring, with the hillsides dressed in fiery reds of bougainvillea and royal purple jacaranda. There was a new dryness in the atmosphere, and Stevie often had a sore throat, worried about her voice.

During the studio routine, Stevie was getting to know the band's longtime crew. In addition to Judy Wong, who handled logistics for Mick, there was a studly lighting director called Curry Grant, lots of hair and big eye contact, who was also working on concert production. (*Dangerous,* thought Stevie.) Fleetwood Mac road manager John Courage, known as JC, was the key man in the organization, responsible for almost everything outside the studio and much inside as well. He was twenty-five, blond and handsome, the son of a British army officer, and a member of England's famous Courage brewing family. JC had come up through the ranks of the English touring bands, and he knew how to give orders to burly roadies with names like Rhyno and Earthquake. Fleetwood Mac's production schedule demanded dependable deliveries of fresh marijuana, vintage wine, and premium English ale; acquisitions were a crucial part of JC's portfolio, in addition to seeing that the recording sessions ran somewhat on schedule. (Fleetwood Mac would later become famous—notorious—for cocaine consumption, but these were early days. Cocaine was then scarce and very expensive, and musicians at Fleetwood Mac's then-current level couldn't generally afford the energizing medicament that had captivated Sherlock Holmes, Sigmund Freud, Aleister Crowley, and the Rolling Stones. Still, friends of the band would bring coke by the studio, and Stevie was usually up for a bump in the night, or early morning. She often took a puff on one of Lindsey's tightly wrapped joints when it was passed around the studio.)

And so work continued on the new album, in a general atmosphere of expectant tension, with everyone in Fleetwood Mac being hyperaware that their careers were on the line this time.

## 2.6    Fleetwood Mac

Work progressed on the new Fleetwood Mac album through June 1975. These were the days of Led Zeppelin's masterpiece *Physical Graffiti* and the Eagles' radio dominance with "Lyin' Eyes." Linda Ronstadt's "You're No Good" was #1 for several weeks. But even by April of that year Fleetwood Mac felt they had something special going on. Sound City's customized twenty-four-track Neve console enabled the musicians and engineers to produce the clearest, most mellow, and most sophisticated sound then commercially available, anywhere in the world. They were astonished at the sonic miracles they were hearing on the playbacks, especially in the triple harmonies they were singing. It was a sweet, caramelized sound, with bell tones and high-end timbres the Mac veterans had never experienced in the studio before.

That the studio could produce this sound was amazing, considering what a chaotic scene it was. Sound City worked on the apprentice system, which meant there were always young runners, tape operators, and assistant engineers in and out. Despite the efforts of glam receptionist Suzanne Salvatore, the studio was famously dirty, littered with empty bottles and cans, ashtrays always full. Every time she came in, Stevie reflexively wanted to vacuum the grubby shag carpeting. Even smoking a joint outside in the hazy San Fernando Valley smog meant enduring the manure-like smell of baking hops wafting from the vents of the nearby Budweiser brewery.

By May, though, they had enough tracks to begin sequencing the album. Lindsey's hard-rocking "Monday Morning" would open the LP's first side, as it would have on *Buckingham Nicks II*. Christine's gentle ballad "Warm Ways" was next, a lush, vaguely tropical ballad, one of her trademark pleas for the love she needs as a woman.

Next was "Blue Letter," borrowed from the Curtis Brothers, who had recorded it at Sound City as a demo with Stevie and Lindsey while they were all signed to Polydor. It was a faux-Eagles radio rocker that owed a debt to its mellow prototype, Jackson Browne's "Take It Easy." But "Blue Letter" swung harder than the Eagles, was a great vehicle for the three singers, and would become a fan favorite in concert.

Then came "Rhiannon," Stevie's mythic paean to the old Welsh witch: four minutes and twelve seconds of goddess evocation for singer and rock band. Her lyrics are almost whispered at first, with verses repeated, a tasty solo guitar, and then the chorus, the first time the new band's soaring, harmonic vocal prowess comes forward on the album. There's some more Clapton-inspired guitar, the cat in the night and the fine sky lark, and then, after "taken by the sky," the song fades to "dreams unwind, love's a state of mind," with no hint of the demonic possession dance that Stevie was already choreographing in her mind for when "Rhiannon" would be presented in concert performance as the climax of the new band's new show.

Christine's powerful love song "Over My Head" came next, with Lindsey's deft finger-picking acoustic guitar over the seductive drone from Chris's electric organ and her brilliant keyboard arrangement. In her early thirties now, and childless by choice, Christine's voice was maturing into a mesmeric English alto that still conveyed maternal affection and spiritual comfort, perfect for love ballads and lullabies.

The album's first side ended with a remake of Stevie's "Crystal," again sung by Lindsey, but played in 4/4 instead of the 6/8 time that appeared on *Buckingham Nicks*. The song's message—"special knowledge holds true"—implied a metaphysical utility and a female intuition that love is driven by a magnet, and that for a rock & roll woman like Stevie, love is more powerful than reason, and then beyond reason, and for that reason it is a holy thing, something to be cherished if not worshipped.

Christine's "Say You Love Me" would open the album's second side, and then would go on to launch and cement the soft rock radio format in the United States when the song was released as a single later in the year. Lindsey's guitar echoed the sound pioneered by Roger McGuinn of the Byrds, the first of the California folk rock bands. The "fallin' fallin' fallin'" tag—repeated six times by the singers—was hypnotically seductive. (Who were Christine's new love songs about? Stevie had, of course, noticed Chris exchanging private glances with the band's sexy lighting guy, Curry Grant, whenever he was around, and surely the superheated passion expressed in "Say That You Love Me" and "Over My Head" couldn't be inspired by her bleary, taciturn old man, John McVie.)

"Landslide" followed, the new band's first breakup song, inspired by Stevie's lonely sojourn in Colorado. The guitar sounds far away from the fragile young singer as she reveals her heartbroken prophesy of the impending end of a long relationship, and that there might never be another one like it for her. The song was a recollection of emotional torment that still promised a hope of recovery and renewal.

The album wound down with "World Turning," a jam by Chris and Lindsey that would become Mick's drumming star-turn in future concerts, and Chris's "Sugar Daddy," a lyric by a woman who is yearning for someone while unsure of her passion. (Waddy Wachtel would be credited on rhythm guitar.) The finale would be Lindsey's cod-monumental "I'm So Afraid," with its multiplanar electric guitars and expressions of existential angst. The song and the album would end with chilling banshee wails provided by Stevie Nicks, in rare form.

The first time the band listened to the album, everyone seemed satisfied, but Mick was enthused. This record could be a fucking monster, he kept repeating. A week or so later they got first pressings of the album, white labeled acetates in plain sleeves. Stevie recalled, "I took it home when I got my first disc, to my apartment. And I laid on the couch, and I closed all the doors, and put all the shades down, and lit a candle, and listened to it all by myself. And I said, 'This is a really nice album. I really like it. It's really . . . pretty. It's got some really pretty songs on it. And the voices sound beautiful. And yes, in fact we *have* added something. We have *enhanced* Fleetwod Mac.'"

Stevie had hoped she would be on the cover of the album, which they were calling *Fleetwood Mac* for continuity's sake. Similarly, the jacket would feature only Mick and John and a crystal ball, in a distorted black-and-white photograph by Herbie Worthington, who had worked with the band before. For the back cover the whole band would later be photographed backstage at a Texas concert, with Stevie in her current performing outfit of dark curly hair worn long, a floral top, and bell-bottom jeans.

Even before the album was pressed, Mick Fleetwood was pressing Warner Bros. for attention, begging them to think of Fleetwood Mac as a new band, not the old one with predictable sales figures. Mick: "They thought of us as a solid opening act who broke up and changed personnel with every new album and tour. This typecasting drove us mad." They took the album to Warner executive Joe Smith, who was enthusiastic. "Hey, this is a good record," he said. "Maybe we could do 400,000" instead of their usual 350,000. "He wasn't being flippant," Mick said later. "He thought that was our limit!" No one ever thought of selling millions of Fleetwood Mac records except the band, and record execs were used to the inflated fantasies of musicians. "Maybe," Smith had said, "we could move an extra 50,000 albums if we had a hit single." Fleetwood Mac had never had a hit single in America, and the last one in England had been in 1970, five years earlier. The band hadn't even chosen their album's first single at that point.

Mick also wanted to take the new band on tour, even before the album came out. He was determined to take the new music to their loyal audience, and the new band had never played onstage as a working unit before. Mick: "I said, 'We've *got* to risk it, and go out and play—as a band. No one has ever seen Stevie and Lindsey before, outside of Alabama. It'll be a great training ground for when the record comes out.'"

Warner Bros. told Mick he was crazy. They told him they didn't want Fleetwood Mac to tour prior to the record's release date, and they wouldn't advance the band any touring money because they'd seen too many Fleetwood Mac disintegrations on the road. They said the band was suicidal if they thought they could tour without their new music to sell. They said it was crazy to tour without a manager. Mick told them that the band had had nothing but trouble from managers, and that Mickey Shapiro would be looking after their interests.

Fleetwood Mac's low regard at Warner Bros. was confirmed when the label took out an ad in *Billboard* magazine announcing the new album, and the photograph caption identified Stevie as Lindsey and vice versa. They were both mad as hell.

## 2.7   The Road Warriors

And it came to pass that in mid-May 1975, the new Fleetwood Mac began its touring run in Stevie's old hometown of El Paso, Texas. Traveling in two station wagons, one for the girls driven by John Courage and one for the boys driven by Richard Dashut, they played shows all over the state, getting good notices in Dallas, San Antonio, and especially the university town of Austin. Then they flew to Detroit, where John Courage rented two more wagons that ferried them all over the Midwest and Northeast until early July, playing almost the same show every night.

Yet, they all agreed that the band sounded amazing as they gathered afterward to hear the tapes of the concerts. They'd rehearsed themselves exhaustively until Stevie and especially Lindsey were familiar with the band's older music that the longtime fans expected to hear. They would open with "Station Man" and older songs from the albums *Bare Trees* and *Kiln House*. Lindsey presented his take on Peter Green's epic "Oh Well," which usually drew a big response. From the new, unreleased album they delivered "World Turning," "Blue Letter," and "Crystal."

It took Stevie a few weeks to realize "Rhiannon" in performance. Working in tight jeans and printed and fringed cotton blouses, she parsed the song's different sections in different ways almost every night until she distilled her vocal and dance movements into a kind of a spell only broken at the end, "all the same, Rhiannon," when Lindsey amped up the guitar and Stevie put her arms back and wailed into the microphone, marching in time, screaming as she invoked her Welsh goddess.

The first audiences the new band faced didn't quite know what to make of Stevie's intense, almost pentacostal fervor, but they were rock fans and appreciated the obvious passion the band put into the song. Also, Stevie and Lindsey had been working together for years at that point, and this unity was apparent as they began to front Fleetwood Mac with greater confidence as the tour moved about the country. They took every decent job their agents booked them into, appearing at three-thousand-seat theaters: Seattle Paramount, the Wichita Century, and the Albuquerque Civic Auditorium, mostly as opening act for Loggins & Messina, the telegenic pop-rock act famous for their hit song "Your Mama Don't Dance." Fleetwood Mac opened for British blues blasters Ten Years After in Minnesota and then through Canada's western cities. They opened for the Guess Who? in Missoula, Montana. The band was making three hundred dollars per show, but if they didn't sell out the hall, Mick and JC would sometimes return their fee to the promoters, to build loyalty for Fleetwood Mac's next headlining tours.

At every stop, Christine (who was the voice of the band onstage) told the audiences about the band's next record and said they'd be back to play for them after they'd heard it.

After six weeks of being in a band of hard-touring English road warriors, Stevie Nicks was a wreck. Her throat hurt, her voice was ragged, her nerves were shot, Lindsey had his own problems, and for the first time ever she was experiencing stage fright. She wasn't eating and was losing weight. Still, there would be another show that night.

Stevie wasn't the only one. The McVies' marriage cratered in San Francisco when John was abusive to Christine after a show at the Oakland Coliseum. She decided she'd had enough and moved out. It was handled quietly by JC, who just let everyone know that John and Chris would be in separate hotel rooms from then on. Stevie asked Lindsey if this meant the band would break up, and Lindsey thought not. They had too much to lose to let this derail the band. Everyone just tried to keep calm and carry on.

Meanwhile, *Fleetwood Mac* was in the shops and selling the usual numbers, but it wasn't on the radio. At a band meeting Mick explained that their touring work would be in vain if they couldn't get songs played on the FM rock outlets and AM Top 40 stations. Rock radio was then dominated by the Eagles, so the band hired an Eagles associate

(Paul Ahearn) to do promotion, calling up industry contacts to get people to actually play the record on the air when Fleetwood Mac came to town. Ahearn also insisted they remix "Over My Head" so it would sound hotter on a car radio. The song got a new guitar intro and different harmonies, and began to get some serious airplay when Warner/Reprise released the single in September.

Fleetwood Mac spent the remainder of that year on constant tour, criss-crossing America in a pair of rented station wagons, playing in one college town after another, beginning in September in El Paso and ending, ninety shows later, in December. The band's private promotional efforts continued, and almost every week they would hear that "Over My Head" was being added to some important station's playlist, along with the big hits of the day: the Eagles' "One of These Nights"; David Bowie's "Fame"; Glenn Campbell's "Rhinestone Cowboy"; Bad Company's "Feel Like Makin' Love." Then the radio stations started seeing that Fleetwood Mac's local sales stayed strong, which meant they kept playing the record. Mick was thrilled as he watched his band accumulating momentum. He'd always thought this record was a monster. At the end of October, they'd already sold 400,000 albums, and Mick felt they were just getting started.

And he was relieved. For Mick, a band wasn't about making records, it was about playing for people, and if they could sell records, far out. But the groundswell he was feeling was matched by how great his band sounded live. John was playing well, despite being given the elbow, as he described it. Christine was really fronting the band, with Stevie and Lindsey playing crucial if secondary roles, and she was singing better than ever. Mick realized that Stevie and Lindsey had given them a new lease on life, and a new challenge for Fleetwood Mac to live up to. Lindsey was turning into a tremendous rock guitar player, and Mick was amazed by the almost obsessive amount of effort that went into his playing, with new tricks and licks emerging every few shows.

To Mick, Lindsey was a mystery. He thought of him hunched over his tape recorders for days on end, working on fitting parts of songs together like an alchemist. He seemed to have more time for his guitar than for his girlfriend, who when not working tended to fold herself into a sofa, wrapped in one or more shawls, steaming cup of tea nearby, writing and drawing in ledger-sized books. Lindsey had opinions about things but was mostly withdrawn. Mick would have to drag him out of the hotel room to have the one or two in the bar with the lads. Lindsey clearly was uncomfortable not being the leader of the band, and Mick realized that by coming into an established group he had to compromise certain aspects of his personality.

"And I could see," Mick said later, "as the first days of the tour turned into weeks, that the long-term Lindsey-Stevie relationship was beginning to change as well. When they first joined the band, Lindsey had control. And, very slowly, he began to lose that control. And he really didn't like it. After we made the first record, Stevie began to come out of her shell and talk as a person—in her own right. We'd never heard this before from her."

The one time Mick did get to hang out with Lindsey alone, something weird happened. "On that first tour of the new band, we were staying in the original Holiday Inn, the oldest one, somewhere in Texas. It was a real dump. I ended up in Lindsey's room after the gig. It was the first time I ever sat around and got stoned with Lindsey, man to man. I had stopped smoking years before, and needless to say I got hammered on this joint we're sharing. Remember, this is the earliest days of the new band. We're both sitting there in a fog, and straight out of the blue, he turned to me and said, 'It's you and Stevie, isn't it?'

"I remember this hitting me like a bolt of lightning. I didn't understand this. I hardly even knew her. I could only stammer out something like, what do you mean? Lindsey didn't really answer, but it was clear that it appeared to him that there was something going on between me and Stevie Nicks. Then the moment passed and it was never mentioned again between us."

## 2.8   On the Road

In early October, after a month on the road, a tired and hoarse Stevie Nicks called her mother and described the previous few days on the road in the Midwest. They'd played at Southern Illinois University in

Carbondale, and then the next day at Purdue Music Hall in Lafayette, Indiana. Next day they drove 180 miles to Cincinnati for a show at a big club with lots of radio people there. Next day they flew to Chicago, picked up two cars, and drove to La Crosse, Wisconsin. Next day it was back to Chicago via Mississippi Valley Airways, changing planes at O'Hare Airport to Ozark Airways flight #559 to Moline, picking up two cars and driving two hours for that night's concert at the Orpheum Theater in Davenport, Iowa. Next day they drove 150 miles to play at Illinois State University in Bloomington. The next day they flew to Detroit to play at the Michigan Palace Theater. Next was Bush Stadium in Indianapolis, followed by another long, long drive to Columbus, Ohio.

Stevie told Barbara Nicks that she had little idea that the big English bands worked this hard. She added that the vibes between Chris and John were deadly, and that she and Lindsey weren't getting on that great either. In fact, Lindsey had complained to Stevie that she was being too sexy onstage, and it made him uncomfortable to see the fans fixated on her as she swirled around the stage, smiling and banging her tambourine. He was emotional about this, thought it reflected badly on him as her man, and actually wanted her to tone it down a bit (though no one else did. Christine said to just ignore him). Barbara was as reassuring as she could be and told her daughter to make sure to take care of herself.

Stevie didn't mention cocaine to her mother. The band called cocaine the devil's dandruff, Peruvian marching powder, booger sugar, and other soubriquets. The expensive crystals were doled out to the band in bottle caps before concerts by JC, whose role as band pharmacist and medicine man required a certain amount of care and resourcefulness: "The band kept telling me they needed cocaine, and I was afraid they'd get busted in some little town by some derelict coke dealer with the narcotics squad on his heels." So JC would acquire the drug from reliable sources, "and of course it caught up with me in the end. But I felt my job was to make sure there were no more disasters on the road. I felt protective of them; they were my friends. And the system was safe; it worked as long as it was expected to."

Stevie also found some solace in her new friendship with Jim Recor, the attractive road manager of Loggins & Messina. It was a flirtatious but platonic thing, with possessive Lindsey on hand of course, and Jim reputedly married (after Stevie inquired) to an extremely beautiful girl called Sara (with whom Stevie would become very close, later on). Jim Recor was a sympathetic guy and he had a crush on Stevie, like many of the men who worked on the tour. He could see that Stevie was struggling, and he would go out of his way to see that she (and Christine) were comfortable—opening acts usually had to dress in the toilets of the hockey arenas they were playing—and that they had what they needed from the venues. This didn't stop him from bawling, "All right—*get those fucking broads off the stage!*" at JC when Fleetwood Mac finished their nightly set.

The other rock bands they opened for on that tour couldn't see how it worked with two women in the group. They teased Mick and John about this in the motel bars after the shows. Mick told them it wasn't a problem; in fact it was the opposite of a problem. In fact, it made them bear up a little more. John Courage said the energy that Stevie and Lindsey brought to the band changed everything. "They were younger, they were good looking, they were friendly, and they were fun to be with. Bob Welch had been moody and very serious, and he went through depressing times with us. But now I saw Chris and John and Mick laughing and enjoying themselves again. It was wonderful, after all that we'd been through."

Stevie Nicks, however, was not doing much laughing. By November 1975, even as "Over My Head" reached the Top 40, she was getting tired of pushing their record in what seemed to be an endless parade of college towns across America. She also went through an anxious spell of self-doubt after reading a stream of negative critical opinions about her. Reviewing *Fleetwood Mac, Rolling Stone* was less than kind: "Nicks has yet to integrate herself into the group's style. Compared to Christine McVie's, her singing seems callow and mannered." Most of the album and concert reviews read something on the order of "the raucous voice of Stevie Nicks and the golden-throated Christine McVie, who's the only thing this old band has left."

Mick: "Stevie was extremely sensitive to this, and so we stopped showing her the reviews, even the good ones. She would just go to pieces when she saw these things. She'd say, 'Oh, come on, the only reason you hired me was because I was with Lindsey, part of a package.'

"And I'd say no, we *love* what you're doing, and the punters love it, too! 'Cause it was true. I couldn't take my eyes off Stevie when we were onstage. Remember, we were only the opening act. We didn't have our own staging and only very limited spotlights, so Stevie and her graceful movements were carrying almost the whole visual burden for the band. But she had a hard time believing me and confided to Christine that she was starting to believe that she wasn't all that good." In fact, when she was feeling down, she looked to Christine as a role model, appreciating her strength and her swagger, the ever-present cigarette, the ever-refilled glass of Blue Nun. Christine swore and complained and God help anyone who crossed her or got in her way. (She was also a good cook, shepherd's pie being a specialty.)

Mostly, Stevie was just fatigued. She wasn't physically strong in the first place, and the hardships of touring—four or five concerts straight, with maybe a day or two off—began to take a toll on her. She couldn't sleep during the long car rides between dates. She was cold all the time. The band had no catering, so they lived off fast food and wine. Stevie lost so much weight that her parents were alarmed when they came to see the band when they played Phoenix in early December. Mick Fleetwood became more and more worried that she might have to leave the tour, and the band. He recalled, "I kept telling her, 'Come *on*, Stevie, you've got to eat and stay fit. You're an important part of this band now, we *need* you!'

"And she'd say, 'Mick—when I joined I didn't have a *clue* it would be like this. No one told me. I didn't know me and Chris would be sleeping on amps in back of the truck. But don't worry, because I've decided. I'm gonna make it through. *No one* is going to say, 'Oh, she couldn't cope. She couldn't hack it. She gave up.'"

But she didn't. In fact, she was getting these lyrical brainstorms while sitting backstage, waiting to go on, writing the lyrics to "Sisters of the Moon" in her ledgers, also reworking the lines that would become "Gold Dust Woman." This was December 1975, and "Over My Head" was in the American Top 10 and climbing the charts in England as well. The pretty harmonies Stevie had sung with Chris were considered crucial to the song's success, which tended to drown out whatever jibes the rock critics were aiming at her. Stevie's morale was also buoyed by the choice of "Rhiannon" to be the album's next single at the beginning of February 1976. Judging by the genuinely aroused audience reactions whenever the band played "Rhiannon" live, with Stevie now performing the song wearing a diaphanous pink chiffon cape, Mick was thinking the new single could put the album over the top, saleswise.

Then Stevie started having some serious problems with her voice. During that tour she was taking full advantage of the chance to make the end of "Rhiannon" memorable for the audience (and herself), shredding her voice as she sang to the stars of her love for the goddess. Lindsey monitored this, watching her carefully but sometimes letting her get too crazy before he pulled back and crashed the song to a halt. She also had to sing over the big floor monitors that blasted the sound back to the band, to the extent that she was hurting her voice almost every night. Stevie would later say that her voice didn't recover until she started working with a vocal coach—twenty years later.

Fleetwood Mac opened for Rod Stewart at a sold-out stadium in Anaheim, in Orange County south of Los Angeles. Stevie was pleased to meet Rod, a real English rock star who arrived with all the trappings: limousines, champagne, girls. She laughed as Mick and Rod got loaded and joked about Shotgun Express, the London blues band they had both been in ten years previous. The last show of the tour was on December 22. The next day the band watched JC and Richard Dashut play bumper cars with their two Chevrolet Impala station wagons on the icy parking lot of the last Holiday Inn that Fleetwood Mac would have to endure—at least for a few weeks.

Their album sold tonnage right through the Christmas holidays and then didn't stop. By the end of 1975 they had sold a million and a half records, and found they were getting considerably more respect from Warner Bros. Company president Mo Ostin presented the band with a gold album for *Fleetwood Mac* and was generous when it was time to renegotiate their contract. The band got a large raise in royalty payments and a big cash advance so they could make their next album.

At the same time, the band renegotiated with their newest members, who had been on salary for a year. In fact Warner Bros. had been so blasé about Lindsey and Stevie—*just another guitarist and his chick singer*—that they didn't bother making them sign a "members leaving" contract clause intended to make it difficult for musicians leaving established bands to start solo careers. (This would have serious and fortuitous ramifications for Stevie later on.) So in early 1976, Stevie Nicks and Lindsey Buckingham were made full partners in Fleetwood Mac.

Years later, in 2014, Stevie would tell a writer for *The New York Times* about what she remembered as the "magical" year of 1975, "when I started the year as a waitress and ended it with Lindsey Buckingham and I millionaires."

# CHAPTER 3

## 3.1 Starting Rumours

1976 was an intense war year for Stevie Nicks and the rest of Fleetwood Mac. All five members of the band had split with their partners by the end of the year. The previous months, while they were trying to make a follow-up album while barely speaking to each other, were cruel and unusual punishment for having sold a couple million *Fleetwood Mac* albums. But the end product of these labors, the legendary megaselling *Rumours,* would be one of the most popular and acclaimed song albums in history. It's still one of the greatest achievements of the rock music movement.

It started, of course, badly, when Mick Fleetwood had a massive falling-out with Keith Olsen, and that was the end of working at Sound City for Stevie and Lindsey. The issues were mostly financial, involving disputes over fees and royalties, but there was also bad blood in getting the former Buckingham Nicks out of their contract with Olsen's production company. Stevie felt bad about this—Sound City had nurtured her and Lindsey for years, and the owners and studio staff had been like family—but in the end there was nothing she could do about it except go along with what was best for the band she had joined.

And then Mick insisted that Fleetwood Mac find another studio, preferably out of town, as his wife Jenny had taken their children and gone home to England after Mick had filed for divorce. Likewise, Christine McVie had moved out of the house she and John had bought in rural Topanga Canyon, leaving John to drown his sorrows by himself. This was when Mick decided to work at the Record Plant, a famous studio in Sausalito, the bohemian waterside village near San

Francisco. The Record Plant had a reputation as a favorite of the great Bay Area bands and was a notorious haunt of Sly and the Family Stone, which made many of its epic soul records in the facility. The Record Plant came with a house in the hills that the band and engineers could live in while they worked there, although Stevie and Chris (and their little terriers) preferred to eschew the guys' bunkhouse atmosphere and instead shared an apartment in the village's marina, closer to the studio.

But first Fleetwood Mac went back on tour, promoting the still-soaring *Fleetwood Mac*. Now they were playing in front of their new stage backdrop, a spooky nighttime scene of the full moon illuminating silvery clouds and bare trees, conjuring a feeling of watchful owls and witches on broomsticks. During an early break from the road in Buffalo, New York, Stevie and Chris were shopping for vintage clothes in a thrift store when Stevie came across an antique black silk top hat, the kind a gentleman once wore to the opera. She tried it on and decided it gave her a dramatic, even operatic look. Within months it would become her trademark.

The band sounded better all the time as the musicians bonded and grew into a fluid organic concert unit, moving from Christine's softly rocking ballads to Rhiannon's spiritual tornado. Offstage the vibrations between the musicians were deadly. Stevie and Lindsey were barely speaking; he suspected she was seeing someone outside their "marriage," which she later said wasn't true. What was true was that Christine was seeing Curry Grant on the side while on tour. John suspected something. "He's doing her, you know," he kept saying to Mick, who'd reply, "No John, it's all in your head." Eventually the road crew heard about it and told Curry he was a bastard for fooling with Chris. It got to the point where Grant couldn't ride in the van with the roadies. Mick and JC confronted Chris; she said it was true. JC sent Curry home for being a distraction, and Chris accepted that it was for the best.

The band took a break from the road in a rented house in Florida, a spooky old mansion with overgrown vines hanging from the trees and humid tropical vibes. There were frogs in the green swimming pool and the band's big touring trucks were crammed in the driveway. Barbed wire surrounded the property. Here Stevie and Lindsey had a blowout fight when she heard the lyrics of his new song "Go Your Own Way," which accused her of "packing up, shacking up"— secretly being unfaithful to him. She bitterly denied his accusation, and there were floods of tears. Several other songs that would later appear on *Rumours* were begun in Florida, under psychic battlefield conditions.

Late winter in the Bay Area is cool and damp, with thick fog rolling in from the Pacific, especially in the morning. Stevie and Christine were driven to the Record Plant draped in sweaters, leg warmers, coats, and headscarves. It took a few days for the band to get used to the Record Plant, whose various studios were connected by a dimly lit, cave-like hallway. *Fleetwood Mac* had been recorded in three months. Now the band would take a year to craft a new album during which, according to Mick, "we spoke to each other in clipped, civil voices while sitting in small airless studios listening to each other's songs about our own shattered relationships." Among the Record Plant's curiosities was Sly Stone's "pit," a thickly shag-carpeted sunken lounge into which Sly would disappear when recording. The pit, which had its own nitrous oxide tank, was generally avoided by the band since it was often occupied by people they didn't know chopping cocaine on mirrors.

They had to fire the house engineer after four days, his crimes being too much attention paid to Stevie and being much too concerned with the band's astrological signs. Mick ordered Richard Dashut, who had been running the soundboard on tour, to produce the new album. Richard, understanding that the new songs would need arrangements, and that no one in the band read or wrote music notation, brought in a more experienced LA engineer, Ken Caillat, to coproduce with him.

In the early days it was actually hard to get the musicians in the same space, as feelings were so raw. Stevie especially was upset because of her almost total dependence on Lindsey to shape her written poems, melodies, and chord changes into actual songs. He was so cross with her that he couldn't let himself help her without making her painfully aware of what this hostile dependency was costing him. But after a couple of weeks he started dating a waitress at a local hangout and began to be less unhappy. Stevie didn't like this and would get upset, leading to more arguments, more tears. In fact, she missed the parts of Lindsey that she had loved and so respected, and the two deeply estranged lovers did have a few stoned sleepovers. Stevie recalled, "In Sausalito, up at the little condominium, Lindsey and I were still enough together that he would come up there and sleep once in a while. And we had a terrible fight—I don't remember what about—but I remember him walking out and me saying, 'You take the car with all the stuff [to LA]. I'm flying back.' That was at the end of the first two months of recording *Rumours*."

It was the same with John and Christine, who still had feelings for her husband of seven years and was quite rattled when he took up with an old girlfriend of Peter Green's. Then there was Mick, who described himself as "piggy-in-the-middle" of all this, even as his ex-wife Jenny and their daughters returned to Los Angeles and moved in with Mick's old band mate Andy Sylvester, one of his best friends.

All this was "material" for the songs Stevie brought to the Sausalito sessions. Her favorite of these was "Silver Springs," a ballad of love and revenge directed at Lindsey. The lyrics implied that he was a well-spring of inspiration for her, but that love for him had faded and that he would—forever—be haunted by the sound of the woman who loved him. Lindsey kind of hated "Silver Springs," but he was professionally obligated to work on it anyway.

As the band was settling in, *Fleetwood Mac* was edging closer to *Billboard*'s Top 10 album chart after the remixed "Rhiannon" single was released in February 1976 and got huge national airplay. Album sales were now above the 2.5 million mark, which put enormous additional pressure on the band's three writers, especially Stevie Nicks. This new album had to be even better than their last, which was produced under much friendlier conditions at a studio they were comfortable in. Stevie was really feeling this pressure. To help her, Robin Snyder came to Sausalito and stayed with her, a soothing presence in the studio and at the end of the day. Robin was a good cook and Stevie, who wasn't eating much, usually ate what Robin put on her plate.

The Record Plant sessions included some promising instrumental tracks that would months later evolve into massive singles and album tracks. As yet without lyrics, they were denoted by the titles written on the two-inch tape boxes: "Spinners"; "Strummer"; "Brushes"; "Keep Me There"; and "Butter Cookie." Some of Stevie's new songs were very strong, like "Silver Springs" and the early demo of "Gold Dust Woman." Others were carefully considered, demo-ed, recorded, and didn't make it on the album. Among these were an early version of "Planets of the Universe" and a piano demo called "Sleeping Angel"; an electric piano demo of "Castaway"; and a heart-broken ballad called "Mistaken Love" that riffed on forsaken love, pagan love, heartbreakin' love. "Think About It" was an almost fully realized band track about a love affair in its final moments. So was "If You Ever Did Believe." "Forest of the Black Roses" was a piano demo of a spooky fairy tale. "Blue Water" was an atmospheric country song. They were all experimental, but Stevie thought of her songs as her children, and it never stopped bothering her that her children were at Lindsey's mercy if they were going to turn into works of art.

## 3.2 Is It Over Now?

While all this was happening in early spring of 1976, "Rhiannon" was on the radio everywhere, and her song was climbing the sales charts. The 45-rpm single actually bore the song's original title, "Rhiannon (Will You Ever Win)," an echo of the primal and starkly competitive ambition that drove Stevie and her younger lover south to seek their fortune half a decade before. The song had been remixed for single release, losing half a minute from the album track. At 3:46 the tempo was faster and the vocals mixed higher to soar out of car radios. The guitar mix was different from the album, "hotter," the electric piano "sweeter." The "taken by sky" chorales were celestial mythograms. "Dreams unwind, love's a state of mind" sounded more country, some-how. The engineers who worked on the single assumed that Stevie's original vocals had been doubled, but when they separated the tracks they found that Keith Olsen had used a Lexicon delay unit to achieve the silvery voice that people identified with Stevie's inspiring song. When Fleetwood Mac's pretaped "Rhiannon" concert video was shown on *The Midnight Special* syndicated rock show later in the year, "Rhiannon" reached #11 and sealed Stevie Nicks's destiny for the rest of her career.   .

The working title for the new album was *Yesterday's Gone,* from the chorus of Christine's new song written for unhappy John, "Don't Stop." They were telling each other that their long travail was over, and now tomorrow beckoned and they shouldn't blow it. Work continued amid relative chaos and heroic intake of stimulants, potions, powders, alcohol, preparations, and medications. Stevie was smoking too much, and to soothe her throat she experimented with various tonics made of tea, honey, Courvoisier cognac, herbal elixirs, and lemon.

The Thousand-Dollar Cookie Session took place one evening when Robin Snyder baked a fresh batch of brownies laced with chunks of hashish someone had given the band. She and Stevie brought them to the studio the next day, warning that the brownies produced a stupefying buzz. Sure enough, Fleetwood Mac got so stoned that the songs were forgotten and the engineers left for the night. Stevie and John spent the session on the studio couch, laughing at the jokes and cartoons in a copy of *Playboy.*

Things were getting a bit out of hand at the Record Plant. They spent four eye-wateringly expensive days trying to get the house piano in tune. The studio's tape machine started shredding the tape—they called it Jaws—ruining fresh takes and requiring boring do-overs. Local scene-makers, players, and strangers the band didn't know were in and out. There was a lot of tapping on mirrors. According to Mick, "We were certainly doing our fair share of the old powder [cocaine]. There was one dealer who came around and kept us supplied at generous discounts . . . and we were so grateful to him that we considered giving him some kind of credit on the album jacket, but sadly he got snuffed—executed—before the thing came out. Perils of the trade, we heard."

And Lindsey was losing it, acting like a jerk. Frustrated and anxious about the lax atmosphere he perceived, he vented his annoying opinions in insulting ways and lashed out at people. He grabbed Ken Caillat by the throat in a studio rage. He reportedly hit the pretty waitress he'd been seeing and she walked out. He struggled for control of the production until McVie walked out, and Mick had to sit Lindsey down and ask him if he was really sure he wanted to be in a band.

Mick and John had talked this over, like it was a crisis. If Lindsey was fired or left the band, they decided they would gamble that Stevie wouldn't leave with him. Fleetwood Mac couldn't afford to lose Stevie Nicks, but they'd never had a problem finding good guitar players. The friction between Stevie and Lindsey was getting worse. One night she and Lindsey were singing the backing vocals to "You Make Loving Fun." They were sitting on two high chairs in the studio with headphones on. When Ken Caillat stopped the tape to rewind it, Stevie glared at Lindsey and shouted, "Fuck you, asshole. You can go to hell!"

Lindsey let out a bunch of curses and said, "When we get back to LA, I'm moving out!"

"I don't want to live with you anymore either," she shouted. The engineers behind the glass looked at each other. When the tape was rolling again, they took up where they'd left off about making loving fun.

Late one night, sitting on the studio floor, Mick gave Lindsey an ultimatum. "I said, 'Lindsey, it comes down to this: either you're in a band or you're not. It's neither good nor bad. If you accept the fact that you're working with other people, then that's great. But if you don't, then you shouldn't be in the band.' We looked at each other hard for a long moment. I'm sure we looked haggard, burnt-out. But the matter was resolved, and we continued."

It was storming the night Stevie wrote the lyrics to "Dreams." Thunder echoed through the Record Plant as Stevie made her way through the stygian hallway to Sly Stone's pit with a little electric keyboard and her velvet-covered notebook. Stevie: "There was a big black circular bed with Gothic curtains hung around it. I hopped up on this bed with my little piano and wrote 'Dreams.' I recorded it on a little cassette machine, and then I walked across the hall to the studio and said, 'I think you're going to want to hear this.' They said, 'We're busy.' I repeated myself and said, 'I *really* think you're going to want to hear this.' They listened to 'Dreams' and we recorded it the next day." Amid the drawings of angels, flowers, and fairies in her journal were lines of loneliness and heartache. Her spirits were low and rubbed raw by the coruscating loss of love. Yet there was hope in the rain, that it could wash away the burden of loss and cleanse the soul for a new life. She implies the power of crystal visions, esoteric and secret knowledge that she possesses and keeps to herself. Her dreams are prophetic. The loss will eventually be worse for her lover than it would be for her. "You'll know," she says. "Ahh, *you'll know.*"

Stevie has also pointed out that "Dreams" is the other side of "Go Your Own Way," a song she saw as angry but honest. "So then I wrote 'Dreams,' and because I'm the chiffon-y chick who believes in fairies and angels, and Lindsey is a hardcore guy, it comes out differently. Lindsey is saying go ahead and date other men and live your crappy life, and Stevie is singing about the rain washing you clean. We're coming at it from different angles, but we were really saying exactly the same thing."

("Dreams" would become Fleetwood Mac's only ever #1 single release. Stevie later said that "Dreams" was "totally related" to a song by the Spinners, but couldn't remember which one. Observers have suggested "I'll Be Around" as a possible model.)

Stevie had been putting off recording her first vocal track for a difficult song, "Gold Dust Woman," a lyric she'd been working on for years. She recalled: "There's a street in Phoenix called Gold Dust Avenue. I think that's where I got the idea. . . . That song was about a very heavy, very bad time in my life. The drug addict in 'Gold Dust Woman' is out there, breaking her back, looking for drugs. I felt I wanted to re-create that dark situation, to warn people. I never saw it as a premonition about myself." The lyrics related to girls she'd known, girls she'd seen, the girl she was, the girl she was afraid she might become. The question in the song—*is it over now?*—was a question she'd been, up till now, afraid to ask. Gold dust was pretty and it felt good, but the doom-laden click track Lindsey had come up with foretold nothing good. The track also had a somber, war-dance coda with a subterranean blue streak of electric piano. The singer must evoke dark forces—black widows, dragons—to overcome her destiny as a shadow of a woman. Either that, or it was pick up the pieces and go home. Recording the vocal track for "Gold Dust Woman" was going to be a bitch. Lindsey thought the song was evil.

It was cold and raining heavily the night Stevie tried it first. Mick Fleetwood watched in awe:

"I recall that she started in a fully lit studio. The song needed a lot of power, a lot of emotion. She got halfway through, stopped, and said she wanted to start again. Take followed take, and I could sense that Stevie was transforming, sort of withdrawing inside of herself. She was reaching inside for something—some magic that she kept hidden from us."

At three in the morning she took a break and walked outside, breathing the chilly air. Somebody made her a cup of black tea with lemon and a little cognac. She mentioned that the studio was too brightly lit for her. Mick: "The lights were dimmed; a chair was brought in so she could sit. She wore a woolen cardigan and wrapped herself in a shawl to ward off the predawn chill. An hour later she was almost invisible in the shadows, a tiny figure under the big cans [headphones]. She was hunched over in her chair, alternately choosing from her supply of paraphernalia: tissues, reading glasses, a Vicks inhaler, lozenges for her sore throat, a bottle of mineral water. Gradually she took command of the material. On the eighth full take, exalted, she sang the lyric straight through for the first time."

This gave Fleetwood hope. "We were under pressure. We were going mad. The only thing holding us together was a slender thread of Mac family cohesion. For me, it was Stevie, physically the most fragile of us all, who inspired our collective drive to create, and prevail."

The song Stevie was most excited about was the one giving her the most trouble. "Silver Springs" was intended to be a self-excavating ballad of lost love. Addressed to Lindsey, the song—delivered in a plaintive soprano voice—sought to reestablish a lost intimacy while admitting bitter defeat before literally casting a spell that in time, for the rest of Lindsey's life, beyond his control, he would always hear the music of the lover he lost, "the sound of the woman who loves you."

Stevie thought that "Silver Springs" would be her dominant song on the new album; it couldn't fail. The only problem was that Lindsey hated the song. He said it was too much in his face, and he gave Stevie a very hard time about working on the song in the studio.

To Lindsey Buckingham, "Silver Springs" was not a prophesy. It was a curse.

## 3.3    White Magic Woman

March 1976. Fleetwood Mac was leaving the Record Plant after several tormented months, returning to their homes in Los Angeles to finish the new album. *Fleetwood Mac* was heading toward Triple Platinum status, reaching its three-millionth mark around then, chasing #1 *Frampton Comes Alive*. One night Stevie and Mick were listening to some rough cassette mixes of the work they'd done in Sausalito. Mick told Stevie that he'd had a feeling that this next record would do better, much better. The new songs felt strong, Mick said. They sounded, well, important. Maybe, he said, they could sell eight or nine million if they could keep it together. Stevie just laughed and squeezed his hand, and said, "Good luck."

When they got back to LA, they played their tapes, which didn't sound right in a different studio. There was panic until someone found Producer's Workshop, a mixing room tucked amidst the sleazy porn theaters along Hollywood Boulevard, and their tapes at least sounded good enough to work on. Now, while Stevie took her friends off to a holiday in Acapulco, Lindsey and the two producers basically discarded almost everything they'd done so far except the drum tracks, and Fleetwood Mac began to dub in new instrumental parts and all the vocals. Once more, the subsonic vibrations of group heartache filled the atmosphere as the three writers—Stevie, Chris, and Lindsey—kept telegraphing punches via their new lyrics.

The studio had a pretty young receptionist, Carol Ann Harris. She was in her mid-twenties, smart and blond, with blue eyes and a great smile. Lindsey took up with her, and she began to hang around the studio to be with him after her working hours. Stevie Nicks was not amused and ignored her. The exclusive coterie of young women, who usually formed a protective entourage around Stevie, totally snubbed Carol. Stevie's girls—Robin Snyder, Mary Torrey, Christie Alsbury, and others—dressed like Stevie, in long skirts and long hair with lots of accessories and drop-dead shades. They smelled like her, too, redolent of patchouli oil and sandalwood. They basically controlled access to

Stevie and styled themselves as ladies-in-waiting to a virgin queen, making sure that Stevie felt supported and had what she needed in the studio. They would stare at Carol, giggle and whisper about her as she sat alone in a corner while Lindsey was working. It soon came out that Carol was part of a record bootlegging enterprise, on the side, which sold unauthorized concert and studio recordings by big stars like Bob Dylan and the Rolling Stones to cooperating record stores. Christine McVie thought this was creepy and told her so. But Lindsey didn't seem to care about this. Stevie finally deigned to acknowledge Carol's existence when Carol showed up one night dressed all in black. Stevie had a quiet word with her, informing Carol that it was she, Stevie, who wore black within the Fleetwood Mac bubble, that it was an exclusive thing, and maybe Carol might want to think about wearing a different color the next time she hung around the band.

Despite being firmly put in her place by Stevie and her entourage, Carol Ann Harris would stay by Lindsey's side for the next eight years.

In May the band traveled to Santa Barbara to shoot a promotional film for Warner Bros. in a football stadium. They wanted a live film version of "Rhiannon" to promote the single's release. This was shot with Stevie playing a guiro, a ribbed Latin percussion instrument, instead of her usual black-ribboned tambourine. Right after this Stevie and Christine flew to Hawaii for a two-week vacation. At their rented beach house on the island of Maui they were secretly joined by a smitten Mick Fleetwood, who wanted to hang around with Stevie and keep an eye on the franchise, away from the band and the tensions of the studio.

By June 1976 they were behind schedule and were due to go back on tour, opening stadium shows that summer for the rip-roaring Eagles, who were also recording a new album, *Hotel California,* at the same time in LA. Some songs were finished, some weren't. "The Chain" was still a bunch of unconnected riffs and ideas with no lyrics. "Don't Stop," written by Christine to cheer up John McVie, was only half finished. "Silver Springs" was way too long—the demo was something like ten minutes—but Stevie didn't know how to cut it back because every line held breathtaking importance for her.

Warner Bros. released the third single from *Fleetwood Mac,* "Say You Love Me" and Christine's love song went straight into the Top 10, giving the album another big sales boost.

At the same time, Stevie was devoting major energy to devising a new look, especially after she was told their first album was likely to sell another million records that summer. She began to work with a young dressmaker, Margi Kent, a stylish local designer who liked to glue little jewels under the arches of her eyebrows, a look that Stevie loved the minute she saw Margi for the first time.

What Stevie wanted now was what she called "a uniform," a stage outfit that would get her through the occasional bouts of stage fright that came with playing big places. She told Margi Kent that she wanted "something urchin-like, an English street urchin out of *Great Expectations* or *A Tale of Two Cities.*" She drew a stick figure of what she had in mind: a handkerchief dress under a jacket with long, droopy chiffon sleeves, like a cape or like bat wings. (This idea came from old photos of the exotic Hungarian silent film star Vilma Banky, whose Spanish Colonial house in the Hollywood Hills Stevie would later buy.) They tried out several raggedy skirts made of chiffon that looked good with the black velvet platform boots that a famous Hollywood cobbler was making for her because she didn't want to wear high heels. They experimented with various fabrics: lace, tulle, organza, rayon. "We came up with The Outfit," Stevie said later: "a Jantzen leotard, a little chiffon wrap blouse, a couple of little short black tailored jackets, two skirts, and the velvet boots. That gave us an edge. I could be very sexy under layers of chiffon, lace, and velvet. And nobody will know who I really am."

But this process caused troubling feelings for Stevie. She complained to Margi that she thought her hips were too wide for someone her height, and that she had no bust. They started talking about breast augmentation via plastic surgery, and Margi allowed that it would be easier to dress her if Stevie added some letters to her bra size.

There was also a major rethink about Stevie's hair, which she usually cut herself. "I'd gather up the top, measure it with my fingers, and just chop it off. I did it pretty well." But Margi brought in a stylist, who recommended that she try a frayed and layered "shag" cut. The shag was considered a Bad Girl haircut, having originated with the English rock stars and then made iconic by the 1970 movie *Klute,* in which Jane Fonda portrayed a call girl threatened by a stalker. The stylist told Stevie that when you cut long bangs and put layers around the face, a girl becomes more assertive, more confident about herself. The shag is also almost permanent, in that you can't really do anything else with the hair, so it takes some courage to take that road. Stevie's hair was cut into a shag and considerably lightened, and she loved the way it looked with her future trademark, the formal top hat. (So also would Chrissie Hynde, Debbie Harry, Patti Smith, and the other shag-sporting lady rockers who came after Stevie.)

Fleetwood Mac began tour rehearsals in early June 1976, before their new album was in the can, and the band exploded back into form after half a year cloistered in stuffy, smoke-filled studios. They began a leg of Midwestern sports fields, opening for Jeff Beck at Royals Stadium in Kansas City. They continued through Wisconsin, Minnesota, and Illinois, with Stevie's "Rhiannon" often stopping the show for extended applause. On June 29 they opened for Jeff Beck, Ted Nugent, and Jefferson Starship at Busch Stadium in St. Louis. The next night the same four acts played Riverfront Stadium in Cincinnati.

Beginning in July Fleetwood Mac played a series of huge outdoor concerts, opening for the (wildly popular) Eagles. On July Fourth, 1976, the American Bicentennial, Stevie Nicks fronted Fleetwood Mac before 37,000 fans at sold-out Tampa Stadium in Florida.

Mick: "This was truly a gig I'll never forget. As I looked out from my drum riser at the crowd that jammed the huge football stadium, I realized I was looking at hundreds—no, *thousands*—of girls dressed exactly like Stevie in black outfits, many sporting top hats, Stevie's new stage costume, which they must have seen in magazines and on TV. At the point in our set when Lindsey played the guitar intro to 'Rhiannon,' and Stevie stepped to the front of the stage and told them that this was a song about an old Welsh witch, these girls went bonkers—barking mad!—swaying and singing along and really giving themselves to the spirit of the thing. With the success of the ['Rhiannon'] single, it was becoming one of the focal points of our set. Graceful and mysterious in translucent dark chiffon, Stevie's acted-out song could only be described as mystical, or a rite. I looked at her, twirling across the stage with her tambourine, her eyes closed during the guitar solo, and I could tell that she was in heaven."

Fleetwood Mac stayed on the road for the rest of the summer, opening for the Eagles, Loggins & Messina, the Beach Boys, The Band, and Santana (who played Peter Green's "Black Magic Woman." Fleetwood Mac didn't, having a white magic woman of their own). The *Fleetwood Mac* album was said to be edging closer to four million in sales. But underneath remained this grinding tension between Stevie and Lindsey, especially when the band had time to get back to recording. The most toxic issue between them, as they tried to somehow renegotiate their relationship, was their codependence in the artistic sense. They would be trying to build something in the studio and Lindsey might say—with total condescension—"Well, *that'll* never work. Why don't we do it *this* way?" He would play it on the piano, and Stevie would just glare at him, speechless with anger.

Mick Fleetwood would try to smooth things over. "C'mon Stevie—what's the matter?"

"Oh nothing, really," she would answer, "I just feel like he's hijacking my music, that's all." Lindsey would lose patience and walk out. Or he would pass some nasty remark and Stevie and her girls would rush away in a flurry of dark glances and tears. Most people thought this evolved from Lindsey's feeling humiliated that Stevie had walked out on him, but insiders knew that this was aggravated by jealousy. Rumors had spread that Fleetwood Mac's golden pair had split up, and now the most attractive and successful men in the LA music scene were drawn to Stevie Nicks like bears to honey.

Lindsey was most jealous of Don Henley. He had reason to be.

The rumors started with the roadies. The Eagles' crew told Fleetwood Mac's guys that their studly singing drummer was hot for the opening act's cute chick singer. Henley had called Stevie before the tour, according to Mick, and they had spoken on the phone a couple of times, but they had never met when Stevie's band opened for Henley's in Greensboro, North Carolina. The two bands were in adjacent dressing rooms. When Stevie walked into Fleetwood Mac's, she saw a large, garish bouquet of roses waiting at her dressing table. Attached was a card: TO STEVIE: *THE BEST OF MY LOVE*—TONIGHT? LOVE, DON. She stared at this, obviously angry at this uncool, awkward, corny approach. She couldn't believe it. Flushed, she looked around the room until she beheld Mick and John almost soiling themselves with laughter in the corner. Christine explained that Don didn't send the flowers and the note. Mick and John did, a stupid prank. Stevie wouldn't speak to either of them for a while, because she was indeed starting to have feelings for Don Henley, who was said to be a really nice young gentleman from Texas.

A few weeks later, Fleetwood Mac and the Eagles found themselves in Florida on a break from the tour. By then, Stevie and Henley had been on a few dates and were getting along. She recalled: "Here's one thing that Don did that freaked out my band so much: we're all in Miami. They're recording at the gorgeous pink house they're renting. It's right on the water, totally romantic. Anyway, he sends a limousine driver to our hotel with a box of presents for me, and they're delivered right to the breakfast room where everyone's eating. There's a stereo, a bunch of cool records. There's incredible flowers and fruits, a beautiful display. The limousine driver is putting all this out onto the table and I'm going, 'Oh please . . . *please* . . . this is *not* going to go down well.' And they want to know who this is from. And Lindsey is *not* happy.

"So, yeah, I started going out with [Don]. Sure. Lindsey and I are totally broken up. I have every right in the world to go out with people. But I spend most of my time with the band, and it's not real conducive to having a relationship. So, yes, I did go out with Don for awhile."

Stevie didn't like to bring her men friends to the house she was then renting in West Hollywood. She preferred spending occasional nights at the house Henley shared with Glenn Frey in Coldwater Canyon. She was amused to see they were an Odd Couple, with Frey the household slob and Henley emptying ashtrays and washing the dishes so they'd be clean. For the next year, Stevie Nicks and Don Henley were a semisecret, superheated Hollywood rock & roll couple. On several occasions when the Eagles were on the road, love-struck Don had lonely Stevie flown to his side in a superexpensive private Lear jet. (The Eagles' roadies called this extravagance "Love 'em and Lear 'em.") Stevie and Don were often apart, and then she went out with his friend John David Souther, who wrote for the Eagles. "We had an *incredible* time together," she remembered, referring to the tall, sexy, broodingly handsome Mr. Souther.

## 3.4   Time Casts a Spell on You

Fall 1976. Jimmy Carter, governor of Georgia, is trying to replace President Gerald Ford in a campaign in which Carter openly evokes his love of Led Zeppelin and revels in the support of the Georgia-based All-man Brothers Band. Carter would be elected in November, but until much later nothing political ever penetrated the bubble that the members of Fleetwood Mac were now living in. "It was a nether world," Mick Fleetwood would remember, "and it mostly existed at night. We in the band and the management and the crew either lived on the road or in the studio, a permanent semi-stoned caravan that rarely permitted the light of the real world to penetrate into our sacred space. At that point we felt we were progressing to a goal, and so we all tried to stay in a kind of glazed state of what I used to call 'transcension.'"

A month earlier Stevie had bought an old mansion in the hills above Hollywood. She called it El Contento. (Mick and Chris also bought new homes. John bought a forty-one-foot sailboat and had moved into Marina Del Rey.) She started to furnish her house with antiques and a new grand piano. Her mother gave her a blue Tiffany-style glass lamp that looked like it belonged on a film set, and this became her favorite possession. Her old friend Tom Moncrieff, who had played bass with Fritz, moved in with her as a housemate and sound engineer. He built a small recording studio in the basement and started helping her with song demos—Lindsey's old job. They came up with a song called "Smile at You" and brought it to the band. Everyone loved it but Lindsey, who refused to work on it when he learned that Tom Moncrieff was helping Stevie.

Late September: Fleetwood Mac appeared at their first TV awards show, *Don Kirschner's Rock Awards*. (Pre-MTV, Kirschner and a few other producers had a lock on which rock bands would get on television.) The event was uncool and very Hollywood—fake glamour and lots of hype. Fleetwood Mac collected awards for best group and best album. To Stevie it all felt unreal, and she only stayed a few minutes at the afterparty. Riding home with her brother in a long black limousine, she had a panic attack. She was frightened. They'd just been on TV, had just been glorified, and everyone seemed to love them. But all she felt was lonely. She told Mick Fleetwood later that she now had an idea how Marilyn Monroe might have felt.

The sessions at Producer's Workshop were almost complete. Stevie suggested calling the album *Rumours and Heartaches*. In October Fleetwood Mac took a week off and flew to London to meet European media in advance of a summer tour. This was Stevie's first trip to London, where the younger kids had turned away from the older rock bands—Zeppelin, the Stones, Elton John—and begun to support the new bands of the punk movement—the Sex Pistols, the Clash, the Slits. But the press seemed interested in the new look of Fleetwood Mac, with the band posing for pictures and trying to look cool. Christine took Stevie shopping at the Antiquarium on the King's Road in Chelsea, where they bought vintage lace and jewelry. They also shopped at the famous flea market along the Portobello Road in Notting Hill. When the band flew back to Los Angeles, the British members—Mick, John, Chris, and JC—were denied entry by immigrations officers. They'd arrived on tourist visas two years earlier and hadn't bothered to get green cards, so most of the band were now illegal aliens. They were detained for hours at LAX airport and almost deported back to England. (Eventually it took the intervention of a powerful U.S. senator, Birch Bayh from Indiana, to get them regularized as legal immigrants. Then, some discreet months later, Fleetwood Mac played a couple of sold-out concerts in Indianapolis in aid of the senator's campaign debt.) In October Mick remarried his ex-wife, Jenny, mostly so she and their daughters could return to live in

America. He had also fallen madly in love with Stevie Nicks, but Mick tried to keep this to himself.

At the end of November they began sequencing the new album, now called *Rumours*. This was a nod to the endless gossip in music circles about who was sleeping with whom in Fleetwood Mac: whether Stevie Nicks had left or was about to leave the band and embark on the expected solo career; whether Stevie Nicks was indeed a witch (because when you portray a witch on late-night rock shows, a lot of stoned fans buy it and start thinking of you as a witch, or at least someone with "special knowledge").

Lindsey's "Second Hand News" would begin the album with a Southern California rock shuffle and a frank admission of getting dumped by his girlfriend. Stevie's "Dreams" came next, her "little" voice and sad lyrics set to the "Spinners" track from Sausalito. (She'd written "Dreams" just after she started going out with Don Henley.) Crystal visions were kept to herself, her dreams dashed, and described as reveries of loneliness and heartbreak. The great "thunder always happens" chorus segues into a prophecy that the rain will wash away one's romantic woes.

The album's first side continued with Lindsey's defiant "Never Going Back Again" and then Christine's rousing anthem "Don't Stop," urging her husband and everyone else to keep going, whatever obstacles fate throws in the road. Lindsey's angry "Go Your Own Way" came next, with its lurid, "shackin' up" accusation of infidelity that was so upsetting to Stevie; she thought it made her look like a tramp, which she never had been. The song would become emblematic of the famous romantic irruptions in the band; from then on "Go Your Own Way" ended Fleetwood Mac shows into the next century. The side ended with Chris's lovesick piano ballad, "Songbird."

The second side began with "The Chain," a compilation of various riffs and vamps (notably Christine's "Keep Me There") with a melody and lyrics adapted from Stevie's notebooks at almost the last minute. Lindsey sings lead vocal while Stevie dominates the accusatory chorus that ends with the powerful "runnin' through the shadows" refrain. The finished song is basically Stevie's, but the five band members split writing credits, mostly as a way of bringing in Mick and John to share lucrative publishing rights. "Keep us together" was the band's prayer for stability and unity in the face of almost impossible odds.

Christine's "You Make Loving Fun" came next, a love song for her flame Curry Grant, a song that helped launch the soft rock/adult contemporary radio format beginning in 1977, with great guitar playing and soulful electric piano by Chris.

Next was Stevie's "Silver Springs," a paean to regret over an epochal lost love. At almost eight minutes long, the song was a gossamer spider's web of prophetic emotion and blunt warning: "Time cast a spell on you . . . you won't forget me . . . my voice will haunt you . . . you'll never get away." Lindsey supplies a very moving guitar solo that seems to weep with deep regret, along with Stevie's "fragile" vocal persona. This stark incantation was followed by Christine's "Oh Daddy," which insiders knew was a heartfelt night letter to Curry, whose eye was said to be always roaming elsewhere in the band's incestuous circle.

*Rumours* was programmed to end in a very dark place with Stevie's terror-stricken "Gold Dust Woman." A sinister rhythm track evolved into a doom-laden, sepulchral vision of crying, addiction, and agony. When the tribal tom-tom signals the dance of the Gold Dust Woman and her weird familiars—the black widow, the dragon, the shadow of a woman—the track ends with tormented harpy-like screaming, banshees wailing over forbidden moors, discarnate spirits seeking to inhabit vulnerable souls. At the end of *Rumours,* all that was left for the emotionally exhausted listener was to pick up the pieces and go home.

When they played this sequence for Warner Bros., Fleetwood Mac was told their album was way too long. Each side of a vinyl album could only be about twenty-two minutes long, or the audio quality would deteriorate. Something would have to be cut or replaced. The obvious choice for the production team was "Silver Springs." First, the song was way too long; second, Lindsey hated it.

Mick knew that "Silver Springs" was Stevie's pet project. There would be a big fucking row if they took it off the album. They wrestled with the song for days, trying to get it down to manageable length. Verses were dropped, the guitar solo cut way back. They finally got it to just over four-and-a-half minutes. But it was still too long for either side of *Rumours,* and at Warner's insistence the song was dropped. To try to placate Stevie, who they knew would be crushed, "Silver Springs" would appear as the B-side of the album's first single, "Go Your Own Way." (This pairing was considered apposite by some: letting Lindsey and Stevie fight their problems out on opposing sides of the 45.)

To replace "Silver Springs" they recorded "I Don't Want to Know," an older song of Stevie's, without telling her. Sung by Lindsey, it sounded great, real cowgirl rock with soulful words—"Take a listen to your spirit / It's crying out loud." At just over three minutes in length, it fit nicely between the other songs on the LP's second side. Warners signed off on this sequence, and they finally sent off the *Rumours* tapes to be mastered and pressed.

Now someone had to tell Stevie Nicks that her special song "Silver Springs" wasn't going to make it onto the new album. This task fell to Mick Fleetwood, who dreaded being the deliverer of a message that he knew must break her already burdoned heart. The day came, and Stevie arrived at the studio with her whispery gaggle of girls. Mick took Stevie out to the parking lot and gently tried to explain the situation, and that it was a done deal. Stevie took it calmly, not saying anything. She stared at him for a while, then gathered up her entourage and left. Mick Fleetwood had a horrible feeling that she might not come back.

Stevie was furious. She told her friends that she would never forgive Fleetwood Mac for this disrespect. She blamed Lindsey for making the song too long. The worst part was that she'd given the song's publishing rights to her mother. She explained, "When I first recorded 'Silver Springs,' I gave it to my mother as a present. My mother would never take a penny from me, so I figured the only way I could actually give her some money was to give her a song to put away for a rainy day. She got the whole thing—publishing, royalties, everything. It was her favorite [of my] songs. She'd even opened an antique store and called it the Silver Springs Emporium. Then they took it off the record, so it was very much a dud gift. It was like, 'Well Mom, guess what? It's not going on the record, and I'm really sorry.'"

This was humiliating because it showed Barbara Nicks, who always advocated an independent life for Stevie, how little control her daughter had over her music. It also cost her a fortune when *Rumours* took off the following year. But Stevie's mother continued to own the song, and it paid off twenty years later when a reissued "Silver Springs" became a big hit.

## 3.5   Crystal Ball

Before the 1976 Christmas holidays, Stevie Nicks underwent a breast augmentation procedure in which silicone implants were inserted to increase her bust size. She was assured that this was safe and that the implants would never leak. Both she and her dressmaker were happy with the resulting change in her body image. "I had them done in December 1976," she recalled (ruefully) later on. "I'd only been in Fleetwood Mac for one year and I was getting a lot of attention. I had always thought my hips were too big and my chest was too small, so we went ahead with it."

The surgery came at around the same time she realized that she had broken with Lindsey Buckingham for good. She had harbored a faint hope for a possible reconciliation with him, but it wasn't going to happen. They weren't speaking anyway, and he and his girlfriend were living with Richard Dashut and were said to be looking at houses in the Hollywood Hills. Stevie wanted the world to know that she had left Lindsey and not the other way around. This was important to her. "I broke up with him," she told a TV interviewer. "He didn't not want to be with me. We'd been uncomfortable together for a while."

It was also at this pivotal time that Stevie firmly decided that she would dedicate herself to her muse and to her career, and that she would never bear children. She even said that she probably would never marry. She told close friends that this feeling dated to when she'd first joined Fleetwood Mac. At that decisive moment she saw only one way forward for her, and the burdens of motherhood would be nothing but an impediment to her ambitions. (Like many rock stars, who remained somewhat childish into adulthood, Stevie didn't even like children that much.) She later explained that she needed a certain kind of autonomous authority to be in a band: "I wanted to be respected, as a musician, by every single dude on that stage. And if I walked out, and if I'd made that choice, the dynamic would have been much different."

In late November, Stevie and entourage turned up at photographer Herbie Worthington's studio to shoot the *Rumours* album jacket. Mick had said he wanted something Shakespearean, so this was Mick in his black waistcoat and breeches, with Stevie in her stage outfit without the top hat. Her velvet boots were replaced by black ballet toe shoes; her hair fell down her back in a feathered shag; and she posed with her leg draped provocatively over Mick's left knee. Mick held the same crystal ball featured on the *Fleetwood Mac* album, which was now well over four million units sold and still counting. The band photos on the back cover portrayed the newly buxom Stevie in a beige rayon wrap-dress drawn in at the waist by a scarab brooch, showing a hint of cleavage—*to die for*.

Lindsey Buckingham was angry. He felt the whole band should have been on the cover of *Rumours*.

Another photo session was scheduled for the cover of *Rolling Stone*. The idea was to show Fleetwood Mac in bed together, so Stevie arrived at photographer Annie Liebovitz's studio in a sexy pink satin nightgown. Shooting from above the bed, she posed Stevie nestled up against half-naked Mick, with her legs resting on John, who was reading *Playboy*. Chris and Lindsey were cuddled on Mick's other side. Not everyone in the resulting image was smiling, but Stevie and Mick were all grins. Much later Stevie confided that this first horizontal body contact with Mick Fleetwood felt good to her and would lead to mischief later on.

To everyone's astonishment, after the shoot Stevie and Lindsey were the last ones on the bed. They got to talking, quietly. He asked her about what he called "the boob job," and implied that it was a turn-on. There was intimacy in the air, and so everyone else left the room.

Then Stevie and Lindsey started making out. Then it became heavy petting. There was some embarrassed coughing outside the door. Then one of the assistants came in and said they needed the room for another session. The moment subsided, and Stevie Nicks was driven home with a case of lover's remorse. She tried to make a song out of it, but inspiration was slow to arrive.

Stevie spent that Christmas in Phoenix with her family. Her mother asked about Lindsey. Stevie said that it all came down to a big fight they'd had in their apartment when they returned to LA from Sausalito. Lindsey had been really angry with her. There was a lot of yelling. It had gotten physical and he'd thrown her down to the floor. "That's when it all blew up," she said. "That's when I stopped it." That's when she walked out on him.

It had been a horrible breakup, and still hurt. Her brother Chris, whom Stevie kept close to her, idolized Lindsey and was crushed. Stevie felt bad about saying good-bye to this guy—her man and friend of seven years. All the normal assumptions—marriage, kids, family—were out the window. Yet she still loved him and felt she always would. And worse, she needed him for her music. She relied on his innate ability to understand her intentions, what she meant to convey musically in her songs. Nobody else had this.

As for Lindsey, he was angry about everything. He blamed Fleetwood Mac and the pressures of being in the band for the breakup with Stevie. He told his girlfriend Carol he didn't like Stevie, but he was still in love with her. Even decades later, he confessed to an interviewer: "I was *devastated* when she took off."

February 1977. Stevie Nicks was twenty-eight years old. Warner Bros. shipped 800,000 *Rumours* albums to record stores that had placed advance orders, the largest such in the company's history. The FM soft rock stations that had been playing "Rhiannon" for eighteen months now began to play "Dreams" and "Go Your Own Way." The album's first single, "Go Your Own Way"/"Silver Springs" (released in December) was in the Top 10. The band was on the cover of *Rolling Stone*, which praised *Rumours* to the skies and glamorized it (and especially Stevie Nicks) as the sexiest group in the booming music business—a business that in the mid-1970s had become a major industry, one that was outperforming the movies, the theater, publishing, everything.

That month, after collecting a shelf full of Grammy awards for *Fleetwood Mac,* a somewhat rusty Fleetwood Mac convened at SIR Studios on Cahuenga Boulevard and played together for a month, preparing for the long international tour promoting *Rumours.* Concerts would begin with "Say You Love Me" and feature songs from both albums. Lindsey played Peter Green's "Oh Well." The encores would begin with "Go Your Own Way" and end with "Songbird," a lullaby that said goodnight to the fans.

By the beginning of March the band was sounding like one of the best rock groups on the planet, but there was serious concern for Stevie's voice. It sounded raw to those who knew her, and somewhat forced on the higher notes. She had basically shredded her vocal cords on the long previous tour, declaiming "Rhiannon" to the skies night after night. She was trying various therapeutic elixirs of cognac and honey to ease the strain, but Mick Fleetwood was worried, and rightly so; they would need to cancel weeks of shows later in the year so Stevie could rest her voice.

She had vision problems as well. A few days before playing A Day on the Green, a big show promoted by Bill Graham in the Oakland Coliseum on May 7, she hurt her corneas when she left her contact lenses in while partying for two days. She was almost blind as Graham carried her piggyback from the band's trailer to the outdoor stage. She managed to get through the show in front of seventy-five thousand, but only just. Then the doctors ordered her eyes to be bandaged for a few days, during which Stevie groped her way around. The band played pranks on her, teasing her, putting things out of her reach. Even her trusted girlfriends dressed Stevie in mismatching outfits and assured her that she looked great.

They spent the next six weeks playing all over the United States, traveling by expensive chartered aircraft, playing mostly arenas holding around fifteen thousand fans. Stevie was accompanied by Robin Snyder and her dog Ginny. The audiences were fervid, mad for Fleetwood Mac, especially in the South. Jefferson Coliseum in Birmingham, Alabama—erstwhile stronghold of Buckingham Nicks—had sold out in an hour. It was the same with Madison Square Garden in

New York City on June 29. (Newspaper reviews of this show noticed Stevie's vocal strain. *Rolling Stone* said that she "lurched" around the stage, monitored by "frantic" roadies to prevent her from falling.) The sports arenas and university halls were packed with young girls in witchy hats and black capes, mimicking Stevie's stage clothes— the black chiffon ensemble, the five-inch heels, the wickedly formal man's top hat with its voodoo associations. The fans stood for all her songs, sang all the words, waved to her, cried out to her, begged to hear "Rhiannon" and the new single, "Dreams," released April 1, 1977. Stevie's girly fans waited for her by the stage doors, straining against metal barriers, hoping to catch her. Sometimes she paused to speak with the girls as JC hustled her, exhausted (exhilarated), from the venue to her limo; the girls told her they loved her, gave her flowers, slipped silver bracelets onto her wrist, or pressed turquoises into her hand for luck.

Not all the early shows on the *Rumours* tour were brilliant, sometimes reflecting tensions within the band. One night Stevie threw a postshow tantrum. She'd missed a cue during "Rhiannon" and Lindsey had to cover for her, which she found humiliating because she had to apologize. She was weeping and wailing in the dressing room, a major drama, and then melted into the arms of Robin Snyder, who cradled her like a child.

Some of Stevie's most crazed fans were young men. One of the wildest shows the band played that month was at the U.S. Naval Academy in Annapolis, Maryland. "When they saw Stevie walk onstage," Mick remembered, "the roar that came out of nine thousand midshipmen can only be described as inhuman. We'd never heard anything quite like it." When Stevie performed the rite of the Gold Dust Woman for the young sailors, dozens of floral bouquets (and a roll of toilet paper) came flying onstage.

After the shows, Stevie and Christine usually rested in their hotel suites, avoiding their exes drowning their sorrows in the bar. Stevie had steam treatments in the bathrooms for her sore vocal cords, and she and Robin did ballet exercises to keep limber. "As of the *Rumours* tour," Stevie later recalled, "if there was a presidential suite, the girls got it. Or two presidentials, we got them, me and Chris. That was the way of the world. For women, it's harder. You have makeup, hair, nails, all this shit you have to do. The boys bitched about this, but in the end it was like: happy wife, happy life."

By then *Rumours* had sold a million albums after only a month in the record stores. The remixed "Dreams" single, with Stevie's fragile vocal, got played on AM radio now, and went to #1 on the *Billboard* chart, which boosted *Rumours* into a huge sales spurt, moving another million or so albums in May. (As of this writing, "Dreams" is still Fleetwood Mac's only #1 single release.)

The band next flew to England, where they played in London to a house full of their old fans, to whom Fleetwood Mac meant a British blues band. Stevie was very touched to see how much this meant to Mick, Chris, and John. A little more than two years after fleeing England, Fleetwood Mac had returned as big stars, playing in Birmingham, Manchester, and London. During a night off they spent a (freezing) night as houseguests in Eric Clapton's (unheated) country house, where he was living with Patti Boyd Harrison, Mick's sister-in-law. Fortunately, cocaine elevates the body's temperature, so everyone survived this rock & roll house party. Then it was on to European gigs in France, Germany, and Sweden. There was a horrible problem in Holland when Dutch customs stopped the band at the airport. Looking for drugs, acting on a bogus tip, they strip-searched Stevie, Christine, and the wardrobe and makeup girls. John Courage swore this would never happen again. Next time Fleetwood Mac played in Europe, the band traveled in private train cars, exclusively.

*Rumours* reached #1 on the *Billboard* and *Cashbox* sales charts on May 21, 1977, knocking off the Eagles' *Hotel California*. As Mick had predicted back in damp and cold Sausalito, *Rumours* stayed at #1 for the next eight months, a historic position for a band that had been written off a few years before. The passions that the band had suffused into their new songs sounded real to their audience, who picked up on the raw authentic feelings that were on offer. "The truth about *Rumours*," Stevie said later, "was that *Rumours* was the truth."

Fleetwood Mac stayed on the road for the rest of the year to promote their album, sales of which were bumped up by two more hit singles, "Don't Stop" (#3 that summer) and "You Make Loving Fun" (also in the Top 10 in October). Everyone in the band, including Stevie, felt like they were on an unstoppable rocket to stardom, powered up by the Heineken bottle caps brimming with star-quality cocaine that were distributed to the band by JC before the shows. "This was the heyday of Fleetwood Mac," Mick recalled of 1977. "It was full-on work, touring, airplay, success. We all felt we were on the old roller coaster, and we were heading up."

In June the band took a break. Stevie and Lindsey both worked on new albums by local rocker Walter Egan and their old friend Warren Zevon. (Walter Egan fell crazy in love with Stevie, ruining his marriage. His ardor wasn't really returned, and he was reportedly crushed.) Then Stevie met a young record executive, Paul Fishkin, when Fleetwood Mac attended a big Warner Bros. convention for its affiliated labels in Los Angeles. Paul was about thirty, well dressed, soft-spoken, darkly handsome (everyone said he looked a lot like Lindsey), and the president of Bearsville Records. Stevie was taken with him, asked to meet him, and started an affair with him that would later prove to be pivotal in her career.

Paul Fishkin, when he got to know Stevie and her scene a little better, was amazed by how she was treated by Fleetwood Mac. She was the band's big draw, but she had zero pull in the group. She couldn't get the songs she wanted on their album. She had no management of her own to help her in dealing with Mick, who was managing the band, which to Paul seemed like a major conflict of interest. He could hear that her voice was almost completely shot, but when he went to a few Mac concerts, the band played on as if this vocal problem wouldn't be a big fucking issue someday soon. Stevie kept belting out the raving, shredding finale of "Rhiannon" at the climax of every show, as if she could grow new vocal cords overnight. When Stevie told Paul Fishkin that she didn't quite know what to do about any of this, he vehemently suggested that she should consider leaving the band and starting a solo career if she was so unhappy. She told him she didn't have the confidence and the wherewithal to do this. From what he'd observed, he told Stevie that someday she was going to be a bigger star than Fleetwood Mac. If she kept writing on the level she was working in, she could even have her own boutique record label, and could keep some of the money skimmed off the top by Warner Bros. Of course he offered to be of help to her with this monumental decision.

This gave Stevie Nicks something to think about. And she continued the romantic interlude with intelligent and astute Paul Fishkin, which lasted until Fleetwood Mac went to Australia later in the year.

### 3.6   Behind the Curtain

For her whole life, Stevie Nicks had always been a self-described girly-girl, but when she broke up with Lindsey Buckingham she assumed a new persona of public and private hyperfemininity that she would become famous for. She would take up the ballet and be photographed in lace, pink leotards, and toe shoes. She still enjoyed the company of men and needed them for her work, but in her private home life she surrounded herself with attractive and artistic females who looked after her and whom she could sing and dance with all night. She told her close friend, the beautiful, ultrafeminine former model Sara Recor, that she didn't think she would ever fully trust a man after what she'd been through with Lindsey, who now seemed so against her all the time.

This coincided with a considerable shockwave-of-fame mystique as her songs became more and more well known. Fans picked up on the "special knowledge" and her "crystal visions" and started bombarding her with mail containing esoteric material, as if her special knowledge embodied mystical, theosophical, alchemical, and astrological doctrines. Fanzines sprouted up with weird interpretations of her songs, as if Stevie Nicks was a hierophant, an interpreter of sacred mysteries and principles. Her fans started thinking of themselves as adepts of a secret society, initiates in a cult, sisters of the moon. Even an acerbic rock critic like Lester Bangs would headline an essay in Detroit-based *Creem* magazine—"Stevie Nicks: Lilith or Bimbo?"

Of course there was backlash, too, from the rock press. This was

1977 after all, the year two sevens clashed, the year of the punky reggae party. *Creem:*

> Yes it's 1977 and Stevie Nicks is the most popular,
> most visible, woman in rock. And she's a joke.
> She's an airhead, a puffball. . . . Stevie is a
> California girl prone to writing songs about
> witches, mysticism, and all the other shit one
> would conjure while sautéing in a Jacuzzi. . . But
> although Big Mac's sound has been consistently
> bland, you can't blame Stevie—she's tried to
> provide some comic relief. . . . But punk is coming,
> and it's gunning for mega-ultra-supergroups like
> Fleetwood Mac. A new generation of women
> rockers will rise and they will play unpretty,
> untwirly music. Nicks' reign will soon be over. In
> the future, she and Fleetwood Mac will be a
> footnote, a footprint frozen in the tar pits of the
> bloated corporate rock age.

At some point that year Stevie Nicks became pregnant by Don Henley. This was weird since she'd decided she didn't want to have children of her own. She'd sometimes stay with him when they were in town at the same time during tour breaks. By then he was living in a wing of Eagles manager Irving Azoff's house in Benedict Canyon while he was building a new house of his own off Little Ramirez Road in Malibu. One night they were having supper with Azoff, and Stevie spoke with him about possibly managing her, if she ever went out on her own. Later, when she told Don about the baby, she said she thought it was a girl named Sara. At first Don was good about it. There were gifts, flowers, more private planes (she would fondly remember a little red Lear jet), and attentive phone calls. But then, as time passed, Don seemed less than thrilled about this idea; he started keeping his distance, and Stevie—disappointed after his immediate, enthusiastic assent—underwent a procedure to end the pregnancy. The Eagles went back on tour, Fleetwood Mac returned to the road, and she didn't see Don Henley for a while after that. Years later, after

Henley had spoken publicly about this pregnancy, Stevie gave an interview to *Billboard* during which she was asked about this in reference to one of her songs. She replied, "Had I married Don and had that baby, and had she been a girl, I would have named her Sara. But there was another woman in my life then named Sara; so it's accurate, but not the entirety of it."

Stevie never forgot those Lear jets. "I was on the road, he was on the road. It picked me up after my show, flew me to Atlanta. I stayed there that day and his show, and then right after the show that little cranberry red Lear jet was waiting for me. It was wonderful. It was one of the most romantic things that ever happened to me in my whole life. It'll pass before me on my deathbed."

Fleetwood Mac toured all that summer, emotionally ravaged but playing great shows. Stevie felt bad after her ordeal with the pregnancy but was more concerned about her band mates. Mick's (re)marriage was coming apart. Described in the press as a glowering, heavily bearded Svengali, he was spending more time at Stevie's house than he was with his family. Christine was in the process of dumping the lighting guy, another trauma in the touring party. McVie, listening nightly to his wife's love songs about the lighting guy, was drinking. They all were, except Stevie, who said she only took a shot of tequila before going onstage. Lindsey was drinking more than she'd ever seen. Her large velvet-covered journal for August 24, 1977, contains drawings of birds, angels, flowers, and stars, plus the entry: "One more time, on the plane. As usual, Lindsey is his usual asshole self. I am slowly coming to the conclusion that Lindsey and I are at an end. So sad to see good love go bad. . . . Worried about Christine. Wishing some spiritual guidance would come from somewhere. Where are the crystal visions when I need them?"

Kenny Loggins (now gone solo) was opening for Fleetwod Mac, and Stevie enjoyed hanging out with Sara Recor, whose husband was his road manager. Stevie recorded (uncredited) vocals for Loggins's disco-tinged "Whenever I Call You Friend"—"sweet love showin' us a heavenly light"—which would be a Top 10 record the following year. Fleetwood Mac also played a benefit concert in Tucson promoted by her father in connection with a foundation for heart disease. This began a long association with Jess Nicks, who in retirement was getting into promoting concerts in Arizona with his brother Gene.

The exhausting tour continued into the autumn of 1977. At one point they played a month of concerts with only one day off. Then Lindsey—spent from leading the band every night in a haze of drugs and alcohol—fainted in the shower in a Philadelphia hotel suite, and some shows were postponed. His doctor later told him he had a mild form of epilepsy, which some thought might have been causing Lindsey's sometimes violent mood swings.

In late October Warner Bros. released "You Make Loving Fun," which was another hit single, and quickly sold another two million copies of *Rumours* by Thanksgiving. By the end of the year the album would have sold its eighth million copy and been at #1 for thirty-two weeks in 1977. At that point, an emotionally depleted Fleetwood Mac took ten days off before heading out to Japan, New Zealand, Australia, and Hawaii.

Sometimes on those darkening November evenings, as storm clouds gathered to pour rain down on the hills above Santa Monica and landslides closed the Pacific Coast Highway, Stevie could hear the feral roar of Mick Fleetwood's black Porsche 911 as it climbed the steep road to her house. This was "the great dark wing" that would surface later in song. He took her on long rides along Mulholland Drive, running above the Hollywood Hills with sparkling views of the lights of the San Fernando Valley in the dark. The vibrations between them were uncertain, weird. He knew she was seeing a record executive. She knew he was sneaking out on his wife and children. Mick's parents, who often toured with the band and whom Stevie adored, were living with him as well.

They didn't talk much, Mick later said. They were just getting comfortable being together, away from the high tensions in the band and the demands of touring. Anyway, cocaine sometimes inhibits conversation when taken in quantity. Everything was very secret. It wasn't physical, this thing, at least not yet. Stevie's girlfriends were sworn to silence.

The late-night rides continued after Fleetwood Mac's sold-out concerts in New Zealand. Stealing out of the hotel's basement garage at midnight after the show in Wellington, so as not to upset Lindsey, they were driven by a Samoan chauffeur on a long journey through mountain ridgebacks and valleys. It was spring in the Antipodes, and the windows of the Daimler limousine allowed fresh air into the dark cabin where Stevie sat holding hands with Mick Fleetwood, breathing. When they arrived at a famous lookout just before dawn, they got out and strolled along a deer path, waiting for the sun to break through the clouds overlooking a vast, greening landscape. Then the morning mist condensed into a cool shower, and the couple's clothes stuck to their skin.

The ride back to the hotel was in a hellacious lightning storm, Mick later said, like something in *King Lear*. Shakespeare sometimes used tempests to separate or unite his characters, and so it happened here. After clinging to each other in the limo, Mick accompanied Stevie up to her suite. She lifted her face to him, and he said, "I think I'd like to stay here tonight."

This was now a love affair, and it continued in a haphazard way after Fleetwood Mac arrived in Australia that December. Christine found out about it but kept quiet. Lindsey and John were in the dark. There wasn't much band interaction in the hotels, anyway. The shows were rowdy, as the Australian fans embraced Fleetwood Mac as if they were mystic emissaries from their ancestors' Wales. "Rhiannon" often stopped the shows, as audiences wouldn't cease clapping and demanded encores of a spent Stevie Nicks, who was struggling with vocal strain. Then Jenny Fleetwood arrived in Sydney, had no idea what was going on, and was sort of awkwardly kept out of the way at the concerts by John Courage until one night Jenny and Mick were standing behind the curtain, holding hands, waiting for the band to go on. Mick gave Jenny a squeeze, stepped around the curtain, found beautiful Stevie Nicks waiting there, ready for action, and the secret lovers embraced in a lascivious soul kiss, with Mick's wife only mere inches away from them behind the scrim. Ten years later, Stevie told Mick it was one of the most amazing moments of her romantic life.

Back in California for the holidays, they all tried to settle down. Stevie retreated to her house and began making song verses out of the writings in her journals. "Sara" would come out of this; also "Angel," "Storms," and "Fireflies." Stevie and Mick kept their affair private, and very on-off, which was most convenient for Stevie; but she insisted Mick have a quiet word with Lindsey, fearing that her former boyfriend would freak out and quit the band if he found out any other way. Mick sat Lindsey down and told him that he was in love with Stevie, and that was that. Mick didn't mention this to his wife, and for the next six months he would try to be two places at once while Fleetwood Mac made their difficult and flawed next album.

Stevie broke up with Paul Fishkin but kept him as a friend. She told her new boyfriend Mick Fleetwood—who was suspicious Fishkin might be encouraging Stevie's much rumored future solo career—that she might need Paul again someday.

# CHAPTER 4

## 4.1 Special Knowledge

Stevie Nicks gave a big New Year's Eve party at her house to celebrate the massive professional successes of 1977 and welcome in 1978. Guests curious about her house on El Contento Drive passed through imposing metal gates, meandered along a gravel drive, passed Stevie's VW in the driveway with its BBUNNI license plate, and were welcomed into a pinkish Spanish Colonial mansion softly lit by fabric-covered lamps and furnished in contemporary California décor. Persian carpets covered the blond parquet floors. Vintage wicker seating was upholstered in flowery chintz with pillows covered in Hermès silk scarves. There were flowers on every table, stained glass in the windows, scented candles everywhere, silver-framed photographs of friends and family. The circular entrance hall contained Stevie's Bosendorfer baby grand piano (the first thing she bought when the staggering seven-figure royalty checks began to arrive), covered by an amber-colored antique shawl. In the living room an Art Deco glass table featured an ancient-looking tome titled *Magical Beings*. Stevie circulated among her guests with a gilt-edged mirror bearing mounds of cocaine and rolled-up twenty-dollar bills. She was trailed by her little dog, who was rumored to have an appetite for cocaine herself. A splendid buffet laid out on the dining room's antique sideboards went almost untouched. Linda Ronstadt's recent smash album *Simple Dreams* was on the stereo, featuring the expert guitar work of Waddy Wachtel (especially on "It's So Easy").

Even Lindsey and his girlfriend Carol came to the party. (Carol later wrote that Stevie glared at her every time they were in the same room, as if Stevie was telling her that she wasn't good enough for him. Carol devoutly wished they could be friends, but of course it never happened.)

They all had a lot to celebrate. Warner executives at the party told them *Rumours* was expected to sell ten million records by the end of January 1978. (Indeed, as the year went on, the album would become, for a time, the best-selling album in recording history.) Stevie, Lindsey, and Christine each made about six million dollars apiece from album sales and publishing, with nonwriters Mick and John making about half that. Within a few weeks Fleetwood Mac would sweep the televised American Music Awards and then the Grammys, and would reappear again on the cover of *Rolling Stone* under the headline "The People's Choice." And the future was rosy. Record retailers were screaming for new product to sell. Advance orders for Fleetwood Mac's next album were expected to be the highest ever. They would make a new album in 1978 and sell it all over the planet in 1979, playing what would be the most lucrative concert tour ever. After that, the sky was not even a limit, but the pathway to the stars.

There were a few people at the party that Stevie didn't know, well-dressed couples schmoozing with the Warner Bros. staffers. They turned out to be executives from Warner's film division who had inveigled their way into her house in a desperate attempt to try to get a meeting with her. For now Stevie Nicks was considered to be a prime catch in Hollywood. Movie bosses had seen her clips on TV, had heard her music on their car stereos as they drove to work in Burbank, Hollywood, and Universal City. Stevie Nicks was red-hot in 1978 and could've been in pictures, if she had the slightest interest. "I'm no actress, believe me," she replied when asked about this. Since Stevie had no independent representation, she didn't know that inquiries about her availability from movie guys, talent agents, and casting directors were referred to the Fleetwood Mac office and fended away by Judy Wong, since Mick Fleetwood had no intention of losing the band's cash cow to a Hollywood film career.

There would be no meetings with Stevie at her New Year's party. Well before the witching hour she and her simpering female entourage disappeared into her private quarters for the evening, where they gathered in the luxurious master bathroom with its superior acoustics and sang together late into the new year.

For all of Stevie's disinterest in appearing in films, there was, in 1978 Hollywood, this idea about a major movie based on her Rhiannon material. Stevie had started thinking about this idea after seeing the amateurish, clumsy "fantasy sequences," imbued with ancient ruins and romantic decay, in Led Zeppelin's 1976 concert movie *The Song Remains the Same*. (She really liked the bit where guitarist Jimmy Page, who was famously obsessed with black magic, morphed from a costumed wizard into the laser-wielding Old Man of the Mountain.) Then, toward the end of 1976, a fan sent her a novel, *The Song of Rhiannon*, published in 1972, the year before Stevie wrote "Rhiannon." The novel was part of the Mabinogion Tetrology by Evangeline Walton, a four-book retelling of the ancient collection of Welsh myths known as the Mabinogion. These stories provided Stevie with much more information about the Rhiannon energy than she had ever known. It became "a project": a movie deal. Stevie contacted the seventy-year-old author, and in early 1978 embarked on an epic road trip to visit Walton at her home in Tucson, Arizona. Evangeline Walton—white-haired, adorned in turquoise and Indian silver, heavily made up to disguise a chronic skin condition—received Stevie and her friends graciously and spoke with her about "special knowledge" for what seemed like hours.

Stevie remembered this meeting years later: "She was living in this little tract house in a subdivision, and you went inside, and it was all dark, gothic and curtains." Candles provided the only light. "On the mantelpiece was a big stone lion inscribed with the words 'Song of Rhiannon.' I thought, *this is so wild*. The world is small somehow, you know? If you look at the dates, it was kind of like Evangeline's work ended on Rhiannon, and then mine began. It's almost like this has been laid out for me, by the gods—or whoever."

Walton (who lived until 1996) later described Stevie's approach as well-meaning, commercialized, naïve. Certainly, she told Stevie, there were people who called themselves "witches," and wrote books on how to cast spells, and even held so-called coven meetings here in

Tucson, but this was understood to be play-acting. They were harmlessly pretending to be witches, not fearfully accusing others of bewitching them.

But still, this was a risky business, Walton advised. Most humans think of themselves as a vortex of some kind of power, and some believe their feelings and intentions can influence human affairs in supernatural ways. Some people can project their power, and if they are malevolent, they believe they can blight crops, curse houses, and cause human suffering, even death. It was also dangerous to its practitioners. She reminded Stevie that twenty innocent people (and two dogs) were hanged for so-called witchcraft in Salem, Massachusetts, in 1692. You can sing a song about an old Welsh witch, Evangeline Walton told Stevie Nicks, but you'd better not encourage people to call you one. In essence, Evangeline advised Stevie that it was in her best interest to lay off the witchy hokum.

At some point during this encounter, the idea was broached to buy the film rights to the Mabinogion Tetrology. Evangeline Walton told Stevie Nicks that she would think about it. Stevie left Tucson and was driven north to Phoenix, determined not to let this energy go.

Early in 1978 Stevie bought a big Mediterranean-style house in Paradise Valley to be near her family when she was in Arizona. The 7,200-square-foot house was in a gated enclave with mountain views and an enormous sky. Construction began immediately on a new kitchen, a mirrored ballet studio, and also a small recording room for making song demos. The basement was converted into the Song Vault, which held Stevie's growing archive of tapes, journals, notebooks, and costumes. Among her friends, Stevie was notorious for never throwing anything away.

Around this time Stevie also bought a new Jaguar sedan. When she and her girlfriends—big hair, big heels, flashy clothes—entered the Beverly Hills Jaguar showroom, the salesman thought they were secretaries on their lunch hour and ignored them. It took awhile for Stevie to persuade him to sell her a car. When she gave him her driver's license, he told her it had expired the year before. Someone else had to drive the Jaguar back to the house. Stevie Nicks never bothered to renew her driver's license, since she was driven every-where by friends, lovers, or chauffeurs. She considered herself almost too blind to drive. "I see things mostly in soft focus," she told an English interviewer. "I see things like in a dream."

In February Stevie and Sara Recor and some other girls flew to Hawaii, where Stevie rented a beach house on the paradisiacal island of Maui, elysian star of the islands. There were hammocks slung from the palm trees on the beach in front of the house, and they enjoyed sipping wine in the dappled light while watching the spectacular purple sunsets as Pacific breezes caressed their bodies and souls. Stevie was convinced she was overweight and wouldn't go out unless wrapped up in full skirts and layers of blouses. Then, totally lovesick Mick Fleetwood rang up and said he was coming, too, and would they please meet his plane. But on the day he arrived, the girls dropped some acid and went to the wrong airport. Somehow Mick found his way to Stevie's house, and she could see he was in bad shape, done in by alcohol, guilt (he'd lied to his wife about why he was going to Hawaii), and the pressures of managing the band and other clients like Bob Welch, whose new solo album *French Kiss* was about to become a big success. Mick told Stevie that he needed her and desperately needed to be near her. He said he felt their affair was cooling down and he didn't want that to happen. But the thrill of hidden, reckless romance still appealed to both of them, and all Stevie could do was try to reassure him that everything would work out in the end. She felt sorry for the overwhelmed drummer, who'd left school at fifteen to make it as a musician in Swinging London. Stevie told Sara and the other girls to be nice to Mick.

Mick knew his former brother-in-law George Harrison was vacationing in Maui, so Stevie invited him over. They spent a memorable afternoon by the pool, Stevie in pigtails, nicely tanned, smiling, flirting, teasing the relaxed, bare-chested, chain-smoking Beatle, trying to get him to write a song with her. This didn't work, but it was fun.

Gradually Mick began to relax and feel better in the tonic of the islands. He began to hang out by the pool with Sara Recor while Stevie was working on songs. According to Mick, "Sara was a good singer, and she knew all the old country songs that Stevie liked. They'd sing all night, calling themselves the Twang Sisters. At the time Sara was working as a model for the Elite and Casablanca agencies. She was gorgeous, charming, gregarious, funny, and extremely warm." Fleetwood couldn't help being enchanted by Sara's beautiful full-breasted figure. In fact, he couldn't take his eyes off Sara, and Stevie noticed and teased him about it.

The next day something fateful happened. They heard there was a fun nightspot called Blue Max in the village of Lahaina; there was a band on that night, and they decided to go. They piled into a couple of cars and arrived just as the band was going on. Stevie was instantly recognized at the door, and they were given tables by the little stage. Stevie was immediately taken with the band's girl singer, an exotic-looking, black-haired twenty-two-year-old who looked like a madonna in a Renaissance painting. This was Sharon Celani, from Los Angeles, whose band had been working Hawaii's steak-and-luau circuit for a couple of years. And she was a great band singer. What pipes! Sharon's movements were subtle, understated, and very sexy. She was a true star. Stevie liked her so much that when the band lit into Linda Ronstadt's big hit "Poor Poor Pitiful Me," she grabbed a tambourine and climbed onstage in a chintz skirt and a pink blouse and started to wail backup vocals for Sharon on the chorus. The Blue Max crowd went crazy. "She *sang* with me," Sharon said later. "No one could believe it. We did all her tunes."

Sharon and Stevie talked between sets. Stevie mentioned that the tropical atmosphere was a temptation to try to write but that she didn't have a piano to work on. Sharon remembered, "I called up a friend and arranged to get a piano brought to Stevie's place. When she got the piano she invited me over to sing with her on a new song idea, and I've been singing with her ever since." Over the next few weeks, Sharon Celani quit her band and returned to Los Angeles with Stevie Nicks. She moved into Stevie's house, joined the entourage as a trusted junior member, and started singing with Stevie on the home-studio demo tapes that would evolve into Stevie's songs on the next Fleetwood Mac album. The relationship between Stevie and Sharon has remained strong for forty years and continues through this writing.

## 4.2  Wait a Minute, Baby

Stevie Nicks stayed in Hawaii to write when Mick Fleetwood returned to Los Angeles. He had to find a studio to record the band's next album, and then try to figure out what that album was going to be like. The label and their fans wanted it to be like *Rumours,* still selling millions in the agora. But Lindsey Buckingham declared himself in open revolt. He'd seen the manic energy of punk heroes the Clash and their spitting young fans in London, where Fleetwood Mac, the Rolling Stones, Led Zeppelin, Paul McCartney, Elton John, and all the older musicians were mocked for being out of touch with their audience and reviled as "dinosaur bands" and Boring Old Farts. In New York young groups like Talking Heads, Television, and Blondie were turning punk rock (which didn't get played on the radio or sell many records) into New Wave, a power-pop movement that both got on the radio and sold albums. Fleetwood Mac's *Rumours* sound was now old hat to Lindsey, and he insisted it would be prostitution if they tried to duplicate it. It would, Lindsey told Mick, be mortifying to be called a boring old fart. The era of the longhaired, spangled rock star was over. Now he was David Byrne from Talking Heads, a cool guy in short hair and a loose suit. Elvis Costello had just arrived in LA from England with a dazzling songbook of short, sharp tunes. Waddy Wachtel told Lindsey that Linda Ronstadt was going to do three of Costello's songs on her next record.

Lindsey was basically saying he wanted to return Fleetwood Mac to the harder, adrenalized sounds of "Oh Well" and "Rattlesnake Shake" via new ideas and maverick invention. His ambition was to somehow graft a punk/New Wave sound onto their band's soft rock ambience—and make it work.

Mick bought into this, because Lindsey was right. You're either an artist or a whore in the music business, and Mick knew that Lindsey's intentions were pure. Besides, who could now tell Fleetwood Mac what to do? They had been a blues band, then a jam band, then a rock band, then a soft rock supernova. The *Rumours* groove had to be part of a progressive continuum, not the endgame. And there was more: Lindsey wanted to work on his songs for the next album at home. He wanted to avoid being in the band's studio with Stevie;

he somehow even wanted to avoid producing her songs, but Mick told him he had to.

Then Stevie came home, and was driven to band meetings at Mick's mansion on Bellagio Drive in exclusive Bel Air by Sara Recor. Mick wanted the band to buy a studio of its own, but this was vetoed as too expensive. Instead they invested over a million dollars to customize Studio D at Village Recorders in Westwood during that summer. A new recording console was bought and installed. Rare woods from Brazil and volcanic stones from Hawaii went into the décor. The control room was comfortable, like a rock star's home. The lounge had English ale on tap and a display of Africana and weird objects. The as-yet untitled next album would be one of the most expensive ever, before anyone played a note. (Mick: "When it was all over more than a year later, we'd spent one-point-four million on the studio, and we didn't own it. The questions changed from 'When are you breaking up?' to 'How much did that album *really* cost?' ")

*Rumours* sold two million more records, cassettes, and eight-track tapes that spring.

May 1978. Stevie is writing as the band starts experimenting with new music. She wanted to revive "Smile at You" and "Sorcerer/Lady of the Mountains," both rejected from *Rumours* by Lindsey, who didn't like them. She had the beginnings of "Angel," about Mick Fleetwood, and "Little Child," about herself. She worked on these with Tom Moncrieff to make demos to take to the band. There was also an as-yet wordless piano demo she was calling "Sara" after her close friend.

That month Lindsey and Carol had a barbecue at their June Street home for the Mac family. Stevie had been invited, but didn't show up after Mick informed her that he'd confessed (almost) everything about their affair to Jenny. Jenny told Carol about this at the party, and the secret romance between Stevie and Mick was hidden no longer. Lindsey said he'd known all along that it would happen. A few days later Stevie attended John McVie's wedding to his secretary, Julie Reubens, at his house in the Hollywood Hills. It was a rock star–studded event with all the big English musicians in Los Angeles drinking to the couple's health. Stevie wore white, upstaging the bride. Then she got into a shouting match in an upstairs bedroom with a distraught Jenny Fleetwood, who lit into Stevie with ferocious intent to shame her. Stevie denied that she was having an affair with Mick, but Jenny wasn't having it. Their raised voices caused alarm among the guests. Robin Snyder was summoned and led a now mortified Stevie out of the room.

In the aftermath, Jenny sent Mick's parents back to England, then she and the girls went home as well. Jenny Boyd and Mick Fleetwood divorced for the second time. Jenny wouldn't speak to Stevie Nicks for decades, a silence finally broached when Jenny asked to interview Stevie for her doctoral dissertation about rock stars and drug addiction. Stevie agreed, and the two old friends made up (sort of).

In the summer of 1978, after they began their next record, Fleetwood Mac went out on tour. They continued to perform before their witchy backdrop of wintry bare trees and a cloudy full moon. They started in Wisconsin before heading to Dallas, Texas, where they were headlining the sold-out Cotton Bowl. Not much conversation on the customized Boeing 737 jet aircraft, a long way from the rented station wagons of yore. At the foot of the ramp a local Dallas TV crew thrusts a camera in just-deplaned Stevie's face while John Courage is distracted. She peers intently through brown eyes without her glasses, longish blond hair flowing in the breeze. She's sporting a red backpack. "We need to go out and play," she tells the reporter. "Fleetwood Mac does not want to be just a recording band." Asked if she liked Texas, she says, "Sure. I lived in El Paso for five years when I was little." Then JC sweeps her away and into a Lincoln stretch limousine, which joins a convoy of six cars taking the group to their hotel.

The Cotton Bowl was the biggest place the band had played, the audience the largest Stevie ever had to win over. She did it with a dramatic, show-stopping dance of Rhiannon. Her voice was a bit ragged but she sounded like she meant it. The stage went dark midway through the song as Lindsey began his guitar solo. The blue light shone on Stevie crouching by the drum riser, waiting for the finale. When Lindsey was done, Stevie drifted across the stage, her black chiffon cape trailing, spinning a bit in her stacked heels, black ribboned tambourine in hand, and then finishing the piece in a shredding rave-up that ended in a deep bow as the band crashed to a climactic thump. Lights out! Standing ovation.

After the show Mick took a call from his sister Sally in England. His father was dying and he'd better come quick. Stevie didn't have time to reach out to him before he'd left Dallas for London. A couple of big shows were postponed, and the tour stayed in Dallas to await Mick's return.

Stevie used this downtime to record the first version of her new song, "Sara." This happened at a Dallas studio owned by Gordon Perry, an old friend of Keith Olsen's whom they'd known from Buckingham Nicks days at Sound City. Perry's studio was in a deconsecrated church, which provided a spooky and charming atmosphere. During the making of the first "Sara" demo—sixteen minutes long and referencing everyone in the band and its extended family's lives and loves—Stevie also became close with Gordon's wife, Lori Perry. Lori was a lovely, fair-skinned redhead, originally from Los Angeles, and a talented singer and trained dancer. In addition to the "Sara" demo, Stevie also recorded the first demo version of a new song (mostly about Mick) called "Beauty and the Beast" in Dallas that night. Stevie would continue working on "Sara" as Fleetwood Mac stayed on the road through August. A later "Sara" demo has her on piano, with Tom Moncrieff on bass and a beat box. Mick overdubbed a drum track and a studio singer named Annie McLoone added harmony vocals.

Stevie's affair with Mick was put on hold while they were touring together, as there is only so much angst that human frailty can put up with. In September Lindsey even helped her think about arrangements for "Angel" and "Beautiful Child" in one of the rare moments when they were in the recording studio together. By then Lindsey had chopped off all his hair and was wearing tailored suits. Gone forever were the floppy silk kimono tops and bell-bottomed jeans. Now Stevie had to admit that her adversary looked pretty damn cute.

But Lindsey was acting out his anger and confusion. His girlfriend Carol later wrote that he had digestive problems, anxiety attacks over the directions he was taking the band, and that one night he had choked her in a blind rage. A few weeks later, she claimed, Lindsey beat her up and dragged her, with her hair caught in his car window, in Christine's driveway. "He was a maniac," producer Ken Caillat said of Lindsey when they began working on the album that would be called *Tusk*. "Early on, he came in [the studio] and freaked out in the shower and cut off all his hair with nail scissors. The first day [of recording] he said, 'Turn every knob a hundred eighty degrees from where it is now and see what happens.' He'd tape microphones to the floor and get into a sort of push-up position to sing. He was stressed out."

In October 1978 Lindsey invited everyone to a Halloween party at his house on June Street. Stevie's faction gathered at her house in the hills for makeup and wardrobe. Stevie would be going as a white witch. Mick would be a vampire in a long cape. Lindsey would be the pope. Christine was Aunt Jemima in full mammy outfit and blackface. McVie was uniformed in full Nazi SS regalia (one of his obsessions). Sara Recor was going as a princess, with her long auburn hair trailing to her waist. Just before leaving in a limo convoy, Stevie noticed Mick and Sara huddling together and wondered what they were talking about.

A month later, in November, Stevie took a phone call from Jim Recor, Sara's husband. He explained that Sara had left him for Mick Fleetwood. In fact, she had taken her things and moved into Mick's house in Bel Air. Jim said he was sorry to be the bearer of such bad news, and Stevie thanked him for letting her know, since no one else had bothered (or dared).

Stevie Nicks was very hurt by this betrayal, and she went into a state of shock, locking herself in her bedroom for two days. She couldn't eat. "I lost Mick and my friend Sara on the same day," she said later. "No one told me, except Jim."

"I had started to see Mick Fleetwood romantically," she later explained to an interviewer, "and I had a very dear friend whose name was Sara, who just went after Mick. And they fell in love, and the next thing is Sara's husband calling me to say, 'Sara moved in with Mick this morning, and I just thought you might want to know.' That was three months into a thirteen-month album. So I lost Mick, which honestly wasn't that big of a deal because that was a rocky relationship. But losing my friend Sara? That was a huge blow. Sara was banished from the studio by the rest of the band. . . . No one was speaking, and I wouldn't even look directly at Mick. And that went on for months, but it was great fodder for writing. The songs poured out of us!"

And later, Stevie Nicks would have her revenge.

## 4.3   Crazy Land

So in December 1978, Stevie Nicks decided to tough it out. When Mick, who looked miserable and terribly rattled, tried to explain, she cut him off with, "Mick, I don't want to talk about it." She worked on a lyric called "Freedom": "My intentions were clear / I was with him / Everyone knew / Poor little fool." Stevie was comforted by Robin, now Robin Anderson, having married Warner Bros. promo guy Kim Anderson a little before.

Then Christine McVie suddenly dumped Mac's veteran lighting director Curry Grant, who moved out of her faux English country house in the hills. Within a few weeks, Beach Boys drummer (and longtime LA wild-man-about-town) Dennis Wilson moved in with Christine and started spending her millions on cocaine, cars, and other women. (Ten years earlier, Dennis had helpfully brought the homicidal Manson Family into the Beach Boys' orbit.)

Now the studio ambience was really deadly, since no one in the Mac circle approved of Mick stealing their friend Jim Recor's wife. Sara Recor was blamed for the whole affair and lost all her friends except Carol Harris. All were fearful that Stevie was now going to quit the band and embark on a much-anticipated career as a solo artist.

Stevie remembered this era with not a little sadness. "That whole thing was a nightmare. I went up and sat on a mountain for three hours and watched my life pass before me. Then I had to get up the next day, get dressed, and go into work, and not ever look at Mick for months. It was horrible, *horrible:* months of sitting in that room, five days a week, all day long and all night sometimes, sitting on the couch just watching, writing in my journal and watching some more, and crocheting scarves by the dozen. It was a very strange atmosphere.

"I'd have been very happy to sit it out in the lounge, but I wasn't gonna *not* know what was going on, not be a part of the music that was being made in my name. So I was gonna sit there and watch everybody. I was like, 'Lindsey, with your new ideas—*be damned*. Mick—you be damned also. Christine, John, and I will watch and make sure you guys don't go round the twist and mess up everything for us. We'll be keepers of the gate while you guys go to complete and utter crazy land.'"

Crazy Land was full of cocaine. The men snorted massive rails of white powder up their noses while Stevie and Christine wore tiny silver spoons on chains around their necks, discreetly sniffing small doses until the men ran out and came looking for theirs.

Another reason Stevie might have preferred to remain in the studio, where a pair of giant African elephant tusks towered over the console, is that handsome young assistant engineer Hernan Rojas had caught the roving eye of a now single (and lonely) Stevie Nicks. This bloomed into a relationship with Rojas (who was engaged) that also contributed (in terms of Stevie's newest lyrics) to the over-egged pudding that became the next Fleetwood Mac album—almost a year later.

Lindsey later maintained that Stevie hardly ever came to Studio D at the Village Recorder, except to work on her own songs. These were songs of heartbreak but also songs of love and hope. The lyrics were stream-of-consciousness poetic phrases that led into other fragments and ideas. "Angel" was an upbeat, funny song about Mick. "Sometimes the most innocent thing . . . wide eyes tell stories . . . a charmed hour in a haunted song." Her singing is strong, passionate, more mature than the voice on *Rumours*. "Try not to reach out . . . Try hard but you never get through." Lindsey's arrangement echoes the colorful chordal textures of Brian Wilson, tending toward the bluer side of the music. (Almost all of Lindsey's songs on *Tusk* would lean toward the Beach Boys' classic groove, overlaid with a saw-toothed edge of New Wave bands Talking Heads, X, and Devo.)

Stevie's "Beautiful Child" was arranged as a soft lullaby, evoking tender memories of being a child and wanting to have a child. "Too trusting, yes, as women often are . . . I will do what I'm told." It's a memory of holding, comforting, and being comforted, and of childhood's loss and end. Lindsey sings the chorus with her, as if holding her hand in reconciliation.

"Storms" was gloomy, pathetic, wonderful; beginning with an organ madrigal, the lyrics evoke empty nights and an empty bed. It's disconsolate storytelling, directly addressing her lover: "Every night that goes between / I feel a little less / As you slowly go away from me / This is only another test . . . So I try to say good-bye, my friend . . . And not all the friends in the world can save us." Stevie uses a soft, girlish voice to indicate the depths of her feelings about what she has gone through in the year 1978. "Those lyrics came out when I was really hurting," she said later.

(The first time Stevie played the "Storms" piano demo for the band, Lindsey told her it was crap—but might be salvageable. This devolved into a scream fest, ending with Stevie in tears and Lindsey storming around the studio in a fury. No one ever told Lindsey that his songs were boring, because everyone was afraid of his withering sarcasm and his rages.)

Then there was "Sisters of the Moon," a stirring rock song about female solidarity and the mystical pull that the lunar orb has on our planet and our women. Here the drums are high in the mix, the electric guitar a wailing banshee of fear. The lyrics are muddy and seem only half finished. Stevie's intent is occluded, like a phase of a waxing moon; her delivery is mysterious. More of a mood than an actual song, "Sisters" would prove one of the most popular and durable of Stevie's songs. (Some observers have related the song's material to *Sisters of the Moon*, a famous series of watercolors from the 1930s by the British artist Leonora Carrington that featured idealized magical heroines and spiritual intermediaries such as Diana the Huntress, Fantasia, Iris, the goddess Rumour, and the Gypsy queen Indovina Zingara.)

Stevie's "Fireflies" was a speeding Southern California rocker with strong harmony singing between Nicks and Buckingham over a hypnotic rhythm track from Mick and John, with a brilliant guitar lick from Lindsey, and with a heroically sung chorus. (The great "Fireflies" would be left off the *Tusk* album but would resurface as a single B-side in 1981.)

"Sara" was the song of Stevie's they worked hardest on. People close to Stevie said that it was typical of her bigheartedness that she could still so ardently declare her love for the friend who had so let her down. Under Lindsey's thumb, and over many weeks, the long piano demo was cut down from a quarter hour to six-and-a-half minutes. It began with "Wait a minute, baby," a shuffle from Mick's brushes, and a calm, measured vocal, drowning in the sea of love. There were magical chordal changes and a floating, soothing, hypnogogic chorale. There's the great dark wing of Mick roaring up the hill in his Porsche or the Ferrari. With total conviction and unshakeable belief, Stevie pours it on. "The night is coming . . . anywhere . . . Ask me and I'm there." Lindsey's ascending triad of chords takes "Sara" and her soft, euphoric mood into ethereal realms of breathless pop atmospherics. *Would you*, she asks as if to herself, "swallow all your pride?"

In the end, "Sara" was Stevie Nicks staking out a new claim, indeed perhaps swallowing her pride about Lindsey's agency in her music. In the future, she seemed to indicate, she would pursue a sort of rapturous grandiosity to which she expected her audience to respond and accept. Big emotions and ardent declarations of love would be her hallmarks. "Sara" would be the template for future songs that would require Stevie to turn deadly negatives into triumphant positives. The song would anchor the first of the four *Tusk* sides after a lethargic ballad, some faux punk rock drummed on shoe boxes in Lindsey's bathroom, and more cod-Wilsonian pet sounds. "Sara" would wake *Tusk* up and give the punters reason to turn the record over.

Over the years, "Sara" became the most asked-about song by Stevie's interviewers, even more than "Rhiannon." Much later, she could laugh about it in a revealing talk with *Entertainment Weekly*:

"It's not about Sara, who was one of my best friends—even though everybody thinks it is. I used her name because I loved the name so much. But it was really about what was going on with *all* of us at that time. It was about Mick's and my relationship, and it was about one I went into after Mick. Some songs are about a lot of things, some songs only have one or two lines that are the main thing, and then the rest of it, you're just making a movie, writing a story about this one paragraph—that little kernel of life. 'When you build your house' was about: when you get your act together, then let me know, because until you get your act together, I really can't be around you."

Was that about Don Henley?

"He wishes! If Don wants to think the 'house' was one of the ninety houses he built and never lived in . . . If anyone said that, they're so full of shit!"

Others mentioned Joe Simon's soul-stirring song "Drowning in the Sea of Love" as an inspiration.

Some time later a songwriter sued Stevie, claiming she'd stolen the song. There was a small out-of-court settlement to make this person go away. Stevie had worked extremely hard on "Sara," and she was hurt by the allegation.

Spring 1979. Fleetwood Mac convened in arid sunny weather at an empty Dodger Stadium in the Chavez Ravine section of Los Angeles to make a promo film for the big-band production number "Tusk." This was an old Mac warm-up riff that had been turned into a mock hoodoo tribal chant. The fully uniformed Trojan Marching Band of the University of Southern California re-created their part from the album in prancing stadium formation while Stevie, lithe and so pretty in much longer hair, heeled sandals, and a cotton summer dress, showed off her considerable solo baton twirling skills. McVie was on his yacht somewhere in the Pacific, and was represented at the shoot by a life-size cardboard cutout wielded by Mick.

It was around then that Stevie and her pretty blond acolyte Mary Torrey found themselves in a cocaine-fueled recording studio late one night with Lindsey and John Stewart, formerly of the Kingston Trio. Stewart's banjo had been a big influence on Lindsey, who was producing Stewart's solo album, *Bombs Away Dream Babies*. As a favor to Lindsey, Stevie attended the vocal sessions for "Gold," Stewart's song about driving over mountainous Kanen Dume Road from Malibu to the Valley, where the great LA studio musicians were turning music into money. But Stevie was tired and stoned and said she didn't much feel like singing that night.

John Stewart: "I had the lyrics to 'Gold' written out on enormous cue cards because Stevie can't see too well. Mary went back in the booth [to sing] and I grabbed Stevie and said, 'Stevie, come on, let's just do the verses on this song, it's not gonna take long.' They turned on the tape and held up the cue cards. I put my hand over Stevie's mouth when she wasn't supposed to sing and hit her in the back when she was. She did it in one take and I got her on the song."

This is also where Stevie first met the great rock drummer Russ Kunkel, one of the most in-demand musicians in town. She liked tall, balding Russ immediately. He was famously a charming ladies' man, and she was a single woman. There was an attraction between Stevie and Russ, an energy that would become a crucial partnership down the road.

"Gold" was a Top 10 hit record when it came out later that year. Stevie's vocal was mixed way high, and the single got on the air, even crossing over to country radio stations. (Stevie also sang on the album's "Midnight Wind.")

Mick Fleetwood claimed that Stevie threatened to quit the band when they decided to name the new album *Tusk*. "I didn't understand the title," she said later. "There was nothing beautiful or elegant about the word 'tusk.' I don't recall it being Mick's joke about a . . . that went right over my little prudish head. I wasn't even told that until after the record was done, and then I liked the title even less." But Fleetwood Mac was still an infantile British phallo-centric imperium, and Mick simply ignored her.

They had so many new songs that Mick and Lindsey decided to make *Tusk* a double album. *Rumours* was still selling in the millions. What could go wrong? To them it made sense. Lindsey wanted the double album for all his new-style songs to make an imprint on their now enormous audience. That summer, they previewed the new songs for the Warner Bros. executives, who vividly foresaw their Christmas bonuses flying out the window as they listened to Christine's moody blues and Lindsey's New Wave rants. They told the band that only four Stevie Nicks songs were not enough; they begged for more and were turned down. It was a time—1979–1980—of economic recession in America; an expensive double album might not be a very commercial proposition. Fleetwood Mac chose to ignore this sage advice from label president Mo Ostin.

In August 1979 Fleetwood Mac convened in New York at the studio of photographer Richard Avedon, who shot the group for their album jacket at enormous cost. Then their label said, "You're going to put a really sexy picture of Stevie Nicks on the album jacket, right?" They said, "No, we're putting on a picture of our producer's ugly dog." *Tusk* would be released in late September 1979, but its fate was already sealed by some dumbly arrogant decisions made that summer.

## 4.4   Secrets

While Fleetwood Mac was busily screwing its new album into the ground, Stevie Nicks spent much of 1979 engaged in a quiet, top-secret campaign to further her own interests and those of her closest friends. By the end of the year Stevie would start her own record label, her own band, a slew of hit singles and albums, and a career as a solo artist that would propel her to even greater fame and fortune than she could ever have aspired to with Fleetwood Mac.

Mick Fleetwood and Lindsey Buckingham would be sorry they had ever crossed little Stevie Nicks.

This process had its beginnings with Stevie's new clothes. After the release of their new album, Fleetwood Mac would embark on its biggest tour yet, a year of a hundred shows in the United States and the Pacific between October 1979 and January 1981. Stevie and her wardrobe designer, Margi Kent, decided that the Welsh witch's black chiffon look and shag-cut hair was now passé. Stevie's golden mane would now be long and fall below her slender shoulders. Stage clothes would be looser, colorful, and flowing, using different fabrics: laces, crepe, leather, organza, satins. The gauzy capes would give way to cropped jackets and corset laced vests, plus layered looks in witchy tones. The iconic top hats would be replaced by elegant feathered berets or fascinators. Different shawls would be deployed to evoke different songs. A beautiful golden shawl was produced for "Gold Dust Woman," and a spectacular wine-red one for "Sara." Stevie loved Margi Kent's designs, loved the fittings and the mirrors and the banter of couture. She felt that Margi—and indeed all her entourage— were artists like herself who deserved the same kind of recognition that she was enjoying. It was this altruistic sense of bringing friends along for the ride that indirectly led to Modern Records, Stevie's new boutique record label.

Fleetwood Mac headlined some big outdoor shows that spring and summer. When the tour hit New York, Stevie called former flame Paul Fishkin and asked him to come over to her hotel. Paul explained that there was a press party for the English band Foghat that night, and since he was the president of Bearsville Records, and since Foghat was their best-selling act, he had to attend. Stevie said she'd tag along as his date. A few hours later she picked Paul up in a black stretch limousine, and he told the driver to take them to Lincoln Center, the gleaming West Side arts complex. (Some livery companies used by Fleetwood Mac in those days were reportedly instructed not to send black drivers for Stevie Nicks.)

The party was in the Performing Arts Library next to the opera house. Stevie, then at the height of fame, caused a stir when she walked in wearing a black velvet dress with a cinched waist, a louche black beret over her frizzy long hair. Paul introduced her to his best friend (and Bearsville publicist) Danny Goldberg, then twenty-nine. Paul mentioned that Danny had worked for Led Zeppelin; Stevie focused her deeply peering gaze on him, and started peppering him with questions about Jimmy Page. Danny was taken aback and then rallied under her onslaught. "I was momentarily intimidated by her glamour," he recalled, "but was soon put at ease by her warm, self-deprecating manner." Paul told Danny that Stevie needed some public relations advice, and Danny agreed to meet them for dinner the next evening.

Stevie liked Danny Goldberg immediately and sensed that he could be a valuable ally and asset to her entourage. At only twenty-four, Danny had been vice-president of Led Zeppelin's phenomenally successful label, Swan Song Records, which not only released the band's albums but also had success with other English acts like Bad Company and Maggie Bell, the British Janis Joplin. Danny handled all of Zeppelin's publicity, but had left Swan Song two years earlier, and now had his own (somewhat struggling) public relations firm specializing in rock bands. Stevie liked that Danny was clear-eyed and didn't take drugs. He was a spiritual guy connected to a fervent group of New Yorkers that conducted meditation meetings in an old church amid the cargo warehouses and sail lofts on Hudson Street, way downtown. Danny was tall, attractive, with long red hair and a funny, reassuring manner.

Over supper in an Indian restaurant, Nirvana on Central Park South,

Stevie told Danny she wanted his advice on how to get Margi Kent's fashion designs into *Vogue* magazine. Danny recalled, "I wondered why she didn't ask the PR person for Fleetwood Mac, or the Warner Records PR department to help, and I was astonished to hear that Stevie had extremely limited clout in the context of the group. Although I, and millions of other rock fans, saw her as the principal star of Fleetwood Mac because of her hit songs 'Rhiannon' and 'Dreams,' she said that she was treated as a space cadet, a 'chick singer.' " Stevie told Danny of her humiliation that "Silver Springs" had been left off *Rumours* after she'd given the song to her mother. Danny was incredulous. *Rumours* had been *Billboard* magazine's #1 album for thirty-nine straight weeks (a run that has never been repeated), largely on the basis of Stevie's songs.

Stevie explained that she had formed her own circle of advisers and was looking to branch out into solo work, fashion, possibly even film production. Danny naturally offered to do whatever he could to help and asked how to contact her. She produced reading glasses, paper, and pen from her pocketbook and—left-handed—wrote her phone number in large, looping numerals. Paul Fishkin winked at him, and Danny sensed a bond between the three of them.

Quicker than you can say Rhiannon, Danny was on a plane to Los Angeles. But before he left New York he kept his word about helping Margi Kent. Nevertheless, *Vogue* didn't want to know about Stevie Nicks or her wardrobe. Indeed, Seventh Avenue thought nothing interesting had come out of California since West Hollywood designer Rudi Gernreich's topless bathing suits in 1966, and even then California was known to be anti-style, just a place where you wanted to take off your clothes and splash barefoot in the surf.

Danny got a warm welcome from Stevie, who'd told her posse to be good to him. "You'll like him," she'd said. "He's vibey. He's very Rhiannon." To ingratiate himself, Danny arrived with a rare video cassette of Led Zeppelin's 1976 concert movie *The Song Remains the Same*. Stevie loved this. The movie had only had a limited theatrical release, and home video cassette recorders were then still so rare that there were hardly any commercial tapes available. The Zeppelin film went into heavy rotation on Stevie's home VCR, along with *Dumbo* and Jean Cocteau's *Beauty and the Beast*.

For the next few months, through 1979, Danny was a friendly presence at the big pink house on El Contento Drive in the Hollywood Hills. He made friends with Robin Snyder, Stevie's best friend and speech therapist, and her husband, Kim Anderson. Tall, bearded, good looking, affable, Anderson had been the local promo guy in St. Louis; Danny surmised he'd been promoted to a national job because he was close to Fleetwood Mac. Margi Kent and Sharon Celani seemed to live at the house. Same with Stevie's younger brother, Christopher. Herbie Worthington, who'd shot Fleetwood Mac's album covers, was the house photographer. There were other girls around, Stevie's acolytes, none of whom seemed to be attached to any man.

Most of the action took place at night in the large kitchen, where Stevie enjoyed preparing fresh tacos and quesadillas for the gang. Music was constantly playing. Stevie seemed to like Tom Petty a lot. (She said if Fleetwood Mac ever broke up, the only other band she could see herself in was Tom Petty and the Heartbreakers.) Then there was the living room, where she kept her Bosendorfer piano. Danny: "I almost stopped breathing the first time I saw her hunched over the piano, singing trancelike a mournful arrangement of 'Rhiannon,' quite different from the recorded version. Many artists are less impressive in person than their image. Stevie was even more magnetic, more compelling, more charismatic. I was besotted."

But it never turned into anything other than a close and trusting friendship. Stevie explained that there were many other written fragments of songs about Rhiannon and other figures in the old Welsh myths. Danny suggested that maybe she could get a movie production deal for the Rhiannon material, and she told him to go for it. She would write more songs for it. So Danny got organized. A writer was assigned to write a treatment. Danny: "I remember the euphoria I felt when I got the signed letter of agreement. Stevie Nicks had publicly said I was someone she was in business with!"

Next Danny flew to Tucson and met with Evangeline Walton, and got her to assign Stevie the rights to her books—for no money unless a movie actually got made. Danny apologized that Stevie's plans were tenuous at that point. "Don't worry, dear," the old Welsh visionary said. "All true artists are a little neurotic." Danny then set up meetings with Hollywood producers who were happy to tell their kids that Stevie Nicks was in the office today, but no movie deals were forthcoming. After a few weeks of this, Danny was worried that he was wasting Stevie's time. It wouldn't be long before the electric gates on El Contento would fail to open for him.

So he was surprised and flattered when she gave him one of her totemic crescent moons. These were 18-carat golden moon charms, copies of one she'd found in London and had a jeweler reproduce. "She presented [the moons] to her close friends with a solemnity like that of an initiation," Danny later wrote. "I was deeply touched the night she gave me one. I'd never worn jewelry, but I bought a chain and wore it around my neck for years."

As a writer himself, Danny was fascinated by the sources of Stevie's inspiration. He would observe her at the piano, zoning out for hours, searching for notes in an intuitive style of composition. And then she'd come up for air with something new. "Stevie's mysticism was entirely self-taught. Not for her studies of Blake, Rimbaud, Ginsberg, nor even the Bible. She was an autodidactic mystic who viewed the universe through the eyes of a middle American," Danny later observed.

Danny had a great mother himself, and knew what a good woman was. He wrote that Stevie "spoke in an intense quiet cadence that conveyed the idea that whatever topic she was obsessed with at the moment was of transcendent importance. But she was also extravagantly generous in her praise of others, laughed heartily at other people's jokes, and created the illusion that everyone in her entourage was somehow her equal."

One of Danny Goldberg's main projects in those days was MUSE, an acronym for Musicians United for Safe Energy, an antinuclear energy group of famous musicians formed after the serious accident at the Three Mile Island nuclear plant in Pennsylvania in March 1979. Danny was on a steering committee that included Bonnie Raitt, Jackson Browne, James Taylor, and others. These in turn recruited Bruce Springsteen, Crosby, Stills & Nash, and Tom Petty and the Heartbreakers (among many others) to perform five nights of benefit concerts in

New York that September. Danny had the notion of trying to get Fleetwood Mac on board, since the *Tusk* tour wouldn't begin until a month later, in October. Jackson Browne agreed to pitch the idea to Fleetwood Mac, and a band meeting was arranged one night in July at Stevie's house.

It was a disaster. The members of Fleetwood Mac and their entourage lived in what Mick always described as "The Bubble," with little or no idea of what was going on in the real world. But a nuclear accident tended to focus the minds even of spoiled rock stars, all of whom had seen the recent Hollywood movie *The China Syndrome* about an atomic meltdown. That night at Stevie's house, as antique silver salvers of cocaine circulated around the living room, the band sat with Jackson Browne, whom they all respected as one of the better LA singer-songwriters, and listened to his passionate plea for help. He had just been arrested at an antinuclear demonstration at the Diablo Canyon reactor in Northern California, and described the feelings of empowerment that were pulling many of their famous peers into the movement. The New York concerts were going to be historic, he told them, and he thought it would be good for Fleetwood Mac to be part of MUSE, and join in the movement against atomic energy in the United States.

To Browne's surprise, Fleetwood Mac seemed uninterested, glazed over, and even bored by the whole thing. Mick told Browne they'd get back to him. Stevie Nicks even gave Browne a piece of her mind. "I said to him, 'But they could have broken your fingers, those beautiful fingers that write all those beautiful songs. Are you crazy? We need you to *write songs*. We don't need you to be in jail.' He admitted this had occurred to him.

"I'm not a martyr," she went on. "I would much rather be around to write the story than die for it and leave nothing behind. I believe you should put your talent where your talent is, and stay out of the rest of it." This was Stevie's credo: stay out of politics. "We're not a political group," she would later affirm. "My mission is not to stand on a political soapbox."

Jackson Browne would report back to his MUSE colleagues that Fleetwood Mac had taken a pass. This episode can be seen as a reminder of those strange days when popular music seemed to have something to do with changing the world.

## 4.5   Modern Records

Paul Fishkin now realized that the time was ripe for Stevie to go solo. When he'd been her boyfriend he never wanted to mention being in business with her. When she'd dumped him for Mick he was too devastated to even think about it. When Mick dumped her for Sara he thought there might be hope. Surely now was the time for Stevie Nicks to raise her banner.

Danny agreed, especially when due diligence discovered that Stevie was signed to Warner Bros. Records as a member of Fleetwood Mac, but not for solo recordings. No one at Warners had bothered to put Stevie and Lindsey under contract when they joined the band in 1975. They were considered just the latest, probably temporary, members of a constantly fluid, midlevel English band. There was none of the usual "Leaving Member" clauses that gave the label the first option on their solo work. Someone in Legal had blown it. Stevie and Lindsey were free agents, able to contract with any label that might want their solo music.

Danny: "Now that Paul and Stevie were no longer dating, there was no reason not to talk to her about forming a small record label revolving around her future solo work. She respected Paul as a 'record man' who knew promotion and sales, and had confidence in me as a PR guy deeply committed to her solo talent. In retrospect, I'm not sure how I had the balls to suggest it to her, but when I presented the idea of the three of us starting a label together she went for it."

The way it was put to Stevie, she would remain in Fleetwood Mac but use her backlog of songs to make solo albums as well. She nodded in agreement when Danny averred that four songs on a Fleetwood Mac album every few years couldn't provide a big enough outlet for her talent. The economics were basic: she would get the same monies—royalties and advances—that she would normally receive, plus own a percentage of the company. The label could also be an outlet for her musician friends in the way Swan Song had been for

Led Zeppelin's. Basically Stevie was being offered more money and more control, which appealed to the independent streak her mother had instilled in her from childhood.

The next step, Danny explained, was to forge a short-term contract for two Stevie Nicks solo albums and then look for a partnership with one of the major labels, based on the relationship Bearsville had with Warners. Their assets would be a signed contract, the piano songs for the Rhiannon film project, and the more polished demos of songs like "Lady of the Mountains" that had been left off Mac's albums.

At this, Stevie led them to her home studio and played them the demo of a song she'd recently written as a duet for Waylon Jennings and Jessi Colter, country music stars who were married to each other. But Jennings didn't want to cut it, so Stevie called Don Henley and he came over and sang it with her. This was "Leather and Lace."

Stevie wanted to know what to call their label. Paul suggested Modern Records, a gesture toward the cool early independent labels out of New York. The industry, he said, would totally get it, but Stevie didn't like the idea. "I like *old* things," she insisted. "I like vibey things, frilly things. I am anything *but* modern." In the end, she never provided another idea, and Modern Records became her bespoke label.

Stevie next told Paul and Danny that *Tusk* was coming out, and she was about to disappear on tour for a year. They said they would pull things together while she was gone and would keep her informed. The three of them put their hands together and shook on it. Stevie murmured a blessing. Danny Goldberg tried not to cry with happiness. True to her word, Stevie Nicks signed the deal documents two weeks later.

October 1979. Stevie was thirty-one years old when *Tusk* was released. Her five songs anchored the twenty-song double album and were probably responsible for most of its meager sales compared to the mighty *Rumours,* still flying out of record stores. Instead of a willowy, mystical Stevie Nicks, the *Tusk* album cover featured coproducer Ken Caillat's mutt, Scooter; this dog was hated by both Stevie and Christine for bothering their little terriers at recording sessions. (Stevie told Caillat that she had a curse put on Scooter. When the dog died a couple of years later, Stevie told a grieving Caillat she was glad the curse had worked.) The album's proto-eighties graphics and messy collages by society photographer Peter Beard left most fans puzzled and unimpressed.

Sales of *Tusk* were slow from the outset, since the sixteen-dollar price tag equals about fifty in current money. The choice of album track "Tusk" as the first single was a mistake; radio programmers complained it didn't sound like Fleetwood Mac and so they didn't play it. Then there was Warner's epic blunder of broadcasting the entire album over Westwood One, a national FM radio network that reached across America and beyond. Almost anyone who had a decent stereo set had a cassette recorder attached to the amplifier and receiver, with the result that millions of fans stayed home that night and taped *Tusk,* the entire album, thus avoiding retail outlets completely. Then the other rock radio networks blacklisted the band for excluding them. Critics savaged *Tusk* as disappointing, boring, and pretentious, at the same time praising Stevie's songs as either touching or rousing iterations of her persona as high priestess of rock. (Some critics also recognized what Lindsey was trying to do—not be boring—while also noting that one only heard Stevie and Christine's songs on the radio.)

Everyone proclaimed *Tusk* would have made a killer single-album release. There was a lot of "I told you so" directed at Lindsey, and at Mick, who had supported his insistence on making it new. Then, after the band started touring, sales picked up. *Tusk* would sell four million albums and tapes in the first couple of years, but it was considered (by some) as a commercial "albatross" compared to *Rumours.* (Later critics would relate *Tusk* to *Rumours* as the Beatles' *White Album* had been to *Sgt. Pepper's Lonely Hearts Club Band:* a challenging, individualistic, experimental collection after a brilliant and wildly successful group effort.)

Other promotional stunts came off better. On a sunny autumn day later in October, Fleetwood Mac arrived on Hollywood Boulevard to commemorate their new star on the Hollywood Walk of Fame. It was a mad scene, with a thousand fans sitting on bleachers and the USC Trojans blaring out "Tusk" in full uniform. The crowd began screaming when they saw Stevie arrive, drowning out Mo Ostin's speech about how important the band was to the label and the industry in

general. They screamed again when Stevie stepped up to the podium, her billowing white satin dress blowing in the wind. "Thank
you for believing in the crystal vision," she told the fans. "Crystal visions really do come true."

The truth was that no one in Fleetwood Mac felt like going on tour
for a year. They were all emotionally exhausted and in some cases
creatively played out. When they gathered at Christine's house for a
photo call for their tour program, no one was smiling. Stevie wasn't
speaking to Mick. Lindsey—short hair, Armani suit—was rude to
her. Christine was involved with Dennis Wilson and was convinced
he was cheating on her—all the time. John was drinking again. Mick
and John Courage tried to soften the blow by chartering a jet airliner
so they wouldn't have to fly commercial. They had some of the
most expensive hotels in the world repaint their presidential suites
and install white grand pianos for Stevie and Chris. Stevie's concert
wardrobe—six costume changes per show—cost well into six figures. The tour's contractual refreshment rider stipulated gargantuan
backstage buffets that no one hardly ever touched because they were
running on the priciest Peruvian cocaine and could hardly look at
food, let alone eat. The backstage bar bill at each show could have
sent someone to college for a year. Their flights were met by so many
black stretch limos—one for each band member and even some of
the support people—that their hotel convoys looked like funeral cor-
teges. If it sounded decadent, Mick said later, well it was: "But it also
helped to keep us going during the most challenging and exhausting
years of our lives."

Still, the band sounded tired during several weeks of rehearsals at
the venerable Sunset Gower Studios complex, where Fred Astaire
danced and Busby Berkeley had filmed olympian movie production
numbers. Stevie (recovering from a root canal dental procedure and
on painkillers) and her ever-growing entourage of ladies would arrive
around eight o'clock. The autumn nights were chilly, and Stevie rehearsed in long tweed skirts and woolen leg-warmers. When she
wasn't needed she'd run offstage and huddle with her girls, safe in their
embrace. She told Mick that most nights she didn't even want to come

and rehearse. It felt more like a job to her than fun. He reminded her that Fleetwood Mac was a job, a good sort of job, but hard work all the same.

Stevie never mentioned to Mick that while they would be on the road, her new partners Paul and Danny were working for her, underground. It would change things around for good. They were keeping her in the loop. Modern Records was going forward.

## 4.6   Not That Funny

Stevie Nicks and Fleetwood Mac took to the air in a chartered jet at the end of October 1979 and played thirty-two shows through mid-December. The first concerts in Utah and Colorado were warm-ups, not sellouts (which worried Mick), more like paid rehearsals. Then in November the band found its strength in the routines of touring, and the set fell into place. "Monday Morning" would start, with Stevie up front banging her tambourine, then "Say You Love Me" would get the fans into a groove. They had to wait for "Dreams," third in, for Stevie to appear upstage in long hanging curls, voluminous berets, cerulean scarves, and diaphanous outfits in beige and teal. The intro to "Dreams" drew a big cheer and an ovation at the end. When Lindsey next fired up "Oh Well," the girls made for the ladies' room. A few songs later, after a costume change, it was time for "Sara," performed in a dark crimson shawl under a red spotlight. The concert arrangement for "Sara" was now oceanic, pulling the audience into a moody slipstream that could last for ten minutes, revealing her (and to be fair, Lindsey's) new masterpiece as both an occult enchantment and a prayerful song of love.

Christine then greeted the audience, still the voice of the Fleetwood Mac onstage. Lindsey took over for a few songs. Then "Landslide," with Stevie in a blue silken shawl and her coiffure piled into a frizzy helmet, like an Edward Burne-Jones painting of a naiad. "Rhiannon" usually got the biggest response. To preserve her voice, Stevie's presentation was now less anarchic. Lindsey took up some of the slack with his blazing guitar solo before the dramatized 4/4 march of "Rhiannon" crashed to a halt with Stevie's deep bow, almost to the tip of her platform boots, amid audience-supplied tumult.

The rest of the concert reprised *Rumours'* greatest hits. A golden shawl covered Stevie under amber light for "Gold Dust Woman." It took a few shows for the band to find its way into spooky, droning "Sisters of the Moon," but the fans responded loudly to this new song of Stevie's, and it quickly found its place in the set as the first encore. Stevie sang the verses while tapping on a cowbell, very cool and poised, telling the story of the song, communicating with the rapt girls and women down front looking at her in pure female rapture. Her subtle, ballet-informed movements, shamanic cadences, and majestic raised palms were mesmeric. The girls up front strained to hear the unheard lines Stevie would chant away from the microphone, as if they feared missing some knowledge too special to be shared with so many. Stevie shouted and wailed the climax to "Sisters of the Moon." The fans roared back at her as she thanked them profusely (and often tearfully) from the lip of the stage. (One astute critic theorized that the dragon in "Sisters" was the anger Lindsey felt for Stevie because she'd left him.) As always, Fleetwood Mac finished with "Go Your Own Way."

By the time they got to St. Louis, where two concerts would be filmed at the Checker Dome, it was clear to everyone who was the star of the show. Audiences responded to Stevie longer and much louder than to the others. Lindsey's new songs in particular were ignored. Water tables in American cities lowered when Lindsey started his angry "Not That Funny" or spiteful "What Makes You Think You're the One?" and thousands headed for arena bathrooms to offload the night's first beer. This caused resentment and silences on the flights between shows. Stevie had Robin along as vocal therapist, and Sharon Celani was her wardrobe mistress, so she could retreat with her girlfriends into her freshly redecorated hotel suites and try to ignore the weirdness of being in Fleetwood Mac. (On this tour Stevie used the pseudonym Katherine DeLongpre when she checked into hotels. Delongpre Avenue is a street in West Hollywood.)

By the time the *Tusk* tour arrived in the Northeast, the concerts were selling out again. "Sara" was released as a single in early December, remixed faster and shorter (but still running four-and-a-half minutes) for radio play. "Sara" reached #7. *Tusk* itself got to #4, but was a #1 album in England. Lindsey told the British music paper *Melody Maker* that he was under a lot of strain and was questioning the decisions he had made about the album. "I was out to do something that had depth to it, but then I realized that people aren't getting the message. You wonder if you've been deluding yourself, especially when the rest of the band starts telling you that it's time to get back to the standard format."

After selling out New York's Madison Square Garden for two nights, the tour moved through the Midwest before returning to California, playing five packed shows at the Forum in Los Angeles. Then it was up to San Francisco for three shows produced by Mac fan Bill Graham at the Cow Palace. Not all the seats had been sold; needing a publicity surge, Graham had arranged a press conference where the same questions were basically repeated for a long, awkward hour: "Stevie, who is Sara?" "Stevie, when are you leaving the band?" "Stevie, when are you making a solo album?" "Stevie, what about the Rhiannon movie?" "Stevie, are you free for dinner tonight?"

The San Francisco critics noted that Lindsey seemed a little weird. He had this mad gleam in his eye as he stared into the crowd, as if he were looking for a friend. He kept pointing at Stevie Nicks during "What Makes You Think You're the One?" She seemed less than comfortable with this. The last show at the Cow Palace was on December 16, 1979. Fleetwood Mac went home and took six weeks off. Stevie Nicks signed a deal with Atlantic Records, rang up Tom Petty, whom she'd never met, and began her solo career.

January 1980. When Paul Fishkin and Danny Goldberg went to mighty Mo Ostin at Warner Bros. to give him first look at Stevie's solo career, they were dismissed as unworthy interlopers. "Maybe I would make a Stevie Nicks solo album," he told them, "but I am certainly not interested in another joint venture." Now the secret was out. Later that night, Danny checked with Stevie to see if she had told Mick about their plans. She looked at him plaintively and said, "No . . . no—I haven't told him. Can you?" She gave Danny Mick's number.

Mick called back the next day. His voice was calm, but Danny could tell he was annoyed. "Well, we actually have a plan, you see, for a new deal, that of course includes Stevie, and that we were *just about* to bring to her." Danny reiterated that they had already made a deal for her solo albums. Mick thanked Danny for keeping him informed, and then Danny let Stevie know that Mick was no longer in the dark about what they were trying to do. She seemed much relieved.

Then Fleetwood Mac's lawyer called Danny to say that their work for Stevie was preventing the band from getting a better royalty deal. The lawyer ridiculed the idea of Stevie making an "artsy-crafty" solo album on her own. Other terms deployed by the horrified Warners and Mac factions to belittle the notion of Stevie recording were "airy-fairy" and "artsy-fartsy." The conventional wisdom was that Stevie's commercial worth was exclusively as part of the platinum-selling formula of Fleetwood Mac.

Then Mick called Stevie and started in on her, made her cry. But any talk of betrayal and backstabbing was pretty lame, coming from a man who had left her and stolen her best friend. She told Mick to call Danny and hung up. When Danny picked up the phone all the English reserve was gone from Mick's voice and he started scream-ing. "YOU DIDN'T TELL ME THAT SHE HAD SIGNED A PIECE OF PAPER!" Danny reminded Mick that he'd told him that they had a deal with her. "BUT YOU DIDN'T TELL ME THAT SHE HAD *SIGNED*!" he shouted. Danny real-ized that Mick probably figured that anyone who spent a lot of time at Stevie's house (like Danny) was too spaced out to produce a con-tract with a valid signature.

Stevie was offended by the dismissive and condescending reaction to her artistic aspirations. If Warners didn't like it, that was too bad. If Mick didn't like it, she was so sorry. "She was impervious to any pres-sure from the group," he recalls. And Fleetwood Mac *was* pretty freaked out by the specter of an independent Stevie Nicks. At a testy band meeting in mid-January 1980, she told the others that she was *not* about to leave the band. She calmly told them she needed another outlet for a big backlog of songs that the band didn't want. She tried to reassure them, saying, "I'm not doing a solo record to turn myself into a solo artist." It also didn't hurt Stevie's cause that Lindsey was also refusing to give up his potential solo career to get a renegotiated deal for Fleetwood Mac. It also didn't hurt that Stevie was now repre-sented by Irving Azoff, the powerful talent manager whose clients in-cluded Don Henley and the Eagles. Now that things were in the open, Danny recalls, "Stevie was enjoying the empowerment that came with doing her own thing. She would show all of them who was 'artsy-crafty.'"

## 4.7   Rhiannon Is Afoot

At the end of January 1980, Stevie wrote a (quite rare) note to Mick. Fleetwood Mac was going back on the road in February, with ten concerts in Japan and sixteen in Australia and New Zealand, and Stevie wanted to settle things before she got back on the plane. In the letter she noted that Senator Ted Kennedy had beaten President Jimmy Carter in the Iowa presidential primary; that the Russians were taking over Afghanistan; and that the American diplomatic hostages in Iran had been held for seventy-eight days. "It is a fearful time," she wrote. "Things are becoming less exciting and more real." She also told Mick that she'd started on her solo album: "Recording has begun, and Rhiannon is afoot." She mentioned that she was selling the house on El Contento Drive and had moved to a duplex condominium on the beach, near Marina Del Rey. She told Mick that he was a cheap bastard and that she'd sent the girls in their office an extra $250. The note was signed "K. DeLongpre."

On February 3, Fleetwood Mac began a three-night stand at the Budokan, the famed martial arts arena in Tokyo. At a news conference they were bombarded with questions from the Japanese press about drugs. Former Beatle Paul McCartney, touring with his band Wings, had recently been held for two weeks in a Japanese prison and then deported after marijuana had been found in his bags at the airport. Fleetwood Mac swore to the Japanese reporters that they *never* touched the stuff. Then they boarded the famous bullet trains for concerts in Kyoto, Sapporo, Yokohama, and Osaka. Stevie was delighted when the Sony Corporation gave them all then-new Walkman portable cassette players. (She bought a lot more to take home to her friends.) The huge problem was that there were no drugs in Japan, or they were impossible to find, and no one wanted to help in the wake of Paul McCartney. They were playing shows without cocaine telemetry for the first time in years. Everyone was in a foul mood. Mick confided to Stevie that he and Sara—who had been forced to stay home or Stevie wouldn't tour—were fighting like tigers, screaming at each other for hours over expensive satellite telephone connections. When they were checking out of one hotel, Mick's bill for a single, miserable all-night call to Sara was over two thousand dollars.

Then it was on to Australia, beginning at Perth on February 21. This was a big market for Fleetwood Mac because the millions of Aussies with Welsh ancestors totally got the whole "Welsh witch" concept and bought the records and concert tickets. The audiences were enormous: Mick claimed there were 48,000 in Sydney, 60,000 at a Melbourne racetrack, with Santana opening. Meanwhile the police were convinced that the band was smuggling drugs into the country. Stevie's rolling wardrobe cases were ransacked by customs officials more than once.

The Australian contract riders became legendary. They stipulated a medieval marquee tent, branded liquors, six dozen cases of Heineken beer, American and English cigarettes, a groaning buffet of roasted meats, cheeses, fruits, salads, and puddings. The band was supposed to be met at Sydney Airport with at least two ounces of high-degree cocaine. After the drug-free Japan shows, the concerts were notably livelier, and longer.

Then it came apart in New Zealand toward the end of the long Pacific tour leg. The first show took place on March 20 in Wellington, before 60,000 at the Athletic Park, a rugby stadium. The opening act was New Zealand bluesman Hammond Gamble and his band, Street Talk. They played well, and were even asked to extend their set by fifteen minutes as there was some problem with Fleetwood Mac. In the rugby dressing room Mick noticed that Lindsey was draining a bottle of Scotch whiskey but didn't think much of it. Their concert set was proceeding normally until they noticed that Lindsey was playing out of tune. Then he began to fool around, trying to trip Stevie as she whirled and twirled about the stage. Then he began imitating her moves and dances. The people up front started laughing, like it was part of the show. When Stevie was hunched down during the quiet interlude of "Rhiannon," Lindsey stopped playing and pulled his suit jacket over his head in a stupid parody of her pose. Then he began trying to kick her when she attempted to salvage the number. He'd aim a boot at her and she'd have to dodge. The rest of the band was embarrassed and furious, glaring at Lindsey, who was now laughing hysterically.

"It was meltdown night for the Mac," Gamble said later. "They deteriorated before our eyes. We heard the crowd chanting 'Bring back Street Talk!' It was my worst live rock experience—ever."

There was no encore that night. The band was in shock. Tens of thousands were outside, screaming for more music, but Lindsey hardly even seemed to know where he was. Suddenly Christine McVie stormed into the men's dressing area, an unheard-of breech of post-show custom. Refreshed cocktail in hand, she strode over to Lindsey, who was dead-eyed and sadly slumped on a bench; she smacked him with a hard right across his cheek. Then Chris splashed her drink in his face. She told him, in a low voice: "Don't you *ever* do that to this band again," and stormed out. Christine didn't even speak to Lindsey for the rest of the tour leg. Lindsey later blamed the incident on "my temper," but he never apologized to Stevie or anyone else.

Two nights later, Fleetwood Mac played another massive show at Western Springs stadium in Aukland. The guys in Street Talk were ordered to play a short set and then leave the backstage area. They could hear raised voices coming from the dressing rooms. "They were arguing among themselves," Hammond Gamble recalled. "We were told to leave them alone; don't even go near them. We went out and watched from the stands, I think. Stevie Nicks came onstage and used all her considerable charm and won the crowd over, and proved she was the rock goddess that we had come to see. But somehow, it seemed forced to us."

They flew to Hawaii, a long haul, for three nights of shows in Honolulu. Everyone was sick of being in Fleetwood Mac. Mick called a band meeting in Hawaii. Stevie reiterated that she was not leaving the band but was going to make her own record next. She told them if her solo career bombed (which many in the Fleetwood Mac camp were praying for), she'd still have a great band to be in. They were all reminded that the *Tusk* tour was booked until the end of 1980. Mick managed to get all five to agree that they would renegotiate with Warners and then plan for the future. There would be solo albums now, a healthy thing, but there were forces that would try to pull them apart, Mick said, but they *must* stick together. No one could break the chain. They made an oath on it.

When Stevie got back to Los Angeles at the end of March 1980, instead of going home she moved in with her future new producer and current lover, Jimmy Iovine. They'd been together, more or less in secret, since the beginning of the year.

Back in 1979, after Warner Bros. passed on a joint venture with Modern Records, Paul Fishkin and Danny Goldberg pressed on. There were a half dozen major labels who might be interested in the multi-million-dollar package they were proposing, but they wanted the next record company they approached to make the deal, since multiple rejections could hurt their cause. Paul knew an exec named Doug Morris, then the head of Atco, a division of Atlantic Records, the pioneering R&B company that had branched out into rock and counted Led Zeppelin as one of its biggest successes. Stevie approved of Atlantic, and a meeting was arranged. Their cause was helped by corporate jealousies; Warners and Atlantic were part of the same giant record company, and Doug Morris was seen by the board members as only a second-tier guy who'd had a couple of one-off hit records. He resented this, and a big success with Stevie Nicks would be a sharp spike in the eye for Mo Ostin at Warners. Morris got his boss Ahmet Ertegun, the suave Turkish diplomat's son who founded Atlantic in 1950, to approve the deal with Modern if Stevie would agree to five solo albums, not two albums as originally proposed. After some hesitation, she agreed. Modern Records would be distributed by Atlantic. (Two decades later, Doug Morris would be the most important executive in the recording industry.)

By then Stevie was already in the studio with Tom Moncrieff, her demo producer who'd worked on the tracks she cut with Walter Egan. One night Danny brought Doug Morris to the studio when they were working on one of Stevie's new songs, "Outside the Rain." Morris was a smart businessman, but he'd also been a songwriter in his younger days. (His biggest hit was "Sweet Talkin' Guy" sung by—*ha ha*—the Chiffons.) Danny remembered, "After a couple of hours lying on the floor listening to what was going on, Doug leaned over and whispered to me, 'We're fucked. He [Moncrieff] doesn't even know she's singing out of tune. We need a *real* producer.' I knew immediately that he was right."

Stevie took this hard. Tom Moncrieff was a trusted old friend from Fritz days who wore one of her little crescent moon pendants. But it didn't take much persuasion in the end to get Stevie to agree. She was in a state of anxiety now about her music. She'd never done anything without Lindsey Buckingham, who'd shaped her sound like a surfboard and knew her in and out. Could she succeed without his brilliant ear and subtle sonic sensibility? (And there were plenty of doubters about this.) But then she came up with the idea of getting Tom Petty to produce the record. She loved Tom Petty, and went to work making this happen.

Tom Petty and his band the Heartbreakers had arrived in Los Angeles from Florida in 1975 and landed a record deal based on their mix of influences: the Byrds' jangling guitars, The Band's Southern soul, and Creedence Clearwater Revival's swampy boogie that bayed like a coon dog. They were an unrepentant Southern rock band in an age of punk and New Wave, and they were FM radio heroes almost from the beginning. Their current album, *Damn the Torpedoes*, was stocked with radio grenades like "Refugee" and "Don't Do Me Like That." The Heartbreakers were one of the bands carrying the swing for rock in America.

"I fell in love with his music and his band," Stevie remembered. "[I thought] if I ever got to know Tom Petty and could worm my way into his good graces, if he asked me to leave my band and join his, I'd probably do it. And that was before I even met him." Now Stevie made overtures toward Petty, phoning his management, but the calls weren't returned. Petty was a truculent, often depressed Southern guy from Gainesville, Florida (aka the Redneck Riviera). He was almost thirty, married to his childhood sweetheart, Jane Benyo Petty, and wasn't interested in associating with LA's veteran rock stars just then because he was busy touring *Damn the Torpedoes* and making its follow-up album.

Stevie met with Irving Azoff, her new manager. Azoff was a famous screamer, a tough little guy with a beard, often called "the Poison Dwarf" behind his back. She told him, "If I can't be in Tom

Petty and the Heartbreakers, I want to make a record that sounds as much like T. P.'s as possible." Azoff told her not to worry. In fact, he'd get her Tom Petty. He'd get her his band, too. He'd get her Petty's next hit single for her own. And he'd get her Petty's producer as well.

Tom Petty protested that he already had too much to do, but Stevie said she could be flexible in her schedule to accommodate him. Petty eventually agreed to produce a track for Stevie, to see how it might work. He brought in organist Benmont Tench and guitarist Mike Campbell from the Heartbreakers as well. They cut Stevie's new song "Outside the Rain" under the watchful eyes of a dozen of her entourage, who to Petty and Co. seemed to be mostly overdressed young women wearing too much makeup.

Petty wasn't that impressed. He later recalled, "I realized I couldn't do this. There were too many hangers-on, just too many to have to get through. We never had guests in the studio. I wasn't used to it." Tom Petty sat down with Stevie Nicks and explained. She was disappointed but accepting. And then he highly recommended to her the producer who'd collaborated on *Damn the Torpedoes*: Jimmy Iovine from deepest Brooklyn, New Yawk.

## 4.8   "Is This What You Want from Me?"

Tom Petty knew he was taking a chance. First, Jimmy Iovine was supposed to be working on the fourth Heartbreakers album, not the first Stevie Nicks album. Second, in terms of personality and style, city slicker Jimmy Iovine didn't believe in fairies. He was like the Anti-Nicks. Crystal visions were not for Jim. He wasn't a drug addict. But if Stevie Nicks really wanted to make an album that sounded like Petty, there was no one else who could do this. And Petty liked Stevie enough to try to make this happen for her.

Jimmy Iovine was born in Brooklyn to an immigrant Greek-American family. His father was a longshoreman who worked along the fabled New York waterfront. He was also supportive of his son's interests, coaching his Little League team, even managing the garage band Jimmy started in high school. Jimmy was a good musician, but he was more interested in sound than he was in playing. In 1973, when he was nineteen, an aunt got him a job sweeping floors and emptying ashtrays at the Record Plant, the elite studio on Manhattan's West Side, and Iovine was off. His talent was spotted early. By the mid-seventies he was helping engineer tracks for John Lennon's solo albums. John became a friend and mentor to Jimmy, who'd never dreamed he'd be working with one of the Beatles. In 1975 he collaborated with Bruce Springsteen and his manager Jon Landau on Springsteen's epic (and career-saving) album *Born to Run*. Iovine moved up to production and made "Because the Night," written by Springsteen and beat-poetical rocker Patti Smith, which became her sole hit single.

Iovine was famously Street—a brash and caustic twenty-five-year-old New Yorker whose idea of style was sweatshirts and trucker hats. When he had arrived in Los Angeles to make *Damn the Torpedoes* with Tom Petty at Sound City in 1978, he took one look at the crummy studio with the legendary Neve board and loudly proclaimed that Sound City should be firebombed.

At first Stevie had to be talked into even meeting with Iovine. She had other ideas about production. But Danny asked Tom Petty to come to the studio and talk to Stevie. Tom described Jimmy as a detail-oriented producer who would be great with her because—Petty was plain-speaking—he wouldn't put up with any of her bullshit. Did she want to speak with John Lennon? John would be glad to tell her about Jimmy. Tom Petty could be charming in a Southern way, when he wasn't depressed or angry, and Stevie was susceptible to Southern charm. Finally she agreed to meet with Jimmy Iovine—who had his own reservations about working with the Welsh witch; Iovine thought her rock & roll enchantress shtick was corny and not for him. This was the eighties, man! In New York the industry heavies told him that nobody wanted to listen to more than four songs in a row by Stevie Nicks. According to Danny, "Out of Stevie's earshot, Petty called Iovine from the studio and dissipated any lingering doubts about making the trip to LA. 'Get your ass over here,' Tom drawled. 'Her voice sounds . . . *just like it does on the radio.*'"

Stevie had installed her precious piano in her new condo on the beach. Danny drove Jimmy over to the Marina and sat with them while they looked each other over. Stevie liked what she saw—a small, skinny man, about five-foot-four, not much taller than she was, with

jet black hair, a macho attitude, Brooklyn-style repartee, funny stories, and a high-pitched laugh. She played some of her new ideas for
Jimmy, then she invited him to take a walk with her and her dog along
the boardwalk. When they returned after a couple of hours, Danny
was relieved to be told that Jimmy would produce Stevie's album.

But it was more than that. Within a few days, Stevie started staying with Jimmy Iovine at his rented house in the Valley. For the next
year they would be both colleagues and lovers. Stevie told her surprised girlfriends that she was fascinated by Jimmy's "little Greek
body." Behind his back, she referred to him as "the little one."

Danny Goldberg learned of this and was amazed. They seemed
such opposites. Stevie would tell Jimmy—basically a Brooklyn street
kid—that he was "very Rhiannon," and Iovine would snap at her, "No
I'm not!" Stevie gave him a golden crescent moon, but he never wore
it. He mocked some of her mystical stuff as pretentious and creepy.
Yet Jimmy ditched his longtime girlfriend, a famous New York radio
DJ, for Stevie. But it was all very hush-hush. Stevie told Danny this
was a secret affair, and to please keep quiet about it. She really didn't
want Tom Petty to know.

"So Jimmy had this house in Sherman Oaks," Stevie recalled, "and
I was pretty much living there, but whenever Tom would come over
I would hide in the bedroom downstairs. Jimmy didn't even want to
mention me to Tom." Iovine knew full well that the moody Petty
would be really annoyed that Jimmy might have been focusing more
on Stevie than he was on getting the new Heartbreakers album done.
The record was already months overdue. This ruse lasted for weeks. "I
started feeling like I was a kept woman, locked down in a dungeon,"
Stevie recalled. When she returned from the Pacific leg of the *Tusk*
tour and started seeing Jimmy again, she insisted he had to tell Tom
something. But, she said, "I don't think he told Tom he'd been seeing
me for three months." But at least it explained why Stevie Nicks started
hanging around the Heartbreakers' recording sessions more and more,
at least until Fleetwood Mac went back on tour in May 1980.

They hired Caesar's Chariot, a swanky 707 jet, from a Las Vegas
casino and played through Canada and the American Midwest. Some
nights were magical, others sucked. Stevie and Chris dominated some
nights while Lindsey turned others into virtuosic electric guitar re-

citals. Typical headline from Vancouver, Minneapolis, Buffalo, Detroit: FANS FORGIVE FLUBS AS FLEETWOOD MAC POURS ON THE ROMANCE. Stevie poured herself into some of these performances, which sometimes were interpreted by critics as dated hippie rituals. But the band could see the incredible bond she had with her fans as they showered the stage with flowers, notes, and toy animals after her songs.

In June the *Tusk* tour played sixteen shows in Europe, the first time many continental fans had seen Stevie Nicks. Huge audiences quieted to a hush when she sang "Landslide" and erupted into ecstasy at the ritual of the Welsh goddess. The band traveled by expensive private train to avoid body cavity searches at European borders. The old parlor car supposedly had been used by Hitler when he was on the march. Stevie found this creepy and hung out in the dining car with Robin, Sharon, and makeup artist Christie Alsbury instead.

Bob Marley and the Wailers opened the show they headlined at Munich's Olympic stadium on June 1 under stormy German skies. The rain stopped when Mac hit the stage with "Say You Love Me." Mick Fleetwood later recalled that he even saw the riot police dancing that night. These shows finished with six sold-out nights at Wembley Arena in north London. Stevie was in top form despite some vocal problems. She lost her voice completely during "Rhiannon" on the last night; she walked over to Lindsey's side of the stage and hid behind him as he finished the song for her.

July 1980. Stevie had a month off back in Los Angeles, and she began to build a recording band. Benmont Tench, the Heartbreakers' keyboard player and architect of its sound, agreed to act as musical director. Heartbreaker Mike Campbell would be sharing lead guitar work with Waddy Wachtel. Russ Kunkel, considered the best drummer in Southern California (alongside Jim Keltner), dashed Mick Fleetwood's hopes of being asked to play on Stevie's record. Roy Bittan from Bruce Springsteen's E Street Band would contribute keyboards and arrangements. Stevie's assistant Janet Weber worked the Rolodex and roped in members of the Eagles and Elton John's band to play on the tracks.

The early sessions in 1980 were mostly devoted to Stevie's older material. "Think About It" was from 1974, meant for the second Buckingham Nicks album. "Kind of Woman" had been left off *Fleetwood Mac*. "After the Glitter Fades" didn't make the cut for *Rumours*. Same with "The Highwayman." These existed as demos and would get new lyrics and arrangements as the work went on.

But Jimmy Iovine was still working with Petty, and Stevie went back on the grueling final legs of the *Tusk* tour in late summer 1980. They were playing mostly outdoors in the heat; Stevie performed in gauzy outfits of mostly beige chiffon set off with long sashes instead of shawls. Her waist-length blond curls were often topped by a crocheted black snood. (Lindsey left his posh suits at home and mostly worked in T-shirts and a straw cowboy hat.) Stevie's long, rolling versions of "Sara" drew the most energy from the fans. The "Sara" single had been released late in 1979, getting to #7, and was still on the radio that summer, mostly by listener request. When Stevie finished "Sara" in Lakeland, Florida, among the myriad flowers, teddy bears, stuffed rabbits, and clothing hurled onstage was a pair of crutches.

She could hardly sing. All of Robin's elixirs and potions—cognac, hot tea, lemon juice—couldn't help Stevie's voice much after eight months on tour. "Onstage, she's like the queen of whatever," Christine said of Stevie, "but offstage she's more like a little old lady with a cold." But sometimes Stevie had to perform no matter what, especially after Lindsey collapsed in his hotel suite in Washington, D.C. The doctors thought he might have a form of epilepsy, but couldn't be sure. A spinal tap wasn't conclusive. Back on the plane something gave way, and Lindsey found himself crawling around Caesar's Chariot in total agony. That night John Courage had to go out front and tell sixty thousand fans in Cleveland that Lindsey was too ill to play, and *please* don't riot because we'll be back to make this up. In fact, Fleetwood Mac did return and sold out three huge stadium shows instead of one.

In a state of constant motion and fatigue, the touring party turned inward to each other for love. Some noticed that Curry Grant was staying nights in Stevie's hotel suites. Sharon Celani was seeing Lindsey's guitar tech, Ray Lindsey. Liaisons came and went among the core touring group, some lasting a night, some not even that.

With Lindsey barely functioning, Stevie had to step up and steal the show, beginning in Atlanta in August. In San Antonio the audience was so moved by a bluesy version of "Landslide" that they spontaneously produced an ovation that the band found as emotional as the song itself. In Dallas, Lindsey had recovered enough to churn "Rhiannon" into a storm that lashed the Cotton Bowl as Stevie, possessed, chanted, "Is this what you want from me? Is *THIS* what you want from me?" during the screaming-loud finale for the Welsh goddess. Toward the end, the tour played in Tucson and Phoenix, where every known member of the Nicks family convened at Compton Terrace arena and were treated to an affectionate serenade and multiple dedications by their superstar relative, little Teedie.

The final shows of this tour were a pair of concerts at the Hollywood Bowl, the famous amphitheater in the Sepulveda Pass, which separated Hollywood from the Valley. Both *The Los Angeles Times* and *The Hollywood Reporter* published rumors that Fleetwood Mac would be breaking up afterward as word of Stevie's solo career began to leak. Nearing the end of the final concert, Lindsey announced, "This is our last show"—groans from the audience—"for a long, long time." Even Stevie Nicks, performing "Landslide," singing about getting older in a parched voice of uncertain pitch, couldn't be certain she wasn't singing it with this band for the last time. There was jubilation backstage afterward, with the best champagne, affectionate hugs, and feelings of relief and completion tempered by exhaustion. Everyone felt it was the end of an era, and how right this proved to be.

But the band and its affairs were not quite done yet. Mick Fleetwood wanted a live album of the tour, one that captured special moments from Rotterdam to Kansas City, from Baton Rouge, Louisiana, to Zurich, Switzerland. No one else was enthusiastic about a live album, but Mick insisted that it would sell like a Greatest Hits record, and that he personally always bought Greatest Hits records. Stevie's managers were against this, as it could cut into her solo sales, but she was outvoted and the project went ahead. Every concert (and most of the sound checks beforehand) had been taped by Ken Caillat, and they had some brilliant choices for every song they did. The fifth night at Wembley in London yielded the fiercest "Rhiannon." The sixth night provided a particularly plangent "Landslide." The sound check at the Palais des Sports in Paris provided a sparkling, moody "Dreams," and "Don't Stop." The stereo soundtrack of the second filmed St. Louis concert provided an up-tempo, tinkling, seven-minute "Sara" of special distinction, and so on.

Warner Bros. insisted the double live album (which some executives were already calling *Tusk Sales Albatross Vol. II*) contain some new material, so Fleetwood Mac set up their concert rig in the Santa Monica Civic Auditorium, invited crew, family, and friends to a lavish buffet supper, ingested mass quantities of the best cocaine that JC could obtain, and cut two new songs: Stevie's epic "Fireflies" (one of her best, say many fans) with a stirring arrangement by Lindsey and great singing by them both; and Christine's "One More Night." Christine's hopelessly louche boyfriend Dennis Wilson was on the scene in Santa Monica that night; Denny was popular with everyone (who were also well aware he was running around on Chris). During a break, in Dennis's honor, Lindsey began the droning surf-guitar part to "Farmer's Daughter," a lovely Celtic melody by Dennis's brother (and Lindsey's idol), Brian Wilson. Stevie grabbed a microphone and sang along in harmony. It sounded great, so they backed up and recorded the whole song, which was one of the highlights of *Fleetwood Mac Live* when it appeared in December 1980. Sales were surprisingly strong, and the album quickly sold a million copies and reached #14 against strong competition from a hot new band from England called the Police. Mick's enthusiasm for a live album had been proved right, but Stevie and the rest of Mac hated it.

Late in 1980 there was a revolt in Fleetwood Mac. A few weeks after the end of the *Tusk* tour the band's accountants claimed that the tour hadn't made any money. Eight months on the road, and there was very little to show for it. The tour had been one of the most expensive ever, as the band traveled by chartered jet and indulged in every sort of expensive folly they could think of. Sometimes the empty jet had been sent to LA to fetch a cocaine dealer on the band's payroll to renew supplies in Midwestern cities. Millions of dollars were said to be unaccounted for, as cocaine merchants on three continents were reluctant to provide receipts when JC paid top prices, in cash, for their medicaments. There were those who inferred that Mick Fleetwood abused his fiduciary role as band manager. Some thought he'd taken money from the band's accounts to pay for things like the tax-dodging apartment in Monaco or the multimillion-dollar cattle ranch that he'd bought on a whim while they were in Australia, among other rock-star extravagances.

There was a terrible meeting at Mick's house. Stevie brought along her pit bull of a manager, Irving Azoff, who dominated the tense gathering of band, managers, accountants, and some staff. The atmosphere was ghastly. Where was all the fucking money? It could not possibly have all gone up their noses. "You should have made more money," Azoff scolded Mick. "Why isn't there more money after a year on the road?"

Mick tried to put up a defense, but it was feeble. Yes, they'd had huge grosses, but the overhead was murder. The tour had run on rock cocaine, high-degree marijuana, French wine, Dutch beer, and Russian vodka. You couldn't tell Stevie Nicks she couldn't have a grand piano in the repainted presidential suite of the Waldorf or the Ritz or the Four Seasons Hotel in Tokyo. You couldn't do that at the Holiday Inn. Caesar's Chariot for months on end—what did that cost? Did any of the lawyers and bean counters know how to run a rock tour by the planet's biggest band?

At the end, of course, Mick couldn't account for a lot of money after a year on the road. No one actually accused him of stealing, but it was a scandal that would remain secret for a long time. John Courage was fired at the end of the meeting. No one thought JC was anything but honest, and no allegations were ever made against him; JC was a star-quality tour manager who had taken good care of his band on the road. And yet, he had to go.

Mick was next. Some saw this as Stevie Nicks's revenge. (Sara Recor, meanwhile, had had enough of Mick's lunacy and had run off to Hawaii with one of the tour technicians, leaving Mick despondent.) At a subsequent band meeting at Mick's Bel Air mansion, with all of them sitting in a circle like an Indian powwow, Irving Azoff read the riot act as Mick realized with dull horror that Stevie had given Azoff the power to leverage a position within Fleetwood Mac. He said something like, "Hey Mick—it's over. I represent Stevie and she ain't doing nothing unless things change. From now on, we ain't paying no management commission, no office overhead, no legal fees, no accounting fees—nothing. She's gonna make a record and we're out for now, good-bye."

Mick remembered thinking that this was also the manager of their great rivals, the Eagles. Maybe it wasn't only Stevie who was avenging something. In the end, Mick later wrote, "Now I was off the throne. It was the democratization of Fleetwood Mac. Ever since, we've had review by committee—managers, lawyers, accountants. The Gang of Four."

When this meeting wound down, Mick went into the back garden of his house and had a cry. The rest of them came out and sat with him. Stevie held his hand and said they weren't mad at him. It was just that there was no money, no cash flow from the long tour. Stevie told him she knew he'd provided what they'd needed, like a sugar daddy. No hard feelings . . . OK, maybe just a few.

With that, a humiliated Mick Fleetwood put his too-big house on the market and flew to Hawaii to try to get wandering Sara Recor to come back home. As for Stevie, her solo career and lots of hard work loomed in the future. But some of her most ardent longtime fans feel that Stevie Nicks's best work was already behind her.

# CHAPTER 5

## 5.1  Stevie Faces Death

Now it's late 1980. Ronald Reagan, the arch-conservative former California governor, has been elected president of the United States. The American eighties are under way and would be nothing like the sixties and seventies. For an ambitious, hard-charging rock star like Stevie Nicks the eighties would be big hair, big tits, new styles, swagger, and pomp. The music would be more pop than rock—synthesizers, synth drums, sequencers, Duran Duran, Michael Jackson, Cyndi Lauper. MTV would start broadcasting music videos around the clock in 1981, which meant the wardrobes got brighter, with more pastels, big shoulders, hard edges. Stevie's new eighties styles would explore the implications of the feminine as applied to power and strength, and her stage clothes would become an even more iconic part of the self she would project to her fans through song and presentation.

On December 8, 1980, Stevie and Jimmy Iovine were at his house in the San Fernando Valley when someone called to tell him that John Lennon had been shot in front of his apartment building in New York. Jimmy went into shock. They turned on the TV to hear that the former Beatle was dead, murdered by a fan. Jimmy had been one of Lennon's favorite studio engineers on his mid-seventies solo projects, and the two had grown close. Now Jimmy was inconsolable.

She'd been living with Jimmy for about six months when this happened. "He was finishing Tom Petty's album," she recalled, "and since nobody really knew where I was, I was starting to get itchy to begin work on *Bella Donna* and it seemed like it would just never happen. Jimmy had told me many times about his incredible friendship with John. It was a real-life fairy tale that ended one gray day. A terrible sadness came over the house; there was simply nothing I could say." Stevie packed up and went home. Jimmy would have to do this by himself.

But Stevie would face death herself in the next few weeks. Her mother called to say that her Uncle Bill was in the hospital with cancer and wasn't expected to live. Stevie was on the next plane to Phoenix where she joined her parents, Aunt Carmel, and cousin John at her uncle's bedside. Late one night Stevie and John were keeping vigil when Uncle Bill went into cardiac arrest. They called for a nurse but there was no response. Stevie dashed into the hall and ran down the long, shadowy corridor, but it seemed no one was on duty. She plunged down some dark stairs, but the door to the floor below was locked. In a panic, she came back up again. She ran back down the hall to her uncle's room, but when she walked in he was already gone. Bill Nicks was her favorite uncle, and Stevie now went into mourning herself, appearing mostly in black for a while.

The deaths of these two men were intense for Stevie. That empty hospital hall would soon be featured on one of her best songs.

Jimmy Iovine took control of Stevie's recording sessions with a steely will. He expected her to show up on time so they could stay on budget. Most of the girls in the entourage were banished from the studio. He'd instructed the Heartbreakers and the studio players to ignore Stevie's attempts to make friends and get them under her spell. He told her, "Look, if we're gonna do this, it's not a part-time job. We have to approach it like you've never made an album before. This band—you can't trick them. You can't trick seasoned musicians. They have to *believe*. If they feel this is a hobby of yours, they're gonna treat it like a hobby, and everyone around it will treat it like a hobby."

It addition to the half-dozen songs from Fleetwood Mac sessions, Stevie brought in several new ideas. "Outside the Rain" with the Heartbreakers, originally produced by Tom Petty, got a makeover by Jimmy Iovine that softened Petty's guitar band sound. "Bella Donna" would introduce the album as a somewhat murky meditation on mystical love and a plea to "come in, out of the darkness." The late *Tusk* outtake, "How Still My Love," was almost an homage to Lindsey Buckingham's celestial chord structures.

"Edge of Seventeen," originally a slower piano ballad, gathered elements from Stevie's journals: the white winged dove was both John Lennon's spirit and the archetypal dove of peace; there was also a type of white dove that roosted in the Saguero cactuses of the Arizona desert. The call of the night bird was Death in the hall where no one was left standing in. Then drummer Russ Kunkel came up with a harder rocking drum track. Waddy added a saw-toothed guitar stutter, and Jimmy Iovine changed "Edge of Seventeen" to a powerful, poetically rambling song about (what seemed to fans like) a romantic coming of age.

But the title came out of a misunderstanding. It was an accident. It happened that Stevie felt she wasn't getting much warmth from the musicians working on her songs. She wasn't used to it. Benmont Tench and Mike Campbell sort of ignored her. Shelly Yakus, whom Jimmy brought from New York to engineer the sessions, hardly looked at her. Even Tom Petty seemed cooler to her. (She didn't know about Jimmy's harsh instructions to leave her alone.) Stevie, accustomed to the drama kings of Fleetwood Mac, wasn't used to this kind of blank professionalism. But she still wanted to be in the Heartbreakers, and she wasn't backing down, or going away. So, as Tom Petty later recalled, "Stevie went to work on Jane."

Jane Benyo Petty had been Tom's high school girlfriend back in Gainesville. At her family's insistence, he married her before they left for fame and fortune in California in 1975. She was slender and pretty, tall and blond like Tom, and spoke with an even thicker Southern drawl than her husband. Stevie invited Jane into her private, enchanted world of Tiffany lamps and Persian carpets, candles and incense, girlfriends in long dresses, and midnight metaphysical speculations on various occult matters, all documented with Stevie's ever-present Polaroid instant camera. Jane Petty liked the high-speed cocaine as well.

One night, Stevie asked Jane when she met Tom. She replied, "Ah met him at the edge of seventeen."

Stevie, puzzled, said, "Did you say the 'edge' of seventeen?"

Jane laughed. "No, Ah said Ah met him at the 'age' of seventeen. He wasn't no more than a baby then."

Stevie told Jane that "Edge of Seventeen" would make a killer song title. Jane told her to go ahead. Such is fate. Stevie invited Jane to come down to the sessions and gradually the atmosphere loosened up. Stevie even got dour Ben Tench and Mike Campbell to smile at her at the end of a good take.

Late winter 1981. Warners Bros. released a single from *Fleetwood Mac Live,* "Over My Head" and Stevie's "Fireflies." A twelve-inch 45-rpm single was also issued to radio stations, the first appearance of Stevie's music in this format. The single only got to #60, and was considered to have bombed.

Around this time Stevie got tired of the so-called "marine layer," the almost daily fogbank that rolled in from the Pacific most mornings and covered the beach towns—Santa Monica, Venice, and Marina Del Rey. She went house-hunting—maybe her favorite activity outside of music—and was shown a colonnaded mansion in the hills above Pacific Palisades with a great view of Santa Monica and the ocean. It was in the middle of its own land, reached by a long drive, and the big white columns holding up the entrance porch reminded her of Tara, Scarlett O'Hara's house in *Gone with the Wind.* She bought the house for the asking price and moved her piano in a month later.

Her recording sessions continued, with an inspiring new presence.

When listening to vocal playbacks in the studio, Stevie and Jimmy thought the singing could be stronger, meatier, deeper in timbre. Stevie and Sharon Celani sounded great together, but a third element was needed to complete the triad of womanly harmonic convergence they had in mind.

Two years previous, during a tour break, Stevie had recorded the piano demo for "Sara" in Gordon Perry's studio in Dallas. At the same session she made a rough demo for a new song, "Beauty and the Beast," which touched on her relationship with Mick. The title was appropriated from one of her favorite old movies, Jean Cocteau's surrealist 1946 masterpiece, *La Belle et la Bête.* While in Dallas, Stevie got to know Perry's wife, Lori, a beautiful redhead who sang on the radio spots and commercial jingles produced at the studio. Stevie was really taken with Lori Perry—everyone was. Lori was from LA, had grown up in the San Fernando Valley, and had worked in the trenches of the music business as a production assistant and secretary. She had her own (understated but sexy) style, was a natural singer, and moved with the easy grace of a trained dancer. At age thirty Lori was a bit younger than Stevie, but she was quickly deemed to be vibey, and *very* Rhiannon.

When Fleetwood Mac moved on from Dallas, Stevie left the "Beauty and the Beast" piano demo with Gordon Perry and suggested that Lori work on the song, adding backing vocals and instrumentation. Lori recalled, "I was so flattered, but a bit reticent . . . I really didn't feel I had the talent to sing on a Stevie Nicks song." But Gordon insisted that Lori should at least try it, so she enlisted her singing best friend, Caroline Brooks, to sing with her. They overdubbed harmonies and ran a simple keyboard vamp over Stevie's piano demo. They sent the tape to Stevie and didn't hear back until she called to say that she'd started her solo record, and she wanted to hire Lori to sing with her and Sharon Celani on the album and the tour. Soon Lori Perry arrived and was absorbed into Stevie's hermetic, insular clique of strong, creative women—the ones who sang at night, and who with Stevie Nicks lived a California rock & roll fantasy of fun and success, and the endless promise of more the next night, too.

## 5.2   Vengeance

Spring 1981. Jimmy Iovine was worried.

They were sequencing Stevie's album. The difficult, almost tuneless new song "Bella Donna" would open the first side, at Stevie's insistence, then "Kind of Woman," "Think About It," and "After the Glitter Fades." Side two would be "Edge of Seventeen," "How Still My Love," "Leather and Lace," "Outside the Rain," and "The Highwayman," the old-fashioned ballad on which Don Henley had been persuaded to play drums and sing. There were also three strong new songs in reserve: "Blue Lamp" was about guardian angels and "a lamp I carried from my mother's home"; "Gold and Braid" was a keyboard-driven, All-man Brothers–style pastiche about a strong man who would "like to make her better, and hold her like a child"; and "Sleeping Angels," a passionate ballad dispensing hard-won pearls of wisdom—"Real love affairs are heavy spells / For a woman and a man."

But Jimmy Iovine didn't hear a hit single in any of these songs. What about "Edge of Seventeen?" Stevie asked. Wouldn't work, he said. "Edge of Seventeen" was too much of a gamble for the first single. She wanted to gamble. Danny explained that solo albums by members of big groups usually only did so-so in the market, unless propelled by huge nationwide radio airplay. *Tusk,* he pointed out, was a "multiplatinum disappointment" compared to *Rumours,* so Fleetwood Mac's stock was perceived by radio program directors to have fallen. Stevie needed an instant radio smash, or their hard work was all in vain.

Jimmy wanted Stevie to cut two new songs Tom Petty and Mike Campbell had written for the Heartbreakers. She was resistant and told them bluntly, asserting herself, leaning in, "I don't *need* to do other people's songs." But Jimmy leaned back—his career was potentially at stake—and soon Stevie and Petty were in the studio with his band. They cut a track called "The Insider," a noirish look at the music world, and the first time anyone had heard the thrilling mix of their two voices. Still, Jimmy said, they didn't have the single.

Somehow, Jimmy Iovine got Tom Petty to record "Stop Draggin' My Heart Around" with Stevie: an organ-driven, duet-format breakup song with a "one-listen hook," destined for Petty's next album. Memphis bass guitar master Donald "Duck" Dunn played on the track, under one of Stevie's most powerful vocals. Petty's lyrics described someone he must have known well, someone beautiful, sexy, seductive, and unobtainable; then sleazy and unwanted, but ultimately haunting. When Petty finally gave into intense pressure and gave Stevie the track, she had achieved everything she'd set out to do when she broke free from domination by Lindsey and Mick. Feminine wiles: she was almost a Heartbreaker now. Some of them were even in her band. She'd co-opted their producer and stolen their best new song. *Bella Donna,* her new album, would be released that summer. Lindsey's first solo album would be out a few months later. Ambitious, super-competitive Stevie Nicks would give them all a run for their money.

Then someone at Atlantic Records had a problem with *Bella Donna* as the album title. Danny Goldberg did, too. Los Angeles' demimonde was rife with rumors of drug-taking at Stevie Nicks's house, and there were also stories going around about experimentation with herbs and plants said to have magical or psychotropic effects. The poisonous black fruit and pear-shaped leaves of the belladonna plant (*Atropa belladonna*) were traditionally associated with witchcraft, used for inducing visions and hallucinations, even when just rubbed on one's skin. President Reagan and his publicity-seeking wife were rabid antidrug campaigners ("Just Say No"), and Danny warned that the title could bring unwanted negative attention to a great album. He finally persuaded an unconvinced Stevie to change the title (and the album track) to a more neutral *Bella Donna,* "beautiful lady" in Latin and Italian.

Prior to release, they shot a video of Stevie and Tom performing the song with the Heartbreakers. This was a few months before the new cable channel MTV began narrowcasting music clips twenty-four hours a day, so the video was aimed at the late-night syndicated rock shows. The director told Stevie just to mime the words and flirt with Tom. Stevie wore an off-white lacy outfit with silvered leggings and stacked heels, a new look she and Margi Kent had come up with for her solo work. This style partly derived from a young Fleetwood Mac fan Stevie had seen in the audience from the stage at the Hollywood Bowl. This girl was dancing in layers of cream chiffon and snowy lace, her long hair piled up on her head like a Gibson Girl, her legs encased in big silver boots. Very Rhiannon, she was. Stevie pointed this girl out to Margi Kent. That was how she wanted to look in front of her own band, and that's how she appeared in the "Stop Draggin'" video. (When MTV did go on air in August 1981, "Stop Draggin'" was one of the few videos available by famous musicians, and the new channel played it almost every hour for the first year of MTV's febrile, exciting, must-watch existence.)

The album photos were shot at Herbie Worthington's studio. Stevie portrayed herself as a bejeweled white witch against a dark, blue-black screen, holding aloft her brother Chris's white toucan, Max. Other props included a crystal ball, Stevie's tambourine, and a clutch of white roses. The inner sleeve depicted Stevie in black lace along with Sharon Celani, looking like Mona Lisa with her olive complexion and black dress, and also Lori Perry, long auburn curls falling over a blue silk dress. The album bore this dedication: "And once again / this music is dedicated / to my Grandfather / and all his children."

Unlike most musicians in rock bands, Stevie was something of a national celebrity, and Danny was able to use this with mainstream media as opposed to the music press. Stevie flew to New York and appeared on ABC's *Good Morning America*, then the highest-rated show on breakfast television. This and heavy airplay helped propel "Stop Draggin'" to the top of the charts in both rock and Top 40 radio when the single was released by Modern Records in June 1981.

*Bella Donna* the album came out at the end of July and was met with strong (but cautious) reviews. Doug Morris made sure Atco's publicity and sales teams worked the record hard. It began selling strongly as legions of Fleetwood Mac fans began buying copies, but it was lagging at #3 behind big albums by Foreigner (#1) and Journey (#2), mainstays of big-time corporate rock. In those days before barcode scans made accurate counting of record sales possible, the *Billboard* and other sales charts relied on phone calls to record stores and other semireliable sources. But Danny Goldberg and Paul Fishkin were determined to get *Bella Donna* to the top. They had almost promised this to Stevie, two long years before.

Danny: "Hundreds of stores were called for information, but the final creation of the chart was done by one guy named Bill Wardlow. Doug [Morris] took Stevie to dinner with Wardlow, and as a quid pro quo for personal attention, the next week *Bella Donna* was officially the number-one album in the country according to *Billboard*, despite the fact that reports indicated it was really number three." Foreigner and Journey angrily protested, to no avail. "*Bella Donna* was number one for only a single week," Danny sagely observed, "but that still made it a number-one album."

Jubilation and relief reigned in Stevie's camps in LA and Phoenix, and at the LA and New York offices of Modern Records. They had done it. Speaking of himself and Paul, Danny later said that they had risked their careers on Stevie, and their faith had paid off. *Bella Donna* would sell up to three million copies by the end of the year. After MTV kept playing the video, the album sold three million more. Stevie Nicks now was an established star in her own right. She was thirty-three years old.

On the day *Bella Donna* went to #1, as Stevie remembered, "my very best friend [Robin Anderson] called me and told me she had terminal leukemia, and might last three months. So without a doubt it was the absolute high and low of success. I never got to enjoy *Bella Donna* at all because my friend was dying. Something . . . went out that day. Something just left.

"They said Robin had the worst leukemia UCLA Medical Center had ever seen," Stevie recalled. "She was sicker than you could believe." The doctors told Robin there wasn't much they could do for her. Then Robin got pregnant. Her doctors advised her to terminate the pregnancy if she wanted to prolong her life. Robin ignored this advice, which set off a mad scramble for alternative therapies and healers as well as months of worry and anguish for Stevie. Robin Snyder Anderson was determined to live long enough to bear this child.

Danny Goldberg loved Robin, who'd even worked for his PR firm, and felt terrible for Stevie. "She had this huge success with *Bella Donna* while trying to manage her unhappiness over her best friend's predicament. It was a very trying time for everyone involved with Stevie and her project."

When Stevie received the first finished copies of her album, she wrote and drew elaborate dedications to each member of Fleetwood Mac, and took them over to the studio where they were remixing possible further singles from the *Live* album. She handed a copy to Lindsey, with a fulsome inscription thanking him for all the inspiration over the years. Lindsey seemed preoccupied with the knobs on the mixing desk; he barely glanced at *Bella Donna*. He put the record on the floor, leaning it against the console. She waited around for him to pick it up and read what she had gratefully written. He never looked at the album for two hours and then went home without it. Someone told Stevie that Lindsey was calling her Top 10 single "Stop Dragging

My Career Around." She was mad as hell. "I never forgave him for that one," she seethed.

"My old journals tell the story of the way things changed when *Bella Donna* came out," Stevie said later. "No one in the band ever said a word to me about my solo career. They were keeping quiet, out of their own interests. No one even said they'd listened to my record. They knew that if they ripped *Bella Donna* apart, I wouldn't give them any more songs. No more 'Dreams'—the only #1 single that Fleetwood Mac ever had. That was me."

Stevie's feelings were hurt. She felt really wounded by her friends' reaction to her album.

She might have taken some small notice (and satisfaction) when Lindsey's solo album was released that October of 1981. The first single, "Trouble," got to #9, but the *Law and Order* album stalled at #32, while *Bella Donna*'s second single, "Leather and Lace," the loving duet with Don Henley, was hot on the radio and peaking at #6.

Vengeance—a dish best served cold.

### 5.3   "The Reigning Queen of Rock & Roll"

Stevie Nicks's newly appointed music director, Waddy Wachtel, began rehearsing the first Stevie Nicks Band in early November 1981. Everyone had played on *Bella Donna*. Waddy was on lead guitar, with Bob Glaub on bass. Swinging Russ Kunkel was the drummer, perfect for a dancing singer like Stevie, with Roy Bittan from the E Street Band on keyboards. Heartbreaker Benmont Tench played atmospheric organ and synthesizers, which made the Stevie Nicks Band sound a lot like Tom Petty's. Bobbye Hall, a striking black woman, played congas, with Sharon and Lori singing at the right side of the stage. Waddy was concerned about Lori actually upstaging Stevie with her unusual beauty and sensual movements while singing backing vocals. He told the girls in no uncertain terms to stay in front of their microphones and not distract the audience's attention away from Stevie. "Take it down a step," he ordered. He didn't want the girls to gesture or wave their arms, either. "Keep those fuckin' arms *down*," he insisted, "or I'll fuckin' cut 'em off."

While the band was rehearsing, something happened that gave

Stevie a jolt. "I came out of the stage door and a girl was crying hysterically. I can never walk away from someone in tears, so I asked what was wrong. She said, 'Will you sign my arm?' So I did. The next night she was back with her arm tattooed with my name!" Stevie scolded the girl, which prompted more floods of tears. Another night, a different girl asked Stevie to sign her arm. Stevie said, 'I did that the other day and the girl went out and had her arm tattooed.'"

That was my best friend, the girl replied. Stevie: "So I told her, 'I'm not touching your arm. Don't put that on me. I'll sue! That's *pain*. I'm not here to bring pain. I'm here to bring you *out* of pain. It's not funny—it's stupid.' It bummed me out. I felt like I'd come out the wrong door."

Stevie and the band performed a concert for an HBO special that was shown several times on America's most important cable channel, increasing sales for *Bella Donna*. (This was directed by Marty Callner, one of a new breed of video auteurs whose small-screen visions—often grounded in TV commercials—would come to dominate Western visual media in the next decade.) Stevie was dressed in white, like a bride, with leggings covering stiletto-heeled boots. Her big hair was blown out backstage between numbers. She wrapped herself in a white shawl for the show's finale, "Edge of Seventeen," which featured a stirring, repeated, priestess-like warning of impending death—"I hear . . . the call . . . of the nightbird"—by the three singers. At the end of the song, as the band vamped behind her, Stevie began a tradition—"The Walk"—moving across the front of the stage, accepting bouquets, toys, notes, and framed pictures while discretely shadowed by Dennis Dunston, a beefy (and married) Australian security expert who'd been working with Fleetwood Mac. He was popular with the band, didn't drink and drug, and now was minding Stevie on her tour.

The White Winged Dove Tour consisted of only eleven shows in Texas, Arizona, and California in late November and early December; the tour went by fast and everyone had fun. Shows began with "Gold Dust Woman" and introduced "Think About It" and "Outside the Rain" to Stevie's audience. Rapturous cries from the seats greeted "Dreams," and then "Angel" from *Tusk*. Three new songs followed: "After the Glitter Fades," "Gold and Braid," and "I Need to Know." More rapture for long, swooning versions of "Sara," taken fast by Russ Kunkel, followed by "Blue Lamp" (just out on the *Heavy Metal* movie soundtrack album) and "Bella Donna"—unfamiliar songs that sent her audiences to the bathrooms. Back at their seats, they heard "Leather and Lace" (the Don Henley part sung by Benmont Tench), "How Still My Love," and "Stop Draggin' My Heart Around." They ended with "Edge of Seventeen" (after a heroic, hand-wrenching, three-minute guitar stutter from Waddy while Stevie refreshed and switched shawls backstage). "Rhiannon" was the encore most nights. The final concert was at the Fox Wilshire Theater in Hollywood on December 13 before a hometown crowd rabid for Stevie Nicks and her band.

Right after that, Stevie went to Phoenix for Christmas, and then she and her assistant flew to Paris via Air France. They were met by a black Citroen limousine and driven for an hour to a remote country castle, the Chateau d'Herouville, in the dead of winter, to help make the next Fleetwood Mac album.

Mick Fleetwood arrived the next day. He remembered the long, tree-lined drive to the chateau and then getting out of the car and looking up to see Stevie peering at him from the leaded-glass windows of her turreted bedroom, looking like Queen Guinevere in the foggy country morning light. He had asked the band to record outside the United States because of his ruinous tax liabilities and increasingly desperate financial concerns. He'd chosen the studio at Le Chateau, a late medieval French castle near the town of Herouville, about sixty miles from Paris. Elton John had famously recorded there and renamed it "Honky Chateau." Other rock stars (with tax issues) who had worked there included David Bowie, Pink Floyd, the BeeGees, and the Dead. The modern recording studio offered the privacy of a fifty-acre deer park, good food, and a romantic atmosphere appropriate to Fleetwood Mac's quest, which was basically to try to remake *Rumours*. They were booked in for a month. Stevie's and Chris's bedrooms had been redecorated at the usual expense. Stevie found the chateau to be chilly and damp, haunted, a little creepy, and she had a cold and a runny nose most of the time she was there.

No one was happy. Stevie, Christine, and Lindsey had all interrupted solo work to be in France, for Mick's sake. Christine was sad, having recently dumped Dennis Wilson, a true cad, who'd used her credit cards to buy stuff for young girls and also put out the malicious story that he'd had a relationship with Stevie Nicks. (Apparently not true. Later Dennis would drown in a pathetic boating accident in Marina Del Rey.) There weren't much drugs to be had. With the excellent JC's contacts and international dope expertise having been forfeited, Mick would have to be driven into Paris on sleazy, dangerous cocaine forays, often returning to the chateau with dubious powders that seemed on nasal ingestion to be infant laxative cut with speed. Delicious communal meals with superb wines in the castle's ancient kitchen were eaten mostly in silence. Mick later remembered one of the only light moments being when Stevie "borrowed" his rented gray mare and galloped down the long drive in the morning mist, a flowing auburn cape streaming behind her.

And yet, here she was   the woman whom *Rolling Stone* had just put on its cover and proclaimed her "The Reigning Queen of Rock & Roll"—back under Lindsey Buckingham's . . . law and order. She was sick, and having trouble breathing, and didn't know whether she had asthma or bronchitis. She joked that she was a career invalid.

She'd brought three songs to France for Mac's consideration. (They'd asked for four.) "That's Alright" was a laconic, country-style rocker, a breakup song with an organ and banjo groove, originally called "Designs of Love" and dating from the 1974 Buckingham Nicks sessions. "Straight Back" was a new song that seemed to conflate the dwindling of the romance with Jimmy Iovine amid the anguish of having to rejoin the Mac in France in the midst of her epic new solo career. It was sung in a low and fierce voice, set off with Lindsey's clever countermelody, an angry soul singer searching for lost dreams.

Then there was "Gypsy," considered by some to be the greatest of the heroic musical collaborations between Stevie and Lindsey. The gypsy was a visionary metaphor: youthful innocence floating away, inchoate, calling out, but then just an echo or maybe a wish. Only visible by lightning, the gypsy was elusive, fugitive, just a feeling and a desire expressed in a sparkling arrangement for guitar and keyboard, bass, and drums. For many, Fleetwood Mac's "Gypsy" bottled a moment, the early eighties crystallized in a haunted song.

Lindsey was with his girlfriend, Carol, who later reported that he was in a bad mood in France. Fleetwood Mac's mandate to recapture the "soft rock/adult contemporary" *Rumours* groove, he felt, was a slap at him for the less-than-magic experiments of *Tusk*. Lindsey took out some of his frustrations on stressed and ailing Stevie, who bore his insensitive sarcasm and toxic indifference until she could stand it no more. She called Front Line Management in Los Angeles and sent for Jimmy Iovine, who soon appeared at her side at Le Chateau. That shut Lindsey up. Stevie had been visited in the studio by love interests before, but this was another matter: a boyfriend who was a respected producer, even a rival, and one who had just made Stevie's solo album a number-one hit record, proving—forever—that Stevie wasn't commercially dependent on Lindsey's production of her music.

Stevie and Jimmy sat close together on the Chateau's commodious studio sofa, sipping champagne, whispering to each other as if in a conspiracy . . . *ssss, ssss* . . . which drove already deeply stressed Lindsey crazy while he was trying to mix tracks at the console. When the month at the chateau had expired, Stevie was relieved to go home and begin work on her next solo album for her label, Modern Records.

Los Angeles, 1982. While Lindsey, Christine, and Mick spend the next seven months at the Record Plant working on the Fleetwood Mac album, Stevie was trying to write her new record, which was difficult because she was preoccupied with trying to help look after Robin Anderson, now visibly pregnant. Robin's cancer doctors were telling her that carrying the baby to term would likely shorten her life, but she wanted the child and had found some strength and solace in her born-again husband's ardent Christian faith. All the songs and verses Stevie was coming up with seemed to be for or about poor Robin. Stevie took her friend to Hawaii for a few restful weeks late in the winter, and it seemed to do them both some good.

Modern Records released two more singles from *Bella Donna* that year, which kept the album in the stores and selling well. "Edge of Seventeen" reached #11, and later "After the Glitter Fades" got to #32. "Sleeping Angel," which didn't make it on the album, would be released on the *Fast Times at Ridgemont High* soundtrack album in June.

In March Fleetwood Mac made their first videos for MTV. Stevie was already a mainstay of the network because of the ubiquity of "Stop Draggin' My Heart Around." (The "Edge of Seventeen" video had been lifted from the HBO special's footage.) Stevie was well aware that the cable music channel was the immediate future of getting her music out to the world. "I was living in the Pacific Palisades [when MTV began in August 1981] and I would just sit there, on the end of my bed, watching video after video, just stupefied," she recalled. The first clip MTV played was "Video Killed the Radio Star" by the Buggles. "When that came out, we took it with a grain of salt. We thought, *Well, video's not gonna kill the radio star.* But it did! The song was prophetic."

Russell Mulcahy directed both of the *Mirage* videos. Stevie appeared only tangentially on the first one, Christine's "Hold Me." It was shot in 100-degree heat in the desert. Stevie refused to walk in the sand in her stacked heels, and indeed seemed so stoned she could barely walk at all. John McVie got drunk and tried to punch the director.

Right after this, Jimmy Iovine got Stevie into rehab for cocaine addiction. She remembered, "I was in Corona del Mar [California] in self-imposed rehab for two weeks. I wanted to stop doing coke. But then the 'Gypsy' video was scheduled and there was no getting out of it." The shoot was for three days. At the end of the first day, Stevie was tired and asked for some cocaine, which was procured. She wrapped the little phial in a tissue and hid it behind the makeup mirror. When she was called back to the set, someone cleaned the dressing room and threw away the tissue with the cocaine. "I said to the person that got it for me, 'You have to get in the garbage dumpster and find that little bottle.' But this person refused." Stevie refused to return to rehab.

The "Gypsy" video was all Nicks: a ballet studio with dolls and crystals; cut to a soup kitchen in the black-and-white rain of a forties movie; then a swank nightclub, with the other Macs as bit players; cut to Stevie in a manic Nirvana, dancing on the edge of a cliff with little white fairy children twirling about her. Stevie: "There's a scene in 'Gypsy' where Lindsey and I are dancing. And we weren't getting along very well then. I didn't want to be anywhere near Lindsey, and I certainly didn't want to be in his arms. If you watch, you'll see I wasn't happy. And he wasn't a very good dancer."

The long (five and a half minutes) "Gypsy" video, said to have been the most expensive clip to date, was MTV's first "World Premier Video." It helped propel *Mirage* to a legitimate #1 *Billboard* chart position when the album came out that summer. "Gypsy" generated the most replay requests in MTV's young history when it went into heavy rotation in September 1982. *Mirage* would spend eighteen weeks in the U.S. Top 10, five weeks at #1—the first time in five years. Mick Fleetwood remembered, "It felt great to be back on top—at least for a while."

He was less than thrilled when Stevie told him that she would only do a short tour with Fleetwood Mac, just shows in North America: no Europe, no Pacific. She said that her friend was sick, she wasn't feeling well herself, and she had her own album to do now. It was another way of Stevie telling him that Fleetwood Mac was lucky to get her at all.

## 5.4   Kim and Sara Anderson's Honeymoon

The *Mirage* tour, originally about thirty shows in the summer of 1982, was booked around two big outdoor festivals, one in Florida, and the US Festival in California, a mammoth concert in the California desert produced by Steve Wozniak, who had invented the Apple II computer. (The band received $800,000—more than $4 million in current money—for their single show closing the three-day festival.)

For Stevie Nicks the tour was an ordeal. She'd been diagnosed with what she called bronchial spasmodic asthma. She told a *Playboy* magazine interviewer, "I have to take these miserable pills that make you feel like someone put something weird in your Perrier." Her singing voice was torn and frayed, and her trusty vocal coach Robin was dying at home. So Stevie used the lower range of her voice to sing and got lousy reviews in the press. But *Mirage* was still #1 after three weeks and many of the shows sold out. Two nights were filmed by Marty Callner, and his cameras captured some memorable moments. There was Stevie glaring with hatred at Lindsey during "The Chain," in whiteface makeup, dark eyeliner, heavy rouge and lipstick, wearing a silver-spangled black dress under a black shawl as if she were in mourning. There was Stevie, barely able to sing "Gypsy," in woolen leggings and a pink mesh top over a cleavage-revealing beige camisole. She was leaning forward for emphasis as she sings, legs wide apart, drugged eyes dead to the camera. They caught Stevie singing "Rhiannon" in a white shawl, barely moving, with only a slinky and subdued dance at the end. During "dreams unwind," she looked over at Lindsey and sang, "You don't change / I don't change / All the same, Rhiannon," finishing the song in a woozy collapse at the microphone stand. She put on her signature top hat and a black cropped jacket for "Go Your Own Way," walking the edge of the stage at the end, accepting presents and flowers as in her solo concerts. The first encore was "Sisters of the Moon," Stevie in a black silken shawl, looking blasted, stricken, tears in her eyes, offering trans-lexical singing, like talking in tongues with a voice that didn't quite work. Christine ended the shows with "Songbird." Some of these shows earned Stevie Nicks some of the worst concert reviews of her career.

Fleetwood Mac usually went out on the road for a year to promote a new record. But Stevie's management took notice of her fragile condition and basically canceled the tour after only eighteen, mostly apathetic, shows. When the brief *Mirage* tour ended, *Mirage* had been #1 for five weeks. It almost immediately dropped off the charts, and that was that. Mick Fleetwood told Stevie he was heartbroken that they couldn't stay on tour to promote their best record in years, but she told him she had other matters to attend to.

When Stevie arrived at her mansion with the great view in Pacific Palisades, the place was dark. The Mac tour had ended quickly, and no one had time to prepare the home for her. The big house was cold, and there was no heat, no firewood either. The refrigerator was empty, and Stevie couldn't even call for a pizza because the phone didn't work. She decided she hated the house. "I was all alone up there with nothing, like a mountain woman. So I freaked out and wrote 'Sable and Blond' and the verses to 'Wild Heart,' just me and my piano."

On Sunday, September 5, 1982, Stevie boarded a helicopter with her friend Robin and flew to a remote desert site near San Bernardino, where Fleetwood Mac would headline the last day of the US Festival before more than 600,000 fans. Robin had been part of the Mac family since the rainy nights back in Sausalito, and the musicians and crew were told that this was probably the last time they'd be seeing her. Now, with child, she looked frail but beautiful as her fate began to close in on her. Fleetwood Mac's show was a bit shorter than usual, and Stevie and Robin were on the first chopper heading back to LA afterward. Mick Fleetwood had a jeweler make a crucifix of gold and rubies for Robin; he was able to hand it to her just before takeoff from the festival site. Robin Anderson died holding the little cross a month later, in October 1982, just after giving birth to a son, Matthew.

Stevie was disconsolate, and could not be comforted. She spent hours talking to her mother on the telephone, sobbing long distance. No one had ever seen her like this. Stevie had met Robin at Arcadia High School when they were in the tenth grade. Later, she tried to describe the loss she felt to the school's alumni magazine.

"[Robin] had just been in my life since I was fourteen. She was the one person who knew me for the person I really was and not the famous Stevie, and it was good to have someone who knew the real you besides just your Mom and Dad. She kind of walked me through life. Robin is also my speech therapist, and the lady who traveled with Fleetwood Mac during the time when my voice just seemed to give up. My friend saved my voice, with a lot of patience and love. She listened to me sing the first song I ever wrote. She taught me how to sing. She taught me how to use my voice. She made sure before she left this planet that I was all right. I don't have any problems with my voice now, but I did and it took us years to fix it. . . . Robin was one of those people, when she walked in the room everybody looked. She was breathtaking, and that's why it's so wild that she possibly could have died. It just doesn't make any sense at all."

Not knowing what else to do, Stevie moved in with widower Kim, ostensibly to help look after the baby, a child with whom she was emotionally hyperinvolved. Then, confused and addled by drugs, she proposed marriage to Kim Anderson, and to everyone's horror, especially their families', he accepted. No one could believe this. Mick burst into tears when Stevie called to tell him this news. (She'd started by asking if he was sitting down.)

Everyone thought it was a crazy thing to do. "We were all in such insane grief," she said later, "just completely deranged. In a lot of people's eyes, it was very blasphemous. But I didn't care." Their families were outraged. Some friends avoided Stevie's wedding in January 1983. The bride seemed dazed and disconnected from the event. The heavily bearded groom looked forlorn. Stevie's mother came, and her brother. From the band, only Mick and Christine McVie attended the simple ceremony in what Mick described as "some born-again type of church. Stevie's bridal veil was one of sorrow. I could see on her face that she knew it was a mistake."

That night Stevie and Kim left for their honeymoon at San Ysidro Ranch near Santa Barbara, a resort popular with newlyweds. On the way north, driving along the coast, Prince's new hit song "Little Red Corvette" came on the radio, and Stevie spontaneously started humming "Stand Back" to the track of Prince's naughty but clever double entendre. "The entire song," she later said, "just wrote itself right then and there." Stevie told Kim that they had to get off the highway and buy a cassette recorder—right away. They also bought a tape of the album *1999*, which contained "Little Red Corvette."

They checked into one of the ranch's honeymoon suites as Kim and Sara Anderson. Stevie spent the first night of their stay writing and recording the four verses of "Stand Back," which describe the approach-avoidance stage of a man-woman relationship, or, as she later wrote, "some kind of crazy argument." At the end she asks for sympathy then acquiesces to the inevitable (or is just weary), and says to her man, "Take me home," which—Stevie later explained—meant "Let's make this work."

Back in Los Angeles, Stevie knew she'd found the key song of her next album. The *Bella Donna* songs had been written over the course of a decade and more. The new album would rely on songs written during the previous tortured and tumultuous year. (And she certainly wasn't getting any hit songs from Tom Petty, whose album she'd just eclipsed with her own.) She went into Sunset Sound Studios with Jimmy Iovine, who got Prince's phone number through Warner Bros. Records. Stevie called the number, and was amazed that Prince actually answered himself. She told him about hearing "Little Red Corvette," and tried to explain that on her honeymoon she "became" the lady in "Stand Back" during the long night she was writing, as if a whole new character had taken hold of her through the inspiration of his song. Stevie was even more amazed when Prince agreed to come to the studio and listen to what she was doing.

Danny Goldberg went to the session that night. "I arrived at the studio to find a giant, white-haired bodyguard hulking over the lithe, petite, doe-eyed superstar [Prince] as he added a driving synthesizer beat to 'Stand Back.'"

"Prince is *exactly* like Jimmy," Stevie announced. Danny looked at Iovine, who just shrugged his shoulders and rolled his eyes.

Stevie: "He played incredible synthesizer on 'Stand Back' . . . and then he just walked out of my life, and I didn't see him for a long time." Prince refused to be credited when "Stand Back" was released as the first single from *The Wild Heart* in 1983. Prince's ardent, orchestral synth licks would be credited instead to Stevie's newest collaborator, Sandy Stewart, a talented singer and songwriter from deep in the heart of Texas.

Stevie later told her trusted Australian minder, Dennis Dunstan, that she knew her marriage wouldn't work when she arrived home from the studio one night and found that her husband had moved a giant Sony television set to the foot of the marital bed. Kim explained he liked to watch TV before he went to sleep. Stevie moved to another bedroom. As the weeks moved along in early 1983, Kim began complaining that Stevie was spending too much time in the studio working on her album. "He was like, 'There's no time in your life for anybody. There's no time in your life for Matthew and me.' And I thought to myself, 'Well, boy—are you right. There's not.'"

Then she got the feeling, from beyond the grave, that Robin was less than thrilled by the situation. "One day I walked into Matthew's room and the cradle was not rocking," she said later. "I know this sounds crazy, but the cradle always started to rock a little when I came in the room, and I knew that Robin was there. And one day it wasn't rocking, and the room got very dark, and the baby was very quiet. And I said, 'Robin wants this to end—*now*.' I felt it as strongly as if she'd put her hand on my shoulder. It was absolutely a sign."

After about six weeks, Stevie moved back into her own house and instructed her lawyers to file for divorce. She told Kim to take the baby and go home to Minnesota, where he was from and had family. She tried to explain that she'd sold her soul to the devil long ago, as she put it, "so I could follow this dream fully and completely and not be wrapped up in children and husbands and all of that." She told him, "Kim, I'm a rock and roll star. It's what I do, and who I am." The marriage with Kim Anderson had lasted about three months. Later in the year Stevie was granted an annulment by a California family judge. Legally, the marriage had never happened.

Some years later, in 1990, Stevie told a version of this story to a reporter from *Us* magazine: "Robin was one of the few women who ever got leukemia and then got pregnant. And they had to take the baby at six and a half months, because Robin died two days later. And when she died, I went crazy. I just went insane. And so did her husband. And so we got married three months after she died. And it was a terrible, terrible mistake. We didn't get married because we were in love, we got married because we were grieving and it was the only way we could feel like we were doing anything. And we got divorced three months later. I haven't seen Kim or Matthew since that day. I suppose that Matthew will find me . . . when he's ready." (Years went by, and Matthew Anderson did contact Stevie; she later helped put him through college.)

## 5.5    Blame My Wild Heart

During this sad and difficult period, Stevie kept working on her next album, recording in Los Angeles, Dallas, and New York. Recognizing that recent traumatic events were affecting her writing, she accepted help from a collaborator for the first time, and the creative partnership with Texas singer-songwriter Sandy Stewart was crucial in getting Stevie's second solo album made in the first half of 1983. Anticipation for this record was very high, so much so that some radio stations were playing the *Mirage* album track "Straight Back" just to keep Stevie's voice on their air in the first part of the year.

Sandy Stewart was twenty-five and living in Houston when she was introduced to Stevie by Gordon and Lori Perry. Sandy was a big-boned, pretty brunette with dark eyes, an unusual alto singing timbre, and a direct Texan style. She came to LA in the immediate aftermath of the death of Stevie's outré marriage. She was quickly assimilated as a Sister of the Moon by Stevie and her initiates, and she proved to be a bulwark of calm and much needed artistic inspiration. With Stevie, Sandy Stewart cowrote and sang on three of the best songs on *The Wild Heart*.

The album was made half on the run between making videos. The operatic "Wild Heart" and "Gate and Garden" were both produced in Gordon Perry's Dallas studio and then further worked on by Jimmy Iovine at Studio 55 in LA, where *Bella Donna* had been recorded. Same with the final version of "Stand Back," with its offhanded tribute to the gentle, pulsing Juju music then being introduced from Nigeria; and "Nightbird," cowritten with Sandy, who had a solo role and even a countermelody of her own, on what Stevie has many times said is her favorite song on the album. She has also said that "the ones who sing at night" do so because they're too busy to sing during the day.

The stately, droning, faintly Celtic "If Anyone Falls in Love," an evergreen fan favorite, was also written with Sandy Stewart. It was cut at the Record Plant in Hollywood with soaring backup vocals by Carolyn Brooks, a classically trained singer. (The song was dedicated to Waddy Wachtel and the lyrics are a paean to Stevie's friendship with him.) The same studio produced the third collaboration with Sandy Stewart, "Nothing Ever Changes," with its pleading bridge that sounds like a Carly Simon song. "Sable on Blond" was also recorded in Los Angeles, a Fleetwood Mac knock-off with Mick on drums, even, and Sandy's washes of synthesized orchestration, "in the sacred name of love."

The remaining songs were all cut in New York studios familiar to Jimmy Iovine, who sometimes had to fit Stevie's sessions in between other projects. "Enchanted," Stevie's funny piece of cheerleader rock, was done by her touring band at the Record Plant in Manhattan. She recorded Tom Petty's song "I Will Run to You" with the Heartbreakers at the Hit Factory on the West Side. And for the orchestra featured on "Beauty and the Beast"—violins, violas, cellos, a harp—Jimmy booked the big room at venerable A&R Recording.

The "beast bridegroom" fable is one of the older European fairy tales. The most famous one, *La Belle et la Bête*—"Beauty and the

Beast"—was written in France in 1758 by a woman, Jeanne Marie Leprince de Beaumont. (Some scholars think the story was designed to reassure girls facing arranged or dynastic marriages, that in time they could come to love their husband, even if he seemed bestial. Stevie's reference was more to the surrealist film version; in later years she would project scenes from Cocteau's film behind her as she performed the song.)

"Beauty and the Beast" ended *The Wild Heart* and was the album's big statement. Originally written about her relationship with the giant, heavily bearded Mick Fleetwood in 1978, the song first saw light as a piano demo in Dallas. Stevie later said it was more a generalized feeling about the way the Fleetwood Mac family related to each other. To realize the emotions she wanted to express, Jimmy Iovine brought in the protean young English arranger-conductor Paul Buckmaster, famous for his work with the Rolling Stones, Elton John, and Miles Davis. He gave Stevie's disjointed lyrics a romantic platform of vamps and rising scales, playing to the gauzy sensibility of the piece— something barely there and hard to grasp. Stevie later wrote: "We recorded this live in New York, with Roy Bittan playing a grand piano and Paul Buckmaster conducting the [seventeen-piece] orchestra, and me and the background singers. It was like we had gone back in time. We all wore long black dresses and served champagne, and recorded it all in one room. When it was all over I walked out with this elderly gentleman who played violin and the generation gap ceased to exist."

There were a few songs left off the album that Modern Records would place on Hollywood movie soundtracks over the next year and a half. "Battle of the Dragon," about a struggling soul with too many friends, with programmed rhythm and Mike Campbell on guitar, would be used in the film *American Anthem*. "Violet and Blue," produced by Jimmy Iovine, would be in *Against All Odds* the following year. And "Garbo" was a sad little waltz about Hollywood—"a town full of fools"—that referenced icons Marlene and Marilyn in a teary and wistful way. "Garbo" would be the B-side of "Stand Back" when the smash single was released ahead of the album in June 1983.

"Stand Back" was another huge radio ear worm, getting to #5 and staying in the Top 10 for weeks. Likewise, *The Wild Heart* was #5 for two months in the summer and would spin off two more Top 40 singles, "If Anyone Falls" and "Nightbird." Reviews were respectful and often glowing, which made thirty-five-year-old Stevie Nicks feel a little better as her crucial second record hit big and her solo career was so firmly now established.

Now airplay on MTV meant almost as much as on the radio, if a record was going to sell. The first attempt at a video for "Stand Back" was titled "Scarlett" and was an expensive costume drama involving the American Civil War, the burning of Atlanta, ghosts in the rented Beverly Hills mansion they were using (and which the film crew set on fire by mistake), and a wild ride on a white horse that literally ran away with Stevie during the shoot. "I almost got killed riding that horse," she laughed. "He bolted into a grove of trees and the crew in the car driving alongside were screaming at me to jump off." The storyline was confused, the lighting was amateurish, and the video was spiked at enormous cost. "This can never come out," Stevie told her manager. "I don't care if it cost a million!" Irving Azoff told her she was an idiot. A new video had to be made quickly, so Jimmy found Jeffrey Hornaday, who had choreographed *Flashdance*, a sexy recent blockbuster, and now had ambitions to direct. He and Stevie came up with a simple performance video, intercut with a troupe of dancers. Stevie sang straight into the camera with big hair and clear eyes, her most intense gaze, wearing the "Stand Back shawl," translucent black tulle with appliquéd silver polka dots. The dancers performed flash, troopstyle coordinated movements behind principal dancer Brian Jeffries.

There was a meeting in the editing room a few days after the shoot for Jimmy, Paul Fishkin, and Danny Goldberg. Hornaday—twenty-six, long blond hair, self-absorbed—screened the edit, and to his annoyance Jimmy criticized it, took it apart, telling him what changes Stevie would want him to make. Hornaday was furious because he had a vision, *a concept,* of what the "Stand Back" video should look like. When Stevie arrived soon after and viewed the edit, she echoed exactly the same changes that Jimmy had suggested. Hornaday began contradicting her, trying to explain his higher ideals of cinema.

Jimmy the scrapper from Brooklyn jumped up and stuck his finger in Hornaday's face and told him, "There is *no* argument from you. This isn't a fuckin' movie. This is *Stevie's* record. This is *Stevie's* video. You do what *Stevie* wants."

Hornaday was shocked by this and said, "Fuck *you*, man." Jimmy punched him in the face and knocked him over. The others restrained the combatants as a tearful Stevie jumped in between them, and the fight was over. Danny later said that "when the changes Stevie wanted were made, Hornaday's choreography had given Stevie the modern effect the song needed" to get played on MTV.

*The Wild Heart* album jacket, with its three images of Stevie, was shot by Herbie Worthington after he and Stevie worked out that she wanted a triad of personae. (One wasn't enough.) The sad and crouching figure on the left with the shag perm is grieving Stevie. On the right, in a long gown, flowing curls, décolletage, and pouting lips is Stevie the Reigning Queen of Rock. The middle figure, wearing a hooded robe and making an esoteric gesture with her hands, is the transmigrated soul of her late friend Robin, always borne within Stevie's deepest being. The reverse bore an image of Stevie in Lori's arms, with Sharon just behind, and the dedication: *And . . . "Just like the white winged dove" / This music is dedicated to Robin—for her brave, wild heart / And to the gypsies—that remain*. And at the top of the *Wild Heart* jacket verso, Stevie wrote: *Don't blame it on me . . .* (The inner sleeve listed credits for hair design, hands, makeup, wardrobe, boots, and inspiration—Sulamith Wulfing.)

Stevie Nicks and her band spent the rest of 1983 on tour. The lineup was pretty much the same but for New York drummer Liberty DiVito replacing Russ Kunkel. (Jimmy Iovine wanted a more animated drummer for the visual effect, to get the audience's attention away from Stevie now and then.) Caroline Brooks joined the chorale. The two-hour shows (introduced by the Police's "Every Breath You Take") began with "Gold Dust Woman" and ranged through Fleetwood Mac songs (especially "Gypsy"), the hit singles from *Bella Donna* (and "Outside the Rain"), and introduced new standards like "If Anyone Falls" and the midset thriller "Stand Back." The tour's contract rider with local promoters specified a hundred hibiscus candles for back-stage, white drapes for Stevie's dressing room, five bottles of French cognac, six bottles of wine, five bottles of Russian vodka, and seven cases of beer.

The first show headlined the second US Festival on May 30, 1983, again in the California desert near San Bernardino, and went on through the mid-South and Northeast through early summer. In June and July they played almost every night in the Midwest. On July 15, after a sold-out show at the Met Center in Minneapolis, Stevie was "kidnapped" from the tour by Prince and taken to his studio for an all-night recording and jam session. Stevie was between relationships at that point and told friends she was a little disappointed when Prince showed her to her car just before dawn.

The tour had a month off in August, but Stevie had been creative while on the road, filling journals with paintings of sad angelic beings with downcast eyes surrounded by colorful robes and floral gestures. She also worked on poems and lyrics, some of which she put into demo form during that month. Some of these titles were realized later, others filed away. They include "Mirror Mirror," "Running Through the Garden," "Greta," "Listen to the Rain," "Thousand Days," and others. It was a highly productive period for Stevie, and the work had the additional benefit of keeping her mind off her considerable agonies. She spent a lot of time at home cosseted in her tribe of women, watching favorite movies like *The Hunger,* a vampire film with David Bowie and Catherine Deneuve; and *Risky Business,* with Tom Cruise dancing in his briefs. Stevie liked that movie so much she bought a 1979 Porsche 928 sports car like the one Cruise drove in the film.

Meanwhile "If Anyone Falls" was at #14 and the video was in heavy rotation on MTV. It was a shambolic affair that featured Sandy Stewart playing a gothic organ, Mick Fleetwood as a giant monk, lots of twirling and ballet (with dancing master Brad Jeffries lifting Lori aloft because Stevie was much heavier), shadows against the wall, and no story line or direction of any kind. Set décor included Stevie's blue lamp and the urn containing her grandmother's ashes. "I have to keep her with me at all times," Stevie explained. And later: "Videos in those days didn't have to make a lot of sense. This one didn't make any sense at all."

September 1983, back on tour. They performed a killer "Stand Back" on NBC's *Saturday Night Live,* with Brad Jeffries leaping into action during the guitar break and dancing a torrid solo around Stevie on the show's small stage. They mimed the new single "Nightbird" for the syndicated rock program *Solid Gold.* Tom Petty showed up for two shows at New York's Radio City Music Hall and sang "I Will Run to You" with Stevie. She sold out the Fabulous Forum in LA on October 2, but the press reviews in *LA Weekly* and *The Los Angeles Times* were less than kind. Stevie's weight was noted for the first time (and this would get worse). Her bathetic "dying swan" posturing and between-song patter were dismissed or ridiculed. "There's always a market for earnest silliness masquerading as poetic insight," opined the *Times's* critic.

Around this time, a bitter Lindsey Buckingham was doing press interviews for a new solo album, *Go Insane.* "I've seen Stevie's show," he said. "To me, it borders on being a lounge act." He went on to claim that she was cruising on Fleetwood Mac's laurels and that she owed it to the fans to try harder.

Lindsey, to another interviewer: "Stevie has never been very happy, and I don't think the success of her albums has made her any happier. In fact, it may have made her less happy. She's flexing some kind of emotional muscles that she feels she can flex—now that she's in a more powerful position. Her success is making her feel that she can pull things that she wouldn't have felt comfortable pulling before. She's venting something—loneliness, unhappiness, something." (*Go Insane* only got to #45 on the *Billboard* album chart when it was released in 1984.)

The Wild Heart Tour spent the rest of the month and most of November 1983 playing coliseums, civic centers, and university arenas all over the South. They finished with two shows in Iowa just before Thanksgiving. By then Stevie Nicks was exhausted, and crazy in love with her opening act, Joe Walsh.

## 5.6   The Joe Walsh Affair

It had begun early in September 1983, the start of the Wild Heart Tour's second leg. Irving Azoff wanted one of Front Line Management's clients to be the opening act, and he and Stevie picked Eagles guitarist Joe Walsh, who was promoting his solo album, *You Bought It—You Name It.* Walsh was thirty-six, a year older than Stevie. He was originally from Ohio, where he'd starred with local heroes the James Gang. He came to LA and was invited to join the Eagles when original guitarist Bernie Leadon left the band in 1975.

Joe Walsh was famously goofy, with a toothy, houndlike smile and long brown hair. When he walked into the room one expected him to start chewing the furniture, then the wallpaper. He was an all-star lead guitar player, well respected for musicianship, and so was able to hold the stage between the monumental egos of Eagles band mates Don Henley and Glenn Frey. Even Led Zeppelin's enigmatic Jimmy Page was Joe's friend, the two often dining together when Page was in Los Angeles, and gifting rare and vintage electric guitars to each other.

Stevie usually preferred to rest in her hotel suite after concerts, but in Dallas on September 5 she decided to change clothes and go down to the bar of the Mansions Hotel and greet her old acquaintance and new support act, Joe Walsh. She left her eyeglasses in the suite, figuring she'd be downstairs for just a moment anyway. But then Stevie was delayed.

Joe Walsh was sitting alone at the bar. "I walked across the room toward him," she recalled. "He held out his hands to me, and I walked straight into them." She sat on the bar stool next to him. "Two seconds later I crawled into his lap, and that was it." Cradled in Joe's strong arms as he smiled down at her, she could see a lot of hurt in his eyes. "I remember thinking, *I can never be far from this person again.*" It would be a few amorous hours before Stevie could see properly again, once she'd regained her spectacles.

As the tour moved on that month through Rhode Island, New York, and the Midwest, Stevie's affair with Joe Walsh was a closely held secret, played out in post-midnight backstairs journeys between hotel suites. Dennis Dunstan would escort Stevie between floors, then wait for the call to bring her back. He'd asked some of Joe's road crew about

Joe and was told Walsh was on his third marriage. He mentioned this to Stevie, to make sure she knew, and she—echoing Dennis's Australian lingo—told him, "No worries, mate." The tour's cocaine specialists were also aware that demand had made a dramatic jump; Stevie and Joe seemed almost in competition to see who could snort the most Andean alkaloid without dying.

Stevie was surprised at the passion she felt for Joe. "Why do you love somebody?" she asked, years later. "Why do you love them so much that when they walk in the room your heart jumps out of your chest? I don't know, but I fell in love with Joe at first sight from across the room. It went from 1983 to 1986. It's crazy, isn't it?"

The affair's most ardent passion—Stevie's compassion for Joe—stemmed from a journey after a concert in Denver, Colorado, on September 19. Stevie had been grousing about some tour conditions, and Joe asked her to go for a ride with him. His tour manager got him a rented Jeep and Joe whisked Stevie off to Boulder, a couple hours away. (This made Stevie's people, especially Dennis Dunstan, very nervous. Joe Walsh was a loopy space cadet. Could he be trusted to get her back safely? Dennis had his doubts, but his boss was determined to be alone with Joe.)

As a light autumn snow began to fall in the foothills of the Rocky Mountains, Joe told Stevie about the little girl he'd had with his second wife. Her name was Emma; in 1974, when she was three years old, she had been killed in a road accident as his wife was taking her to preschool. Stevie: "And he drove me to this park [North Boulder Park], and I knew he was going to show me something that was going to freak me out, because I was already totally upset by the time we got to Boulder. We walked across the park, and there was this little silvery drinking fountain. A plaque nearby read: TO EMMA KRISTIN FOR ALL THOSE WHO AREN'T BIG ENOUGH TO GET A DRINK.

Joe explained that he used to bring Emma to this park, her favorite place to play, but she was too small to reach the park's drinking fountain, and this was his tribute to his poor child. As they stood by the fountain, Stevie was weeping, her head on Joe's shoulder, and he was crying, too. It was still snowing. After a while in the park, they drove back to Denver in silence. Michael Jackson's "Thriller" was on the radio.

There was a short break in the tour, and Stevie wanted to see her mother and write in her house near Phoenix. She was in love with Joe Walsh and so deeply felt his loss. Hadn't she, herself, just lost a child—baby Matthew—Robin's son? When she walked into her big house in Paradise Valley, she lit some candles, sat at her piano, and wrote most of "Has Anyone Ever Written Anything for You," one of her most trenchant songs, in about five minutes. It was the only way she could respond to the suffering to which she'd been exposed. The song was ostensibly about Joe Walsh, but it was also about herself.

Stevie was also at home for a business meeting. She had invested in a concert promotion business with her father and his brother Gene. Jess Nicks was said to have been dumbfounded by the money his daughter was making and had wanted to get into the business for some time; he'd even gone on the Bella Donna Tour as an observer. But he was dismayed by some of the ways things were run. He began to complain, and was gently advised to butt out. "So he went home," Stevie commented later.

Stevie put up the money and her father and uncle bought (or leased) an amphitheater (a "shed" in concert parlance) called Compton Terrace in some scrubland near Tempe, Arizona, and began putting on rock shows. Aerosmith played Compton Terrace, also Bruce Springsteen. Stevie took a night off from her tour and did a free benefit there for the American Heart Association, a charity her father favored. Joe Walsh and Kenny Loggins played for free as well. (The Compton Terrace Amphitheater was judged by the bands and crews that played there to be a dump, with bad acoustics, poor sightlines, and inadequate facilities for both artists and their audiences. It has since been demolished.)

Over the years, Stevie has often forcefully stated that, for her, Joe Walsh was The One. "We were probably the perfect, complete, crazy pair," she said. "He was the one I would have married, and that I would probably have changed my life around for . . . a little bit, anyway. Not a lot. But he wouldn't have changed his life either."

During the rest of that tour, she tried to look after crazy Joe, buying him clothes, making sure he got what he needed because opening acts—even if you were in the Eagles—were often bullied or neglected by the promoters and the headliner's crew. "I *loved* him," she told an interviewer later. "It was a great secret, which made it even better." To another: "I really looked after him, and that's what probably scared Joe the most. I was *too* in tune with him, and he was so out-of-tune—*with everything!*"

But the drugs got in the way. Rock cocaine was a powerful energizer that opened up grand vistas of production and helped make everything happen. Stevie: "We were busy superstars, and we—everyone—were doing way too much drugs. We [her and Joe] were really, seriously drug addicts. We were a couple on the way to hell."

The biggest problem Stevie had with Joe was getting him to pay attention to her. He seemed distracted when they were together, always playing with some gadget that he'd just bought. The first time she visited him at home, the first thing he showed her was his music room, which was actually a computer lab. With all the metal cases, dials, and winking lights, she thought it looked like the spaceship from *The Jetsons*. Joe had some new gear, "samplers" that would soon replace the programmable OBX-A and DMX drum machines and the postmodern synthesizers that had featured on Stevie's records. Joe wanted to demonstrate the future of electro pop. He told her to play a melody on a sampler's keyboard; he then turned a knob and she heard the tune—fully orchestrated. Stevie: "I looked at him and said, 'So—we've all just been replaced by . . . whatever this is?'"

Wrong thing to say to a gear head. Joe Walsh ignored her for the rest of the day, lost in the novelty of his samplers. Stevie was mortified. Thirty years later, Stevie told England's *Mojo* magazine that she has distrusted computers ever since.

At least she had someone to write about besides Lindsey, and the affair with Joe Walsh certainly gave her plenty of first-rate cad-lover material over the course of three years, during which Stevie said she mostly worked on songs and waited by the phone in case Joe called her, which he rarely did. She also started eating and gaining weight. A friend told her she was "stuffing her feelings," using food as an antidepressant, but she said she didn't care. Toward the end of the Wild Heart Tour, Joe Walsh's opening set was cut down to half an hour, so if there was a short break in the tour Joe and his band would play a solo show—two hours of Eagles songs and roadhouse rock. After one of these in the Midwest, some local journalists were taken backstage for a meet-and-greet. Also waiting for Joe in the hospitality room, to their amazement, was Stevie Nicks. When Joe came out, he completely ignored Stevie, who cut herself a hefty slice of a chocolate cream pie that was laid out on the buffet. The scribes then watched in disbelief as Stevie proceeded to eat the entire gooey dessert, by herself, over the course of an hour.

Much later, Stevie was talking with collaborator Sheryl Crow about this period, and speaking of Joe Walsh, she recalled, "I look back at all the men in my life, and there was only one that I can honestly say I could truly have lived with every day for the rest of my life, because there was respect and we loved to do the same things. I was very content with him all the time. That's only happened once in my life. The point is, it can happen—this kind of love. This man, if he'd asked me to marry him, I would have."

To *People* magazine: "There was nothing more important than Joe Walsh—not my music, not my songs, not anything. He was the great, great love of my life."

They broke up in the middle of 1986, almost in public. Joe had been out on tour, and she was working in the studio with Waddy. Joe came over, got high, and was entertaining the studio crew while Stevie patiently waited for some time with him. Finally she got tired of Joe ignoring her, told him she was leaving, and asked him to come with her. Joe said, "Oh, I meant to tell you—I can't see you—I'm leaving tomorrow to go back on the road."

Stevie looked at him for a moment and muttered, "I don't think this is working." As she headed for the exit, Joe called after her, "If you walk out that door, you cease to exist." She kept going. (And later used his line in a song.) The next day Joe Walsh flew to Australia, having left a message for Stevie (through their management): she was not to follow him or even try to contact him. Their thing was over. Joe went to the far side of the world "to get away from me, basically," Stevie said. "He thought—or so I'm told—that one of us was going to die, and the other person would not be able to save them. And I did think I was going to die—absolutely."

"It nearly killed me," she told another interviewer. "We had to break up, or we thought we'd die. We were just too excessive. But there was no closure. It took me years to get over it—if I ever did. It's very sad, but at least we survived."

Twenty years later, in 2007, Stevie was still in love with Joe Walsh. "There was no other man in the world for me," she told London's *Telegraph* newspaper. "And it's the same today, even though Joe is married and has two sons. He met someone in rehab and got married. And I think he's happy."

CHAPTER 6

## 6.1 Battle of the Dragon

Stevie Nicks spent most of 1984 working and worrying about her third solo album, a crucial project for her long-term career whose working title was the ultrawitchy *Mirror Mirror*. She started the record with Jimmy Iovine, but when Iovine realized that his sometime girlfriend had fallen for totally uncool Joe Walsh (most everyone in New York hated the Eagles), their personal relationship was finished. Nevertheless, they worked on some of the new music she had, mostly "Battle of the Dragon," "Reconsider Me," "Violet and Blue," and "Love Is Like a River." They reworked "Sorcerer," originally "Lady from the Mountains," and her record label placed it on the *Streets of Fire* movie soundtrack in mid-1984. Then Stevie decided she hated all the new music they'd recorded. "It didn't sound right," she said. "I can't tell you why; it just didn't sound right." She decided to warehouse these songs and start over.

Jimmy Iovine called Tom Petty at home in Encino and asked about a new song for Stevie. Petty suggested that Iovine call the guy from the Eurythmics. This was the now broken-up English synth-pop band, all the rage on MTV, consisting of Scots singer Annie Lennox and Dave Stewart, originally from Sunderland in the far north of Britain. Dave Stewart and Annie Lennox had been a power couple like Stevie and Lindsey, but their massive success had split them up. Dave Stewart moved to Los Angeles, bought a big old Cadillac, and started throwing great parties at a rented house in the Hollywood Hills. Dave was a bluff, extremely smart, and funny guy. He charmed everyone and was a really talented musician, arranger, and producer. Jimmy listened to the Eurythmics' big hit, "Sweet Dreams (Are Made of This)," and knew that Dave Stewart could write with Stevie.

Stewart came to see Stevie one evening at her house. She asked him about the breakup with Annie Lennox, and he ended up staying the night. Stevie seemed surprised to see him in her bed the next afternoon. To him, she looked dazed, otherworldly, out of it. She told him not to come back to the house, that she'd see him at the studio later. (Decades later, when they were working together again, Stewart reminded Stevie that they'd once made love. No, she answered, they'd done it twice.)

Dave Stewart started working with Stevie and Jimmy. He had a drum program they were working on, without much success. Stewart called Tom Petty at home and invited him to the studio, just to hang out and lend his ears. Petty, glad to get out of the house, agreed. He arrived at the studio around two o'clock in the morning.

Stevie: "Tom liked what we were working on. I was writing, madly. I had my little book. I was writing, writing. But it was five in the morning and I was really tired." Stevie went home, and Dave and Jimmy worked all morning, producing a track that Dave called "Don't Come Around Here No More"—based on Stevie's order not to come back to her house after their night together. Tom sang on the track as a guide vocal: this was meant, after all, to be a Stevie Nicks song.

Stevie: "When I got back the next day at three in the afternoon, the whole song was written. And not only it was written—it was spectacular. Dave was standing there saying to me, 'Well, there it is . . . it's really, really good, and now you can go out and *you* can sing it.' [But] Tom had done a great vocal—a *great* vocal. I just looked at them and said, *I'm going to top that? Really?* I got up, thanked Dave, thanked Tom, fired Jimmy, and left. That all went down in about five minutes."

"Don't Come Around Here No More" would be a big hit single for Tom Petty and the Heartbreakers. (In the psychedelic video produced for MTV, Petty famously played the Mad Hatter from *Alice in Wonderland*.) It was a good payback for Stevie's theft of "Stop Draggin' My Heart Around."

After Jimmy Iovine left, Stevie got a case of writer's block and was advised to take some time off. Mick Fleetwood called to ask if she would play some shows with a moribund Fleetwood Mac to help him stave off imminent bankruptcy. Stevie had heard Mick was in trouble, with rumors of bounced checks and canceled credit cards, and his house in Malibu was facing foreclosure. The rumor was that he'd lost eight million dollars, and that most of it had gone up his nose. Stevie wanted to help Mick, but her representatives had to tell him, because she wasn't taking his calls, that she was in no shape to play shows with Fleetwood Mac that year, or the next.

Stevie needed inspiration. Her assistant Rebecca Alvarez reached out to Sandy Stewart in Texas, but for unknown reasons (reportedly related to songwriting credits on *The Wild Heart*) Sandy declined to make herself available. Stevie did find some magic in Don Henley's new album *Building the Perfect Beast*, chock full of great songs, contemporary LA ennui, and an intelligent, world-weary sensibility. The hit single "Boys of Summer" was based on a track that Henley had got from Heartbreakers guitarist Mike Campbell, and Stevie took notice of this for some future project.

Around this time, Stevie went to see a mystic and had a "life reading," which purported to reveal a person's previous life incarnations. She took this sort of thing very seriously and was moved by what was revealed to her. Some of it was interesting. She'd been a high priestess in ancient Egypt, living in a stone temple. She'd been a famous concert pianist. On the other hand, she'd been a German "who went through some of the atrocities. I *know* I experienced it. Every time I go to Germany, I feel it." She was also told that the life she was living now would be her last.

Beginning in November 1984, suffering from various ailments and thinking of herself as a captive spirit chained to a recording contract, Stevie resumed work on her music, using other collaborators to help her assemble enough songs to fill out an album that only had two strong songs. The first of these was "I Can't Wait," which began as a backing track sent to her by a friend from her teen years called Rick Nowels. He'd been a friend of Robin Snyder's younger brother, and now worked on commercial jingles in Los Angeles. Jimmy Iovine heard the tape of the backing track he'd sent to Stevie, and thought it might work on radio and the dance floor. It was a typically "eighties" track informed by machines rather than instruments. Computer rhythms underlay skittering Oberheim 8, Prophet, and Emulator II synthesizers. Stevie sings the impatient lyrics—Joe Walsh *always* kept her waiting—in a cracked and wasted voice, the best she could offer at the time. All this was overlaid by lashings of glistening glockenspiel, for that Springsteen High School marching–band feel so popular in those times.

The other strong track they had was "Talk to Me," written by Chas Sanford, an English producer who had cowritten John Waite's massive hit "Missing You." "Talk to Me" was basically the same song, but kind of sung like video star Cyndi Lauper. The song had come through Jimmy, who rightly thought it could be a hit for Stevie. The backing track was recorded in France and featured Parisian jazz master Barney Wilens playing the saxophone solo. Again the lyrics were a message to Joe Walsh: "You can set your secrets free, baby." While recording the vocal track, Stevie was having trouble with the lyrics, trying multiple times and failing to get them to scan with the backing track. (This often happened when she was singing words written by someone else.) Also working in the studio that night was the great LA session drummer Jim Keltner. Stevie spoke with him, told him of her troubles, and he said to her, "Come on, try it again. I'll be your audience." Reassured by Keltner's presence and encouragement, Stevie nailed it on the second try. This worked out so well that "Talk to Me" would become one of Stevie's most popular, and requested, songs: an expression of her sympathetic attitude toward her fans.

Another fan favorite is "Has Anyone Ever Written Anything for You?" By the time in 1985 that they were working on this track, Jimmy Iovine was gone, so Stevie turned in desperation to her old producer, Keith Olsen—who happened to be working with Joe Walsh on a solo album at the time. Stevie begged both Joe and Olsen, and Joe agreed to step aside for her—for a week. They worked at Olsen's new studio, designed to produce digital music for the new compact disc format that was replacing the old analog record. Unfortunately, Olsen had built his studio right next to Sound City, taking business from his old friends and generally drawing hatred from them. Olsen was also upset because Stevie was so high on cocaine that she couldn't sing in tune. One night he got so angry that he ordered her out of the studio and told her to come back sober, or don't come back. When the song was finished, Olsen left the project, and their old friendship never recovered.

Keith Olsen had adapted her piano demo for "Has Anyone" (written in Phoenix in early Joe Walsh days) and helped with the verses. The synthetic orchestral background was produced by Rick Nowels. Olsen also cowrote "No Spoken Word," the only track on *Rock a Little* that sounds like a real Stevie Nicks song.

The title track, a reggae-flavored tune sung in Stevie's most frail register, was strung together from fragments, somehow congealing like ingredients in a murky soup. "Time to rock a little," her tag-along father had urged her when she needed to be onstage during the Wild Heart Tour. Using her then-current hotel pseudonym, Jess Nicks would say, "Go ahead, Lily—time to rock a little."

The album's remaining tracks were mostly filler and lesser songs, unusual for a Stevie Nicks record, recorded by studio pros and informed by production styles similar to that of Michael Jackson, the Police, Duran Duran, and other MTV stars. These included forgettable numbers like "Sister Honey," written with guitarist Les Dudek; "I Sing for the Things," another torn-up ballad; "Imperial Hotel," a generic rock song with Stevie's lyrics applied to a Mike Campbell backing track (for the first time) by Jimmy Iovine; "Some Become Strangers"; "The Nightmare," written with her brother Chris; and "If I Were You," another collaboration with Rick Nowels.

Three good songs were recorded at this time but remained unreleased. One session produced "Are You Mine," a duet with the young rockabilly star Billy Burnette, on a song first taught to her by her grandfather when Stevie was about five years old. "Reconsider Me" was a rocker by Warren Zevon that Jimmy Iovine brought to her late in the 1985 sessions, which they recorded with Don Henley's vocals and a full band; and which she then left off *Rock a Little* mostly because she and Jimmy were fighting again. (He stayed mad at her for a long time about this.) Finally there was "One More Big Time Rock and Roll Star," a sarcastic and angry song about Joe, who played a symphonic guitar solo for her bitter song that evoked candles and crystals, an abandoned woman, and the wistful observation, "I was anyone's fantasy." The track was good enough that it was on the B-side of "Talk to Me" when the first single from *Rock a Little* hit the market in late October 1985.

MTV was quick to play the new videos for "Talk to Me" and the album's second single, "I Can't Wait." These were choreographed, troop-style dances, directed by Marty Callner, starring Stevie and her girls along with dancer Brad Jeffries and her brother Chris. (Originally Stevie's management wanted her to work with a different director, Bob Giraldi, who had made the earliest Michael Jackson clips. Giraldi came to Stevie's house, as he later recalled: "I had a meeting with Stevie Nicks where we sat on her bed. I've never seen a woman that stoned in my life. She was so wasted, we couldn't even communicate."

Marty Callner set "Talk to Me" in a stark, claustrophobic setting, like a rehab in an office park. Cut to Stevie and her crew, walking to the beat with a simple little back step. "I Can't Wait" had them climbing and descending a precariously steep staircase, which she almost fell down. Then she was on a treadmill, then in a claustrophobic trap, pounding on enclosing walls to get out. Both (highly successful) videos radiated an unusual (for MTV) anxiety and lack of contact with the viewer.

Later Stevie had her own point of view: " 'I Can't Wait' is one of my favorite songs, and it became a famous video. But now I look at that video, I look at my eyes, and I say to myself, *Could you have laid off the pot, the coke, and the tequila for three days so you could have looked a little better? Because your eyes look like they're swimming.* It just makes me want to go back into that video and stab myself."

## 6.2   The Survivor

Late 1985. *Rock a Little*, which had cost Stevie Nicks almost a million dollars to make, was released for the holiday market. The album sold well in both vinyl and CD formats, if not as well as Stevie's first two solo albums. *Rock a Little* got to #12 on the *Billboard* album chart, while the first single, "Talk to Me," got major national airplay and rose to #4. The reviews were mixed but mostly favorable, except for her image on the album jacket, a heavily retouched photo of Stevie in whiteface makeup and wearing a layered black dress and a cloche hat. (This had been shot in London by fashion photographer Tony McGee. The reverse of the sleeve had a downcast, spectral portrait of Stevie by Herbie Worthington.) The album jacket also featured a crystal ball supported by a pair of bronze dragons, and an off-the-wall dedication to all those who had survived the Vietnam War. One reviewer observed that Stevie—in her music and her presentation— had now come through a portal into mainstream, corporate rock, a move away from quirky, semi-gnarly Fleetwood Mac and the thematic unity of her first two records. Now thirty-seven, Stevie Nicks was seen by some as another cog in a megacorporation that viewed music as "product" and churned out soulless pablum for mass consumption on schedule. Sometimes Stevie Nicks must have wondered if she felt that way herself.

Now scheduling became a problem. Stevie's management team at Front Line didn't quite know what to do with her. Stevie preferred to tour in the American summer, which was months away. Then she announced that she was going on Bob Dylan's Australian tour, which began in late February 1986. Dylan was using the Heartbreakers as his band after Tom Petty opened. But Petty had started having problems with his wife, Jane, and was saying he wasn't going on tour without her. One evening Stevie was at their house in Encino and told Petty he was crazy to even think about canceling. "I told him, *Oh yes, you are going. You can't cancel on Bob Fucking Dylan.*" He told her he was going through a rough time and needed to be with Jane, who didn't want to go because she was having mental problems, and also she had more freedom to be herself when Tom was away on tour. Acting as a go-between, Stevie negotiated a settlement where she would go to Australia and look after Tom. They wouldn't be a couple, she assured Jane (who didn't seem to care). Stevie would be more like Tom's big sister, his sidekick. That's the way it worked out in the end. Stevie, her assistant Rebecca Alvarez, and a big wheeled wardrobe case full of stage clothes flew to Wellington, New Zealand, for the first show of Bob Dylan's True Confessions Tour on February 5, 1986.

For the next three weeks, Stevie and Rebecca looked after Tom,

Stevie haunting Lindsey as Fleetwood Mac is inducted into the Rock & Roll Hall of Fame in 1998. (*Photograph by Timothy A. Clary/AFP/Getty Images*)

Stevie with producer Jimmy Iovine in 1983. (*Michael Ochs Archives*)

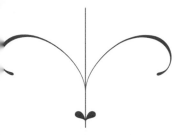

Stevie with Don Henley in 2002. (*Photograph by Ray Mickshaw*)

Stevie and her mother Barbara at the 1998 Grammy Awards.
(*Photograph by Ron Galella*)

Singing "Sara" with Lindsey on the Tusk Tour in 1980. (*Photograph by Richard E. Aaron*)

Stevie singing on New Year's Day, 1990.
(*Photograph by Mick Hutson*)

Stevie and Taylor Swift, one of many younger female stars who say they were inspired by Stevie from childhood. (*Photograph by Kevin Mazur*)

Stevie with her husband
Kim Anderson, March 1983.
(*Photograph by Ron Galella*)

Fleetwood Mac in 1982, the *Mirage* band. (*Photograph by David Montgomery*)

Rhiannon comes alive in 1975.
(*Photograph by Fin Costello*)

There are fan websites dedicated to Stevie's performing shawls. This dark shawl was worn in 2012 at an AIDS charity concert in New York. (*Photograph by Kevin Mazur*)

This golden shawl was worn at a charity gala in Los Angeles in 2012. (*Photograph by Jason Merritt*)

The Fairy Godmother of Rock in 2013. (*Photograph by Danny Clinch*)

Stevie and Mick Fleetwood on Broadway in 2015. (*Photograph by Walter McBride*)

Stevie with her long-time music director Waddy Wachtel performing on CBS's *The Late Late Show with James Corden* in October, 2016. (*CBS Photo Archive*)

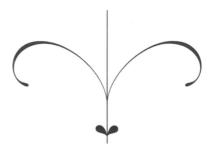

Stevie Nicks at the microphone during a tribute to Tom Petty, Los Angeles, February 2017. (*Photograph by Michael Kovac*)

Stevie and Tom Petty, February 2017. (*Photograph by Lester Cohen*)

kept him on track, got him to the gigs on time, and then helped him feel like going onstage. Stevie was always in full wardrobe, hair, and makeup as she stood in the wings and watched the concerts. She sometimes sang with Dylan's backup singers—three black women— as they were warming up before the shows. (This tour had happened so fast for Stevie that they didn't have time to get her work permits for New Zealand and Australia. She didn't even have a valid passport when she decided to go, and they had to really scramble to get her on the plane.) One night Stevie saw Dylan waving her onstage to sing with him, and all she could do was wave back because she didn't have papers. But she was a hoot at the hotel bar afterward, when Ben Tench took over the piano and led a late-hours oldies sing-along with her and Dylan and Tom and their backup singers.

As the tour progressed and the shows got better, everyone was glad to have Stevie Nicks on the tour. Even the enigmatic Dylan was smiling when he saw her at the gigs, all dolled up. "I tend to get dressed up every single night," she said, "so that everyone knows that when I walk in the room, this is serious—even if I'm ten pounds overweight. If I'm dressed up and I look pretty, everybody in that room says, 'Wow! She must have really thought she was going somewhere.'"

"Having Stevie along was very good for me," Petty later told his biographer. "It changed the channel. Stevie was lighthearted, and she so loved music. She figured out before I did that we had a blend as singers. She'd come over and we'd sing old songs, and it could sound so good. She also knew more than most that I was in a delicate mental spot."

It was also a creative time for her. Stevie wrote "Whole Lotta Trouble," one of her best songs in years, with Mike Campbell on a day off.

The tour's best moments were the four nights in Sydney, Australia's biggest city. On the second night, Stevie could no longer stand by, waiting in the wings, all dressed up and no place to sing. They were singing the show's first encore, "Blowin' in the Wind" (which she used to sing with her folk group, the Changin' Times, in junior high school). Stevie walked on to sing but realized the only standing microphone on the stage was Dylan's. So she climbed on the drum riser and sang backup vocals using drummer Stan Lynch's microphone for two songs. Finally she was invited to center stage to join Dylan and Tom for the finale, "Knockin' on Heaven's Door."

After the concert, Stevie was threatened by a low-key but firm representative from the Australian authorities for working without a permit. Stevie countered that she wasn't working, because she wasn't being paid, but it didn't matter. Stevie was told if she got onstage again while a guest of the tour, she would never sing professionally in Australia again.

Like many couples, platonic or romantic, Stevie and Tom had their disagreements, often over music, during late, postconcert conversations. "She got really mad at me one night in Australia," he remembered. They were talking about Fleetwood Mac, and Petty said something dismissive, like: "Yeah, but the Heartbreakers are a *rock & roll* band."

Stevie took real offense at this. What was Fleetwood Mac? *"I'm* in a rock & roll band," she insisted. "Not really," Petty advised, twisting the knife. To Petty, Fleetwood Mac was a corporate English group pedaling soft rock music to the ladies, much different from a rock & roll band that could play a high school prom. Stevie was mad now, and she spat, "How *dare* you say that to me?"

Petty pushed on. "And this long debate ensued about how you get those credentials. And I love that band, have the greatest respect for Lindsey and Mick, but I didn't see them as a rock & roll band. I thought her journey was different than mine. I didn't always agree with her musical taste, and she didn't always agree with mine. My frustration with her was, 'You need somebody to remind you what you're capable of. You get too easily distracted by bullshitters that want to make a hit. I don't know why you're doing all this synthesizer rock.'" This was a stab at *Rock a Little,* which Stevie should have been promoting at home, especially her new hit single "I Can't Wait," instead of pretending to be Tom Petty's road wife on the other side of the planet.

There was a bit of a furor over this issue in the Los Angeles and New York offices of Modern Records. "I Can't Wait" was a Top 20 single in America and the video was in constant rotation on MTV. A twelve-inch single, released with three dance floor remixes, was selling well and especially popular at gay discos; to her amazement, an aging Stevie was becoming an icon of female sympathy for homosexual men under threat from the AIDS epidemic of the eighties. Also wanting Stevie was comedian David Letterman, host of NBC television's *Late Night* program. *Letterman* repeatedly showed clips of Stevie's modest cleavage (edited from her videos) and demanded she come to New York and sing "I Can't Wait" with the show's house band. Stevie: "But I was gone, out of touch with the world, and it got into the papers that I'd disappeared. I'm in Australia with Tom Petty and Bob Dylan, having a great time—*oblivious*. This is how important Tom Petty and the Heartbreakers are to me. I was completely willing to get in the way of my own single."

Then Irving Azoff managed to reach Stevie on the phone and literally ordered her to come home. Stevie did as she was told, flew to New York, and sang "I Can't Wait" on Letterman's show, which had its best ratings of the year. From then on, Stevie could count on David Letterman's crush on her when she needed to promote a new album.

No one was happier when Stevie came home than the cocaine purveyors who counted on her, their best customer—ever. Less happy was her musical director Waddy Wachtel when Stevie came to the first band rehearsals for the Rock a Little Tour in the summer of 1986. Stevie looked wasted and haggard without her stage makeup, and her scratchy voice needed work. She was going on the road with a six-piece group anchored by the New York drummer Rick Marotta, who often worked with Carly Simon and other lady singers. Bobbye Hall on percussion was the only holdover from the old band; Elisecia Wright, a powerful black singer from the Dylan/Petty tour, augmented Lori and Sharon's vocals. Margi Kent had fabricated some beautiful new shawls and costumes: a black dress and shawl for "Talk to Me," set off by a red trailing scarf; a crimson shawl for "I Need to Know"; a white spangled wrap for "Beauty and the Beast"; a black and golden shawl for "Stand Back."

Stevie got her demon down far enough to play some good concerts that summer. Others were less than enchanted. Stevie could seem obviously intoxicated, slurring her words, dancing so close to the edge of the stage that she fell a couple of times, always caught by Dennis

Dunstan, who had to carefully shadow Stevie from the security pit in front of the stage so she didn't hurt herself. (Another of Dennis's duties was helping to put Stevie to bed, since she had to sleep in an awkward sitting position due to both a back problem and an acid reflux condition.) Her road crew joked that you could drive the equipment truck through the hole in her nose. They'd heard the rampant rumors about Stevie's drugs back in LA: that her face was falling off; that she was absorbing cocaine in unorthodox applications—anally, or through her vagina.

The last concert was in early September at the Red Rocks Amphitheater at the foot of the Rocky Mountains near Denver, Colorado. Mick Fleetwood joined the band on percussion and Peter Frampton played a little guitar as well. Mick was alarmed by how much Stevie was drinking and snorting and smoking so she could perform. He'd seen a couple of her shows and was scared that her increasingly dizzying spins would propel her off the stage. Before the Red Rocks concert, he managed to take her aside.

"I said to her, 'Stevie, you're gonna hurt yourself. You've got to work on getting away from being so high while you're on stage.' And she cried, and said, 'Oh Mick—I know it. I don't want to be like this. I don't want to need this stuff so much. I'm going to do something about it.'"

This concert was filmed by director Marty Callner for video release the following year. The set blended Stevie's older songs—"Dreams," "Sisters of the Moon"—with mostly new material, especially "Stand Back" and "Talk to Me." During "Beauty and the Beast" Stevie looked over at Mick and sang, "I've changed, baby / Or at least I'm *trying* to change." She delivered "Has Anyone Ever Written" with a bathos that seemed genuine, and the audience responded with whoops of appreciation and affection for her. The concert ended with an epic "Edge of Seventeen," with fresh blooms on the microphone stand and Stevie twirling in a creamy fringed shawl and lacey half-gloves, singing in crazy tongues, bringing down the house before the nightly ritual of The Walk, just as it started to rain.

Now it was cold and everyone went home except Stevie, who had her makeup reapplied and stayed to shoot some grueling hours of close-ups and inserts for the commercial video. She was relieved and grateful to see that Mick had stayed behind to keep her company on the now empty Red Rocks stage. He'd wanted to leave with the rest of them but stayed when he saw how alone and fragile his beloved Stevie looked, with more work to finish that night: she seemed to him ghostlike, a distant glimmer of her former self, on the fugitive threshold of the drugs that barely sustained her.

After this, the Rock a Little Tour moved on to Australia. With no cocaine, Stevie began to drink more, and she fell off the stage twice.

Back in Pacific Palisades later that month, the people closest to Stevie—friends, musicians, management—staged an intervention at her house, and she was reluctantly persuaded that her very life was in danger, that her entire face was at risk from her perforated nasal septum and a possibly subsequent brain hemorrhage, and that she must enter a detox and rehab unit immediately. Within a few days, she checked into the Betty Ford Center, the famous rehabilitation clinic in Rancho Mirage, California, under her married name.

It seemed clear to everyone that Stevie wouldn't be working for some time. Dennis Dunstan left Stevie's employ and went to work for Mick Fleetwood, who was trying to re-form Fleetwood Mac, confident that Stevie would recover and join the Mac for another big payday. Waddy would join the X-Pensive Winos, Keith Richards's solo band. Sharon and Lori sang backing vocals for Mick Jagger and others. Irving Azoff was out because Stevie hadn't liked being forced into treatment, even though she admitted it was the right thing for her. Danny Goldberg sold his share of Modern Records and later went on to become president of Warner Bros. and other major labels. Modern released "Has Anyone Ever Written Anything for You" as a single and it bombed, only reaching #60 in America.

The fifty-seven-minute video *Stevie Nicks Live at Red Rocks* was released early in 1987, heavily doctored with reshot close-ups, cut-ins, and overdubbed new vocals. The VHS tape sold well, and today its DVD edition provides stark visual evidence of an old Welsh witch hitting the very bottom of her career.

## 6.3   Too Special for Words

"Sara Anderson" checked into the Betty Ford Center, hardly knowing herself. She sat through an orientation session in a daze. Someone explained that Betty Ford was the wife of former President Gerald Ford. She was a longtime alcoholic and Valium addict who wound up in a naval hospital after hitting bottom because there was nowhere else for her, other than private clinics that could wean people off drugs and drink but offered little or no help afterward. In 1982 Mrs. Ford and some doctors founded the Betty Ford Center, where Stevie Nicks now was surrounded by people like herself: helpless addicts in need of a fix and redemption. The current poster children of the mid-eighties rock star sobriety movement were Aerosmith, the famous band from Boston, who were a year into recovery from addiction to everything, and now making chart-topping singles and albums after a decade of sludge and despair. Look, the drug counselors told their resistant clients, if those toxic junkies in Aerosmith can get sober and create again, then anybody can got sober and get their lives back.

After the intake procedures, someone dressed like a nurse helped Stevie make her way to the spartan quarters where she would spend the next twenty-eight nights. The nurse opened the door for her and said, "Welcome to the room, Sara."

"Betty Ford was not easy," Stevie later recalled. "I called it the Betty Ford Boot Camp." Stevie soon found herself swabbing floors with a mop and cleaning bathrooms alongside tired businessmen, desperate housewives, sick rich kids, some athletes, and one of James Taylor's backup singers. No one got preferential treatment. (Stevie didn't even mind cleaning since she used to do it professionally.) Everyone had to do chores in housekeeping, or buildings and grounds. "It's what I imagine it's like to be in the army," she remembered. "There's four dorms, twenty people in each dorm. Everyone does the dishes, makes the coffee, vacuums the carpet. And it was tough. But two weeks in, you start to think, *Oh my God, I'm getting better*—because when you first get to Betty Ford they basically tell you that you're dying. And that's not an easy thing to hear."

In the group meetings, Stevie was frank about what she had done with cocaine. "You could put a big gold ring through my [nasal] septum," she said later. "It affected my eyes, my sinuses. It was a lot of fun for a long time because we didn't know it was bad. But eventually it gets hold of you, and all you can think about is where your next line is coming from.

"All of us were drugs addicts," she explained. "But there was a point where I was the worst drug addict. I was a girl, I was fragile, and I was doing a lot of coke and I was in danger of brain damage."

Later she was asked about the persistent rumors that she was being administered cocaine anally. "Well, it's just not true," she insisted. "I'm a lady, and I'd never do such a thing. But I have to say, when I heard that rumor, it made me decide, *OK! Enough!* I checked into the Betty Ford Center soon after."

Stevie shared a room with a fifty-five-year-old alcoholic woman whose snoring kept Stevie awake at night. One morning the alarm went off at seven o'clock. It was Stevie's turn to swab down her dorm's interior patio. She quietly dressed, folding her fading blond curls behind the shawl over her shoulders. She was glad she'd packed her brown suede platform boots, so her feet wouldn't get wet in the desert's morning chill. At seven thirty she slopped her string mop into her bucket and got to work.

Back in her room, she applied some lipstick, rouge, and kohl to a face she barely recognized. During the day she had psychotherapy, group therapy, and attended lectures. Lunch was the major meal of the day, a bountiful buffet surpassing even the legendary uneaten backstage repasts at Fleetwood Mac concerts. Afterward was the daily walk around the duck pond. Later she had tea with her new gang: three millionaire drunks from Texas, two oilmen and a cattle tycoon, old guys in their sixties with rheumy eyes and rough, course hands from working the ranch and the oil patch. She enlisted them to help her distribute the dozens of bouquets, plants, cacti, and flowers that started arriving daily at Betty Ford from friends and fans since word got out that Stevie was at the clinic. The four of them would fan out to the dorms and give the stuff to patients who were alone and far from home.

No one at Betty Ford had ever seen such an outpouring of gifts for a patient. Some of the staff blamed Stevie for leaking her whereabouts to the media; they preferred to keep treatment confidential. There was one mean nurse who seemed to dislike Stevie; she would say to her, when she was gathering up her horde of flowers and stuffed animals: "Oh my, aren't you just *too special* for words?"

But it didn't matter. Four weeks after she arrived, Stevie Nicks left Betty Ford and went home to Phoenix, sober. Her coke dealers were astounded that their best client had given up their product. But everyone around Stevie (except her mother) was certain she would relapse. It was just a question, they were sure, of when. But it didn't happen.

Three months passed, and it was now early in 1987. She was still off the devil's dandruff, as Dennis Dunstan used to say. Dennis was now managing the career of Mick Fleetwood, who was desperate to get out of bankruptcy and seemed to be succeeding in putting Fleetwood Mac back together for another go at the punters. And it would work. Cue *Tango in the Night*.

Fleetwood Mac had been inactive since the end of the truncated *Mirage* tour in 1982. The next time all five members were in the same room was when Stevie and her band played a benefit gig in 1985 (the cause was environmental, "Mulholland Tomorrow"), and the vibes between them in the hospitality room were uptight. Then, while Stevie was promoting *Rock a Little,* four-fifths of Fleetwood Mac helped Christine cut an Elvis song for a movie soundtrack, and they thought they sounded good. Christine had gotten off cocaine, and Mick almost had. John McVie was drinking less after an alcoholic seizure almost scared him to death. Even the great tour manager JC had been recalled from his Hawaiian exile and was managing Christine's affairs. Stevie was approached to re-form the band while she was in Australia, but she wasn't returning calls. But she did let Mick know through Dennis Dunston that she would try to do whatever he needed to help him, once the band was back together.

Lindsey was the most reticent about Fleetwood Mac. He was enjoying his independence, writing new songs like "Big Love," and working on his third solo album. Then Mick played him some of Christine's new songs—the best of her career. Mick convinced Lindsey that they might have enough momentum to carry on without him. Lindsey thought about this for a couple of days, and renewed his membership. They began recording—without Stevie—at Rumbo Recorders (recently vacated by a new band called Guns N' Roses) in the Valley, and then moved to Lindsey's hillside garage studio for overdubs and mixing the tracks.

Soon Stevie began getting cassettes—working tapes—of new Fleetwood Mac songs at her home in Paradise Valley. She was astonished by what she heard. Christine had "Little Lies," "Everywhere," and "Isn't It Midnight," cowritten with her new husband, Eddie Quintella. Lindsey had written his best music in ten years: "Big Love," "Caroline," and "Tango in the Night." If they could get a few songs from her, Stevie realized, this album could be another number one.

She got to work on her piano and came up with some demo-quality tapes. "Welcome to the Room Sara" was a faltering, nightmarish recounting of her experience in rehab. "When I See You Again" was another of her frail songs of parting, closely related to "Silver Springs." Sandy Stewart sent Stevie a demo of "Seven Wonders." Stevie wrote some new lyrics and shared the songwriters' credit. A fast rocker called "What Has Rock & Roll Ever Done for You" wouldn't make it on the album.

The night before Stevie was due to work in the studio with Fleetwood Mac for the first time in five years, she called Mick and told him she was dreading having Lindsey lord it over her with sarcastic and jaded remarks in his capacity of producer. She didn't have to remind Mick that she was a bigger star than any of them and wasn't going to put up with any disrespect.

"We only had a brief few days with Stevie," Mick recalled, "and we'd been working for about six months. When she finally came to us Lindsey made an effort not to be as much of a martinet as he was with the rest of us. He was under some strain with this project and lost his patience occasionally, but with Stevie we wanted him to be more objective and professional. He tried to make her feel good in the studio, got some good vocals from her, and it seemed to us that they got on well." Stevie and Lindsey even wrote a song together, really more of a wordless melody, called "Book of Miracles." The real miracle was that they could be in the same room.

The truth was that Lindsey was sick and tired of Fleetwood Mac. He'd actually found postrehab Stevie to be a tranquilized zombie, and drug-addled Mick Fleetwood had spent most of the recording period nodding off in his Winnebago, parked outside Lindsey's garage. Now Lindsey was forced to remix their tapes to make it sound like Stevie was singing on songs that she'd never even heard.

Late in March 1987, Stevie came to the studio to listen to the mixdown before the new album, *Tango in the Night*, was released. There was a row. After the closing strains of the album's last track, Stevie looked like she was about to explode. She got up and stormed around the studio, fighting tears.

Mick: "All right, Stevie, tell us what's wrong."

"It's not even like I'm on this fucking record. I can't hear myself at all!"

Mick: "Stevie, we only had you for a couple of days in the studio. We have a deadline."

"All right," she said, really angry now, "maybe I wasn't able to get to the studio that much. You know how fucking sick I was."

Silence. She went on, "But how is it going to look when the record comes out and I might have to tell *Rolling Stone* that I didn't work on it?"

Christine McVie, hardened road warrior, wasn't used to being threatened. Plus she'd had two glasses of wine. "OK, Stevie. What *specifically* are you so upset about?"

"I should be singing harmony on 'Everywhere,'" she said, bitterly. "You should hear me singing harmony on that song."

"I wanted you to sing on it, too," Christine said, "but you weren't there. In fact we've been working on this record for almost a year, and you were only with us for a couple of days. Now why don't you just tell us you're sorry and we'll work it out."

Stevie looked deflated, but then gave up. They went back into the studio and dubbed her harmony vocals into the final mix of the album. "This was a good thing," Mick said later, "because the album sounded much more like Fleetwood Mac. Stevie had been right after all, and so had Christine."

## 6.4   Last Tango

*Tango in the Night* was a Top 10 album by early summer 1987. Fleetwood Mac borrowed a quarter-million dollars to make a surreal video for the first single, "Big Love," which got on the radio and reached #5. *Tango* got the best reviews ever for the band. The glistening tintinnabulations of Lindsey's arrangements were in sharp contrast to machine-driven contemporary pop, and the press took notice. "Fleetwood Mac Shimmers Back," sighed *Rolling Stone*. *The New York Times* accurately observed, "Mr. Buckingham's arrangements . . . evokes the members of the group calling to one another from mist-shrouded turrets, across vast distances."

The second single from *Tango* (whose sleeve illustrated an African jungle scene in homage to the French surrealist Henri Rousseau) was Stevie's "Seven Wonders," alive with the astonishment of life and hope for the future. "Seven Wonders" got immediate airplay, the video was a hit on MTV, and was a Top 20 record by July. A 12-inch disco version was remixed by Jellybean Benitez, Madonna's dance floor producer. *Tango in the Night* would go on to sell millions, and it reestablished Fleetwood Mac as a major radio hitmaker.

They began to talk about a world tour now, like in days of old. Lindsey again was the least enthusiastic because he wanted to finish his own record. Stevie was into it, but was perceived as the band's weakest link. There were lots of meetings about this, some behind her back. She was now represented by Tony Dimitriades, a Front Line agent who had been Tom Petty's manager for ten years. Dimitriades was an English lawyer who had watched Stevie's decline and fall in horror. (Tom Petty had told him to call right away if Stevie was found dead from drugs.) Tony was concerned for her, and neither he nor anyone else could see Stevie, at almost forty years old, surviving a long road campaign without relapsing on cocaine, thus probably dying in the process.

More meetings of what Stevie calls "the powers that be"—her management, the Mac, her doctors and advisers, "the people around me"—decided she should be medicated if she wanted to stay in the business, and she insisted that she keep working. She was too young to retire, she told them. Getting onstage and singing for people and being the star and the center of attention was what she still wanted out of life. Everyone around her agreed that it was best—for everyone who made money off her or were dependent on her generosity—that Stevie Nicks keep working.

Stevie started seeing a psychiatrist—"the shrink of the hour" as she later said—whose office was off Robertson Boulevard in Beverly Hills. This doctor saw a lot of patients from the music world and Hollywood, and he was chummy, knowing, and liked to gossip with Stevie. He suggested that she was vulnerable to cocaine relapse and offered effective medication. Later she remembered what happened. "When I came out [of Betty Ford] I was happy and felt good about myself. But when I didn't go to AA [Alcoholics Anonymous], my friends pushed me to go to a psychiatrist, who wanted me on tranquilizers. First there was Valium, then Xanax, and then there was Klonopin. I asked why I had to take it. He said, 'Because you need it.' So I took it for seven years—until I just turned into a zombie."

So Stevie Nicks spent the next seven years—between the ages of thirty-nine and forty-five—habituated to a powerful antipsychotic drug, prescribed by a doctor she later called "a groupie shrink," in ever-increasing doses. She later would claim this ruined her life.

In July 1987 Fleetwood Mac began having meetings about touring *Tango in the Night*. Warner Bros. Records was adamant that the band had to tour America, selected European cities, Australia, and Japan. Everyone was keen except Lindsey, who was still saying that he wanted to stay home and make his own record. Unsaid at the meetings was Lindsey's refusal to play second fiddle to Stevie Nicks, whose management now insisted that Fleetwood Mac tour with her two backup singers and nightly perform "Stand Back" and "Edge of Seventeen" in their concert sets. (Otherwise, it was made clear: no Stevie Nicks.)

No one minded this—anything to fill seats with punters—except Lindsey, who told Mick that he wouldn't play Waddy Wachtel's bone-crushing, three-minute guitar stutter on "Edge of Seventeen" while Stevie took her usual coke break backstage. Lindsey didn't even like "Stand Back," he insisted. Lindsey had recently been quoted in *Creem* magazine that he didn't think he could create at a peak level with Fleetwood Mac anymore. This was heresy—a low blow. "To the rest of us," Mick later said, "it was like he was giving notice in the press, which was very poor form."

Recently, during the first half of 1987, to get back her stage flexion Stevie was appearing with Mick Fleetwood's Zoo, a pickup band that Mick had maintained, on and off, for a few years. The Zoo had released an album on RCA Records, and the gigs brought in much needed cash to keep Mick in cocaine and a roof over his head. Stevie liked the Zoo's guitarist and lead singer, Billy Burnette, an affable young musician from Memphis. Billy had style, an impressive mane of jet-black hair, and impeccable credentials as the son of Dorsey Burnette, who with his brother Johnny formed the original Rock & Roll Trio back in the mid-1950s. (The third member of the trio was guitarist Paul Burlison. Their biggest hit was beyond-legendary "The Train Kept a-Rollin'.") Billy Burnette was rockabilly royalty, and also a really nice guy and songwriter.

Mick Fleetwood's Zoo mostly played in upscale bars in places like Lake Tahoe, Las Vegas, and Aspen. Once, in Hawaii, the Zoo was booked into a restaurant on Maui, and word got out that Stevie would appear. Three thousand people showed up, the restaurant opened all the windows, and the Zoo played on. When Stevie came onstage half-way through, the girls went crazy; it was like monkeys in the jungle after the bananas had fermented.

Late in July, there was a Fleetwood Mac meeting at Stevie's house. The band, John Courage, and management (Dennis Dunstan, Tony Dimitriades) were seated on the big white leather sofas in her Pacific Palisades living room. The issue was the *Tango* tour. Mick started: "Lindsey, we want to go back to work, as you know, and I think it's about time that you . . . gave us an answer about your intentions."

Lindsey looked miserable. He didn't like it that Stevie was peering at him, down her nose, through her eyeglasses. Fidgeting, he answered that he was being put under pressure, and he didn't appreciate it. He'd just finished *Tango;* he'd given Fleetwood Mac all his primo ideas, and now he had to make his own record. "Why," he asked, "should I go out and kill myself on the road?"

Mick pressed on, telling Lindsey that it seemed that he'd been telling the press different things from the band. Mick asked him again, "Why don't you give us a clue?"

Lindsey: "Mick—you're not letting go of this, are you?"

"No, Lindsey. I'm not. It's not fair to the rest of us. The days of five years between albums are over, man. We're musicians—we want to go back to work."

Stevie was nodding in assent.

Lindsey let out a sigh. He didn't know what to do. "I don't want to tour. I don't need to tour. But I feel funny leaving the band. I might regret it—later."

Stevie said, "You sure would." Lindsey glared at her. Then he asked Mick, "Are you gonna go on the road without me?"

Mick said yes.

"Yeah, yeah," Lindsey said, stalling for time. "Uh . . . how long do you want to go out for?"

They looked at John Courage, who answered, "Eight months, give or take."

Mick suggested he do the tour with them and then leave the band.

Lindsey said again, "I don't *need* this." His implication was that he didn't need to do profligate, insanely bankrupt Mick Fleetwood any major favors.

Stevie swallowed her pride and had a go. "Hey, Lindsey, c'mon. It won't be so bad. We could have a *great* time out there. Let's try it for old times' sake—just once more!"

She stopped, her cheeks reddening. They all laughed. It was so corny. Even Lindsey had to smile. Everyone knew the *Tango* tour was going to be another exhausting horror show.

Stevie went on: "Lindsey—I solemnly *promise* you, this tour will *not* be a nightmare."

But Lindsey said he wanted to think about it. He left, saying he would meet them all later for dinner at a restaurant. That night, waiting for their private dining room, they saw Lindsey drive up to the place, but then he gunned his engine and drove off. Over a late supper Mick mentioned replacing Lindsey with Billy Burnette from the Zoo, but the others wanted to keep pressuring Lindsey. Finally, a few days later, Mo Ostin—who had major leverage because he had Lindsey under contract for his solo albums—persuaded him to tour with Fleetwood Mac for ten weeks. The tour was on! They were all elated, especially Stevie Nicks, raring to get back on the road again. There was a reconciliation meeting at Christine's house, and Lindsey even seemed enthusiastic about taking best-selling *Tango in the Night* on the road. They started rehearsing, hiring roadies, confirming bookings, chartering newer and faster jets.

One afternoon the telephone rang in Stevie's house near Phoenix. She had sung with the Zoo in Salt Lake City a couple of nights before, and Mick had flown home with her as a houseguest. (Mick and Sara had separated while Mick was living in comparative austerity during his financial troubles.) Her assistant said that Mick was wanted on the phone. When he came back, he looked ill.

"That was Dennis," Mick told her. "You know, Stevie—I knew we were fucked when he asked if I was sitting down."

"What is it?"

"The tour's off," Mick said, and put his face in his hands. Lindsey had called John Courage and announced he'd changed his mind. He couldn't go through with it. JC tried to talk to him, and Lindsey reiterated he wasn't about to play "Edge of Seventeen" and "Stand Back," or any of Stevie's solo work, during a Fleetwood Mac concert. And that was that, except that JC told Lindsey the band deserved an explanation from him in person, considering his formerly precarious position— one step ahead of the surf-and-turf cover band circuit—when Mick found him at Sound City in 1974. And so a meeting was set at Christine's house. Anyone could have anticipated what happened next.

## 6.5    Shake the Cage

August 7, 1987, will always live on as a sad day for Fleetwood Mac.

It was a big meeting, the whole band, the whole band family, at Christine's house, decorated with landscape paintings and antique furniture like an English country manor. Mick pointed out that it was twenty years, almost to the day, since Fleetwood Mac was founded in a London pub by Peter Green.

The atmosphere was tense. The humiliation of a canceled tour was a disturbing echo from the band's now distant past, and it had been made clear to Lindsey Buckingham beforehand that he would be replaced if he left the band. Fleetwood Mac was going on tour, with or without him.

The meeting went well for about five minutes. Then Stevie Nicks could stand it no more and decided to cut through the bullshit. "Lindsey," she said, trying to remain calm. "You can't do this. Why the fuck are you doing this?"

He answered that he was sorry. "I just can't do it anymore . . . twelve years of my life to this band . . . I've done it all . . . arranged, produced, played guitar, wrote, sang . . . I just can . . . not . . . *hack it* anymore."

This annoyed Christine. It was her songs, not Lindsey's, which got played on the radio. Her tone was measured but withering. *"Done it all,* Lindsey? What do you mean, you've done it all?"

He was silent, looking at the floor. He'd given his final answer.

Stevie spoke up. Mick saw she had tears on her cheeks. She said, "Lindsey, I can't believe this. You've broken my fucking heart on this."

He said, "Hey—don't do this again. Don't start attacking me."

"Watch out," she responded, standing up. "There's other people in the room."

Now he was shouting. "Oh, shit! *Get this bitch out of my way*—and fuck the lot of you." That was the end of the meeting. Lindsey grabbed his jacket and left the house with Stevie behind, pleading with him to change his mind. The two of them spoke briefly, intensely, almost touching each other, in the car-filled forecourt. The others couldn't hear what was said, but finally Stevie shouted, "Hey man, you'll never be in love with anyone—but yourself!"

Stevie later described the scene: "I flew off the couch and across the room to seriously attack him. I'm not real scary, but I can be fairly ferocious, and I grabbed him, which almost got me killed."

Lindsey manhandled Stevie, slapped her face, and bent her backward over the hood of his car. He put his fingers around her neck and started to choke her.

Stevie: "I screamed horrible obscenities at him, and I thought he was going to kill me. I think he probably thought he was gonna kill me, too. I told him that if he hurt me, my family will get you. My father and brother will kill you."

Mick saw this and started out of the house at a run, but Dennis and Tony Dimitriades got there first. Dennis grabbed Lindsey's collar, pulled him off Stevie, and roughly shoved him backward. The burly Aussie, devoted to Stevie, thought about breaking Lindsey's arm but then decided not to.

Lindsey came back into the house, where everyone basically wanted to kill him. Stevie was still in the driveway, rubbing her throat. The guitarist looked crazed, disoriented, distraught. He shouted, as if to the heavens: "Get that woman—out of my life—*that schizophrenic bitch!*"

Christine regarded him with royal contempt. She sipped her wine and said, "Jesus Christ, Lindsey, just look at yourself, screaming like a madman."

No one said anything until John McVie told Lindsey that he'd better leave—*now.* The attack on Stevie had been brutal, and there were men there who wouldn't have minded escorting Lindsey behind the garage and teaching him a lesson.

Lindsey seemed dazed. (There was the epilepsy thing, they all thought later.) He looked around the room, told his friends they were a bunch of selfish bastards, and walked out. He sat in his car for a quarter hour, but no one wanted to comfort him. Eventually they heard him start the engine and drive slowly away.

Stevie was in a state, really angry. But there was something good that the others had finally seen—the unhinged violence Lindsey was capable of with her—why she had left him. They all knew it wasn't the first time he'd hurt her. McVie said it was bound to happen in front of them, sooner or later. Mick gathered them all and said, "We've got a great record, and we're going to look like a lot of bloody idiots if we don't go on the road. Let's keep our momentum and use it to find new people."

Mick had anticipated that Lindsey wouldn't change his mind. He'd reserved a private room at Le Dome, the au courant French bistro on Sunset Boulevard, and had invited Billy Burnette and ace guitarist Rick Vito to see if they wanted to join Fleetwood Mac's first rehearsal without Lindsey Buckingham the following day. Dennis

Dunstan mentioned the dinner to Stevie, and she asked if she could join them.

Stevie remembered, "I walked into the restaurant, sat down, and was introduced to Rick Vito, who I'd seen play with Bob Seger but had never met before. [She had previously recorded "Are You Mine" with Billy Burnette.] What happened was, everyone just started to smile. . . . I thought, *these are going to be really close friends of mine.* I wanted this to work out."

Billy and Rick joined Fleetwood Mac the next afternoon. A few days later they were invited to a big tea party at Stevie's house to celebrate the so-called Harmonic Convergence, a widely hyped astronomical event celebrated on August 16. "I wanted us all to converge," she said later. "So if there's something happening up there, we'd be first on that priority list." Asked about Lindsey, she answered, "You can't ever 'replace' somebody, or their soul, or their historical value to Fleetwood Mac, but you *do* go on."

Later, upon reflection, Stevie sadly told an interviewer, "I should have left, too."


Early September, 1987. Stevie was driven to Venice Beach for secret tour rehearsals with Fleetwood Mac's eleventh lineup. She told Mick she was more than satisfied with Billy's way of handling Mac classics like "Oh Well" and Rick Vito's blues playing on "I Loved Another Woman" and "Rattlesnake Shake." Sharon Celani and Lori Perry (who would soon divorce her husband and marry Stevie's brother Chris) were on hand to sing with the band.

"Stand Back" would become a crucial part of the set when Fleetwood Mac began the Shake the Cage Tour later that month—but not "Rhiannon," which for Stevie was too closely associated with Lindsey's direction and pacing. In fact, Mick found it difficult to completely convince her that this was still Fleetwood Mac, because she was so used to Lindsey being there. The audience was now totally focused on Stevie and Christine, which neither seemed to mind. Stevie was happy to be on tour, because at home she was under a Klonopin haze and tended to stay home all day, no exercise, watch soap operas, and order in from Jerry's Deli. Her weight had ballooned to 150 pounds—

duly noted in most concert reviews. She was performing in big hair and corseted bustiers under blouson tunic jackets, or in crinoline-looking petticoats in shimmering white, prairie chic. Most stage ensembles included silver crosses and black gloves. Reviewers noted her abiding attractiveness and endurance, since the rehab at Betty Ford had been widely publicized. By mid-October, her confidence had been bolstered by some rave reviews, and she began to ask for midtour rehearsals to rethink the harmony singing in new songs like "Little Lies," which was heading to the top of the charts.

After a month on the road, Stevie started to notice something. Nobody, in all the interviews she was doing, ever asked her, "Where's Lindsey?" In fact, without the moody, highly strung guitarist, the tour atmosphere was light and refreshing. Billy's singing and Rick's guitar effectively took Lindsey's place. No audience ever shouted for "I'm So Afraid" or "Second Hand News." No one missed Lindsey Buckingham, which seemed to give Stevie some satisfaction and not a little sadness as well.

The one interviewer who asked her about him was from the BBC, who were filming a documentary on the band called "the epitome of adult rock music."

"I gave Lindsey up," she told the interviewer. "He's a thing of my past. I hope he finds what he's searching for, and I hope he's happy, and I wish him well. And there's nothing left to say."

The tour broke for the Christmas holidays. On New Year's Eve Stevie sang with Mick Fleetwood's Zoo at a little club in Aspen, where she had written "Landslide" in what seemed to her another lifetime. (Eddie Van Halen sat in on supersonic electric guitar. The stage was the size of a mattress in a good hotel.)

The Shake the Cage Tour was supposed to go to Australia and New Zealand in March 1988, but Stevie's health intervened. She was forty years old now and told friends she was feeling her age. She was fatigued, tired all the time. One doctor diagnosed glandular fever, something like mononucleosis. Another told her she suffered from the debilitating Epstein-Barr syndrome. The Pacific tour was canceled.

But Fleetwood Mac did go to England in May, playing in Manchester and Birmingham before a record-breaking ten sold-out nights in London's Wembley Arena. *Tango* had been a #1 album in the U.K., and anticipation ran high for the return of the venerable London blues band that had gone west and conquered the world. Even younger members of the royal family were requesting tickets. Hope sprang high that Diana, Princess of Wales, might come, but she was more of a Duran Duran fan. Instead, her brother-in-law, Prince Edward, the Queen's youngest son, came to the opening night and was graciously received backstage by Stevie, the Queen of Rock, with a modest curtsey after the show.

Stevie later said that this London residency was one of the highlights of her career with the band. Backstage the vibes were high-energy, aided by the vitamin B12 shots dispensed by the comical English tour doc. The band was augmented by an unseen keyboard player who added atmospheric drones to their sound. Stevie's girls were along to add vocal depth to Christine's crystalline "Isn't It Midnight," "Little Lies," plus Stevie's "Seven Wonders" and "Gold Dust Woman." During "World Turning" Mick was joined by West African percussionist Isaac Asante, adorned in cowrie shells and a horned helmet, in a hoodoo drum duet that drew cheers. Fans were spellbound by Stevie's plangent solo on "Has Anyone Ever Written Anything for You." Then they got up and danced when Fleetwood Mac threw its full, prodigious weight into "Stand Back" and "Edge of Seventeen."

Rhiannon, the old Welsh witch, never appeared in London, despite constant fan clamor for her. Ziggy Marley was on the PA leading to the concerts. Afterward, as the fans filed out into the chilly spring evening, the PA played "Albatross," Fleetwood Mac's perennial Top 10 hit.

After the ten nights at Wembley, everyone was relieved and more relaxed. Stevie Nicks didn't know it then, but time's currents would ebb and flow, and after the tense, successful, and highly creative *Tango* era she wouldn't sing onstage with Fleetwood Mac for several years.

# CHAPTER 7

## 7.1 The Writer

While Fleetwood Mac was in London, Stevie Nicks was disconcerted by the presence of a writer who was helping Mick Fleetwood with his autobiography. They didn't usually let writers mingle with the band. "I don't think anyone in the band welcomed it," Mick said later.

He'd recently gone through his second bankruptcy and needed cash. His lawyer, Mickey Shapiro, knew a literary agent who knew a writer, a former *Rolling Stone* editor, who was now a best-selling rock biographer working with Michael Jackson on a memoir. Mick met with the writer, who produced a proposal for the New York publishers that netted a six-figure book deal for Mick's history of Fleetwood Mac. The writer began taping interview sessions with Mick early in 1988 in Mick's rented house near Zuma Beach in Malibu. A few months later, Mick finally married Sara Recor, who'd been living separately in a tract house in Burbank. Stevie attended the wedding at Mick's house, along with the rest of Fleetwood Mac (minus Lindsey).

Gradually, the writer asked to speak with other band members. Christine agreed and gave a funny interview to him backstage at Boston Garden. Wine glass and cigarette in hand, she repeated her oft-told joke that she'd been Perfect before she married John McVie. John in turn made a choking gesture with his hands when asked why Lindsey had left the band. Bob Welch described the band's difficult midperiod of disasters and defections. Richard Dashut—who had lived for years with Stevie and Lindsey when they were a couple—kept saying what a great woman she was. John Courage told about the relentless teasing he took from his fellow road managers in the early days, because JC had two girls in the band. (These rock pirates thought it was bad luck, like women on a frigate.) Dennis Dunston let it drop that Mick had gone through a torrid affair with Stevie Nicks. Then there was the Sara material . . .

"We can't put that in the book," a goggle-eyed Mick told the writer.

"We have to," the writer said. "It's box office boffo." Mick put his head in his hands. The writer said, "You'll have a huge best seller. You'll make a lot of money."

"She'll kill me, or leave the band," Mick said.

"No, she won't," the writer said. "We'll make her look good. No one wants to read trash about Stevie Nicks, believe me."

Weeks went by. Mick invited the writer to come along to London for the band's residency in Wembley Arena. Christine spoke again at length, as did Billy Burnette and Rick Vito, charming guys, ten years younger than the band, who were thrilled to suddenly find themselves in one of the biggest groups in the world. No one wanted to talk about Lindsey. The writer enjoyed eavesdropping on the vocal rehearsals backstage as Stevie, Chris, and Billy worked out different harmonies for new songs like "Little Lies" and "Isn't It Midnight."

One night Stevie Nicks asked Mick about the writer. Everyone was talking to him. People were spilling their guts. Why didn't he ask to interview her? Because, Mick answered, he knows you'd say no. That's right, she said, adding that she was going to write her own book someday. Does he, she asked, know about us? Mick nodded yes. About you and Sara? Yes again. The next day Stevie changed hotels.

"Stevie was huffing and puffing for a while," Mick said later. "And I said, 'Stevie, you've got to trust me. I'm *working* with you. I'd have to be out of my mind to scuttle anyone that was close to me, in a very distasteful way.'"

The writer and Stevie passed each other a few times in the narrow backstage corridors of Wembley Arena. She would give him a little smile, and then lower her eyes as they passed. He noted that she was tiny, overweight, and seemed a little bleary, as if she was medicated. Her eyes were red behind thick eyeglasses and she smelled of weapons-grade hairspray. She was stuffed into corseted stage clothes that displayed a bounteous silicone décolletage, and she wobbled uncomfortably in stacked-heeled boots, trailing scarves, and wore metallic hair jewels in her big coiffure. Even a bit overripe in her current state, there was still something deeply alluring in her presence.

After the last concert in London, the writer had himself introduced to Stevie at the band's glamorous party at the Kensington Roof Gardens. She was wearing a costumey gypsy-rocker black dress, nursing a goblet of white wine, and smoking a filtered cigarette. "Everything they say about me is true," she advised him. Behind her, Sharon Celani and Lori Perry-Nicks, as she was now called, stared at the writer, icy and dead-eyed after a long night's work. The writer wondered what these veteran singers made of him.

When Fleetwood Mac went on to their European concerts, the writer went home and typed up his notes. Then, in the summer of 1988, he received a phone call from John Courage, who wanted to know if he would write the booklet notes for *Fleetwood Mac/Greatest Hits,* a compilation of the current band's best songs, augmented by new tracks from Stevie and Christine, to be released for the holidays in all three formats: compact disc, vinyl, and cassette. Warner Bros. had ordered a huge advance pressing, JC said, and the band wanted the writer for the job. They agreed on a price, and the writer asked for a tape of the album's running order and the new songs.

He wasn't surprised to see that five of the album's sixteen songs were Stevie's: "Rhiannon," "Dreams," "Gypsy," "Sara," and "No Questions Asked." This last was a complex narrative paired with an instrumental track by Kelly Johnston, almost five minutes long, about a fascinating man—elusive, a loner, and she wants him. He's resistant—it sounds like Joe—and she gives in to her needs, then regresses into childhood: "I need you . . . now . . . no questions asked . . . like a little girl." Her singing seems buried in a generic Lindsey-esque arrangement directed by Greg Ladanyi, a sought-after producer favored by Jackson Browne and Don Henley. Stevie's sad song was offset by Christine's more hopeful (and tuneful) "As Long as You Follow," designated to be the package's first single.

The writer duly sent JC a 1,500-word essay about being with Fleetwood Mac in London during their triumphant, sold-out return to the mother country. This was accepted with only one change. The writer had characterized Stevie's most tribal fans—young women tricked out in black toppers, scarves in shimmery, transparent fabrics, and gauzy nomad frocks—as "Nixies," referring to the mythological Celtic fairies of the Western Isles. This was nixed by Stevie Nicks, who didn't want this moniker attached to her people.

Fleetwood Mac/Greatest Hits was released in November 1988. The album reached Billboard's #14 and then proceeded to sell eight million copies over the next few years. The writer felt proud to have been a tiny part of its massive success. A few months later, John Courage sent him a framed platinum record award signed by all the members of the band (except Lindsey Buckingham).

## 7.2   Alice

Beginning after her return from England in the summer of 1988, Stevie Nicks stepped away from Fleetwood Mac and spent most of the next year making her fourth solo album. Later she would assert this album of songs was extra special to her: "The Other Side of the Mirror is probably my favorite album. It was a really intense record. I had gotten away from the cocaine. I spent a year writing those songs. I was drug-free, and I was happy."

She was also in love, or at least infatuated, with her new producer.

It had taken awhile before Modern Records could find one, since no one was exactly lining up to work with Stevie Nicks, generally considered an aging, over-forty diva by the record industry in the late eighties. Jimmy Iovine had moved on. She wanted to ask Tom Petty, but he already had a lot of problems. Keith Olsen had kind of fired her the last time they worked together. Gordon Perry was out because his wife had married Stevie's brother. Rick Nowels was out. She liked Greg Ladanyi, the soft-spoken and handsome Hungarian engineer who had worked on Fleetwood Mac/Greatest Hits, but he was booked. Longtime fans winced when Stevie's publicist announced that cheesy pop-jazz saxophone star Kenny G. would be in the studio with Stevie. There was some relief when they were informed that rugged piano man Bruce Hornsby would be there, too. (Stevie had liked his hit "The Way It Is" in 1986.)

Eventually Doug Morris suggested they hire Rupert Hine, an English producer who had produced some of the decade's biggest British pop acts—the Fixx, the Thompson Twins, and Howard Jones. He was best known for writing the hits on Tina Turner's hugely popular comeback album, *Private Dancer*. Rupert Hine was forty-one, handsome, tall, a musical intellectual with an air of command, like a veteran RAF pilot who had survived the war. He preferred to work in his own studio in the countryside near London but agreed to cut the basic tracks in Los Angeles if they could make a deal. Stevie agreed to meet him for dinner at Le Dome, and that was that—a *coup de foudre*. She remembered: "The night I met Rupert Hine was a dangerous one. He was different from everyone else I've ever known. He was older, and he was smarter, and we both knew it. I hired him to do the album before we even started talking about music. It just seemed that we had made a spiritual agreement to do a magic album." Stevie told friends that she could feel that this was going to be more than a working relationship.

Rupert Hine preferred not to record in studios, and Stevie wanted an intimate atmosphere because *Rock a Little* had been recorded all over the map, so she took a half-year lease on a fake castle high in the Hollywood Hills for twenty-five thousand dollars a month. Built in 1974, the crenellated house was mostly used for film and video shoots, especially blue movies. Stevie moved her own bed into the master bedroom; also in residence were her brother Chris and sister-in-law Lori, plus her longtime production associate, Glenn Parish, and her new personal assistant, Karen Johnston. Herbie Worthington was installed in the coach house.

Paul Fishkin persuaded Jimmy Iovine and engineer Shelly Yakus to help set up a recording studio in the castle's long dining room, lined with solemn old portrait paintings of somebody's ancestors. The recording console was in the middle of the room, under the chandelier. This became "Castle Studios," where the basic tracks for the new album were cut with an assortment of local musicians, joined by Waddy Wachtel, on leave from his axe-hero gig with Keith Richards's X-Pensive Winos.

Stevie wanted a theme that would tie her new songs together, but she was having trouble focusing. The success of *Rock a Little* was three years in the past, and this time she didn't have a big backlog of songs. She was anxious about writing, she told the psychiatrist she saw twice a month, so he increased her Klonopin dosage. This made her listless in the studio and ultratranquil upstairs. The take-out orders from Jerry's Deli increased, and Stevie put on more weight. Mick Fleetwood later observed that the drug that was supposed to keep Stevie productive was making her useless instead.

But then, in October 1988, under pressure to create, she found her theme.

In 1862, an eccentric Oxford University mathematician named Charles Dodgson took a little girl named Alice Liddell and her sisters on a rowing journey up the Thames River from Oxford to Gostow. Charles was close to the Liddell family, and indeed had photographed Alice naked when she was seven. While rowing, he told the children a story about Alice's tumble down a rabbit hole and her descent into an underground world peopled by fantastic creatures: the Mad Hatter, the March Hare, Humpty Dumpty, the Red Queen, Tweedledum and Tweedledee. At a Wonderland tea party, Alice was given potions that altered her body, first growing tall, then growing small. Alice always maintained her dignity while undergoing various ordeals, like a spooky journey through a mirror, or looking glass, but all came out well at the end. Dodgson later said that the real Alice begged him to write down the story so she could hear it again. He published *The Adventures of Alice in Wonderland* in 1865 under the pen name Lewis Carroll, with illustrations by John Tenniel, followed by a sequel, *Through the Looking Glass,* in 1871. The books were enormously popular and have remained so for 150 years. John Tenniel's imagery of Wonderland, with its chessboard landscape and ludicrous characters, became iconic for multiple generations, especially after Walt Disney's animated version was broadcast on television while Stevie was growing up. Then the sixties counterculture focused on the proto-psychedelic visions of mind-altering substances, giving Lewis Carroll's fantasies new life a hundred years after they were written. (No one in that generation can forget watching a bloated caterpillar smoking a hookah while seated on a giant mushroom.)

Stevie knew the stories of *Alice in Wonderland* from being read to by her grandmother Alice Harwood, during hot summer childhood visits to Ajo, Arizona. Alice and Stevie liked to disappear down the rabbit hole together, into a world where the looking glass both makes everything double and also reverses things. It was a world that now made perfect sense to an increasingly medicated Stevie Nicks, who understood Alice's discovery while in Wonderland: that "I say what I mean is not the same as I mean what I say."

Also, Stevie's grandmother—Crazy Alice—had recently died. Stevie told friends that she had never heard her own mother (whose middle name also was Alice) so upset on the phone before, because Alice Harwood had had such a hard and difficult life. So Alice's adventures in Wonderland supplied the context for some of the new songs that would reflect Stevie's own woozy adventures across the other side of the mirror as she made her new album of songs.

She liked working with Rupert Hine from the start. He was quiet, deferential, and sympathetic about getting ideas out of her journals and notebooks and into an arrangement. They sat together at the piano; he played and she chanted from her written notes. They worked under the old-fashioned portraits that lined the gloomy room. "We never felt alone," she mused later. Soon she was wanting to get closer to his intelligent energy. There seemed to be a glow of empathy about him, especially given the castle's dark, cloistered atmosphere. She later wrote, "It always seemed to me that whenever Rupert walked into one of those dark castle rooms, that the rooms were on fire. There was a connection between us that everyone around us instantly picked up on, and everyone was very careful to respect our space."

Stevie wasn't reticent or circumspect about expressing her feelings for Rupert Hine, who recalled the period to an interviewer. "Stevie's so open it's impossible not to fall for her. She's just completely herself, and you fall for that honesty. That 'magical quality,' the phrase that everybody uses, is simply because she is true to who she is. If she cared about how she came across, she wouldn't have it. It's all real."

One evening after supper, Stevie was working with Rupert on a passionate new love anthem, "Rooms on Fire." Sitting next to him at the piano while he was playing a possible arrangement, she told him, "You know this is about *you*, right?" He was so moved he had to stop working on the song. Stevie and Rupert remained close for the next four months as they lived and worked at the castle in the fall of 1988.

It wasn't all work. Energized by her new relationship, Stevie began to emerge from her medicated world and just get out more. Rupert Hine was someone she could be seen with around town, at restaurants, openings, and industry events. In late October she threw a Halloween party for the Fleetwood Mac family. Everyone had to wear an outfit of some kind. Stevie found hers at Western Costume in Hollywood: a billowy scarlet ball gown with short puffed sleeves and a vampire collar. Stevie loved this dress for her party costume as Scarlett O'Hara; she also wore the red dress for the jacket photo of her new album, and in the first single's video. (Rupert Hine came as a World War I biplane pilot. Mick Fleetwood arrived as Jesus Christ entering Jerusalem. "Mick was riding an actual donkey," Hine recalled. "These people didn't do things by halves.")

Then, in early November, Stevie gave an A-list Hollywood party at the castle for the Irish band U2, then the biggest rock band in the world. They'd come to LA to preview their new album *Rattle and Hum*. Stevie—all dolled up and looking great—attended U2's show at the Wiltern Theater on the arm of Rupert Hine, who found himself in *People* magazine a week later. Stevie's party for U2 started at seven the following evening at the castle. Rupert was at the front door when Jack Nicholson, Hollywood's biggest star, walked in promptly on time. Hine later remarked that, after making records in the fastness of Buckinghamshire for ten years, he knew he had finally hit the big time when he found himself directing Jack toward the bar.

Rupert Hine was really charmed by Stevie's natural ways. He told an interviewer, "We'd go out to dinner and she'd suddenly just start singing to me straight into my ear, things that she was either thinking or just little ideas . . . [she was] only able to tell me what she was thinking by singing."

Rupert went back to England in December. Stevie joined him after spending Christmas in Phoenix with her family. Her new album would be finished and mixed at Rupert's rural studio, away from the temptations of London. Stevie arrived the following January with a small entourage and twenty pieces of luggage, planning for a few months' stay in England in early 1989. They were driven to Farmyard Studio, Rupert's house near the village of Little Chalfont, in Buckinghamshire, about an hour's drive north of London. Rupert wanted to re-create the familial atmosphere of the castle sessions, but in the context of a romantic old English farmstead. He had one of the farm cottages upgraded and redecorated for Stevie, and hired some jolly local ladies from the parish church to keep the studio's kitchen open at all hours.

At first Stevie was disoriented, dazed, ensorcelled by the ancient landscapes of the quiet, rural shire. The English winter is mostly mild; she took long walks along sere fields and fallow pastures, then over turnstiles with the farm dogs, and she wrote in her journal about the swirling mists and the morning fogs of the gently rolling countryside, with the blue hills of the Chilterns rising in the distance. The musicians quickly fell into a working routine, spending the most time on the strongest of the new songs: "Whole Lotta Trouble," "Alice," "Rooms on Fire," and "Ooh My Love." Rupert brought in British musicians, like guitarist Jamie West-Oram from the Fixx, to add colors and accents where needed to fill out the castle tracks.

After a month, to stay on the production schedule, they needed to dub in Bruce Hornsby, who was supposed to be on two tracks, "Juliet" and "Two Kinds of Love." But Hornsby was having second thoughts about being featured on the same record as the dreaded Kenny G., who was regarded as a hack by most serious musicians of the era. (They may have been jealous, too, since his sugary "smooth jazz" recordings were shipping gold.) Hornsby's management said his schedule was tight, so he couldn't work in England just then. So Stevie (really annoyed) and Rupert boarded the supersonic Concorde at London's Heathrow Airport, and flew to New York for two days' work at the Hit Factory with Mr. Hornsby. (Rupert noticed that Stevie traveled with only six suitcases for the two-night visit.) Hornsby was truculent, and the sessions were tense. But they got his piano stylings and vocals down and then flew the Concorde back to London in just over three hours.

Then something happened that remains a mystery. Stevie and her people suddenly left Rupert's studio in a flurry of hired cars. They checked into a London hotel, then flew back to Los Angeles. The reason for Stevie's quick exit has never been explained—there were rumors of a medical diagnosis of some kind—but two years later Stevie had this to say about the scene with Rupert Hine in England: "[It was] somewhere outside London. It was like being in a cottage in Wales, it was a little spooky . . . the atmosphere was like nothing I had ever experienced. Then something happened to him [Rupert] that simply made it impossible for us to ever be together again. I left him there . . . the rooms were still burning, but the fire had been stolen from us. It wasn't over love, in fact, it had nothing to do with love. It was just a bad situation. I came back to Los Angeles a very changed woman."

## 7.3   What Price Glory?

When the tapes of Stevie's new music came back to Los Angeles, they didn't sound quite right, and so they were remixed by Chris Lord-Alge, an up-and-coming young LA engineer much in demand for his "ears." Rupert Hine was said to be offended, but Stevie didn't return his calls. Some of her new songs were strong, and potential hit records. "Rooms on Fire," written with Rick Nowels, was a blank verse narrative with a chorus that echoed the Searchers' version of "When You Walk in the Room." It had an orchestral palette and a Spanish guitar, and would be the album's first single.

The lyrics for "Whole Lotta Trouble" were written in Mike Campbell's hotel room in Australia during the Dylan/Petty tour five years before. The line, "You're not living in the real world," had been spoken to her by Tom Petty during one of their heated disagreements on nights off. Stevie and Campbell had recorded a hotel-grade demo of the song on Mike's four-track recorder, with Stevie playing her guitar. Then he wrote a bridge and expanded the demo into a backing track, developed further by Rupert Hine. To Stevie it came out sounding like an old John Lee Hooker song. "Whole Lotta Trouble" was a breakup message, a threat display, a power play. "When I want something," Stevie declares, *"I get it."* The LA Horns, a trio of session players, were overdubbed as a tribute to Atlantic Records' classic R&B band sound.

Equally strong was "Ooh My Love," with its rhythm following "If

Anyone Falls in Love," and words about romantic memories of creating art with a new lover in dark castle chambers. Other tracks included the cowgirl rock of "Long Way to Go," "Ghosts," "Fire Burning" (both, again, with Mike Campbell), and "Alice," a dreamy séance using the "Sara" template, with a journey to the other side of the mirror. "Run for your life, said the Mad Hatter," Stevie sang as Kenny Gorelic warbled his insipid soprano saxophone cadenzas.

"Two Kinds of Love" and "Juliet" were the two duets with Bruce Hornsby. In the first, Stevie is a widow contemplating a fatal love. "Juliet" (one of Stevie's names for Robin Anderson) is a rocker about a crying blue sky and getting one's life back on track. Three more songs complete the album. "Cry Wolf" is a cover of a song recorded by Laura Branigan, an Atlantic singer who was said to be close to the label's chairman, Ahmet Ertegun. "Doing the Best I Can (Escape from Berlin)" is a somber portrait of distress and addiction. "I paid a price for it," Stevie comments ruefully. The record ends with a reggae version of "I Still Miss Someone (Blue Eyes)," tacitly dedicated to Lindsey Buckingham, according to Stevie in a later interview.

Herbie Worthington shot the cover of *The Other Side of the Mirror* in his studio, using a black backdrop and a checkerboard floor to simulate Wonderland. Stevie wore her outrageously red Halloween dress, with a crimson fascinator sprouting from her big, late-eighties shag perm. Diamonds sparkled on her fingers. The (beautiful) inside-sleeve portrait showed a melancholy rock star in a dark beret, revealing an alluring, deep décolletage. Stevie dedicated the album to her grandmother Alice, "the Queen of Hearts."

Stevie made an expensive video for "Rooms on Fire" (shot mostly at the faux castle), and featuring boudoir scenes, Stevie dancing on the water of a swimming pool, an adorable baby girl, and Stevie—as an old lady—being led into the white light of a mystical landscape by a caped stranger. She called it "the What If video," meaning *what if* she had married Rupert Hine, something she seems to have considered. But when they screened "Rooms on Fire" at MTV's weekly editorial meeting in New York, someone suggested Stevie looked way too fat in the clip, and that it would hurt her career. Some in the room remembered that when MTV began ten years earlier, the only good clip they had was "Stop Draggin' My Heart Around." Stevie Nicks had friends at MTV, which, for whatever reason, did not play the "Rooms on Fire" clip in heavy rotation.

*The Other Side of the Mirror,* Stevie's fourth solo album of songs, was released in May 1989 when she was forty-one years old, and it proved a great success for her. The first single reached #16, while the record was a Top 10 album by July. It was a smash in Europe, Stevie's first record ever to sell really well on the continent. It got to #3 in England after Stevie flew to London and sang "Rooms on Fire" on the BBC's *Top of the Pops.* Her first solo European tour followed during that summer and fall, playing in England, France, Sweden, and Holland. Opening for her were singer Richard Marx and the Hooters, and these two bands got better press reviews than Stevie, who was described as clumsy and distracted. The American leg of the Mirror Tour extended into the autumn months, with Russ Kunkel on drums and Carlos Rios on guitar. Sara Fleetwood, now separated from Mick, joined Sharon and Lori singing backup onstage.

Her fans were still eager to see Stevie, and she sold out arenas and amphitheaters that big acts like Tom Petty and Bon Jovi had failed to even half-fill (in a recessionary national economy that year), especially in the South and Midwest. The two-hour concerts included several costume changes and mostly fan favorites (but not "Rhiannon"). Stevie and the band worked out stage arrangements for several new songs. Russ Kunkel propelled anthemic "Rooms on Fire" with a hard-rocking, four-on-the-floor beat, and played "Whole Lotta Trouble" with a rumbling menace, like war drums. He gave "Ooh My Love" almost a striptease rhythm, which Stevie, Lori, Sharon, and Sara all agreed they liked to move to. Stevie's fans seemed attentive and appreciative of the first new songs they had heard from her in four years.

But there was also a spate of awful reviews of some of these shows, cringe-inducing notices of Stevie's increasing weight, her tightly girdled or corseted costumes, her overdone makeup, her rigid hair. Some critics accused Stevie of letting down her fans with less-than-magic performances. There was even a contentious press conference in Europe where disrespectful reporters kept shouting rude questions about what drugs she was on when she went to rehab at Betty Ford. Stevie refused to answer, got annoyed, snapped, "I didn't go there to have a good time. I went because I wanted to." Then she walked out.

"Two Kinds of Love" (with Kenny G.) was released as the album's second single, and it bombed: it was the first Stevie Nicks single not to make the charts of either *Billboard* or *Cashbox* magazines. The industry maintained a disciplined radio silence. (Some said it was the curse of Kenny G.) They made another video, shooting "Whole Lotta Trouble" while playing in Houston that fall. Veteran fans noticed that Stevie's band was much more animated without Waddy Wachtel in charge. Sharon and Lori waved their arms around and danced with more abandon. The musicians threw themselves all over the stage, vogueing, rockin' out. "It was much more of an R&B band than I usually had," Stevie said.

At the end of 1989 Stevie went home to Phoenix, where her mother was recovering from open-heart surgery. It had been a long, hard year. Even Western civilization itself had shifted seismically when the Berlin Wall came down that year, followed by the collapse of the Soviet Union and the rest of the communist nations. Stevie Nicks was herself a troubadour in the Western romantic tradition, and that she was affected by major political changes would soon be reflected in her songwriting.

When family members asked how the *Mirror* tours had gone, Stevie replied that she had no memories of even being on tour. She said she couldn't remember a thing.

But later, she wrote that she had fond memories of making *The Other Side of the Mirror:* the spooky faux castle, the old pictures on the walls, dinner dates at actual restaurants with dashing Rupert Hine, the U2 party where movie stars had come; and then the haunted winter landscape of rural Buckinghamshire. Years later she told *Rolling Stone* that *Mirror* was her favorite album of her solo career. And she wrote, "Now I remember the rooms, the music, and how magic the whole thing was . . . 'All right, said Alice, I'm going back . . . to the other side of the mirror.'" Followed by, "'What price love . . . what price glory . . .'"

## 7.4  Desert Angel

Now it was 1990, and Fleetwood Mac came calling. The new Mac album would follow *Tango in the Night,* the band's best-selling album after *Rumours* and *Greatest Hits,* which also had sold in the millions. Mick Fleetwood was nervous about the new record, the band's first album without obsessive-compulsive producer Lindsey Buckingham in control. Mick asked Stevie to give them three or four new songs. But she was mostly living in Phoenix, concerned for her mother's health, and existing in a haze of psychotropic medication. Stevie was now wracked by bodily spasms, and her hands sometimes shook, which frightened her. She was finding it very hard to write something new.

Stevie did fly to Los Angeles and meet with Greg Ladanyi, who was producing with Fleetwood Mac. She wanted to write with Rick Vito and Billy Burnette, and invited them to her rented estate in the Valley for long sessions with their guitars and her journals. She enjoyed it, she told Rick and Billy, because she could never work this way with Lindsey anymore. First, he would never come to her house, and even if he did, all she and Lindsey would do was get into heated arguments about why they broke up, years before, and whose fault it was.

Stevie did come up with new music during that winter in 1990. She wrote "Love Is Dangerous" with Rick Vito and sang the somewhat generic lyrics with him. She wrote "Freedom" to a killer track sent by Mike Campbell. The lyrics dated to the stunned and heartbroken era when Mick had dumped her for Sara: "My intentions were clear / I was with him / Everyone knew / Poor little fool."

"Affairs of the Heart" was credited solely to Stevie, a passionate appropriation of an old saw that probably came from deep in the heart of Shakespeare: "'Tis better to have loved and lost / than never to have loved at all." But with a passionate attack and a Rick Vito guitar break, Stevie somehow transformed the Bard's timeless sentiment into something fresh and moving. She also wrote (with Vito) the sad, sweet ballad "The Second Time," about a woman who had regrets but still never looked back.

Stevie stayed in Paradise Valley, keeping out of the warm winter sun during the album's production. When it was time to add her vocals, Greg Ladanyi came to Phoenix and recorded her at Vintage Recorders' studio there. *Behind the Mask,* Fleetwood Mac's fifteenth album, was released by Warner Bros. in April 1990. Reviews were mixed, most noting that Lindsey's not being there made the band sound more like a team of individuals. *Rolling Stone* (which had never really embraced the abrasive Lindsey) said that Rick and Billy were the best things to ever happen to Fleetwood Mac. Somewhat tellingly, the actual group wasn't depicted on the album jacket.

But sales proved disappointing. *Behind the Mask* barely grazed the Top 20. Christine's single "Save Me" got on Top 40 radio, and her "Skies the Limit" made it to the adult/contemporary FM radio format, but none of Stevie's songs were much played. Meanwhile, Stevie Nicks joined Fleetwood Mac for a long and successful international tour that, on and off, lasted for the rest of 1990. Once again, some fans missed Lindsey Buckingham's steely presentation and clever guitar playing, but the band agreed the touring atmosphere was less tense and more fun. As for Stevie, she still donned her iconic top hat for the encores, but she mostly preferred to sing wearing slouchy black berets adorned with jewels or feathers or beads. "Rhiannon" was never on the set lists, so the old Welsh witch's gossamer capes stayed in the wardrobe cases.

Fleetwood Mac was on a private plane between European concerts when Mick Fleetwood came out of the lavatory and beheld the entire band and entourage reading the hot-off-the-press British edition of his just-published autobiography, *Fleetwood: My Life and Adventures in Fleetwood Mac*. Mick gulped. He looked at Stevie, who was avidly absorbed in his gentle recounting of their affair. No one looked at him. This was mostly a prank staged by John Courage, who'd gotten hold of a case of books, but actually they were all engrossed in Mick's recounting of the often dramatic story of the band. Mick was immediately concerned about Stevie's reaction. Would she freak?

Mick: "When she actually read the book, we were on this private jet and she said, 'I've just finished the book.' And I was dreading it. I thought she was going to bat me around the face, or something. But she said, 'Well, you could've put *more* in about you and me. What about that kiss we had behind the curtain in Australia, with Jenny inches away?'"

Mick laughed and looked at her. Stevie winked at him.

But their friendship was about to fray into enmity and revenge over—once again—her mother's song, "Silver Springs." By the time the dust settled in 1991, Stevie Nicks had quit Fleetwood Mac, and she would not come back for seven years.

It all began in late 1990, while Fleetwood Mac was still on the road. Stevie's health became more of an issue, and her manager convinced her to stop touring with the band. Stevie was persuaded that she only needed one career—her solo work. Christine McVie decided that she wanted out from touring as well. (Touring was better left to the competition, which in those days meant Wilson Phillips, the daughters of Brian Wilson and John Phillips.) On December 7, before the tour's last show in Los Angeles, it was announced that Stevie and Christine would record with the band but would stop touring with Fleetwood Mac. That night, Lindsey Buckingham joined his old band for an emotional "Landslide" with Stevie, and then "The Chain" with the whole band. In her dressing room afterward, Stevie wept with relief and sadness that this might have been her last show with her old band.

In early 1990 Modern Records was intending to release Stevie's first compilation of hits from her solo career, augmented by a few new songs with famous cowriters and some remixes of familiar tunes. Then Stevie had the notion of including "Silver Springs," her 1977 song left off of *Rumours*. "Silver Springs" had never had an album release: it had been the B-side of the "Go Your Own Way" single. Stevie had given the publishing income of the song to her mother. If "Silver Springs" appeared on her possibly mega-selling solo compilation, her mother could be in for considerable income, and everyone would be happy. Stevie asked her new manager, Howard Kaufman, to propose this idea to Mick Fleetwood.

Mick said no. He refused to let Stevie use "Silver Springs." His exact words were that she could have "Silver Springs"—over his dead body. It was a Fleetwood Mac song, he tried to remind her, and he wanted to release it on a Fleetwood Mac compilation in 1992, commemorating the band's twenty-fifth anniversary. This made Stevie very angry. She just could not catch a break with "Silver Springs." There was a

lot of pleading, cajoling, and begging over this, but Mick was determined to maintain control over Fleetwood Mac's legacy.

Stevie threatened to quit Fleetwood Mac. Mick failed to respond.
Howard Kaufman told her it was her decision if she now wanted to
let go of Fleetwood Mac entirely. It could mean a cut in income for
her, he advised, but Stevie was adamant. So she announced her departure in early 1991. Rick Vito left as well. Then Christine McVie told
the London press she was leaving, too. "Fleetwood Mac just kind of
fell apart for various reasons," Rick said at the time. Years later, Stevie
told a reporter, "I didn't leave Fleetwood Mac. My brain left me."

Winter 1991. Stevie was working on her hits compilation. She spent
two weeks in the studio, working on a song she didn't much like,
"Sometimes It's a Bitch," with its writer, Jon Bon Jovi, the telegenic
New Jersey rock star. She didn't even want to sing the word "bitch,"
but her people convinced her that this was a Garden State product
worthy of mighty Bruce Springsteen, and a sure-fire radio rocket. "I
had to be talked into it," Stevie later explained. At first she didn't really
understand what his song was about. What did "Well, I've run through
rainbows and castles of candy" actually mean? Later she said she
thought it was about an earlier version of herself—"the notorious
Stevie Nicks," as she put it. (Stevie and her girl singers enjoyed inspect-
ing Jon's shapely bottom as he leaned over the mixing console. "He
was nice to all the ladies," Stevie later said of him, "and he had the best
butt of all time.")

Then there was a collaboration (and some semi-motherly infatua-
tion) with twenty-seven-year-old Bret Michaels, pretty-boy lead singer
of Poison, the LA glam rock band that everyone who liked Guns N'
Roses loved to hate. Michaels and Stevie worked on his song "Love's a
Hard Game to Play," which would be a late addition to the hits package when they needed an extra track. Stevie really dug this kid. Just
after cutting his song, she wrote (or dictated): "This song was brought
to me barely two weeks ago by a most extraordinary young man. One
of those men who have everything . . . beauty, sensitivity, warmth,
and a love for life that I had not seen in a long time. I recorded his song,

singing it for him to the best of my ability . . . hoping that people would love the song as much as we loved doing it."

Stevie wrote "Desert Angel" in a hyperpatriotic mood during Operation Desert Storm, the 1991 Gulf War between the United States and Iraq, after Iraq had invaded U.S. ally Kuwait. It was her first overtly political song, referencing recent events like the fall of the Berlin Wall. She wrote the words at her house in Paradise Valley after reading about a local support group for the troops called Operation Desert Angel, and recorded the vocals with Sharon Celani at Vintage Recorders in Phoenix in February. She was even inspired to write a passionate letter in support of the military that was published in the Army newspaper, *Stars and Stripes*. Describing herself as among those who felt "helpless and scared" by the onset of war, she was motivated to patriotic fervor in part by the hypnotic track Mike Campbell had sent her, and by a growing sense of dedication to her American homeland, especially politically conservative Arizona. Her blank-verse lyrics refer to National Guard units being called up and the anxiety of those whose family members go to fight in a foreign war. "You should know how much we love you," Stevie sings to the departing soldiers, and then simply, "Come home."

"Desert Angel" was the closing track of *TimeSpace/The Best of Stevie Nicks* when the compact disc was released, worldwide, in September 1991. This was ten years after *Bella Donna* had launched Stevie's solo stardom in 1981. *TimeSpace's* first single "Sometimes It's a Bitch" was disappointing, and wasn't helped by an uninspired performance video that mixed childhood photos with quick cuts of film clips from Stevie's career. Radio didn't seem to want to play a song with "bitch" in the title. The album got to #30 in *Billboard,* and was a Top 20 record in England, where interest in her music continued to build. (The London press, the BBC, and TV networks were happy and eager to help Stevie promote her music; some of this was due to her immense popularity in Australia and New Zealand. She also tended to give English reporters chatty and candid interviews.)

The rest of 1991 was devoted to Stevie's Whole Lotta Trouble/TimeSpace Tour in the autumn months. Stevie's old friend Les Dudek, who'd worked on *Rock a Little,* played lead guitar with a broken hand after an accident. The tour manager broke his leg. Other weird stuff happened, like power failures and dead microphones. There were whispers the tour was cursed, but the shows went well, with Russ Kunkel pounding out those hip-swinging rhythms for the girls onstage and in the audience. When it was over, Stevie came home and collapsed. Much later, no one understood how she had been able to perform at her level after five years taking ever-increasing doses of the powerful antipsychotic drug Klonopin. Those who knew her well realized it was sheer will that kept Stevie Nicks in the arena. For her, any other life was not worth living. What price, glory?

## 7.5    Death in Venice

After a period of rest and some time in Hawaii, Stevie was restless and intended to make another record. This was 1992, when Bill Clinton was running for president against George Bush. All that year, Clinton used Fleetwood Mac's catchy, hope-filled "Don't Stop" as his campaign theme, and when Clinton won the presidency in November he wanted Fleetwood Mac to perform the song at his January inauguration in Washington.

The problem was that Fleetwood Mac didn't really exist. The band was down to Mick and John, but the White House wanted the classic *Rumours* lineup with Stevie and Lindsey. When Mick polled the band members, Lindsey reminded him that he'd left the group five years earlier. Stevie was still angry with Mick over "Silver Springs," which had finally appeared on the compilation *Fleetwood Mac: 25 Years—The Chain* in November 1992. Christine was also gone. But Mick emphasized what a huge honor this was for their band and won over Stevie and Christine. But Lindsey didn't want to do it. He said he didn't care about Clinton and that he was making a solo album.

Stevie got Lindsey on the phone and told him that if he deprived her of this honorable moment, she swore she would never speak to him again. Lindsey caved in. People close to the band speculated that he was helped to this conclusion in that he might need to be part of Fleetwood Mac's guaranteed touring cash flow some sunny day in the future.

Fleetwood Mac played for the Clintons in January 1993. Bill Clinton told Stevie that he'd first heard "Don't Stop" while riding in a taxi in 1977 and realized what a great campaign song it could be. He pointed out that he and his wife Hillary were big music fans; they'd even named their only daughter after a Joni Mitchell song. Fleetwood Mac's presidential reunion was nationally televised, and it helped keep the band in the public eye while it didn't really exist. It would be another four years before they would play together again.

Work on Stevie's fifth solo album began in mid-1992, Stevie's sixth year on Klonopin. She asked her psychiatrist about decreasing her daily dose, since the drug was producing side effects that made her look older than her forty-four years. The doctor told her that she would be "nervous" without the pills, and he didn't think that was a good idea if she wanted to keep working. He ran down a gossipy list of rock stars who were supposedly on Klonopin, mentioning Bruce Springsteen, Prince, Michael Jackson, and that crazy guy from Aerosmith. He suggested increasing Stevie's dose instead. She didn't know what to do.

Stevie had liked working with an English producer, so they hired Glyn Johns, who had started out engineering the Rolling Stones' records in 1965 and had gone on to work with the Beatles, Led Zeppelin, the Who, Rod Stewart, Linda Ronstadt, and almost every important musician in rock music. Johns (fifty, attractive, longish graying hair) arrived in Los Angeles and found Stevie eager to work but muddled, unfocused, and sometimes confused. Stevie didn't have much in the way of new material. She and her in-house production guy, Glenn Parrish, had been poring over old tapes, looking for outtakes and demos of songs, some dating back almost thirty years. They had some songs left over from *Rock a Little:* "Mirror Mirror," "Greta," "Listen to the Rain," and "Love Is Like a River." They found "Destiny" on an old cassette, dated 1973. "Rose Garden" originally was a fragment of another song that Stevie wrote in 1965. "Unconditional Love" came from Sandy Stewart's demos for *The Wild Heart.* Newer material included "Street Angel," hard-rocking "Blue Denim" (written to a Mike Campbell instrumental track), "Kick It" (also with Campbell), and "Jane." Glyn Johns brought "Docklands" (by Trevor Horn and Betsy

Cook) from England, and suggested they ask Bob Dylan to play on a cover of his classic song, "Just Like a Woman."

They worked on these songs until November 1992. The album, now titled *Street Angel,* was set for release in March 1993. But then, on December 12, 1993, a seemingly dying and desperate Stevie Nicks disappeared into a locked rehabilitation clinic for almost two months. Glyn Johns went back to London, and *Street Angel*—an album Johns thought was complete—was put on hold. No one knew what would happen next.

These events began one evening when Stevie was entertaining at home. She now weighed 175 pounds and was smoking three packs of mentholated Kool cigarettes per day. She felt cold all the time, so there was always a gas-fed blaze in the fireplace. One moment she was standing by the mantel, wine glass in one hand and lit cigarette in the other, and the next moment she'd almost fallen into the fire.

She remembered this with bitterness. "I was hosting a baby shower in my old house. We had a bottle of Lafite Rothschild, some incredible vintage, and there were probably fifteen of us there. Everybody had a little sip. And that's all I remember. I must've collapsed. The girls said they found me on the carpet, curled up by the fireplace. I'd hit my head, but felt no pain. They got me up to bed. Later I looked at myself in the bathroom mirror and saw I had some blood on the side of my head. I never injure myself, so I was horrified to see that blood. I hadn't had enough wine to pass out like that. I knew it was the Klonopin.

"I'd gone from two blue pills in the morning to four blue pills. Then it was two white pills in the morning and two more at bedtime. He [her psychiatrist] kept upping my dose. If I went without it for two days, I'd start to shake. I was shaking so hard that people would look at me like I had Parkinson's disease. And then I'm starting to think, do I have some kind of neurological disease, and I'm dying?"

Then Stevie had an idea. Her assistant Glenn Parrish, who'd been with her since 1980, was a trusted friend. She now asked Glenn to take her daily dose of Klonopin so she could see what kind of effect it had on him.

"I said, 'It won't kill you because it hasn't killed me, but I just want to see what you think.' Because Glenn was terribly worried about me. Everyone was. At that point, if I could find a Percocet, because I was so miserable, I would take that, too.

"So Glenn proceeds to take all my medicine. He was a very good friend to me. I told him I'd sit with him in case he died. He began setting up a stereo in the living room. And after half an hour, he was just sitting there. And he said, 'I can't fix the stereo, and I don't think I can drive home.' And I said, 'Well, good. Just stay there, because I'm studying you.'" And he was almost hallucinating. It was bad. Then he just passed out.

"I called up my psychiatrist, and I said, 'I gave Glenn everything you prescribed for me.' And the first words out of his mouth were, 'Are you trying to kill him?' And the next words out of my mouth were, *'Are you trying to kill me?'* So I decided to get off Klonopin."

She went to this doctor for the last time the next day. "I told him I was going into rehab and he said, 'No, I can cut your dose way down.' But I had made my mind up. I felt like this jerk had taken away eight years of my life." Shortly afterward, Stevie was admitted to Daniel Freeman Memorial Hospital in Venice Beach, where she remained for the next forty-seven days.

In some primitive societies, shamans are intermediaries with the invisible realm of spirits and ghosts, healers who often take on themselves the sufferings and illnesses of their patients. Sometimes, aided by potions and herbals, the shaman must "die" to the material world and enter the dangerous, supernatural, often hellish underworld in order to restore and bring back healing energies to the regular world. Some fans speculate that this is basically what happened to Stevie Nicks in those forty-seven days, purging her body of an addictive benzodiazopine before returning to resume her songs of hope and consolation.

She recalled, "They said I'd nearly died. My hair had turned gray and was falling out. My skin molted and had started to peel off. I was in terrible pain. I couldn't get out of bed. I couldn't stand up in the shower. I thought I *was* going to die. I felt like someone had opened a door and shoved me into hell. But after forty-seven days, I came out shining, on the other side. I had a new lease on life.

"I learned so much in that hospital. I wrote the whole time I was in there, some of my best writing ever. I learned that I could have fun and laugh and cry with amazing people, and not be on drugs. I learned that I could live my life and still be beautiful and have fun and go to parties and not even have a glass of wine. And I never went to therapy again."

And later: "It's been easy for me to stay sober. I could still drink alcohol, recreationally, because I'm not an alcoholic. But I take a drug called Neurontin for my menopause. It handles the menopause [symptoms] brilliantly, but if you take so much as a sip of tequila, it makes you very sick." (After this, Stevie's publicist suggested that she stop talking to the media about menopausal issues, advice Stevie ignored.)

After this, and for the rest of her working life, Stevie constantly expressed a deep bitterness over what she described as a wasted time of her life. She told London's *Telegraph* newspaper: "I think it's very good to talk about this, to get the message out to the world about addiction to this particular drug. That was the worst period of my life. They stole my forties. I might have met someone, had a child, become a mother, made some great music. It was eight completely wasted years of my life. It's very Shakespearean, very much a tragedy."

"It was eight years of my life—gone," she told *The New York Times*. "Your forties are the last vestige of your youth, and mine was ripped away from me." Asked if she was still angry with the psychiatrist, she answered, "If I was driving a car and he was crossing the street, I might run over him." The interviewer asked for the psychiatrist's name. "Doctor Fuckhead," was her reply.

Stevie Nicks came home from the hospital on January 27, 1994. After a listening session for the supposedly complete *Street Angel* album, she said she wanted to go back to the hospital because she hated her new record so much. She said it was the saddest, lowest-energy music she'd ever made.

Atlantic was told the album was delayed while Stevie tried to fix it. Glyn Johns stayed in England and took his name off the record. Tom Panunzio, a Heartbreakers associate, was brought in to supervise. Stevie recruited Waddy Wachtel and former Eagles guitarist Bernie Leadon to overdub some of the tracks. Benmont Tench supplied painterly lashings of his majestic organ sound. Over the next few months they boosted the firepower of the better tracks ("Blue Denim," "Listen to the Rain," and "Street Angel," a pastel portrait of a homeless girl, harmonized by David Crosby.) They completely overhauled songs like "Greta" and gave it a sense of the epic, with a reggae rhythm. Song lyrics were changed to reflect bitter recent experience, referencing addiction, despair, rehab. She substituted "pills" for "pearls" on "Just Like a Woman," sang it in the first person, and indeed got Bob Dylan to play some guitar and (inaudible) harmonica on the track. She recut her vocal on her pretty 1965 ballad "Rose Garden" because her voice was hoarse on the original. (Indeed, there are four or five of her different voices running through *Street Angel*.) She wrote a new song, "Thousand Days," given a terrific, horn-driven production by Chris Lord-Alge—"Why does the greatest love / Become the greatest pain?"—but the song was left off the album.

In the end, Stevie gave up, in part because of the sheer cost of the project. *Street Angel* was released in May 1994, when she was forty-six years old. Stevie and Tom Panunzio were credited as coproducers. No one had high hopes for the record. It had some good songs but was overwhelmed by the sadness of the ballads: "Destiny," "Maybe Love Will Change Your Mind," and "Jane." Stevie was depicted on the Modern Records CD jewel box looking downcast and swaddled in pink, as if she'd break just like a little girl. The first single was supposed to be "Blue Denim," but it was replaced by "Maybe Love Will Change Your Mind," which stalled at #57. That summer, while she was touring (with Rick Vito on guitar), Marty Callner directed a performance video for the second single, "Blue Denim," showing Stevie wearing a black Bedouin tent to disguise her full figure, upstaged by stunning Sara Fleetwood, who was singing onstage with Sharon Celani and Mindy Stein.

*Street Angel*, Stevie Nicks's worst-selling album, peaked at #45 on *Billboard*'s chart. The "Blue Denim" single—one of Stevie's best rock

& roll songs ever—didn't even chart at all when released during the summer tour.

Stevie gave a lot of interviews that year while selling her album and promoting the Street Angel Tour, explaining her medical problems and why her new music wasn't up to her usual standards. "I'd been taking Klonopin for almost eight years," she told *Time Out* later. "*Street Angel* was done in the last two years of that, when it had kicked in to the point that it took away my soul and my creativity." When she came out of rehab, "I listened to the record—I'm off all the drugs—and I knew it was terrible. It had cost a fortune.

"So I went back in and tried to fix it. If you're taking a lot of tranquilizers every day, it only makes sense that the music will be [slurs] ver-r-y tranquil. Trying to fix it was like redoing a house. You end up spending way more money than if you had just burned it to the ground and started over. It wasn't fixable. Then I had to go do interviews for it, and it was everything I could do *not* to say to the interviewers, 'I hate this record.'"

Nevertheless, and despite an onset of periods of extreme fatigue, Stevie and her band spent the three summer months of 1994 on tour. At 175 pounds, Stevie knew she would look fat to her audiences. Margi Kent sewed and stitched a new wardrobe that emphasized bodily freedom for a plus-sized rock star. Her hair was dyed blond and frizzed in a "root perm," which took two hours a day to braid for the stage.

Since *Street Angel* hadn't taken wing, the tour was downsized from arenas to theaters, amphitheaters, sheds, music and arts centers, or auditoriums. (The fans loved being closer to the band and sometimes got rowdy down front.) Shows started with "Outside the Rain" and proceeded through "Dreams" and "Rooms on Fire." "Rhiannon" was back in the set, the old Welsh witch now appearing in a shorter, non-hysterical rendition, timed to the second by Rick Vito. They tried out various songs from *Street Angel* but mostly stuck to the hits: "Gold Dust Woman," "Stand Back," and "Edge of Seventeen." The encores were usually "I Need to Know" and "Has Anyone Ever Written Anything for You."

To save money, they traveled by bus from city to city. The two tour buses—one for her, one for the band—cost seven hundred dollars a day instead of the five-thousand-dollar airplane. They started in the Northeast in July, moving South and then to the Midwest in August. Stevie sang "Blue Denim" on David Letterman's *Late Night* TV program in New York on August 2. She said later she liked the new routine of keeping all her tons of gear on her bus and only taking a few things into the hotel: shawls for the lamps, extension hair plugs, snacks, candles, and incense. She also said that she had a torrid romance with a band member and spent a lot of driving time making out in the back lounge. She said he asked her if he should leave his girlfriend, but she said no. "It wouldn't have worked, off the road," she recalled later.

Then it was on to the West, with dates in California, Texas, and Arizona, where Stevie performed at her family's Compton Terrace shed in the desert. They finished with two nights at the House of Blues on Hollywood's Sunset Strip. The last show was broadcast on FM radio and got huge ratings. Stevie was exhausted and her muscles ached, but she kicked it, and Rick Vito in his bright red jacket carried the swing, a real blues-rock hero. The audience—two generations now, old Mac fans and their daughters—was cheering, and a few people were crying with relief that Stevie had saved herself from dying like all the other wasted rock stars. Stevie and her people were buoyed by the passion they saw in the fans; it was an indication that Stevie could regain her standing once she got the rest of her life in order and started writing hit songs again.

The Street Angel Tour was profitable, but Stevie was super upset when the reviews emphasized her weight gain and personal problems as much as they did her shows. Stevie was already aware that she *had* died, and that a new, sober, and much wiser persona had to be established for her career to resume properly. She recalled with bitterness, "When I walked off the stage after the last show, I told my assistant that I would never sing in front of people looking like that again." So in early 1995 Stevie quit smoking cigarettes (again), and installed treadmills in her houses in Phoenix and Los Angeles. She started Dr. Atkins's then-faddish low-carb diet and managed to lose thirty pounds by the middle of the year. She told *People* magazine, "I've accepted the fact that I'm not going to be picture-perfect. I just want to be strong."

Then she finished this transformational era—menopause, detoxification, rehabilitation, major attitude adjustment—by restoring her breasts. Her mother had suspected that Stevie's chronic fatigue might not be the Epstein-Barr virus. Barbara had read that leaking silicone from the breast implants Stevie had received in 1976 might be to blame. Stevie: "It was like cocaine—everyone was getting [implants] back then, and everyone was told they were safe." The doctor told her the procedure was painful and wasn't worth it to get them out. Stevie insisted and had the surgery, and for good reason. "They were totally broken," she said of the silicone implants, which were preserved and deposited in her doctor's freezer in case she ever wanted to sue.

# CHAPTER 8

## 8.1   Trouble in Paradise

"It takes all the running you can do, to keep in the same place," the Red Queen told Alice. "If you want to get somewhere else, you must run at least twice as fast as that."

For the next two years, Stevie Nicks would have to run twice as fast to get her career going again. Beginning in 1995 she returned to her double-winged home in the gated community at the foot of Camelback Mountain in Phoenix, and lived in the care of her brother Chris and sister-in-law Lori and their five-year-old daughter, Jessie Nicks (plus two dogs). She tried various diets and physical therapies such as movement and massage. She told friends she wasn't even tempted to think about cocaine. She wanted to think about writing songs, but her recovery was slow, and her doctors told her not to be concerned with work. She was forty-seven years old, had plenty of money, and her whole family behind her. Yet she desperately wanted to write but felt blocked and less than inspired. She told everyone she needed a collaborator.

Back in late 1994, Stevie had sung on "Somebody Stand by Me," a new song by the Missouri-born singer Sheryl Crow, whose "All I Want to Do" was one of Stevie's favorite recent songs. With Don Was producing and Ben Tench playing organ, Stevie delivered an unusual (for her) soul-style vocal, more Mavis Staples than Welsh Witch. The song was on the soundtrack for the movie *Boys on the Side*, released in February 1995. (This was a quasi-lesbian road movie with an HIV subtheme.) Stevie Nicks realized that glamorous and talented Sheryl Crow would be a good writing partner for her and vowed to make it happen.

Stevie recorded music at Vintage Recorders in Phoenix in April 1995, with Lori and guitarist Jesse Valenzuela. She found the ex–Gin Blossoms front man a tonic for her postrehab depression. She recalled, "I was sad and I was trying to figure out how to get my voice back, and if that was even possible." They cut a six-song demo that later yielded up a snazzy version of Dorsey Burnette's rockabilly classic "It's Late" (a hit for Ricky Nelson in the fifties), but when she listened to the playback at home, Stevie wasn't impressed with what they'd done. "That's where Jesse came in. He was so cool, a really strong force in taking me out of that negative thing. Jesse just said, 'Don't be stupid. This is *good*. Let's get your singing chops going and get the excitement back.'"

Then, on April 24 the Heartbreakers were playing in Phoenix, and Stevie had dinner with Tom Petty at the Ritz-Carlton hotel. Petty had gotten divorced from his wife under battlefield conditions, his house had burned down, and there were rumors someone had done it. Petty told Stevie he was in no shape to try to write with her. Instead, he delivered what Stevie later described as an "inspirational lecture," reminding her of her deeply felt obligation to her fans and urging her to go and write her own stuff. Petty knew what it was like to have a band and a road crew and about a hundred people depending on you for food on the table that night. Tom was sympathetic but steely; Stevie had to keep working or get out of the game.

"I returned home," she later wrote in the notes to her next solo album, five years in the future, "and began writing these songs." Her brother and assistant Karen began helping her find themes. One of the first to coalesce was the idea of "trouble in paradise," meaning Paradise Valley where she lived. Over the next five years, Karen Johnston and Chris Nicks recorded dozens of demos in Stevie's home studio. Some of these new songs would be featured on *Trouble in Shangri-La* in 2001.

Through all of this, Stevie kept tabs on Fleetwood Mac. She knew they'd recorded an album of new songs, some by Christine and her husband. They'd toured (opening for Crosby, Stills & Nash) with Mick's old mate Dave Mason (ex-Traffic) on guitar and the terrific twenty-seven-year-old singer Bekka Bramlett fronting the band alongside Billy Burnette. Bekka was the good-lookin' daughter of sixties rock stars Delaney and Bonnie Bramlett. She'd been singing with the Zoo and worked steadily as an in-demand backup singer in the LA studios. Bekka Bramlett had a great voice, but in the hot summer of '94, half the audience left the sheds when they realized the slender beauty in the skin-tight red leather cat suit wasn't Stevie Nicks, and Christine McVie wasn't onstage, either. Mick begged Bekka to sing "Dreams" and "Rhiannon," but she wisely refused to step into Stevie's stacked-heel stage boots. (Bekka did allow herself to perform "Gold Dust Woman.") In the 1995 touring season, the floundering Mac embarked on a semi-humiliating package tour with REO Speedwagon and Styx.

In October, Warner Bros. released a twelve-song Fleetwood Mac album called *Time*, which became the first Mac album not to make the charts at all. No one had the heart to tour after that. Billy, Bekka, and Dave Mason all left the band by the end of the year. This was described in the press as a stunning reversal for the twenty-year-old megaband.

Stevie Nicks loved Christmas and, with a little girl in the house, she lavished a lot of attention on Yule decorations and traditions. Then she made her first public appearance since rehab at the Herberger Theater in Phoenix, where she played the Ghost of Christmas Past at KTAR radio's annual broadcast of Charles Dickens's "A Christmas Carol." Afterward, she told a reporter from the weekly *Phoenix New Times* that she was sure 1996 was going to be a good year, because she was already starting to feel better.

Then, slowly at first, a momentum began in early 1996 to reunite the *Rumours* band. It started with a simple phone call from Lindsey, asking Mick to play on the solo record he was making. Mick said yes, put down the phone, and had one of his premonitions. He *had* to make this work, this time. Mick had to get Stevie and Christine back in the band. "It's victory or death for Fleetwood Mac," he told his friend Richard Dashut.

Stevie met Sheryl Crow at a post-Grammys party in Los Angeles, where Crow (who'd started out singing backup for Michael Jackson) was a hot pop commodity. As Sheryl recalled the meeting, "Stevie had just recorded 'Somebody Stand by Me,' a song of mine. I liked her immediately, and she said, 'We should get together and work some time.' I thought, Great! But then I didn't hear from her—for two years."

Meanwhile, Stevie and Lindsey were circling around each other, treading lightly. (Stevie's spies reported that Lindsey had a new girlfriend, Kristin Messner, a pretty blond photographer, and that they were living together.) In April, while she was staying in a rented beach house overlooking Sunset Boulevard and the ocean, Stevie sent him a demo of a song called "Twisted" that she'd written for the storm-chaser movie *Twister*. He agreed to produce the track and play on the song, which described "chasing down the demons / crying out for love." (The song wasn't used in the film but appeared in the soundtrack release.) Then in May, she and Mick performed together in Louisville, Kentucky, at a private party just before the Kentucky Derby.

Stevie owed Atlantic Records one more album and then was free to sign with another label. It was agreed that her final album under her Atlantic contract would be a multidisc compilation. But for her next solo albums, she was induced to sign with Warner Bros. after the two guys that ran the label came to her house and told her that they believed in her. They also offered her what they called "synergy." This meant they could attach her songs to Warner Bros. movies, increasing her revenue stream. Stevie told Danny Goldberg that she would miss the people she'd worked with at Atlantic for fifteen years, but that she needed a lot of new inspiration, so it was an auspicious time to make a change.

Stevie was still vexed by a creative blockage. If she was going to switch labels at the age of almost fifty, then the next solo album had to be terrific. However, she still wanted someone to work with her, someone supercreative like Lindsey, or Jimmy, or Rupert—someone who could bring out the best in her. She was still convinced the best person for this role was Tom Petty.

But Petty had just left his family and moved out of his house; he was staying by himself in a miasma of guilty pain and hard drugs in a secluded, rustic cabin on some overgrown land in Pacific Palisades, near where Stevie was living. He had a fourteen-year-old daughter and couldn't cope. He didn't even know how to buy groceries. Stevie went to visit him one day and saw her old friend as a really broken man. She decided it might help them both if they could try to write together, despite the fact that he'd told her to forget it a year earlier.

Stevie told Petty's biographer, Warren Zanes, what happened next: "I said, 'Let's just write some songs. I don't write songs with anybody, and really, neither do you. Let's write some.'

"He said, 'Well, okay. Maybe.'

"So I went home, thinking I'm going to go there every day until six o'clock at night and we're going to write. The next day I arrive with my grocery bags, with Hershey's chocolate syrup, instant coffee, and the kind of milk I like. He's looking at me like I'm crazy."

Petty was horrified. It looked like Stevie was moving in with him.

"I say, 'I'm going to be here, so I need my supplies.' He's like, 'Your supplies?' I say, 'Supplies! Like when you go camping.' I'll never forget the look on his face. So I said, 'Okay, so we're not going to write songs together. But I'll come visit you, and I'll keep in touch.' "

Stevie was disappointed and alarmed at her friend's mental state and near complete isolation. But she was still determined to find someone to help her find her voice again. And soon she was relieved to hear Petty had a new woman in his life, and she was someone with whom Stevie could be friends.

## 8.2   The Dance

Lindsey Buckingham hadn't seen Mick Fleetwood in almost eight years, except for a few hours at the Clinton inaugural in 1993. "He didn't want me turning up at his house, coked out of my head," Mick explained. When they bumped into each other in March 1996, Lindsey could see that Mick had cleaned up his act. Lindsey explained, "I was just about to go into the studio with [producer] Rob Cavallo, and I said, 'Why don't you come down, Mick? Let's cut some tracks.' So we started, and it was going great. And then we got John [McVie] down to play some bass [on Lindsey's 'Bleed to Love Her']. Then somebody at Warner Bros. said—and this was probably their agenda all along—'Do you want to do a live Fleetwood Mac album?' I was like, 'No—but okay.' "

Of course The Dance, as the project was termed from the begin-

ning, would be more than just a live-hits album, recorded on a Warner Bros. soundstage. It would also be a huge payday, a lucrative tour,
a long-form video, and a celebration of a resurgent Fleetwood Mac's
achievements two decades after *Rumours*. Stevie Nicks was over the
moon with relief about the reunion, since it meant putting her next
solo album on hold. It meant she didn't have to come up with lots of
new songs right away. It meant she could enfold herself in the first-
class luxuries of a big Mac tour without having to make any decisions
or take on the daunting responsibilities of a band leader. (Less enthusiastic about The Dance was Christine McVie, who confided to Stevie
that she had developed a phobia about flying in airplanes and really
wanted to retire.)

As soon as everyone had agreed, Mick got the band into a rehearsal
studio to see what Fleetwood Mac sounded like. They hadn't played
together since Lindsey had quit ten years earlier. They hadn't toured
since *Mirage* in 1982. Christine began to play "Say You Love Me,"
and Stevie stepped up to the microphone and started to sing. When
they were finished, Lindsey smiled and said, "Pretty great!" Lindsey
was excited because this would be the first time he would play the
*Tango in the Night* songs—some of his best work—with Fleetwood Mac.

To prepare for The Dance, Stevie started working with a new
vocal coach, Steve Real, who emphasized tone control, breathing, and
conservation. He gently taught her various techniques to expand her
range and refine the various timbres in which she sang. She also resumed a strict diet and lost thirty pounds. She also wrote a new song
called "Sweet Girl," and cut a demo in Phoenix with Big Al Ortiz on
guitar, in March 1997. The song was autobiographical: "I chose to
dance / Across the stages of the world." This was the song that Stevie
brought to the first rehearsal (April 1, 1997) for the two studio concerts that would be recorded and filmed for The Dance. She also
brought her singers Sharon Celani and Mindy Stein; Mindy was in
Lori's place while Lori stayed home to care for her daughter.

Also missing were veteran Mac producers Richard Dashut and Ken
Caillat, since Lindsey wanted to produce the record by himself. Even
Herbie Worthington was passed over for the more au courant fashion photographer David LaChapelle, who posed the band in a studio
painted pink.

It was hard work preparing for this next phase, but Stevie was enjoying doing it sober for the first time. She was in her element: rehearsals, repetition, learning other people's new songs, hair and wardrobe, the discipline of a new campaign. Lindsey seemed slightly more mellow, and Stevie even liked his girlfriend (although she did ask her not to take her picture with her ever-present camera). At the same time, Lindsey could still be sarcastic and condescending to Stevie when he was frustrated. She chose to ignore his boorishness as much as possible. She was used to it.

And so, after a ten-year hiatus, Fleetwood Mac returned for two concerts filmed on consecutive evenings in late May 1997 in Burbank before an adoring audience of friends, family, label staffers, and fan club members. The band was augmented with synths and percussion. Both concerts were filmed by an MTV crew, since *The Dance* would have its video debut on the cable network. "Welcome to our little soirée," Christine told the audience after the second song.

Stevie appeared in witchy black widow's weeds, with long, tousled blond hair and clear eyes. Gold chains dangled from her neck and bangles from her wrists. There was a glint of a diamond on her right hand. A black silk scarf hung from her mike stand. She still looked heavy, but was very pretty at age forty-nine, and her movements were predicated on modest twirls and gestures. Her vocal coaching had improved her voice and returned it to an echo of what she had sounded like as a much younger singer. She used a speak-sing technique on hypnotic "Dreams," which brought out more of the song's expressions of deep regret. She sang glistening backup with her girls on "Everywhere" from *Tango*. Mick pounded muffled drums to give "Rhiannon" her aura of bare ruined choirs and romantic flight. Singing at a lower pitch, Stevie deployed vibrato effects to say, in the intro, "and I still cry out for you—don't leave me—don't leave me." The formerly Dionysian "dreams unwind" finale was now a more tensile, vestal ritual—"Take me by the wind, child, take me by the sky, take me now—and he still cries out for her—Don't leave me—now . . ."

Stevie wore a gorgeous reddish gold jet-beaded shawl for "Gold Dust Woman" and danced a staggering parody of dope addiction before she snarled the "running in the shadows" chorus as if she were trying to teach a hard-won lesson to her audience. They played "Gypsy" fast and straight ahead, with Stevie twirling ecstatically during the guitar solos. (And it has to be said that Lindsey's always clever playing had reached some kind of apex as he bore down to amplify the lead guitarist's role of rhythmic drive and musical impression.)

Stevie and Lindsey played "Landslide" by themselves on a dark stage, after Stevie looked over at her father in the audience and said, "This is for you, Daddy." The fans whooped at the line, "I'm getting older, too." At the end, after a slightly wobbly vocal rendition of "Landslide," Stevie embraced Lindsey with what may have been genuine tenderness, or a gesture of reconciliation for the fans and the cameras. A few days earlier she had told an interviewer that she was conscious that the band's fans valued the epic romance of herself and Lindsey Buckingham. It was part of the legend and had to be respected.

Lindsey switched to banjo for "Say You Love Me," then took over and played his new song, "My Little Demon." Then Stevie offered a slow and stately "Silver Springs," which sprouted wings and soared with five voices on the chorus. The cameras captured Stevie glaring at Lindsey, and roaring at him as she sang the ominous warning that he would never get away from the sound of the woman who haunts (and still loves) him. "Thank you very much," she told the cheering audience, "we really appreciate it. 'Silver Springs' is a great old song." Then Stevie performed a clunky dance with her tambourine during "You Make Loving Fun," before delivering her new song, "Sweet Girl," which describes her global travels, "always on call / missing whole cities."

The concerts wound down with a supercharged "Go Your Own Way"; the arrival of the uniformed USC Trojan band for "Tusk"; the finale of "Don't Stop"; and the classic Fleetwood Mac encore: Christine McVie at the piano by herself, lulling her listeners with "Songbird."

The album and video releases of *The Dance* were delayed when Lindsey decided the band hadn't performed to his standard in either concert. When they chose the best songs, they replayed and re-sang almost everything. Using Pro Tools and Auto-Tune digital engineering, almost the entire show was "repaired, replaced, and retuned" (according to the disgruntled Ken Caillat) until Lindsey's perfectionist vision had been attained. But this paid off when *The Dance* was released the following August. The album debuted at the top of *Billboard's* chart. "Silver Springs" was released as a single and also sold well, which meant that Barbara Nicks would finally get paid royalties for the song her daughter had given her.

Stevie Nicks and Fleetwood Mac spent the autumn of 1997 on a forty-four-concert tour, which was fine with her. Cosseted and pampered by private planes, five-star hotels, and an attentive road crew, all she had to do was show up and sing, and she said later this period was crucial to her continuing recovery. The tour also grossed a reported $36 million. Reviewers were generally kind to the aging musicians, but some mentioned Lindsey's showboating and overextended guitar solos. One review of a Texas concert noted, "Unfortunately, some incredibly self-indulgent moments ruined the band's pleasant, if nostalgia-driven spell, which was primarily woven by the tambourine-playing gypsy that is still Stevie Nicks at forty-nine. Every time she twirled [in] her chiffon and velvet outfits while teetering in suede platform boots, the entire arena went nuts."

About halfway through the tour, it started getting to Lindsey that Stevie was getting all the love from the fans, who responded to the tormented howling of his own songs by making beer-and-bathroom runs. Acting out his rage with his guitar, his segments were likened to exorcisms by more than one newspaper critic. Around this time Stevie stopped embracing her old boyfriend after "Landslide." Instead, the duo exchanged perfunctory nods and Stevie walked back to her place on the stage.

Mountains of cocaine were no longer served at the preshow buffets. John Courage by now had retired, and the band now kept a greater distance between themselves and the crew. By the end of the tour Stevie noticed that Christine was unhappy and drinking more than usual. And Stevie told her people that Lindsey had been sullen or mean to her on almost every occasion when they were together off the stage. After the final show, Stevie pointedly told Mick that this was going to be her last Fleetwood Mac tour—for a *very* long time.

## 8.3   Hall of Fame

On January 11, 1998, Stevie Nicks and a small entourage flew from Los Angeles to New York, where they checked into the Waldorf Astoria hotel on Park Avenue. The next night, all dressed up in black velour and lace, Stevie took the elevator to the ballroom downstairs, where she and Fleetwood Mac were inducted (by Sheryl Crow) into the Rock & Roll Hall of Fame. (The actual hall had opened in Cleveland in 1995.) Fellow inductees included Santana, the Eagles, Gene Vincent, the Mamas and the Papas, and Lloyd Price. This is where Stevie recruited Sheryl Crow to work on her next solo album, and where Don Henley recruited Stevie to sing at benefits for his Walden Woods project, which sought to protect forest land adjacent to Walden Pond in Massachusetts, made famous by Henry David Thoreau. In the postinductions concert, Stevie and Lindsey sang "Landslide" and pretended to be civil to each other, before the whole band played "Big Love." Mac's founding guitar hero Peter Green played his "Black Magic Woman" with Santana, who'd had a Top 10 single with the song in 1970.

Now her new label Warner Bros. wanted Stevie's new solo album, her sixth, but she put them off to spend the winter compiling a megacompilation to complete her contract with Atlantic Records. Stevie, her brother, and her assistants spent several months in her Paradise Valley house, choosing songs from hit singles to deep album cuts to studio outtakes and demos; also single B-sides, live tracks, and movie songs; also picking snapshots (mostly Stevie's Polaroid prints) and primo images by Herbie Worthington and Neal Preston that depicted Stevie in all her varied personae: hieratic priestess, noir femme fatale, Scythian princess, Will o' the Wisp spirit, satanic abbess, Astarte, Alice, the Queen of Sheba, prima ballerina, atomic cowgirl, waif, wraith, fairy godmother, et cetera. Stevie wrote and dictated an introduction and expressive production notes for some of the forty-six tracks on three compact discs, which would feature in the box set's sixty-four-page booklet. She asked Danny Goldberg to write a short history of Modern Records. Stevie remixed "Blue

Denim" and other *Street Angel* mixes that she'd never approved because she was just out of rehab and totally dazed, and also cut a new version of "Rhiannon" that would set a certain record straight. She wrote, "With all the bootlegged versions of 'Rhiannon' out there, I just decided to go into a studio with a great grand piano and play 'Rhiannon' to you now, as she is today. I feel her wisdom is much evolved . . . and you will hear that in the piano, and in my voice. People say, 'Do you really want to go through that again?' And all I can say is, 'It is my pleasure.'"

This solo piano variation on a theme of Rhiannon is chunky and chordal, with Sharon Celani descanting harmonically, and some new ideas: "Dream on silly dreamer / Try hard, try harder . . . you can't leave her." Stevie accelerates the tempo after a repetition of the first three verses, providing a stark and minimalist rendition of the wild-eyed dance of Rhiannon that she recycled every night onstage as an ingénue singer with Fleetwood Mac. This was Rhiannon in 1998—an older and wiser Welsh witch.

*Enchanted* was released by Modern/Atlantic in April 1998, just as Stevie Nicks was turning fifty. It was one of the most ambitious, vault-emptying CD compilations that any rock star had yet attempted, and it met with quick success for an expensive package, reaching #85 on *Billboard*'s chart. Superior digital mixing technology gave a newly haunting majesty to great songs like "Nightbird." "If Anyone Falls" roared like a pride of lionesses. "Stop Draggin'" and "Stand Back" were luridly brighter, and "Rooms on Fire" sounded like it was cut in a cathedral. "Reconsider Me" (by Warren Zevon, a *Rock a Little* reject), was released as a single and didn't chart. Late that summer, after a blistering "Stand Back" on Jay Leno's *Tonight Show* on NBC, Stevie and her band began a thirty-seven-concert solo tour on May 27 in Hartford, Connecticut. Slimmed down, with long straight hair, traveling with her seven-piece band and her vocal coach, and fighting an unusual bout of stage fright, Stevie was able to unleash a new, throaty singing energy that her fans didn't think they would hear from her again.

She was also working on a new way of presentation. The stage was ultrafeminine, with rose-colored fabric and doily patterns. She began in a tight black bodice, as if to reclaim her old figure, and then added layers of shawls, waistcoats, and more shawls as the evening went on. In Hartford she gave the fans a seminar on her shawls. The golden shawl for "Gold Dust Woman" was so old, she said, "that it should be falling apart, but it isn't—just like me." This provoked general laughter. The crimson "Stand Back" shawl was from her earliest days with Fleetwood Mac. (Her truest fans knew this was a departure, since she'd always sung "Stand Back" in a classic polka-dot shawl.) She said she was through with her stacked-heel boots after the previous year's Mac tour. From now on she would play in black high-top Nike boots. For many the highlight of the show was when the band "unplugged," and sat on bar stools around Stevie for an acoustic set that included quieter songs like "After the Glitter Fades" and "For What It's Worth." The encore was usually the Heartbreakers' "I Need to Know."

Fans and reviewers who had seen Stevie playing less-than-stellar shows in their towns with Fleetwood Mac the year before were now happy to see her return to form with her own musicians. A perceptive Chicago reviewer covered her concert at the World Music Theater in the city's near suburbs:

> The endlessly blond rock diva muscled into upper registers that were only rumors for her last year, whirled and twirled unencumbered by ancient feuds and ambivalent band mates, and glided across the stage visibly thrilled to be emancipated from another greatest-hits set list. Turning 50 appears to have lit a fire under those 5-inch heels and rivers of flowing shawls.
>
> Wrapped in a lacy black antique dress and adorned with wispy layers of earth-toned scarves, Nicks baby-stepped her way onstage, her trademark elbow-length blond mane brushed exquisitely. Watching Nicks sing her classic "Rhiannon" convinces the most rational skeptic that she'd lose her voice if you cut off her hair.
>
> Touring to promote a new retrospective CD box set, Nicks sounded innocent, even nervous as she told the crowd that she intended to perform

some songs she'd never sung onstage before.
Where Nicks appeared drained and weary last
November [1997] with Fleetwood Mac at the
Horizon [venue], she looked radiant at the World,
as if she were auditioning for a gig with a band
she'd been dying to join. That edge made the
evening.

On July 21, a Colorado fan/stalker was held by security when he tried to get into Stevie's show in Englewood, near Denver. A judge had already granted Stevie's lawyers a petition for a restraining order against the fan, who was obsessed with meeting her. Hauled before the judge, the fan explained to the court that Stevie Nicks was a famous and well-known witch, and she had the power to cure him of his unwanted voices and his homosexuality.

Late in the tour Stevie and her girls were in a helicopter making a descent onto a large field in the upstate New York town of Bethel, where the Woodstock Festival of Art and Music had been held on Max Yasgur's farm in 1969. Stevie told the girls that she'd wanted to do this ever since she saw the choppers ferrying the big rock stars onto the site in the 1970 *Woodstock* movie. She was headlining the first night of a weekend festival called A Day in the Garden, along with Don Henley, Ten Years After (who'd played in 1969), and Ziggy Marley & the Melody Makers. Stevie later said that she got chills when she and Don sang "Leather and Lace" a hundred feet from where Jimi Hendrix had blasted out a war-cry version of "The Star Spangled Banner" at dawn, almost thirty years before.

When the Enchanted Tour finished, Stevie returned to Paradise Valley to rest. There she learned that Christine McVie not only had quit Fleetwood Mac, but she had sold her house in Beverly Hills, her cars, and her grand piano; she was divorcing her husband and moving back to England. She told Mick that at age fifty-five, she'd had enough of Fleetwood Mac. Her father had died the year before, and there was an old ruin of a house in Kent that she wanted to restore, and then re-tire to an English countrywoman's life of damp tweeds and wet dogs.

Christine had also given interviews that indicated she may have gotten tired of Stevie and Lindsey. She complained of Stevie's dabbling in "astrology and stuff" and Stevie's "so many boyfriends." She said the trouble with "the Americans in Fleetwood Mac" was that they had little sense of humor and took themselves "much too seriously."

"Christine just flipped out," Stevie recalled, "and said, 'I can't do this anymore. I'm having panic attacks.' She moved back to England, never to be heard from for years. Mick stayed in touch with her, so we always knew she was okay. I never expected her to come back, and I missed her a lot."

Then Lindsey's girlfriend had a baby, Lindsey's first child, and this is when Stevie finally said that she accepted that there was no way that she and Lindsey were going to grow old together in an old folks' home. Stevie had never consciously given up on Lindsey Buckingham, until then. The next time an interviewer asked her about their old romance, she answered, "It's over. It doesn't mean the great feeling isn't there. It just means that . . . you know, we're beauty and the beast. It means that the love is always there, but we'll never be together, so that's even more romantic." Asked when she knew it was really over, she replied, "The day his first child was born. I knew that was it. *That* was the definitive thing."

For a little over a year Stevie had been seeing a much younger man, a divorced waiter with two children, who was twenty years her junior. She liked him, but he wasn't someone who could escort her to the Grammy Awards and other industry functions she was asked to attend. She recalled, "I went out with somebody for a little over a year who was quite enamored with me. He was way too young for me, though. I was nearly fifty and he was nearly thirty. We had a riot, but I said eventually he would make me feel extremely old, so I ended it. But I'm never not open to the possibility of romance." She told friends that the waiter was an embarrassing situation for her. "He really cared about me," she said.

Then she started seeing an old flame. "I'd had a relationship with someone I'd gone out with a long time ago. It didn't work out then, and it didn't work out now. It just proved my theory that you can never go back." Stevie's next boyfriend was a younger musician whose career was stalled. Stevie was mentoring him, offering love and encouragement. Then she was offered a huge cash advance in a new publishing deal, and she didn't feel she could share her delight with this person. "I was tickled and thrilled and I made the mistake of telling someone who was struggling in this business. As the words came out of my mouth, I could see that he didn't think it was funny. So I knew our relationship was never going to happen, because I can't be a person who is not going to share that moment."

For the next three years Stevie would turn these and other loves into material: ideas and lyrics that would become the inspirations for the twelve songs on *Trouble in Shangri-La,* which took so long to make it wouldn't come out until 2001.

## 8.4   Adult Contemporary

Sheryl Crow was thirty-six years old when she started writing and producing new tracks with Stevie Nicks in Hawaii in late 1998. Stevie loved Sheryl's songs like "Everyday Is a Winding Road" and "My Favorite Mistake," and she pressed Crow for details of her life. Both Sheryl and Stevie were baton-twirling teenage prom queens who went on to sing in local bands. The difference was that where Stevie wanted to go to hairdressing school, Sheryl went to the University of Missouri and then taught music in grade school while honing her skills as a multi-instrumentalist. Stevie ruefully told Sheryl that when she was thirty-six, back in 1984, she was hopelessly addicted to cocaine and about to have a breakdown that landed her in rehab. She said that in another year she would have died from overdosing on something stupid, like too much cough syrup. Stevie said that at thirty-six her life was slipping away, and what saved her was her music. It gave her the strength not to let go and made her realize she wanted to stay in the land of the living, write more songs, go on tour, and have some more fun. They talked for hours about having children (or not), with Sheryl concerned that her biological clock was ticking louder every day and Stevie relieved that her time had run out. Stevie did tell Sheryl that she was almost sure that she would have met someone, and might have had a child, but for her eight wasted, heavily medicated years.

As for Sheryl Crow, she took a hard look at Stevie's life: near total freedom, international fame, growing respect as a wise woman of rock, a legend in the Hall of Fame. Crow came to the conclusion that for a female rock star, staying single and childless wasn't the worst thing that could happen.

For most of 1999 Stevie's year-old Yorskhire terrier, Sulamith, sat on the studio sofa and listened as Sheryl Crow helped her mistress develop new songs. (Sulamith was adorable, but there were those who were less than enchanted with the grating, squealing "voice" that Stevie used to communicate with the puppy, and vice versa.)

These hard-won tunes were a mixture of ancient melodies from Stevie's past and some new ideas by other writers. The former included "Candlebright," a mandolin- and organ-driven ballad about a wandering dreamer seeking that beckoning candle in a window. It started out as a journal poem called "Nomad" in 1970, continued as a demo for the second Buckingham Nicks album, and was considered for *Fleetwood Mac,* but they used "Rhiannon" instead. Similarly, "Sorcerer" had been first written in 1972. Buckingham Nicks played it live under the title "Lady from the Mountains." It was also made into a demo for *Fleetwood Mac* but not used. Now "Sorcerer" became a blazing anthem proclaiming visions of star streams and snow dreams, propelled by a ringing guitar pattern from Sheryl's Telecaster. It was also a song about Lindsey and control. "Sorcerer—who is the master?"

This was an important song for Stevie, as she later commented: "I always think some of my songs are premonitions, and ["Sorcerer"] is one of them. It saw the future. The lady from the mountains was the lady from San Francisco who moved to Los Angeles to follow her dream—which was to make it as a rock star—and a rock star she became."

Sheryl Crow also had major involvement in "That Made Me Stronger," a churning, Beatles-influenced song about Tom Petty telling her to pull herself together and write her own stuff. Stevie put her words on a demo track by other writers and Sheryl pulled it together in a rocking arrangement. Sheryl also contributed one of her own songs, "It's Only Love," which Stevie sang in a voice that expressed great sympathy for the passion of Sheryl's lyric.

When Stevie sought a song from Sandy Stewart, someone who never let Stevie down despite some conflicts and disappointments, Sandy sent her "Too Far from Texas," a hard-rocking love song that Sheryl got deeply into, and to which Mike Campbell contributed lead guitar. They recast "Too Far from Texas" as a duet between Stevie and Natalie Maines, the spitfire singer from the Dixie Chicks. Then they got most of the Heartbreakers to play on the track, with Steve Ferrone on drums and Sheryl on bass guitar. The song was about a girl in Texas missing her man in England under questionable circumstances, and it was by far the best production Stevie Nicks had been involved with for years. Another track coproduced by Sheryl Crow was "Touched by an Angel," which appeared in the 2001 movie *Sweet November*. Another was a rethink of Stevie's ancient (and prophetic) song "Crystal," with Stevie singing this time in place of Lindsey Buckingham.

They worked on this new music until the end of 1999. But Sheryl Crow was booked through 2000, and she regretfully had to leave Stevie's new album in the hands of other producers. Stevie and her band embarked on what was called the Holiday Millennium Tour, playing mostly her hits in California and the Southwest.

Stevie then spent most of the year 2000 shuttling between a dozen different studios in Westwood, West Hollywood, and the Valley as she wrote and rewrote, pulling new music out of her workbooks and ledgers. The musician-producer John Shanks, who was associated with singers Bonnie Raitt and Melissa Etheridge, now became Stevie's arranger and friend. They started working on the title track, "Trouble in Shangri-La," building a militant choral wall around Stevie's wordy text about a lover getting between her and her friends. Then they cut "Planets of the Universe," which was written during the 1976 *Rumours* sessions, when Stevie first realized that she would leave her relationship with Lindsey. "Planets" was a complex song about vengeful feelings of being wronged. "You'll never rule again / The way you ruled me." (The accompanying guitar lick echoed Lindsey's distinctive style.) "Planets" was also about a woman's resignation to a different romantic existence: "Yes, I will live alone." The original version had some especially spiteful lyrics. An angry verse would be removed by Stevie at the last minute before release, after she decided the song as it stood would be too hurtful to Lindsey.

"Fall from Grace" was another collaboration with John Shanks, and one of Stevie's fiercest expressions of her will. A furious lyric paired to an incendiary guitar track, "Fall from Grace" was written in a Nashville hotel suite at the end of The Dance Tour, when Stevie felt she wasn't getting the respect she deserved. The song reminds a lover—or a band—that she was the reason they made it this far. "Maybe the reason I say these things / Is to bring you back alive / Maybe I fought this long and this hard / Just to make sure you—survive / Just to make sure you survive." (Another song from this period and subject matter was "Thrown Down," which was filed away for future use.)

Stevie's new song "Every Day" was given a cushion of violins and cellos by John Shanks. Then Stevie turned to another musician-producer, David Kahne, for help with "Love Changes," a ballad in blank verse, like beat poetry. Stevie's pretty and wistful "I Miss You" became a lush ballad under the baton of old friend Rick Nowles, who also added a liquid string section to a questioning song about relationships and travel. Lindsey Buckingham was persuaded to add guitar to "I Miss You," his first-ever appearance on a Stevie Nicks solo album. When she saw Lindsey in the studio, Stevie warmly congratulated him on his recent marriage to his girlfriend, Kristen, thirty. (Lindsey was fifty-one.)

Stevie wrote and produced "Bombay Sapphires" herself. It was a moody piece that echoed with samba feeling, conjuring the Hawaiian islands of Maui and Oahu, where Stevie visited between recording sessions. Stevie's manager asked that his client Macy Gray, the soulful pop-blues singer, appear on the track. Stevie reportedly didn't much like Macy Gray's voice but acquiesced to Howard Kaufman's earnest request.

One of the last tracks completed was recorded in Paris. This was "Love Is," a languid ballad about being awed by love's power. Stevie was joined on "Love Is" by Canadian singer Sarah McLachlan, then thirty-two, who had founded the Lilith Fair, an important, all-female summer music festival. Stevie and (very pregnant) Sarah had bonded over drawing in the studio: Stevie with her stained-glass angels, Sarah with Celtic figures and lettering. Later Sarah would draw the initial "S" in Stevie's name on the album jacket, in the shape of a dancing Welsh dragon.

At the end of the year 2000, Stevie Nicks went home to Paradise Valley for an Arizona Christmas, satisfied that she and her six producers had made her best record in years. "Trouble in Paradise" became *Trouble in Shangri-La*. Stevie had to prepare for the new album's release and promotion, and then another tour with her own band after an absence from the stage of three years, since the Enchanted Tour. But first, Fleetwood Mac reconvened (without Christine McVie) and played for Bill Clinton one last time before he vacated the White House after eight years of peace and prosperity, and a noxious whiff of sex scandal as well.

The first half of 2001 was spent in further production. Stevie was photographed in gauzy taffeta and chiffon on an elaborate, sepia-toned studio set by rock-fashion photographer Norman Seeff, who achieved his trademark foggy effects by stretching a sheer woman's stocking over the lens of his darkroom enlarger. They made two expensive videos, primarily for the cable channel VH-1, MTV's sister station for (supposed) grown-ups. Sheryl Crow returned to appear in the "Sorcerer" video. Sheryl strummed her guitar and smiled while Stevie sashayed in major red lipstick and a low-cut black dress. (The director, Nancy Bardawill, shot the entire video in five hours.)

Stevie hated her next director, Dean Carr, who seemed to take five years to make the "Every Day" video. This was a big production with a water feature, dancers, and a pair of mated black swans. Stevie was in a dire-looking Morgan le Fay dress and long, curly hair extensions; she curtly refused when directed to lie down in the water with the swans. She shouted at the director that she was *not* getting in the water with the fucking swans. "He hated me," she commented later. "I was so unpleasant." She pointed out that swans mated for life, but even the swans were quarrelsome and mean to each other while they were making the "Every Day" video.

*Trouble in Shangri-La* was released by Reprise Records in May 2001. Stevie was fifty-three years old. Her sixth solo album had been mixed and equalized by Chris Lord-Alge, who had to make the work of seven separate producers into one seamlessly flowing and sonically apposite Stevie Nicks album. It was a success. *Trouble* debuted at #5 on the *Billboard* chart, Stevie's best showing since *The Wild Heart* in 1983. "Every Day" was a Top 20 single on the "Adult Contemporary" charts, and then "Sorcerer" got to #21. But "Planets of the Universe," thunderously extended and remixed for the dance floor and issued on two vinyl LPs, got to #1 on the "Hot Dance Music/Club Play" chart. Stevie's music, sometimes remixed without official authorization, had been steadily growing in the discos. There also was this thing, "The Night of a Thousand Stevies," now an annual fetish rite in lower Manhattan, where fans from all over the world danced late into the wee hours wearing costumes based on Stevie's wardrobe. (Rhiannon-looking witches were huge; also Arthurian princesses, Scarlett O'Haras, Ladies from the Mountains, and other personae. Some came as White Winged Doves.) Sometimes at these events, Stevie's male fans outnumbered the ladies. Every year, the organizers implored Stevie to attend, but she always declined, sending loving messages of support instead.

*Trouble in Shangri-La* has been credited with saving Stevie's career. Her comeback was helped by a new liaison with VH-1, which made her its Artist of the Month in May, putting all her videos back into max rotation and booking her for episodes of its hit programs *Storytellers* and *Behind the Music*. Then *People* magazine named her to its "50 Most Beautiful People" list, which led to Stevie being in demand for TV appearances and award shows. The hottest female group in America, Destiny's Child, sampled the "Stand Back" guitar riff for their hit single "Bootylicious," and invited Stevie to appear in the video, miming Waddy's now classic single-note guitar stutter.

The Trouble in Shangri-La Tour began in July 2001 and wound its way around the country, with Sheryl Crow joining Stevie onstage as a guest artist on several concerts in major markets. Stevie's set began with "Stop Draggin'" and continued through "Dreams" and "Gold Dust Woman" before introducing "Sorcerer." Sheryl came out to sing "My Favorite Mistake" and stayed for "Every Day." "Rhiannon" came in the middle of the show, then "Stand Back" and "Planets of the Universe" in a dance floor arrangement. Sheryl came back for "Everyday Is a Winding Road" and a brace of new songs from the *Trouble* album. Stevie gave "Fall from Grace" a ferocious interpretation, leaving some fans wondering what she could appear so angry about. "Edge of Seventeen" ended the concert, with "I Need to Know" and "Has Anyone Ever Written" performed as encores.

But there was trouble with Stevie's voice: the doctors said it was acute bronchitis, and several concerts were canceled. This upset Stevie terribly, because of disappointed fans and a blemish on her reputation with the agents and promoters who ran the concert business. Too many canceled shows could mean no tour next time. Waddy Wachtel then got sick, and then the stage monitors began to fail in the middle of shows. Was this tour also somehow cursed?

By the end of August, the tour was back in a groove. Stevie was unusually chatty with the audiences on this tour, spending long minutes on random monologues and more focused warnings about medication and addiction. She started enjoying the fellowship of the road, even the nightly makeup sessions that began with her naked face and progressed through a base layer, foundation, spot concealer, under-the-eye bag concealer, cheekbone sculpting with three types of blusher, eye shadow, eyeliner, mascara, lip liner and—finally—lipstick, until a full performance mask was achieved. But she was mainly proud that she had fielded one of her best bands ever. But then something happened that cast a long shadow over the whole enterprise.

## 8.5   Terrified

Stevie's Toronto concert had gone well, with waves of cheering even for new songs and an audience that didn't want to let the evening go.

Stevie and her girls did a quick post-show run to the big black SUVs that carried them to Toronto International and Stevie's private jet. It was September 10, 2001, a quiet Monday night.

Stevie slept a little on the short flight to LaGuardia Airport in New York, where the Trouble in Shangri-La Tour would continue at Radio City Music Hall. Stevie was also booked on NBC's *Today* show, a crucial appearance for the success of the tour. More black cars took them through sleeping Queens after midnight and on to the Waldorf Astoria hotel on Park Avenue and 50th Street in Manhattan. At two in the morning, Stevie checked into one of the hotel's presidential suites near the top of the building. She changed into her black lounge clothes while snacks were prepared in the suite's galley kitchen. They chatted about the night's concert, Stevie drawing in her journal, eyeing the grand piano in the suite's wood-paneled living room. Shawn Colvin's new album was playing. Stevie thought about writing a condolence note to Gladys Knight, whose niece Aaliyah had been killed in a plane crash while making a video in the Bahamas. The television was on, sound off. They watched the sun rise over Long Island to the east, a moving display of shifting light. It was Tuesday, September 11, 2001.

Stevie was thinking about going to bed when someone shouted, and she turned on the television's sound. An airplane, a passenger jet, had flown into one of the towers of the World Trade Center in Lower Manhattan. Then another plane pierced the second tower. The images shown on TV were riveting and obscene. Stevie was glued to CNN, the cable news channel, which broadcast images of people jumping from the tallest buildings in New York. Some of the people appeared to be on fire. Then another jet smashed into the Pentagon in Washington, D.C. And another plane—all had taken off from Boston—was missing, presumed hijacked, and down somewhere. Then the Trade Center's South Tower collapsed. A bit later, the North Tower went, too. The TV announcers said the towers were full of people and firemen when they fell. A building across the street then collapsed a few hours later. The air in the hotel suite became degraded as the drifting dust from the collapsed towers spread over New York City like a toxic pall.

America was under attack. Stevie Nicks was very frightened. To calm herself down, she opened her journal and began to take notes on what was happening.

The air was getting worse as a death haze loomed over the city. The hotel staff told the guests to close all the windows and to stay off the streets. The Waldorf went into the lockdown mode used when presidents stayed there, with only one entrance open and guards posted. They heard early that the Radio City concert was canceled. The area's three main airports where closed while Air Force jets buzzed low over Manhattan, prowling for intruders, letting people know the battle was over—for now. Even some of the bridges were closed. The Trouble in Shangri-La Tour was stuck in Manhattan, for the time being.

At a quarter to five the following morning, an emotional Stevie Nicks took up her journal and wrote: "We are a devastated city / I feel I am part of this city / We are a strong, brilliant city / We are watching a piece of history / We are living through a tragedy / Like no one—has ever seen." The wife of one of her favorite Warner Bros. executives had been on one of those planes from Boston, where she'd left their twin daughters at college.

Stevie noted in her journal that the sun rose at 6:10 on 9/12. She wrote, "So today is both beautiful and frightening, looking out from 36 floors up, can I tell you how unimaginable it would be if I looked up and saw a big jet flying toward me, in this country? My question— how could this happen?" And a bit later: "Well, I think I have to sleep now. We are all traumatized. God bless everyone that lost someone . . . and all of those . . . that are gone . . . I am so sorry . . . —Stevie Nicks, 7:06 in the morning . . . P.S. The room is still glowing pink."

When Stevie woke up in the late afternoon, she wondered if she should cancel the tour out of respect to those who died. Her managers advised that she already had canceled some shows when she was ill, and that she should keep going if she was able. So they packed up and drove to Atlantic City for a show at the Borgata Hotel that Saturday. Then it was on to Columbus, Ohio. The fans were turning out for her, selling out shows that still had plenty of availability before the planes hit the buildings. But she was anguished about being on tour. She wanted to be home. She called Don Henley. The Eagles were recording, he said, but everyone was having a bad time.

Stevie: "At first he said, 'Just come home, honey.' But then he said, 'Are people coming to the shows?' I said, 'Yes.' Then he said, 'Well,

Stevie, if you can gut this out and make people happy for a minute, then try and stay out there.'"

She called her mother. "When my mom answered the phone, I burst into tears and said, 'I don't know if I can stay out here. I'm having a really hard time.' She said, 'Teedie, I've had at least ten phone calls from Atlantic City saying they loved it, and that you totally cheered them up. Honey, if you can finish this tour, think how many hearts you can lift up. This is your gift. I know you can do this. You *are* that strong.'"

So Stevie stayed on tour, moving from one Ritz-Carlton to the next Four Seasons hotel and back. Some days she had to force herself to get on the plane to do the next concert. For the first time she copied personal diary entries onto her Web site, nicksfix.com, so fans could follow her travels. The Washington, D.C.–area show sold out and was emotionally wrenching since the Pentagon was still smoldering in nearby Virginia. Stevie was visited backstage by children in wheelchairs, and there were long hugs for all of them.

They were going to return to New York, but *Today* canceled and Radio City declined to reschedule. This was disappointing as Stevie wanted to sing "Landslide" and "Has Anyone Ever Written Anything for You"—which she thought her most compassionate song—for a New York audience. To her fans she wrote that she was having panic attacks, especially on show days, and these feelings didn't let up until she was on her way to her plane after the concert. "That is the only time I can feel calm or safe. That is the time when I reaffirm my conviction to stay out here and finish the tour."

Meanwhile, her band was really hot onstage, rechanneling the crackling electro-spiritual energy coming from an excited rock audience. (Fans who compare bootleg concert recordings think these were some of the best performances of Stevie's career.) Stevie picked up on this: "Anyway, the shows have been good, and I do think I take the people away for a moment, I see them smile, I see them dance, I touch their hands, I look into their eyes, they are suffering, but just for a moment, we are free."

The Nashville show was difficult, but Lori Nicks had joined the tour for moral support, so Stevie didn't cry onstage, even if she wanted to. (She was glad she didn't, she told her journal.) In San Francisco a few days later she was distracted by the TV sound of bagpipes keening at the funerals of firemen killed on 9/11. At 1:20 in the morning of September 28, while watching CNN in her suite in the Mandarin Oriental Hotel, she wrote, "I feel like I have aged five years since Sept. 11th. My skin feels different; my eyes look different to me—my frown is more pronounced." Two hours later she added: "I play tomorrow at Shoreline, San Jose, land of Bill Graham, big rock shows, Janis Joplin and Jimi Hendrix, all those great San Francisco bands we opened for—the place where Buckingham Nicks was born. So this is as close to home as it gets—my dearest friends will be there—San Francisco, here I come."

In early October, the Trouble in Shangri-La Tour moved into the new Aladdin Theater in Las Vegas. Stevie was hoarse and sometimes struggling, but her parents and her brother's family were there with her, so she felt safe. Other times she gave herself pep talks: she was a warrior-queen on a crusade to bring succor and healing to her damaged people. She also was obsessing about those canceled shows and her reputation in the industry. She wanted to make up for all the missed concerts, but the autumn touring season was really over for her.

The last concerts were in Los Angeles. Watching the news in her hotel suite in the San Fernando Valley, where she would play two shows at the Universal Amphitheater, she was informed that although all the 9/11 plane hijackers were from Saudi Arabia, her government was now bombing Afghanistan, whose Taliban government supported Osama Bin Laden, mastermind of the 9/11 attacks. Los Angeles was in fear of retaliation. Streets were unusually quiet. The Emmy Awards broadcast was canceled. But both of Stevie's LA shows were sellouts, and they had to be special. That night she wrote out her prayer:

> Dear God, let me be great tomorrow—let me
> forget about terrorism and sing your songs from
> my heart . . . let me feel good and be happy—let
> me give that to these people—that is my prayer—
> And remember Stevie,—Walk like a queen.

As usual, Stevie was glad and relieved to be home, which was then an apartment with high ceilings in an oceanside building near the Pacific Coast Highway, where Santa Monica meets Pacific Palisades. It was on a high floor, with big picture windows and beautiful, majestic views toward Palos Verdes in the south, and then all the way to Point Dume, the massive promontory northwest of Malibu. Sitting by her window with a glass of wine, watching the serpentine red taillights of the cars moving up the coast, she felt herself in a post-tour twilight zone.

"I am home now," she wrote. "I am starting to calm down a little bit, knowing there is no show tomorrow. Lucky for me and the band that we are doing a few shows between now and December, or we'd all be freaked out. It is always hard to come back into the atmosphere after a tour ends. It's an age-old rock road problem—the road becomes normal, so going home is strange."

The sun was down now, and Stevie got up and lit some candles. She liked watching the mesmeric highway lights, the whites coming toward her, the reds going away, the apartment filled with the candle's pungent scent of *nag champa,* a rare spice from India. The name of the candle was Illumé. She fixed on Illumé's double image, the candle and its reflection in the darkening window. Then she got out her journal and wrote out four long verses of a new song about the last few weeks, a haunted ballad of trauma and remorse, and a thanksgiving for all the love that got her through the ordeal. When she was done, she dated the entry: October 11, 2001.

# CHAPTER 9

## 9.1 The New Deal

In late November 2001, Stevie Nicks returned to Los Angeles from a Hawaiian retreat, determined to make another solo album. She recalled, "What happened was, when I went home to Phoenix for Christmas, I realized I needed to say how I was feeling after that horrendous tour of mine. The way things stood, only one of the songs on the new album was actually brand new, and as a writer that is not acceptable to me. So I went back to my journals and wrote 'Destiny Rules,' then 'Silver Girl,' then 'Illumé,' then 'Say You Will.'" This happened over a six-week period in Phoenix with help from bassist "Big Al" Ortiz. Then Stevie Nicks and Friends were top-billed at a Christmas benefit for the Arizona Heart Institute, on whose board sat Stevie's father, Jess Nicks. Stevie's friends included Sheryl Crow, and Stevie reciprocated by appearing on Sheryl's 2002 album *C'mon C'mon*.

Fleetwood Mac, meanwhile, had come to the end of its contract with Warner Bros. and was currently without a record label. But there was turmoil in the Warner Bros. executive suite: record sales were plummeting with the advent of file-sharing platforms like Napster. Obituaries were being written for the expected demise of the retail record business, with all recorded music becoming free to anyone with a tap of a computer key. No one had seen this coming, and now an entire generation of record guys—Fleetwood Mac's crucial allies in the industry—were being sidelined and laid off, not the least at Warner/Reprise, leading to anxious uncertainty for the label's artists.

One of these was Lindsey Buckingham, who had been working on a solo album for Warner Bros.—the one delayed by *The Dance*—in his

home studio while he was building another house nearby for his growing family. When he played his new tracks for Warner executives,
they were less than thrilled. "They just couldn't hear it," Lindsey
recounted later. "But I knew AOL [America Online] was about to buy
Time Warner, so rather than put the album out with a lame-duck re-
gime I decided to wait for a new one."

Mick Fleetwood was confident that Warner Bros. would re-sign the
band, but he also talked with Jimmy Iovine, currently the president
of major label Interscope Records. (The kid from Brooklyn—"Little
One"—was now one of the top execs in the music industry.) Jimmy
told Mick straight out that Interscope's interest in Fleetwood Mac de-
pended solely on the participation of Stevie Nicks.

But Stevie Nicks was traumatized from her unwanted exposure to
the realities of current events. *You don't live in the real world,"* Tom
Petty had taunted her years before. But now she felt more a part of
things, especially after the dark days of September. She resolved to
start thinking differently. She remembered her fervor for Jack Kennedy when she was twelve years old. She asked herself, was there
anything she could do for her country? Now, a different and more mature Stevie Nicks began to emerge, at the age of fifty-four: a woman
who wanted and needed to see things more clearly.


But it was hard to see clearly from her high-floor apartment by the
beach on an early afternoon in December. The "marine layer" of sea
smog had failed to burn off Santa Monica on a windless day, and the
ocean was shrouded in a thick and fleecy fog. After a strong cup of
tea, Stevie was driven to the offices of her manager, "big bad Howard
Kaufman," as Lindsey referred to him. After greeting the office staff
with hugs and presents, Stevie was shown into an office bare of the
usual award albums and citations and photos with the clients. The atmosphere was cool, professional.

Stevie wanted to speak with Kaufman about her next solo album.
He listened to her pitch and then told her to forget it. He explained
that computers and the Internet and the World Wide Web—only hazy
concepts for Stevie at this point—were destroying the record business.
Kids were getting their music free from file-sharing, and soon their

parents would, too. Something called YouTube was coming along, and then they'd get the videos for free, too.

As Stevie listened, she was angry. It wasn't fair, she said. What about the artists? Don't we have our rights anymore? Kaufman explained that professional paradigms were shifting for musicians. Artists who were used to living on recording and publishing royalties were now going to have to depend on touring for income. The days of the troubadours were coming back, where musicians would have to go out and play for the public to maintain their reputations and their value to the community. There's not much point, Kaufman reiterated, for Stevie to spend a year of blood and treasure on making a solo album that might be great, but that few would pay to hear when they could get it for free.

Then Kaufman got to the point. He had inquiries from Mick Fleetwood about putting the Mac back together as a four-piece, without Christine McVie. Fleetwood Mac was that rarity in show business—a sure thing. People would always come out to hear their old songs of love and hate. Revenue would be split four ways instead of five. She would make more money. He would, too. In fact, the boys were already jamming at Lindsey's house. Kaufman wanted Stevie to say yes to a proposed two albums and two tours. It was a four- to five-year commitment as it then stood. Stevie's heart sank. Another potentially horrible psychic siege with Lindsey Buckingham had appeared on the horizon instead of the solo album she'd come to talk about. She protested that Fleetwood Mac didn't even have a record deal, but he said they would get a deal—*if* they made a good album—*with her.* But before they went for the record deal, they were going to realign Fleetwood Mac's power structure. Stevie now had major leverage to dictate her own terms with Fleetwood Mac. The deal Howard would eventually propose to Mick would basically make Fleetwood Mac Stevie Nicks's band.

There was a certain satisfaction in that, a naked vindication of the angry and taunting lyrics of "Fall from Grace," about how Stevie had worked to make sure that all of them—the Fleetwood Mac family—survived this long. She told Howard that she would think about it, but she knew she would take the deal, whatever it was.

But this came at a price. Stevie Nicks's solo recording career would be put on hold—for years. It would be a decade between *Trouble in Shangri-La* and *In Your Dreams* in 2011.

And there would be major resentment over the financial restructuring of Fleetwood Mac, which reportedly involved Stevie making more than Lindsey, Mick, and John. It was a tacit acknowledgment that there was no Fleetwood Mac without Stevie Nicks. (Some observers noted that they never could have pulled this off if Christine McVie was still in the band. She wouldn't have stood for it.) Another factor was songwriting. Lindsey wanted the recordings to be released as a double album, like *Tusk,* because he wanted to use his (rejected) solo album as his contribution to the new project. Without Christine, all the songs had to be written by Stevie and Lindsey, but Lindsey had many more than Stevie did at that point. Howard Kaufman insisted that the two writers had parity on the next Fleetwood Mac album. This meant that Stevie had to write some more songs, and that Lindsey had to sacrifice some of his.

When this dust had settled, a chastened and put-in-his-place Lindsey Buckingham told *The Guardian* newspaper: "Howard [Kaufman] has his formulas and he's very much in control of certain aspects of the business side. . . . He's concerned with getting this project up and running and making Stevie the money that he feels he wants her to make. There's a strength to that, but there's also a weakness. . . . Let's just say I sense there's something large looming up ahead."

Stevie arrived at Lindsey's home studio on January 28, 2002, with a giant Navajo "dream catcher" from her Phoenix home, as her contribution to the décor. She also had a bagful of new songs and a positive attitude toward developing music with her difficult former boyfriend. A documentary film about the making of the new album was in production, so the house had been fitted with lights and microphones and even a few discreet cameras meant to capture any drama, let alone train wrecks. This also meant that Stevie had unwanted hair, makeup, and wardrobe sessions before leaving for the studio every day.

At band meetings, Lindsey was reasserting himself in his role as producer after a fifteen-year absence from Fleetwood Mac's recordings. He said he wanted the new album to be a double, and the others tried to not groan. He kept saying that Fleetwood Mac had to *redefine* itself and present new styles to their audience. Mick said that was great, but he was forced into praying to the commercial gods. Mick admitted that he had a fear of failure and that the idea of a double album didn't seem right. Lindsey understood but held his ground. "It's my *selfish* idea," he said of the double album proposal. There was a silence in the room as eyes rolled into the back of heads. Then, "No—it's my *ambitious* idea."

Stevie Nicks didn't bother to argue with Lindsey. She knew that it would never happen, because she didn't want it to.


## 9.2   Hidden Cameras

In February 2002 they began working on Stevie's songs, beginning with "Say You Will," "Silver Girl," "Illumé," "Thrown Down," and "Destiny Rules." Jimmy Iovine had heard some of these as demos, and mighty Interscope was now interested in signing Fleetwood Mac. But Warner Bros. came in with more money up front after Rob Cavallo, an ally of Lindsey's and now the chief of the label, came to the studio and heard working mixes of "Say You Will" and "Destiny Rules." Cavallo expressed mild interest in a double album if they had enough songs, but the issue was left open while negotiations began.

Lindsey was being nice to Stevie, perhaps for the benefit of the "hidden" cameras. Sitting with her one night, he got emotional about their coming together, "making up for some of the mistakes we made before." He told her he was "so thrilled, you and me, doing this." She told him it meant a lot to her, to hear him say these things.

But there was still this worry that Warners would pass if Lindsey kept insisting on putting out a double CD. One night, whispering so as not to upset Lindsey, Stevie told the film crew how she felt. "We have to sell our music to [younger] people, not people *our* age, in their fifties. They're not lying around on the floor smoking dope and worrying about paying the rent. . . . And they *don't* want twenty-two songs from us."

And at a band meeting she scolded the others: "You guys *all* have young families. [Mick and McVie, like Lindsey, both had kids with second and third wives.] We *have* to be commercial on this record."

One night the cameras captured a run-through of "Illumé," in which a smoldering Stevie sang in full hair and makeup, in a billowing black dress, with white nails, red toenails, and red sandals, with a gold thumb ring and a bracelet made of delicate white seashells. She was emotional as she sang of the terrors of the Twin Towers, chanting the verses about the serpentine movement of traffic up the coastline as she recalled the fears of those days in September.

March 11, 2002, was the six-month anniversary of 9/11. Stevie flew to New York, her first flight on a commercial airline since then, to perform at the Revlon Breast Cancer benefit with Sheryl Crow. Stevie then stayed in Manhattan for a week to see "my best friend Tom Petty" inducted into the Rock & Roll Hall of Fame in the Waldorf Astoria's ballroom. Two months later, in May, she was back in Manhattan again for a benefit for the Robin Hood Foundation, which helps poor kids with scholarships in New York. In her hotel, she watched TV images of the last steel I-beam from the fallen World Trade Center being lowered onto a truck, covered with a giant flag, and driven away. At the same time an empty gurney was lifted into an ambulance, a gesture toward the many victims never found. She flashed back to the despair they must have felt—"Of how we could make it / Of how we could get out" of the burning buildings on that day: lines from her poem "Illumé." Later she wrote that she was lucky "to come off the road into the dreamlike setting of recording a studio album with Fleetwood Mac. It was a good place to be, after what I had been through—a great tragedy followed by a gift."

Another gift was the Dixie Chicks's massive hit single "Landslide," which reached #2 on both the rock and country music charts and kept one of Stevie's signature songs on the radio during the summer of 2002. (It also fulfilled the prophesy of "Silver Springs" that Lindsey would never get away from the sound of the woman who loves him.)

It was just around this time that the fragile production truce between Stevie and Lindsey began to fray. It started while they were working on Stevie's "Thrown Down," which was explicitly about Lindsey, written about indignities while touring The Dance. Lindsey complained that he was finding it "odd" to sing about himself, and he wanted Stevie to change some of the pronouns and some tenses of her lyrics. Her umbrage at this was caught on videotape. "Would you say that to Bob Dylan?" she rebukes him, visibly offended. (She had worked with Dylan; Lindsey had not.) And Lindsey was like, "Uh, no." "Well," she interrupts, *that's how I write.* This might have reminded Lindsey who was now the real boss in Fleetwood Mac. He may have found this discouraging. Things went downhill from there, with renewed bad vibes and serious enmity between Nicks and Buckingham. (Those close to both of them say they never really recovered from *Say You Will*—a tense period of enforced competition and strife.)

Then Mick walked in one day, wearing a big smile, and said: "We have a label." Warner Bros. had made a deal—but only if the double-CD idea disappeared—and of course, Lindsey caved. Mick was thrilled. He whispered to the camera crew that Stevie's new songs were the best she'd written for Fleetwood Mac since *Rumours*.

Autumn 2002: Stevie's nine songs were finished, some with the help of John Shanks, who was brought in when relations with Lindsey tanked. Then they began dubbing in Stevie's vocals as background to Lindsey's nine songs, with Stevie singing on a high stool under headphones in the tiled entrance hall of the house. Sharon Celani and Mindy Stein came in to add vocals, as they would on the forthcoming tour. Then there was a big fight about who would mix down the eighteen tracks into a cohesive sound. Stevie wanted Chris Lord-Alge, who knew her music and had a track record, but Lindsey dug in his heels and refused to sign a deal memo that would let this go forward. Someone else mixed *Say You Will.*

Then, toward the end of the year, there was another row over the running order. Lindsey wanted two of his songs to come first on the album. Stevie was insulted but caved in. Why fight this anymore? But then she scaled back this whole Fleetwood Mac project, only agreeing to a limited number of concerts in 2003–2004 as opposed to the four-year commitment originally proposed.

*Say You Will,* Fleetwood Mac's seventeenth album, was released in May 2003, when Stevie Nicks was fifty-five years old. The CD jewel-box photo depicted the band looking miserable. Stevie's back was turned toward Lindsey, who was trying to look bored. John McVie and Mick Fleetwood appeared to be clutching each other for dear life.

Stevie's longtime fans listened to the nine new songs she had composed for the album and realized that, by themselves, the songs were of such a high caliber that they alone would have made an excellent Stevie Nicks solo album. (Some fans gave Lindsey credit for this; it seemed to them like the old Buckingham Nicks magic had resurfaced in some of Stevie's new work, as arranged and produced by Lindsey.)

After two Buckingham songs, the album really begins with "Illumé," with its beatnik bongos and images of a coastline like a working river and being alone with the dark thoughts of a 9/11 obsessive. It's one of Stevie's most anguished vocals and most haunted songs. This is followed by the wishful thinking and bitterness of "Thrown Down," a fantasy of a rekindled romance with a man eager to make amends to her in the form of a duet with Lindsey and his sparkling chords. "You can dedicate your pain to him," she sings in a song of touching psychic projection.

Lindsey's "Miranda," a rewrite of the Kingston Trio's moody ballad "South Coast," was followed by his "Red Rover," an anxious paean to free-floating negativity. Stevie's "Say You Will" countered this with a plea for hope and second chances, with backing vocals (and Hammond organ) by Sheryl Crow, plus a children's chorus composed of her niece, Jessica, and John McVie's young daughter, Molly.

Then came Lindsey's creepy song "Come," followed by a run of three of Stevie's: "Smile at You" (dating from the *Mirage* era) was about regrets and missed romantic opportunities; "Running Through the Garden" (written with Rick Nowels) was like a Fleetwood Mac song from 1975 but with a rocking theme of addiction and "turn-around"; "Silver Girl" (sung with Sheryl Crow) was a late-period self-portrait of a girly girl caught in a man's world, a woman of heart and mind who saw herself as an actress—"you cannot see her soul."

Christine McVie had played keyboards on Lindsey's "Steal Your Heart Away," followed by his "Bleed to Love Her," a live version of which had appeared on *The Dance*. Stevie wrote the catty, defiant lyrics for "Everybody Finds Out" to a Rick Nowles backing track. It's a funny song about love in the dark and hiding from decline. Then came "Destiny Rules," one of her great songs, sung in a low voice over a cowgirl-rock rhythm. She travels to foreign countries, she misses an old lover, she follows the rules, and she reprises the powerful imagery of the evening traffic moving up the coast as a glittering diamond serpent that she can see from her high window, "like living by a working river." ("Destiny Rules" was the lone track on *Say You Will* mixed for release by Chris Lord-Alge, at Stevie's insistence, signifying the song's importance to her.)

*Say You Will* winds down with two songs of farewell—appropriate since this was the last studio album Fleetwood Mac has released, as of this writing. Lindsey's "Say Good-bye" was a quiet bolero, Stevie's "Good-bye Baby" a tinkling lullaby. (Another of Stevie's songs, "Not Make Believe," was released on a deluxe version of *Say You Will*.)

*Say You Will* was a hit album in the summer of 2003. It jammed into the *Billboard* chart at #3, something that hadn't happened to Fleetwood Mac since *Mirage* in 1982. The album stayed in the Top 40 for months and was also a Top 10 album in England. They made quickie performance videos for the two singles. "Peacekeeper" wasn't a hit, but "Say You Will" got to #15 and was on the radio for the rest of the year.

Lindsey Buckingham walked Stevie Nicks onstage, holding hands in a false display of amity at the first show of the Say You Will Tour in Columbus, Ohio. Actually they hated each other, but this was show business, after all. Stretching from May 2003 through September 2004, the tour would produce 136 hits-heavy Fleetwood Mac shows in five legs. Stevie's production values were at their peak, with a new flowy wardrobe and black Nike boots replacing painful stacked heels. She sang "Rhiannon" in a black gown and a black shawl, whirling carefully in a subdued manner compared to the crazy maenad of olden times, displaying cleavage during the traditional deep bows at the end, reaching to the audience as she wailed, "And you still cry out for her / Don't leave me." She performed "Gypsy" in a golden shawl and six-inch cream-colored suede boots with a half-moon pendant on her throat. She made "Gold Dust Woman" the tour's show-stopper, sung in a fringed, pearl-beaded cape and danced with two twirls and a half-spin. When Mick hit the pounding backbeat in the shadow/dragon section, the stage went dark and Stevie entranced the crowd with oracular hand gestures that seemed descended from ancient temple paintings. This often provoked the biggest ovations of the evening. Lindsey petulantly refused to play the "Stand Back" and "Edge" guitar figures (Stevie's solo turns were a crucial part of Fleetwood Mac's concert repertoire now), so Carlos Rios from Stevie's band was along to motivate them as Stevie danced in an off-shoulder shawl.

For many fans, the concerts' highlight was "Landslide," with Stevie and Lindsey on a dark stage under a bright spot. Their languid smiles at each other, as Lindsey tenderly kissed Stevie's extended hand while applause washed over them, were totally fake. The concerts ended with "Don't Stop" (Christine's only song in the set, Stevie banging her tambourine, wearing a shawl of royal purple silk), and finally Stevie singing "Good-bye Baby" as a country-flavored ballad.

Fleetwood Mac were still troupers, solid professionals, and the tour would gross twenty-eight million. Stevie's new songs were well received, and without Christine McVie's songs, Stevie had much more time at stage front; this was to her liking because in her solo tours she was used to rapping to the audience about the origins of the songs. There was a glitch in Stevie's crew when backup singer Mindy Stein left in September. Jana Anderson was recruited to sing and sway next to Sharon Celani for the remaining shows. When the tour was over, Stevie Nicks—who had hated almost every moment of the last two years—left Fleetwood Mac for another five years.

## 9.3   Soldier's Angel

After the Say You Will Tour ended in late 2004, Stevie Nicks retreated to her 3,000-square-foot penthouse condominium on Ocean Avenue in Santa Monica, with its slightly better view of the California coastline that she so loved. But Stevie was in a state of depression, feeling tired and bloated after months of being squeezed and tied into stomach-flattening corsets on tour. Some of it was a prolonged, "horrible" menopause, the symptoms of which her Warner Bros. publicist Liz Rosenberg begged her fifty-six-year-old client not to discuss with interviewers, advice Stevie again ignored. One day Stevie and Liz were flipping through a fashion magazine, and Stevie said, "We're too old to wear these clothes." And Liz (whose other main client was Madonna) answered, "No Stevie, we're too *fat* to wear these clothes."

"I looked at her," Stevie remembered, "and suddenly this lightbulb went off. I said to myself, *That's* it. *It's* over. *I'm losing this weight.*" Stevie went back on the rigorous Atkins Diet, about which she said: "When you get into its mindset, you're terrified to even have a potato."

The other causes of her malaise were the bitter feelings left over from the Fleetwood Mac tour, which, she told both friends and journalists, she had hated. She hated the bitter production disputes involving petty and abrasive ego trips onstage. She hated the old wounds and the livid scars that remained. She hated Lindsey bringing his vulgar solo material into the set, and she usually left the stage when he played his tasteless song "Come." She hated missing Christine McVie and the isolation of being the only girl in the band. She told London's *Express* newspaper that she even hated *Say You Will*. "I didn't like it at all," she was quoted. "I didn't like making it; I didn't like the songs, so that tour was very hard for me."

Stevie's estrangement from Fleetwood Mac was such that she shied away from doing publicity for *Fleetwood Mac Live in Boston,* a CD/DVD package released by Reprise in late September 2004. Instead she flew to Hawaii with some friends for three months to try to come up with a project relating to Evangeline Walton's Mabinogion Tetrology, to which she still held development rights. Normally after a tour, Stevie would dress up, with makeup and the candles and the piano, and begin writing new songs for the next solo album. But with no solo material in the near future, Stevie needed some other creative passion, and so decided to realize her long ambition for the Rhiannon energy to be something other than a familiar song. "It could be a movie," she told a reporter. "It could be a record. It could be a couple of records. It could be a miniseries, because the stories are fantastic. We started in that totally scholarly, you-are-a-student-of-Welsh-mythology place. And then I got a call from my manager saying, 'I need you to come to Vegas right now, because Celine Dion and Elton John are playing back-to-back at the Caesars theater, and they want you to do a week there. It's really good money and you don't have to travel very far.'

"And I'm like, 'Howard, I am on a spiritual quest here; I really cannot come to Vegas.' And he's like, 'Stevie, you *have* to; *please*, just come tomorrow.'"

So she and her girly Rhiannon brain trust packed their bags and flew to Las Vegas for a lucrative four-night stand at Caesars Palace, the Roman-themed casino. She has yet to bring any more Rhiannon projects to fruition. (But she says she still wants to try.)

In the spring of 2005 Stevie went house-hunting and found a white family house in the hills above Pacific Palisades. The large house, on Chautauqua Road, had five bedrooms, a nice garden, plus canyon and ocean views. Stevie could see her apartment house by the beach from the second-floor master bedroom. The house was cozy, with stained-glass windows, sofas and fireplaces, with family photos in silver frames, flower arrangements, and freshly baked aromas wafting from the country-style kitchen. Stevie bought the house on impulse for a reported nine million dollars, but when she went to live there after the family had moved out, the place seemed lifeless. She also intuited that the house was haunted.

"There was this big family living there," she said later, "that obviously loved this house. So there was a vibe. And something in me thought, *Maybe I can have that.* I was not there three days before I thought, *What the hell do I do here?* I was too shallow and stupid to realize that it wasn't the house I had fallen in love with, but the mom and the dad and the four kids, and the smells of the cooking. So it was a mistake from day one." Stevie installed one of her goddaughters in the caretaker's apartment above the garage, and from then on she used the big house mostly for guests and parties, preferring to stay in her glass-walled penthouse by the Pacific Coast Highway.

Summer 2005. Stevie and Don Henley teamed up for the Two Voices Tour, a ten-concert showcase whose nightly show-stopper was the tour's two principals meeting onstage during Stevie's set to sing "Leather and Lace." Then something happened that profoundly affected Stevie Nicks.

The tour was in Washington, D.C. It was hot and humid, and no one wanted to leave the hotel. Someone from Walter Reed Army Hospital, which treated and provided long-term care for some of the most grievously wounded soldiers from the wars in Iraq and Afghanistan, contacted Warner Bros. and asked if Stevie Nicks would come to the hospital to visit the recovering soldiers. Stevie immediately agreed and had a car take her and her assistant Karen Johnston to the famous military hospital. She put on a gown and gloves, and spent the afternoon moving from bed to bed in the intensive care unit, talking with the damaged young men, many without limbs, spreading as much cheer as she could. When it was time to leave, Stevie and Karen were waiting for their car in the hospital's forecourt when sirens sounded and the military police closed off the hospital to traffic as medical emergencies began to arrive from Iraq by ambulance from Andrews Air Force Base. These were fresh casualties, hours off the battlefield, some of them bloody, being wheeled into Walter Reed right in front of Stevie and Karen.

With no car to pick her up, Stevie went back into the hospital and asked what she could do, *now.* Comfort these new guys, she was told. So she started greeting the soldiers, talking to them. Some couldn't speak. Some didn't have limbs or faces. She would touch them lightly and say, "My name is Stevie Nicks—what happened?" Some told her of the IEDs—roadside bombs—that had maimed them and killed their comrades. Stevie held a lot of rough hands that night, and new feelings began to build inside her. Maybe the patriotism she had felt in September 2001 could be channeled into something useful for her country—now.

That night she wrote in her online journal: "I look at life through the eyes of a rock and roll fairy princess who lives for nothing more than to sing a song . . . break a few hearts . . . and fly on to the next city and do it all again . . . until today.

"I walked into Walter Reed today as a single woman with no children. I walked out a mother, a wife, a girlfriend, a sister, a daughter, a nurse, a patient's advocate—a changed woman. What I saw today will never leave my heart."

The next night the tour was in Charlotte, North Carolina. Stevie called her mother. Barbara Nicks told Stevie that Americans had to do whatever it takes to keep the country safe. She said, "These young men are in no uncertain terms fighting for our freedom. So what you can do, Stevie, is love them and visit them, and tell the world what you experienced, so that people know what these boys have given up."

Stevie wanted to find some token to give to the patients during these visits and came up with the idea of giving them iPods—small music players loaded with digital lists of her favorite songs: "all the crazy stuff I listen to." Stevie knew that music had gotten her through some of her worst times, and maybe music could help some of her new constituency of wounded soldiers and their families. Later she would incorporate the Stevie Nicks Soldier's Angel Foundation, which purchased hundreds of iPods that she personally distributed to wounded veterans around the country.

After the Soldier's Angel campaign generated national publicity, she returned to Washington to lay a wreath at the tomb of the Unknown Soldier at Arlington National Cemetery—one of America's most sacred places. She was escorted by Mick Fleetwood; he was from an old English military family and understood the gravitas of the event. Afterward, having heard "Taps" played by Arlington's bugler, they went to Walter Reed to visit patients. Stevie: "As Mick and I went from room to room delivering their tiny iPods, they told us their stories. We floated down through the halls of two hospitals over a three-day period. We gave out all the iPods until there was none left." Stevie had been raising funds for Soldier's Angel from her fellow musicians in Los Angeles. When they heard about this in Boston, Joe Perry and Steven Tyler from Aerosmith gave Stevie a pledge of ten thousand dollars to buy more iPods. "In my eyes," Stevie wrote, "they went from the coolest rock stars to generous, great men."

Beginning in late summer 2005 Stevie went back on the road under the banner of the Gold Dust Tour. Opening was Vanessa Carlton, twenty-six, a pop chanteuse and Stevie's new best friend. Waddy Wachtel and drummer Jimmy Paxson had worked out a hot version of Led Zeppelin's "Rock and Roll," which Stevie started doing as an encore after watching a sedate audience explode into agitation when Waddy pulled the trigger on the classic rock masterpiece.

Most of the Nicks family attended Stevie's concert in Reno, Nevada, in late August. The next day Barbara Nicks called her daughter with the bad news that her father had collapsed, was in a bad way, and wasn't expected to recover. Jess Nicks died a few weeks later in September. Stevie told friends that saying good-bye to him had been the hardest thing she'd ever done. She said a bit later, "I always hear my dad saying, 'Ninety-nine percent of the human race will never be able to do what you've been able to do, to see all the beautiful cities, and meet the people you've met. You're a lucky girl, Stevie.' And I just try to keep that very present in my life."

But she carried on, and the Gold Dust Tour stayed on the road into 2006. Stevie was immersed in *Twilight*, the first of a series of novels about teenage vampires, an obsession that would last for the rest of the decade as Stevie identified with the romantic tribulations of the character Bella. And it was around then that they heard that Judy Wong, Fleetwood Mac's friend and secretary since 1968, had taken her own life. There were those who maintained that Judy had asked the band for financial help, and had been turned down.

## 9.4   The Honorary Heartbreaker

The Gold Dust Tour stayed out through early 2006. On February 4, Stevie and the band played for an hour at the Super Bowl pregame show in New Orleans. On the plane home the flight attendant—a big guy—told her how he tarted up—in a chiffon dress—for his annual visit to The Night of 1,000 Stevies in downtown Manhattan. He begged her to come, just once. She told him she was flattered, but it might be too much for a lady her age.

Few of Stevie's American fans were aware of her enormous stature and stardom in Australia, where the tour continued, beginning at the Rod Laver Arena in Melbourne on February 17. Stevie's shows had sold out immediately. Her record sales were strong, and a high-stakes horse race had been named for her. In Melbourne she was backed up on "Landslide" and "Edge of Seventeen" by members of the Melbourne Symphony Orchestra, with string charts by Waddy Wachtel. The audiences Down Under loved her version of "Rock and Roll," and the Led Zeppelin thunderbolt stayed in the set.

Back home in March, with no new music forthcoming from her, Warner Bros. announced yet another Stevie Nicks hits compilation, to be called *Crystal Visions,* also featuring all of her music videos to date. ("These records are *never* your idea," Stevie groused.) For the next few months she would review all the videos, often aghast at how stoned and wasted she appeared in some of them. A few years later she described this in a fan forum online: "Some of those videos are really good, except that I'm high. I'm sorry I let that happen. I ask myself, 'Stevie, could you have just, while you were filming that video, *not* done any cocaine, and *not* drank, and *not* smoked pot?' But I didn't, and now I'm very sorry." Stevie made it clear that years of addiction were a matter of deep regret to her. "If I could have gotten it together a little more, I would have had a better career. I would have made a couple of more great albums. I would have painted more pictures. You are sorry for this, later on."

Later in March 2006 Stevie and the band again appeared at Caesars Palace in Las Vegas, which was becoming one of their favorite places to play, since their most ardent fans came to see them there, some for multiple nights. Stevie was still doing The Walk as the band vamped at show's end, still collecting the bouquets, the stuffed bunnies, and the fervent love notes from the most besotted fans, those clamoring down front to get near to her in person.

Later that spring, she attended the fortieth reunion of Menlo-Atherton High School's class of 1966. She was sitting with a group of her old girlfriends—most of them in their late fifties like Stevie—and one of them said to her, "You know what? You haven't changed *one bit.* You're still our little Stevie girl!"

This made Stevie cry. "It was the nicest thing anybody had said to me," she told an interviewer, "that I'm still the same. Because I always tried very hard to stay who I was before I joined Fleetwood Mac, and not become a very arrogant and obnoxious, conceited, bitchy chick—which many do, and I think I've been really successful."

Tom Petty and the Heartbreakers had migrated from the Florida panhandle to Southern California in 1975, and by the next year had a record deal and a national tour. Three decades later, Stevie joined the band's Thirtieth Anniversary/Highway Companion Tour as a special guest, pleasing Petty's audiences no end when she glided onstage—a vision in black tulle and chiffon—to sing "Stop Draggin' My Heart Around" with him. She was his "special guest" at the massive Bonnaroo festival in Tennessee in June (introduced by Petty as "an honorary Heartbreaker"), and then was in and out of his tour over the next five months. (She was also exploring trying to write with guitarist Mike Campbell, who had started sending her backing tracks again.)

Later in the summer of 2006, the legendary Swiss concert promoter Claude Nobs dedicated an evening of his annual Montreux Music Festival to Ahmet Ertegun, founder of Atlantic Records (and partner of Stevie Nicks in Modern Records). Ertegun had helped launch her solo career, so Stevie was happy to participate, performing "Rock and Roll" with Nile Rogers and his band, Chic. Stevie later observed, "Robert Plant was there on the side of the stage, and he congratulated me after our performance. He told me I did a great job. That meant the world to me—one of the great rock-and-roll moments of my life. I think Robert Plant and I are kindred spirits. I think we are both connected to the mystical side of things—but on different sides of the world."

Stevie spent the rest of that year doing good works, headlining an October benefit for New York City charities, then in Las Vegas for the Epicurean Charitable Foundation in December. But the highlight of that era was the opening of the Arizona Heart Foundation's Cardiovascular Research and Education Building, a project that her father had worked on before his death in 2005.

Stevie and her team spent most of 2007 compiling, promoting, and touring her third compilation album, *Crystal Visions*, released in March of that year. This was a CD/DVD package with extensive booklet notes written or dictated by Stevie, and a collection of her videos with her own (often hilarious) subversive commentary. ("Why is Mick in this one?") Included in the DVD videos was the rejected "Scarlett Version" of "Stand Back," a fiasco that had cost Stevie a fortune in 1982. The sixteen audio tracks collected the usual hits plus two live tracks with the Melbourne orchestra, the "Deep Dish" remix of "Dreams" that had been a dance floor hit in 2005, and her stirring version of "Rock and Roll." The *Crystal Visions* booklet was cluttered with old snapshots and extensive song notes. Stevie dedicated the album to her father and to his twin sister Carmel, Stevie's closest aunt, who had died the year before. *Crystal Visions* entered the charts at a respectable #21, but the singles "Rock and Roll" and the symphonic "Landslide" failed to receive airplay or even make the charts.

Stevie did a round of interviews for the album, receiving interviewers in the lamp-lit living room of her house in the hills, offering them steaming cups of Earl Grey tea as her two terriers listened on the chintz-covered sofas. She was usually dressed in a flowing silk or chiffon blouse and close-fitting black trousers, wearing stiletto-heeled boots, her long hair worn loose and down to her waist. Reporters mentioned how small she seemed as she spoke with them in front of a gas-fueled fireplace. She told them that she was working on children's stories and the illustrations to go with them. "They're my Zen thing," she said, "what I do on airplanes, what I do when I really think about what I'm going to do." Asked about her tireless touring schedule, she answered: "Due to the fact that I never got married and never had children, I do have this crazy world where I pretty much continually work. But I love my work, and it's so different all the time that I really can't complain. And when I do get tired and irritable, I get really mad at myself and stop in my tracks and say, 'You have *no right* to complain. You are a lucky, lucky girl.'"

Asked if she still had any vices, Stevie was candid. "Since I got out of rehab in 1994 I've stopped doing serious drugs. And then as menopause touched my life, I stopped even having a glass of wine. I don't drink at all. I find that I'm spacey enough on my own that I don't need to be drinking and smoking. It just doesn't fit into my life anymore."

The Crystal Visions Tour began on May 17, 2007, in Concord, California, with hunky crooner Chris Isaak opening for Stevie. Her set list now included the furious "Fall from Grace" and Tom Petty's "I Need to Know." "Rock and Roll" was the killer first encore, and Stevie usually closed the show with "Beauty and the Beast" as scenes from the Cocteau movie screened behind her. The brief tour ended in New England in mid-June, after Don Henley bailed on some promised shows with her that summer. But then Stevie stayed on the road, playing dates with Vanessa Carlton until August. Stevie now added covers of Bonnie Raitt's "Circle Dance," and Dave Matthews's big hit "Crash Into Me," which, Stevie told *Rolling Stone,* was about the sexiest song she'd ever heard.

But at the age of fifty-nine, in a profession requiring twirls and spins plus two-and-a-half hours in platform boots, Stevie started having problems with her knees and hips. She fell hard onstage in Toronto when her knee went out from under her, hurting herself, which led her to Power Plate therapy, which required fifteen minutes standing on a vibrating platform that was developed by Russia for its cosmonauts in space. "It's this big-ass machine," she told the *Toronto Sun,* "and we built a big case for it, and we roll it around, and we use it. It fixed my knees, and now I'm in pretty damn good shape." She also told a Canadian audience that she loved Canada because everyone was so nice. "As much as I love my country," she added, "they aren't that nice."

Some of Stevie's fans, as reported on various blogs and Web sites, were upset by the 2007 publication of *Storms,* Carol Ann Harris's book-length account of her troubled years as Lindsey Buckingham's girlfriend. Harris provided meticulously detailed accounts of Lindsey's dire behavior toward her, including beatings, repeated chokings, and mental cruelty, testimony that jibed with some of the stories that Stevie had told friends over the years. Harris generally depicted Stevie Nicks as what one reviewer described as "a bubble-headed nymphomaniac." Asked by an interviewer about her reaction to Harris's book, Stevie told the truth—that she hadn't read it and wasn't intending to. (But a friend later told a reporter that someone had read Carol's book to Stevie.)

In October Stevie and her band were in Chicago to film an episode of *Soundstage,* a concert program with a live audience on PBS in America. Seventeen songs were filmed, including most of her contemporary set. Stevie performed in a cutaway black frock coat over a frilled white dress of crinoline and lace. Her black top hat was adorned with ostrich plumes and peacock feathers. Long blond hair spilled over her shoulders and caught the hot TV lights, shining. The evening's most dramatic shawl was purple with golden trim. Lori Nicks came back to sing with Sharon Celani and Jana Anderson. Highlights included "Sara" (at the producer's request), "Fall from Grace," "How Still My Love," and "Sorcerer." Stevie sang "Crash Into Me" with Vanessa Carlton as an earthy sex chant. "Landslide" was dedicated to her father, as a montage of Nicks family photos was projected behind her. The show ended with "Edge of Seventeen" and "Rock and Roll" in a satisfying TV blast of cathode-ray energy.

Stevie then went to Nashville to embellish a CD version of the concert with producer Joe Thomas, who assembled a small string section to give depth to "Beauty and the Beast," "Crash Into Me," and "Circle Dance." Stevie's *Soundstage* concert was broadcast on PBS in 2008. A DVD was released by Warners in March 2009 as *Stevie Nicks Live in Chicago,* containing eighteen songs. A ten-song CD, *The Soundstage Sessions,* came out at the same time, reaching #47 on the *Billboard* album chart. "Crash Into Me" was released as a digital download single at the same time.

In late 2007 Mick Fleetwood called Stevie to ask if she would be interested in touring with Fleetwood Mac. Stevie replied that she would consider this, but only if Christine McVie rejoined the band. Mick called Christine in her quiet Kentish village and asked her if it was time to come back to the band. "Not yet," Christine said.

## 9.5  In Your Dreams

Stevie Nicks was sixty years old in 2008, spending her birthday on her Soundstage Sessions Tour, again supported by Chris Isaak. She put her house on North Yucca Road in Paradise Valley on the market, and would sell the sprawling property later in the year for about three million dollars. She gave a bunch of interviews that revealed some interesting details. She now considered what she described as her "rock-and-roll penthouse" by the ocean to be her true and probably final home. She said she no longer drove a car or went anywhere alone because she was "very, very famous." She never carried money, she told London's *Telegraph* newspaper, because she had sold her soul to the Devil "to follow this dream." She liked to stay up all night drawing and painting, retiring around dawn and rising around noon. She promoted her Soldier's Angel Foundation as much as she could. She launched into tirades against Klonopin, plastic surgery, and Botox.

She said she had no interest in Fleetwood Mac unless Christine returned to the band. She admitted she was still at odds with Lindsey
Buckingham, adding: "Maybe when we're seventy-five and Fleetwood Mac is a distant memory, maybe then we might be friends." She
denied being a witch or ever practicing witchcraft in any serious way.

Then she changed her mind, having been persuaded that going on
the road with Fleetwood Mac might enhance the prospect of writing
new songs for the new solo album she was beginning to think about.
So Stevie spent a good portion of 2009 on the band's intercontinental
Unleashed Tour, which billed itself as a "global hits" concert for longtime Mac fans. It began in June in New Orleans, where Stevie spoke
passionately from the stage about her feelings for the city in the dread-
ful wake of Hurricane Katrina four years earlier.

But once again, this tour was marred by Lindsey's behavior toward
her, with bad blood and bitterness even noticed by fans and critics, who
saw that they ignored each other onstage and that he seemed mock-
ing and contemptuous of her when introducing her songs. They still
performed "Landslide" as a barely contained duet, continuing the
clenched smiles and corny hand-kissing routine that they both hated.
Stevie said she felt bad about faking love; it felt so false and soul-
destroying. Yet she acknowledged that the fans were still interested
in the Stevie-Lindsey legend, and it was important they be seen as
still able to put aside their unhappy past and perform with each other.
Some reviewers noted that Stevie's heart didn't seem to be in these
shows.

When Fleetwood Mac's Unleashed Tour reached Europe in October, Stevie reconnected with Dave Stewart in London. Stevie had last
seen Dave a few years earlier, when they were both involved in
making a pilot episode for a television show that was never produced.
Stevie: "We talked about everything for two hours. At the end he
suggested I play something at the piano, so I did a fifteen-minute
version of 'Rhiannon.' Then Dave joined in as if we'd been singing it
together for years. I realized then that if I were ever to make a solo

album again—and believe me, I had my doubts—but if that day came, I knew I wanted to have Dave on board."

Now in London Stevie asked Dave Stewart if he wanted to be involved in her solo record. He replied that not only would he help her produce the record, but that together they should make a documentary film of the whole production, using mostly hand-held cameras in natural light. Stevie was enthusiastic, and told him she would reach out to him when she recovered from the current tour. The Unleashed Tour ended in New Zealand in December with two sold-out stadium shows near the capitol at Wellington. It had been a financial success despite some unsold seats in Europe, but the stresses of working with each other proved emotionally exhausting to the band's aging front line, Stevie and Lindsey.

Stevie Nicks went to Arizona to spend Christmas with her mother and brother's family and began to clear out her Paradise Valley house, which held so many memories—good and bad—for her. She told friends that she was going back into the solo album business and that she intended to hit the ground running. She already had a complete song, "Moonlight," written while in Australia after seeing the movie *New Moon,* based on the *Twilight* teenage vampire novels.

Some time now passed. Deal memoranda passed between Stevie's people and Dave Stewart's so they could work together. Stevie took four girlfriends on a vacation to Italy's Amalfi coast, where they stayed in a splendid villa hotel perched on a mountain with a stupendous view of the isle of Capri.

When work on her solo album started, Stevie recalled, music started to flow from the first day. "Dave Stewart came over to my house in the Palisades, and I gave him a binder of my poetry and said, 'See if there's anything that appeals to you.' Dave always has a guitar around his neck, and he started playing, and I just sort of started reciting my poetry, and all of a sudden, in about an hour, we had this amazing song." (This was "Secret Love.")

She continued, "I have never been interested in writing with anybody—not Lindsey, not anybody. And all of a sudden I could actually understand why Lennon and McCartney wrote together, or

Rodgers and Hammerstein, or any of the great songwriting teams. I don't know a thousand chords, and Dave doesn't have a book of forty poems. When you put those two things together, you have this amazing amount of wisdom and knowledge. Those five minutes when it all started was a brilliant moment. Stars went off. When it was done I said, 'Well, I'm a changed woman.' And then we just continued."

The name of the project was *In Your Dreams*. For the next eleven months Stevie turned her house into a home studio, with recordings made in the acoustically bright front hall, various hallways, and in the master bathroom. A chef was hired to provide meals and snacks for the musicians, singers, engineers, and visitors to the production. Stevie said that it was the first time she felt really comfortable in that house, working with Dave Stewart on her first album in almost ten years.

One of the first songs they worked on was "Secret Love," which had origins as a demo from the *Rumours* era and then as an unused lyric in 1980. Now it became a rhythmic plea for romance, "in a timeless search / for a love that might work."

"For What It's Worth" (cowritten with Mike Campbell) dated from 2004, when Stevie had an affair with a band member who offered to leave his girlfriend for her—if she really wanted him. "This man said that to me," she explained later, "but we both knew it would never work off the road." It was an acoustic ballad, full of good intentions and promise, with the risks of forbidden love. And in the end the singer tells the lover, "You saved my life."

The title track, "In Your Dreams," was meant to be comforting despite lashings of tears, pain, and darkness. The track was up-tempo, courtesy of Heartbreakers drummer Steve Ferrone. The hard-rocking "Wide Sargasso Sea" was the album's first Big Statement, with surging power chords and dueling guitars. Stevie sings of burning down the house of an English lover, smoke and fire, before running home to California. (The song's title was appropriated from the novel by Jean Rhys.)

"New Orleans" and "Moonlight (A Vampire's Dream)" were both wistful ballads, both inhabited by blood lust. "New Orleans" was a post-hurricane tribute to "a city of tears," one of Stevie's favorite places. "Moonlight" was more a portrait of a beautiful, insecure, idealized lover and a thwarted romance that could never be. Stevie later allowed that she had lived in the world of the Twilight Saga for at least five years, and "Moonlight" was the song that came out of that obsession.

"Annabel Lee" is Stevie's setting of Edgar Allan Poe's morbid romance that she first tried in high school. Now it totally fit in with au courant teen vampire exotica, as the poet keeps vigil by the cold body of his beloved. Dave Stewart put it in a sparkling framework for the rock audience, and it would become a huge fan favorite, since "Annabel Lee" sounded like it could have been on *Mirage* but for Waddy's "gothic" interlude that captured some of the poem's dead breath.

The song that gave Stevie and Dave the most problems was "Soldier's Angel," an attempt to capture the feelings of sympathy with injured troops that had been so transformative for Stevie, five years earlier. It had to be a somber song, haunting but respectful, but they could not find a way into it. In near desperation Stevie called Lindsey Buckingham, who came over to her house, shook hands with Dave Stewart, was nice to everyone, and played a trolling guitar that turned "Soldier's Angel" into a war threnody, one that reminded some listeners that *The Iliad* was chanted for a thousand years before someone wrote it down. Stevie was grateful to Lindsey for his uncomplaining cooperation. She noted that family life, now with three daughters, seemed to have finally softened the highly strung master musician.

The easiest songs to make were the ones Stevie and Dave wrote together over the course of the year. "Everybody Loves You" seemed like a self-portrait; it ended with the observation that "you're so alone." "Ghosts Are Gone" was hard rock, more Stewart than Nicks. "You May Be the One" was a pastiche of girl-group doo-wop with clever and ironic lyrics, some of Stevie's best from this period. "Italian Summer" was an operatic recounting of Stevie's time in Ravello with her girlfriends, soulful with violins and touristic memories of Chianti and Capri. For some the highlight of the Nicks-Stewart collaboration was a riddling song, "Cheaper Than Free," a country music bar-room weeper complete with pedal steel guitar.

Work on the new album was mostly complete by early 2011. For the album pictures Stevie and the girls dressed up in gowns, posing with a white horse, a snowy owl, and giant mirrors. Then *In Your Dreams* was held back for postproduction work on the *In Your Dreams* documentary so it could be entered at film festivals in Europe and considered for a theatrical release at home.

In the meantime, a restless Stevie Nicks went back on the road, opening for Rod Stewart on what was billed as The Heart and Soul Tour. As the opening act, Stevie and her band were limited to just over an hour, but for Stevie this was mitigated by Rod's gentlemanly insistence on bringing her onstage by the hand, introducing her personally, and proclaiming it an honor to be supported by the queen of rock.

Stevie was determined to make *In Your Dreams*—her seventh solo album and her first in a decade—into a success. In the run-up to its May release she threw herself into promotion mode, appearing on major TV outlets like *Oprah* and *The Ellen Degeneres Show,* singing "Secret Love," then released as a digital single. Then Stevie got the flu and had to cancel appearances around the release date, but she rallied and flew to England, where she was received like returning royalty, doing the important TV chat shows, speaking with the leading papers, and performing before fifty thousand fans in London's Hyde Park.

*In Your Dreams* was a big hit when it was released in May, just when Stevie Nicks turned sixty-three, debuting at #6 on the *Billboard* chart and selling well for months. Critical reception was positive, with some saying it was her best solo album of them all. That summer Stevie continued to promote her record, appearing on the wildly popular TV talent contests *American Idol, The Voice,* and *America's Got Talent* as a coach and mentor to the young singers competing for her favor. Other dramatic TV roles would follow, on the music drama *Glee,* and *American Horror Story.* (On the latter, Stevie was portrayed as a white witch worshipped by all the other witches.) Stevie had never thought of herself as an actress, but now she found that playing herself, projecting a magical, womanly persona she'd honed for decades, wasn't so hard after all.

## 9.6   The Fairy Godmother

With *In Your Dreams* still selling and in the charts, Stevie Nicks told Fleetwood Mac that she wouldn't work with them in 2012 because she was extending her own tour to try to keep her album in play since, at that point, she didn't know if she would ever make another one. The documentary, for which Stevie was credited as codirector, was shown at some festivals but failed to find a distributor for a run in theaters, a disappointment after all the work they'd put into the project. It was released on DVD along with the four music videos produced for "Secret Love," "For What It's Worth," "Moonlight," and "Cheaper Than Free."

Stevie and her band went out that autumn of 2011 on the In Your Dreams Tour, a long run that would extend into 2012. "Secret Love" and other new songs were in the show, and the band was playing with a renewed energy and drive. There was a five-month intermission when Stevie's mother died in December, of emphysema. Stevie was of course disconsolate about "my little mother," who had given Stevie life itself and had never lost faith in her, even when Stevie had lost it in herself. Stevie moved back into her house in the hills where she could be with her tribe and be looked after; the "rock-and-roll penthouse" near the ocean was basically one enormous glass room with statues and images of Buddha everywhere, but Stevie found no place for the sense of loss she was experiencing.

There was another death around then. A son of a friend of Stevie's, one of her godsons named Cory, eighteen years old, had overdosed on drugs at a fraternity party. In her leathern journal Stevie wrote some lines about how she and her people had always tried to be careful not to dance with the devil and his narcotics. It was one of her most bitter poems about the needle, and the damage done. A bit later, Stevie was contacted by Dave Grohl, the former Nirvana drummer, now leader of the serial rock festival headliners Foo Fighters. He explained that Nirvana had recorded its grunge-classic album *Nevermind* at Sound City in 1990, using the same Neve VR-72 console that Buckingham Nicks had used to record "Crying" in 1973. Sound City had closed in 2011, as the analog studio was unable to compete in the world of digital music. Grohl had bought the historic Neve board from Sound City and had installed it in his home studio. Now he was making a documentary film about Sound City and its famous console. Paul McCartney was involved. Stevie said yes, right then.

Stevie arrived at Grohl's studio with an entourage that included hair and makeup. If she was going to be filmed for this, she was going to look good. She had sent them the lyrics she'd written when her friend's son had died, now titled "You Can't Fix This." Grohl and Foo Fighters drummer Taylor Hawkins set her words to a "Rhiannon" chord progression, and Stevie sang them with a passion and intensity that surprised even herself. When Grohl's (excellent) documentary *Sound City* was released in 2013, some fans commented that "You Can't Fix This" had to be the best, most stirring, most emotionally acute song Stevie Nicks had written in thirty years.

The In Your Dreams concert tour finished in the fall of 2012. Mick was after her to play with Fleetwood Mac in 2013, and this time she said yes, under certain conditions. After a band meeting Stevie and Lindsey had what she later called "The Talk."

Stevie did most of the talking as they sat, drinking coffee. She told him she was an old woman now and needed his sympathy if they were going to work together again. She explained that in her world, on her solo tours, she was surrounded by the love of her friends. But in Fleetwood Mac's last tours, she felt surrounded by spite and resentment, and she wasn't going to have that happen anymore. "What can I say?" was Lindsey's comment. Stevie basically told him he could promise to behave decently toward her, and everything would be okay. The Talk was a big moment for Stevie. She could stand up to Lindsey now. She was a much bigger star than he was, by far. Stevie was an American legend, but Lindsey's star would eventually fade away. She could even threaten him a little. "So," she said as they parted, "2013 better be *great*—okay?"

It turned out to be an interesting and profitable year for both Stevie and the Mac. Stevie celebrated her sixty-fifth birthday that May in Las Vegas, where the band was playing that night. The original plan was to stay on the road for a year, but when Christine McVie asked to re-join Fleetwood Mac, after appearing with the band for one song at London's O2 Arena in September (and after John McVie was diagnosed with cancer in October), Fleetwood Mac—all now in late middle age—

would stay on tour for the next two and a half years, playing about 122 concerts for three generations of fans ranging from sixteen to eighty years in age.

Most shows began with "Second Hand News," blending into "The Chain." Stevie delivered a truncated version of "Rhiannon," now a slower rite performed by a venerable celebrant. ("I don't twirl as much as I used to," Stevie told *The New York Times*.) "Sisters of the Moon" and "Sara" anchored the concert, which included a couple of songs from *Extended Play,* Fleetwood Mac's four-song, digital-only EP, released in April 2013. One of these was "Without You," a confessional song of dependence written by Stevie and Lindsey in the earliest days of Buckingham Nicks, circa 1971. It had existed as a ghost demo on the Internet for years and was revived as Stevie's contribution to *Extended Play*. Describing the song (which often took longer than the song itself), Stevie told the audiences, "We were like, crazy in love." They also played "Sad Angel" as the hottest song in the set. It was the first song in decades that Lindsey admitted he had written specifically about Stevie.

The strangest part of the show occurred during "Gold Dust Woman," when Stevie performed what she called her "crackhead dance," lurching around the stage like a demonically possessed dope fiend, hair akimbo, arms flailing awkwardly, acting out her memories of staggering around under antipsychotic medication. Stevie: "The crackhead dance is me being some of the drug addicts I knew, and probably being myself, too—just being that girl lost on the streets, freaked out." When Christine saw this interpretive dance for the first time, she said, "Wow—we've always known that 'Gold Dust Woman' was about the serious drug days, but this depicts how frightening it was for all of us."

Stevie revived herself for "Stand Back," which often got the best ovation of the evening. As ever, the Mac finished with "Go Your Own Way," and Stevie calmed the fans down with a low-key encore.

But then the Australian leg was postponed in October while John McVie underwent treatment for cancer. Stevie rented a beach house in Malibu to rest, away from any distractions, because she was working on songs. She still wrote in longhand, proudly telling interviewers that she didn't even own a computer or a cell phone. But this changed in December when the Santa Ana winds whipped up wildfires in Southern California. A blaze swept through Malibu Canyon, singeing the Cross Creek shopping village and bearing down on the little beachside neighborhood where Stevie was staying. Alone and concerned, she picked up the telephone to call for help, but the line was dead. The fire spared Stevie's house that day, but she always had a cell phone after that.

Christine's request to return to Fleetwood Mac wasn't a cause of joy for Lindsey Buckingham, and he let it be known. Lindsey said he liked the Mac as a four-piece band with hired keyboards. His money would go down when they added another full partner. They hadn't played Chris's songs in sixteen years, except for "Don't Stop." Christine was seventy: could she keep up?

Christine explained that she was bored out of her mind in her quaint suburban English village. The ancient period house had been restored. Every day she walked her dogs in the same country lanes and said hello to the same folks, most of whom were related to each other. She had just been given the prestigious Ivor Novello Award, Britain's highest honor for a songwriter. Some nights she ate supper by herself in the village's pub. She missed her band, she missed singing, and she missed the audiences and their electrical energy.

Lindsey was outvoted, and Chris would be welcomed back into her old band. Mick made the announcement in January 2014. Stevie was content. "I just told Chris that she better start working out," she said, "because some nights we play at least two and a half hours." When John McVie recovered from his cancer treatments, Fleetwood Mac went back on the road. They called it the On With the Show Tour.

There were some losses in this period. Bob Welch succumbed to depression and shot himself. His departure from Fleetwood Mac had prompted the hiring of Lindsey and Stevie. Photographer Herbie Worthington died; his archive comprised thousands of images of Stevie Nicks, most of them unseen. And a curious geneological researcher, working on the Nicks family tree, found the grave of Stevie's grandfather, A. J. Nicks, in a cemetery near Phoenix. It was unkempt and overgrown. She did her best to clear weeds and bracken from the grave and its stone, and wondered why no one looked after it.

## 9.7   Still a Dreamer's Fancy

April 2014. Fleetwood Mac took a four-month break from the road. On April 6 Stevie sang "Rhiannon" with the group Lady Antebellum at the televised Country Music Awards in Nashville. Stevie appeared with Sheryl Crow, Bonnie Raitt, and Emmylou Harris in a tribute to Linda Ronstadt, who had a lingering illness and wasn't present. (Carrie Underwood, considered the only country singer who could match Linda's epic talent, sang lead on "When Will I Be Loved," "Blue Bayou," and other Ronstadt hits.) On May 5, Stevie attended the Rock & Roll Hall of Fame ceremony to see Nirvana inducted. Stevie had played several shows with Dave Grohl while they were promoting *Sound City*, and she was now considered an honorary Foo Fighter.

Then Stevie set herself up in Nashville for nine weeks with Dave Stewart and made a new album of songs she had written over the years but never recorded. Some of them dated to 1969. Some had been lost. One song, "Lady," was found on a cassette in a trunk full of her mother's treasured keepsakes. There was a severe deadline that she had to meet, before rehearsals began in late summer for Fleetwood Mac's fall reunion tour with Christine. Stevie: "I called Dave Stewart and said, 'I've got the songs, but how do we make a record in two months?' He said, 'Nashville. That's what they do.' It's like checking yourself into musical rehab." Lori and Sharon came out from LA to help Stevie, and Waddy as well. Standout tracks included "The Dealer," country rock about being the mistress of her fate; "Mabel Normand," about an old movie star with a taste for cocaine; "Belle Fleur," thumping guitar rock with chanted, underdeveloped verses; "Carousel," a Vanessa Carlton song that Stevie had sung with her niece Jessica at her mother's hospice bedside. Stevie wrote "She Loves Him Still" with Dire Straits' Mark Knopfler, specifically about Lindsey. The best song for most fans was "Cathouse Blues," a faux-Louisiana jazz scat with a whorehouse flavor. Stevie-as-courtesan sang, "I need some new red velvet shoes." And then, "I'm still a dreamer's fancy."

"Lindsey will love this album," Stevie told *Rolling Stone* when her fourteen Nashville songs were released (by Reprise) as *24 Karat Gold— Songs from the Vault* in September 2014. "Half the songs are about him." The album was another Top 10 hit, climbing to #7 on the *Billboard* chart. (In a sign of the times, Fleetwood Mac's old label, and the Warner Music Group itself, were now owned by an international media syndicate controlled by Russian investors.)

Fleetwood Mac began rehearsing with Christine McVie in August. Stevie liked singing the harmonies to "Over My Head" and "Say You Love Me" with her again. Vocal warm-ups now would take a little longer, but their voices still sounded great together, and demand for tickets to this band reunion was very strong.

Stevie did dozens of interviews between promoting *24 Karat Gold* and the Mac tour in September. Some of these were in the Palisades house, with the aging terrier Sulamith resting by Stevie's leg. Reporters pointed out that most of the younger female stars—Taylor Swift, Lady Gaga, Katy Perry, Florence Welch—acknowledged Stevie as a major influence on their careers, and Stevie allowed that this was flattering. A writer who got into Stevie's kitchen noted the refrigerator contained only sealed meals from Weight Watchers. There seemed to be intense curiosity about this sixty-six-year-old rock star's romantic life. "I've narrowed it down to nobody," Stevie joked, but if pressed she would elaborate. She said she loved being a free woman, and that she'd tried every kind of man. Her last real love had been in 2004. She told one interviewer just about all that was needed to know about the subject:

"I'm single. I don't have children, and I've never been married except for three months a long time ago. I live a single woman's life, and yes, I spend a lot of time with myself. I have a few very close friends, most of them I've known forever, and I kind of like it. Would I be willing to have a boyfriend? It would be fun if I could find a boyfriend who understood my life and didn't get his feelings hurt because I'm always a phone call away from having to leave in two hours for New York, or a phone call away from having to do interviews all day long. It's not very much fun to be Mister Stevie Nicks."

"In the last ten years I've just said I'm going to follow my muse. If I want to go somewhere I don't have to worry about anyone being mad at me. . . . If it were to happen to me, I'd be thrilled. But when I'm 90 years old and sitting in a gloriously beautiful beach house somewhere on this planet with five or six Chinese Crested Yorkies, surrounded by all my goddaughters who will at that point be middle-aged, I'll be just as happy."

Fleetwood Mac's On With the Show Tour did great business in the fall of 2014. Their fans cheered the return of Christine McVie, and most of the arenas in America and England were sold out. Things between Stevie and Lindsey were much better, although Christine still described their relationship as "abrasive." They still did the hand-holding bit for the fans after "Landslide," but without the old rancor and phony posturing. Backstage, Lindsey complained that the music in Stevie's dressing room was too loud. (She still liked pushing his buttons.) There was some tension because *Rolling Stone* wanted to put only Stevie on its cover. (It was that, or nothing.) She told the magazine that she smoked a little pot now, when she wanted to write at the piano. She said her brother was in Arizona, being treated for bladder cancer. She said that she was temporarily living in a luxury mobile home near Paradise Cove in Malibu.

In another interview, Stevie was asked why she hadn't written a memoir. She answered, "Because I wouldn't be able to tell the whole truth. The world is not ready for my memoir, I guarantee you. All of the men I hung out with are on their third wives by now, and the wives are all under 30. If I were to write what really happened between 1972 and now, a lot of people would be really angry with me. . . . I am loyal to a fault, and I have a certain loyalty to these people that I love because I do love them, and I will always love them. . . . Just because a relationship ended badly, and shitty things happened, you cannot tell the world. But you can write a song about it, in three verses and a bridge and a chorus, that tells the really magical moments."

Fleetwood Mac kept playing through 2015, and then took a long break. Stevie Nicks could often be found in New York, where she attended multiple performances of *School of Rock*, the Broadway musical based on the 2003 movie in which Stevie's had been the only woman's music played in the film. An exhibit of her Polaroid self-portraits appeared at various galleries in that period. She was completely obsessed with the fantasy TV series *Game of Thrones*. *New York Magazine*'s profile of her was headlined, "The Fairy Godmother of Rock."

In September 2016, Stevie announced a twenty-eight-city tour with her own band. Opening were the Pretenders, with Chrissie Hynde the only original member. Stevie told the press that her solo career was probably the only reason Fleetwood Mac was still together. She said she supported Hillary Clinton's run for the American presidency (and was later disappointed—even stunned—when the glass ceiling held, and Donald Trump was elected early in November).

A week later, Stevie's private jet took off from Washington, D.C., headed northeast to a concert in Boston. She was running late, because it had been raining all day after another sold-out concert on the 24 Karat Gold Tour, with Stevie speed-rapping stories and yarns for the fans about some of the lesser-known songs she was playing on this tour. She was now sixty-eight years old.

Her jet landed, also in the rain, at Hanscom Field in Bedford, north of Boston. Black Escalades transported Stevie and the girls to the arena via the city's grand Commonwealth Avenue, with its nineteenth-century mansions. Stevie told the driver to slow down so she could ogle the gleaming chandeliers in the softly lit rooms of the stately houses. A few hours later, she told the sold-out arena crowd in TD Garden about wanting to buy an old house on Beacon Hill. This drew prolonged cheering: Boston had been a second home for Fleetwood Mac since 1968. Boston had been the first town to play the singles from *Fleetwood Mac* in 1975. Stevie Nicks and Boston had a long history together.

The Pretenders opened the concert with an hour-long jukebox set. Stevie and her band, working in front of colorful animations and psychedelic patterns, launched into "Outside the Rain" as fans ran back to their seats after beer runs and bathroom visits. Stevie told the hall that they had a hard curfew of 11 o'clock, so her raps about the songs might be semi-incoherent. (Some were.) "If Anyone Falls" got the Garden fucking, Stevie explained that she was going to play some songs she hadn't performed onstage before. When the unfamiliar "Belle

Fleur" segued into "Dreams," twenty thousand people sang along, softly, in a genuinely touching outpouring of fandom, love, and respect.

Stevie sang nineteen songs that night. The highest moment came after she and the band played "Crying in the Night," an old Buckingham Nicks song. Speaking to her fans as if they were her comrades and friends, she said, "If you are a creative person—*which you all are*—you can also go out and follow your dream. . . . And, forty-three years later, you can stand on a stage, or in your house, and do something you wanted to do since you were twenty-one years old—when you're sixty-eight years old!"

Friends said that Stevie, who'd always been politically conservative, was upset at the election of Donald Trump, whose comments about and attitudes toward women she found offensive. She wondered if she should vent to her audiences when she added seventeen shows in 2017 to the 24 Karat Gold Tour. There was more upset when her Facebook page was hacked, and what she called "crazy posts" began to appear in her name. Stevie now lived in a world of viral memes, hashtags, tweeting, and complete concerts phone-filmed on iThings. (She barely knew how to make a call on her smartphone.) Her presence on social media went dark for a while after that. Late in 2016, she told the *Miami Herald* that even her participation in a rumored new Fleetwood Mac album was in question, because the others had "gone such different ways."

Tom Petty and the Heartbreakers embarked on a fortieth anniversary tour, which Petty indicated would probably be their last big road campaign. Honorary Heartbreaker Stevie Nicks signed up to open for Petty when they played a massive concert in London's Hyde Park in July 2017. After that, she said, she might try to stay on the road until she was seventy years old, in 2008, and then worlds beyond.

In those days, all her interviewers (annoyingly) asked the old Welsh witch when she was going to retire. To Andy Greene from *Rolling Stone,* she answered, "I work very, very hard. I have a piece of paper here that says, 'You keep going and you don't stop.' You do your vocal lesson. . . . I see lots of people my age, and lots of people who are younger than me, and I think, 'Wow, those people look really old.' I think it's because they didn't try. If you want to stay young, you have to *make* an effort. If I wanna walk onstage in a short chiffon skirt and not look completely age-inappropriate, I have to make that happen. Or you just throw in the towel and let your hair turn white and look like a frumpy old woman. I'm never gonna go there."

And further: "I'll never retire. 'Stand up straight, put on your heels, and get out there and do stuff.' I want to do a miniseries for the stories of Rhiannon and the gods of Wales, which I think would be this fantastic thing, but I don't have to retire from being a rock star to go and do that. I can fit it all in."

Summer 2017. Stevie joined Don Henley onstage at his seventieth birthday celebration in Dallas, Texas. "Some friendships never die," she said, "and this is one of them." Earlier, Stevie had re-recorded "Gypsy" in a different, more haunted voice as the theme for *Gypsy*, a fraught TV series about a beautiful psychiatrist's erotic obsessions that began showing in June. Also in June, *Lindsey Buckingham/Christine McVie* was released, a *Tango*-like album that started as the next Fleetwood Mac project, but changed after Stevie baulked, saying it would take too long to make and no one would buy it. But she evidently decided she wasn't quite through with Fleetwood Mac, and signed up for an eighteen-month Mac world tour in 2018–2019. "And you won't see a poster calling this a farewell tour," Mick said.

And at the end of all that, her most ardent fans knew that Stevie Nicks could retire undefeated, a world champion of rock, a poet of substance, an American legend. Her followers would understand that the events of her life had validated her long-term faith in herself, her unshakeable conviction in her artistic worth, and her magical ability to offer healing, solace, and beauty to the masses with her music, its message, and presentation. Stevie Nicks, this self-described "old woman," had shouldered her burdens, met her responsibilities, and valorized her country in a way few other women have. No other rock star of her charmed generation could say as much.

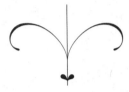

The fact is that nobody has a clue
to what my life was really like.

— STEVIE NICKS


If I should meet thee / After long years,
How should I greet thee?—/ With silence and tears.

—LORD BYRON

Fleetwood Mac kept Stevie Nicks away from interviewers for five years after she joined the band. Mick Fleetwood was the group's spokesman and he wanted it to stay that way. When reporters from the entertainment press did get rare access to Stevie in those days, her interviews tended to be spacey and inarticulate. She was infamously allowed to appear intoxicated and deranged in a notorious Boston TV interview in 1979. This contributed to a generalized image of her as an airhead. But this changed when Stevie started her solo career in 1981 and began giving interviews, a game at which she proved quite adept. For the next thirty-five years she gave intimate, informative, and highly quotable interviews to the media as she promoted her records and concert tours. Interestingly, her most articulate comments tended to be published in English newspapers and magazines, especially if a woman was asking the questions.

Since *Gold Dust Woman* is an unauthorized biography, I have used reliable published interviews, taped interview transcripts, and Stevie's own writings to let the reader hear her "voice" in a consistent register, to get a feeling for her interior life in her own words. I have tried to avoid the suppositional language that some biographers deploy, such as "she must have felt" or "she might have wondered." If the text ascribes a thought or emotion to Stevie, the source is something that she has reliably said, told, or written.

Mick Fleetwood brought me into the Fleetwood Mac orbit in 1987, when we began to work together on his memoir *Fleetwood: My Life and Adventures in Fleetwood Mac*. At that time I conducted interviews with band members, associates, family members, and many others. Our book was published in 1990 and became an international bestseller (and the foundational text for almost every book written since about this band). Mick also asked me to write the booklet notes for albums such as *Fleetwood Mac/Greatest Hits* and *Live at the BBC*. While researching *Gold Dust Woman*, I returned to these original interviews and conducted additional research relating to Stevie's more recent career as a solo artist, mostly with friends, former friends, musicians, and professional colleagues. Except where noted, most of my sources requested anonymity.

Several published books were helpful in assembling the puzzle of Stevie Nicks's life and times:

*Making Rumours* by Ken Caillat with Steven Stiefel (2012) is an in-studio account of the recording of some of Stevie's best songs while she was leaving her long-term romance with Lindsey Buckingham.

*Storms* by Carol Ann Harris (2007) is a diary-informed account of the author's allegedly abusive relationship with Lindsey Buckingham after Stevie Nicks, and a reliable look inside the private Fleetwood Mac "bubble."

*Bumping Into Geniuses* by Danny Goldberg (2008) is a memoir by the famous record industry executive that contains the saga of the founding of Modern Records, Stevie Nicks's record label.

*Petty: The Biography* by Warren Zanes (2015) provides clear details about one of Stevie Nicks's most important professional and personal friendships.

*Stevie Nicks: Visions, Dreams & Rumours* by Zoe Howe (2015) is an unauthorized biography by a British writer that is good on Stevie's reception in England, and the making of her album *The Other Side of the Mirror*.

*Simple Dreams* by Linda Ronstadt (2013) is a heartfelt, poignant memoir about growing up singing in postwar Arizona.

*I Want My MTV* by Craig Marks and Rob Tannenbaum (2011) makes sense of Stevie's crucial early engagement with music videos and the cable channel that played them.

Jenny Fleetwood became a psychologist later in life, specializing in addiction and recovery issues relating to artists. Her book *It's Not Only Rock 'n' Roll* (2013) has revealing interviews with Stevie Nicks and other luminaries of her era.

*The White Goddess* by Robert Graves (1948) is indispensable regarding Stevie Nicks's own source material, and her place in the Welsh bardic tradition. Likewise *The Mabinogion*, as edited by Charlotte Guest (1902).

Interviews and some descriptive material are taken from the following sources, with thanks to the indispensable Christopher B. Davis's hard-working 2012 research blog "The Daily Fritz": ABC, ABC (Australia), *Allure, Amazon.com, American Songwriter, Arcadia Apache, Arizona,* Arizona Music Hall of Fame, *Arizona Republic, Baltimore Sun,* BBC, *Blender, Billboard, Blackcat, Boston Globe, Boston Phoenix, Cashbox, Charlotte Observer, Chicago Tribune, CHUM, Crawdaddy, Creem, Daily Mail, Details, Der Spiegel, Elle, Entertainment Weekly, Guitar Player, Harper's Bazaar, Hartford Courant, High Times, Hollywood Reporter, Houston Chronicle, Indianapolis Star, Independent, International Herald Tribune, Interview,* KCRW, *LA Weekly, London Evening Standard, Los Angeles Times, Melody Maker, Metro, Miami Herald, Microsoft Music, MOJO,* MTV, *Musician, New Age, New Musical Express, Newsweek, New Yorker,* New York *Daily News,* New *York Post,* New York *Times, Newsday, Nixfix.com, Oui, Parade, People, Phoenix New Times, Playboy, Q, Reading Eagle, Record World, Reuters, Rock, Rock Family Trees, Rolling Stone, Salon.com, San José Mercury-News, San Francisco Chronicle, Spin, St. Louis Post-Dispatch, St. Petersburg Times, Sunday Guardian, Telegraph, The Times* (London), *Times Literary Supplement, Time, Time Out, Toledo Blade, Toronto Sun, Uncut, Us, USA Today, Variety,* VH-1, *Village Voice, Vogue, Wall Street Journal, Washington Post,* WBCN, WBZ, WMMS, *Woman's Own,* WZLX.

Honorable mention to researcher Callie Pillar for her work on the Nicks and Meeks families. Archivists James Isaacs and David Bieber both helped with research materials, as did the British Library at King's Cross and the Boston Athenaeum.

Thanks also to Elizabeth Beier and Nicole Williams of St. Martin's Press. This text took a long time to gestate, and their patience was almost infinite. Attorney Eric Rayman vetted the texts whilst touring Andalucia, and for that he deserves mucho gracias.

David Vigliano is my long-suffering literary agent, for whose friendship I have been very grateful; likewise his associates Thomas Flannery, Jr. and Ruth Ondarza. The 77th Street office dogs are called Sunny, Pepper, and Gus. (Pepper's favorite game is called Bite the Client.)

The following are very Rhiannon: Maria Evangelinellis, David Winner, Pat Healey, Patrick Donnaly, and especially Danny Goldberg.

Few authors can write long books without support from their families. My loving clan includes Lily Davis, India and John Goodridge, Chris Davis, Hana and Howard, and the late Judith Arons. They all made inspiration easy to come by.

In the twenty-first century the media and the popular press have become fixated on the female celebrity "trainwreck," defined as a hypersexual, over-refreshed, crazy lady—usually a singer or an actress—whose hell-raising, loony judgments and subsequent flame-outs lead to public suffering and even death. Amy Winehouse and Whitney Houston played those trainwreck roles until they died. Britney Spears and Lindsay Lohan had their moments as well. It has been observed that the outlaw aspects of biography—intrusive, revealing, sometimes transgressive—are the only reason for its survival as a bestselling literary form. With this in mind, I would finally like to thank Stevie Nicks for getting her train back on track when she did, because if she hadn't, this would have been a much, much darker story, one not much fun to tell.

Another nose-bleed on waking.

—ALEISTER CROWLEY

*THE MAGICAL RECORD OF THE BEAST 666*

1918.

# INDEX